Listening to the Silences: Women and War

7-25-2006
WW
$136

International Humanitarian Law Series

VOLUME 8

The International Humanitarian Law Series is a series of monographs and edited volumes which aims to promote scholarly analysis and discussion of both the theory and practice of the international legal regulation of armed conflict.

The series explores substantive issues of International Humanitarian Law including,

* protection for victims of armed conflict and regulation of the means and methods of warfare

* questions of application of the various legal regimes for the conduct of armed conflict

* issues relating to the implementation of International Humanitarian Law obligations

* national and international approaches to the enforcement of the law and

* the interactions between International Humanitarian Law and other related areas of international law such as Human Rights, Refugee Law, Arms Control and Disarmament Law, and International Criminal Law.

Aminatu, Victim of the Sierra Leone conflict, Freetown, 2001.

Listening to the Silences: Women and War

edited by

Helen Durham
and
Tracey Gurd

MARTINUS NIJHOFF PUBLISHERS
LEIDEN · BOSTON

A C.I.P. Catalogue record for this book is available from the Library of Congress.

Printed on acid-free paper.

ISBN 90 04 14365 3.
© Copyright 2005 by Koninklijke Brill NV, Leiden, The Netherlands.
Koninklijke Brill NV incorporates the imprints Brill Academic Publishers, Martinus Nijhoff
Publishers and VSP.

http://www.brill.nl

Cover photograph and frontispiece:
Aminatu, Victim of the Sierra Leone conflict, Freetown, 2001
© Nick Danziger/ICRC/Contact Press Images

Typeset by *jules guldenmund layout & text*, The Hague.

Printed and bound in The Netherlands.

In loving dedication to our mothers

Mary Gurd

and

Christine Durham

Foreword

Some two years after delivery of the *Akayesu* rape judgement, a journalist conducting research for a book on women in Rwanda described to me the fate of women survivors in Rwanda, and in particular, that of Witness 'JJ'. 'JJ' had testified in the *Akayesu* trial to horrific gang rapes perpetrated upon her during the genocide at the Bureau Communal under the orders of Akayesu, the Bourgemestre. The prosecutor's questions proceeded as follows: 'I am sorry to keep on asking you each time – did your attacker penetrate you with his penis?' She answered: 'That was not the only thing they did to me; they were young boys and I am a mother and yet they did this to me. It's the things they said to me that I cannot forget'.

Her words caused me to re-examine the law's perception of women's experience of sexual violence during armed conflict. It seemed to me that the traditional practice of law has not paid sufficient attention to the silences of women. The effect on me, the judge, was a realisation that I too, as a woman in such a situation, would live the entire act of violence as the violation perpetrated upon me.

'JJ''s testimony influenced the definition of rape that emerged in that case.

I am reminded of the words I subsequently heard Meryl Streep say: 'I have come to believe that in the core of our being we as women are profoundly similar, in what makes our hearts beat in rapture, or shame, or content, or what encourages us or makes us proud'.

I have now learned that Witness 'JJ' was living in conditions far worse than that of the other survivors – in a ramshackle hut on bare ground amidst sparse provisions, rejected by and rejecting the society of others. She and other women suffer deprivations of food, housing and medicine for HIV/AIDS and other diseases. The journalist criticised the UN Tribunal for Rwanda for having used and discarded 'JJ'.

The international community had reacted to only one aspect of the aftermath of the genocide: that of bringing perpetrators to justice – but not the reconstruction of the country based on the priorities and needs of women to help feed, clothe, house, educate, heal and rebuild.

In recent times we have seen a pernicious increase of wars and armed conflicts. It is of note that women are no longer prepared to fill traditional roles of victims but are speaking out for themselves. Women's voices are breaking into the mainstream which has, for far too long, been dominated by the propaganda of militarists and beneficiaries of wars. Women and children are the most vulnerable groups in times of conflict – therefore the significance of their experiences must be emphasised.

Listening to the Silences: Women and War is an invaluable collection where women's experiences and demands have a forum. The contributors relate real-life experiences, or are activists, or experts, in their fields. Their stories demonstrate that women can be heroic, courageous, tragic, inspirational, capable of inflicting harm and of doing good.

Aspects of each are captured in the collection. This presentation is important as we learn to recognise and embrace the multi-facets of womanhood in the advancement of International Humanitarian Law.

Navanethem Pillay

Judge on the International Criminal Court
Former President of the International Criminal Tribunal for Rwanda

Table of Contents

Acknowledgements

A book such as this requires the input and assistance of many people. To start with, we owe a depth of gratitude to all the contributors. Without their involvement, enthusiasm and engagement, this book could not have been written. In particular, Georgina McEncroe, who worked as a proof reader and assistant editor, is to be acknowledged for her hard work and superb eye for detail. Elizabeth Grant also needs to be thanked for her role over many years, as does Timothy McCormack for his enduring encouragement and support. Victoria Bannon was significantly involved in the start of this journey and is gratefully acknowledged. Jan Smith and Annmarie Brennan at Hunt Alternatives Fund were very helpful, and Eric Stover at the Human Rights Centre at U.C. Berkeley also provided some valuable suggestions for pushing this book forward. Finally, our publishers – in particular, Lindy Melman – have demonstrated extraordinary patience and commitment to this book and for this we are grateful.

Preface

The genesis of this book began a number of years ago at a seminar hosted by the Australian Red Cross (ARC) and the International Committee of the Red Cross (ICRC) on the topic of women and war. The seminar highlighted the significant work undertaken by the ICRC in this area and also gave voice to victims, academics and professionals working in related fields. It was decided that publishing the papers from this event would be a worthy contribution to the literature on this topic. Five years later, with the addition of numerous other authors sourced from all over the globe, *Listening to the Silences: Women and War* has changed shape, texture and size from the original, rather humble, aim. Yet the underlying philosophy (and feminist methodology) remains the same: to listen to the multitude of women's voices and experiences involved in armed conflict so as to provide a deeper reflection on the ways in which war impacts upon women. It is hoped that in reflecting upon these pieces – some highly personal and some tightly academic – the formulation of responses to further protect and empower women can be more easily achieved.

The book is divided into three distinct sections. The first section emerged from the contemplation of one simple, underlying question – 'whose voices should we be listening for?' Throughout history, women's voices have often gone unheard or have been silenced when it comes to talking about their experiences of armed conflict. They have been stereotyped predominantly as 'victims' in wartime settings, with other roles being regarded as exceptions to the norm. This section, then, attempts to demonstrate – through the inclusion of personal stories recounted by women who have been involved in armed conflict (and its resolution) in differing ways – that the existence of these stereotypes and silences has hindered the evolution of more thoughtful responses to women's needs, ideas and activism in relation to armed conflict. The second section looks at what factors operate to liberate and obscure women's voices, examining this matter in 'the field' as well as in legal theory and practice. The final section deals with the ways in which lessons can be learned by the international community in order to empower women and work constructively towards inclusive forms of peace and security. Each section commences with a short summary of the themes and perspectives to be covered to enable the reader to identify areas of interest.

In the last few years there has been a dramatic increase in the examination of the gendered impact of armed conflict upon society.[1] Concurrently, humanitarian organisations working before, during and after armed conflict have identified the protection of women as a major priority.[2] Sadly, the horror and intensity of the issues facing women during times of war and internal tensions are neither new nor unique to specific situations. What is perhaps unprecedented, and highlighted in this book, is the

---

[1]   See Judith Gardam and Michelle Jarvis *Women, Armed Conflict and International Law* (2001).

[2]   See Charlotte Lindsey, *Women Facing War; ICRC Study of the Impact of Armed Conflict on Women* (2001).

range and seniority of women involved in work relating to armed conflict – as judges; forensic anthropologists; business women; soldiers; humanitarian workers; members of civil society; journalists; eminent academics; legal advisers and politicians. What does this mean for the thousands and thousands of women who *are* 'victims' during the most dangerous and deadly time society can ever experience? Whose voices are speaking on this topic and from this 'noise', whose are being heard and acted upon? How does the international community liberate/obscure/synthesize/silence these views? These are the matters authors within this book were asked to consider in writing pieces in their own areas of expertise.

This book is not consistent in its format. Some pieces are long and some are short, some are personal stories and some rigorous legal analysis. Each author chose to answer the questions – and in many cases break the silence – in their own way: Jan Ruff-O'Herne's heart-breaking experience as a 'sex slave' in World War II; Mimi Doretti's description of the emotional eloquence of the dead; Neela Marikkar's indication of the empowerment women can find in responding to conflict; Kelly Askin's comprehensive survey of the international jurisprudence of sexual and gendered crimes; Judith Gardam's articulate analysis of the ability of international law to protect women during armed conflict. Each woman adds her voice and skills to this troubling area.

There are obviously no neatly packaged answers and this book only touches upon some of the issues. Yet the collection of writings contained here demonstrates that while frustratingly slow, there is hope for improvement in a range of professions dealing with women in times of armed conflict. At the very least, the complexity of issues surrounding this topic is being considered. This will never be enough, however only time will tell whether the gains made can be built upon.

For Helen, the privilege of being able to work for a humanitarian organisation engaged and committed to the improvement of the plight of women during internal and international turbulent and violent times is inspiration enough. The opportunity to also 'dabble' in academic musing on this topic has added an extra dimension to the layers of questions asked late at night. Teaching a post-graduate subject at the University of Melbourne entitled 'Women and War' has allowed me to focus on this topic with theory as well as practice, and most importantly to learn from the extraordinary range of students engaged in reflecting on this area. A number of the contributors have taken the academic journey with me and I would like to thank all the others for their significant insight into an area one cannot but be passionate about. As a co-editor, Tracey has been a delight and I have learnt much from her patience, wisdom and friendship. Family and close friends – especially Greg and Lexi – have shared this interest and been supportive in the dark hours of pondering; listening patiently as I have tried to come to terms with narrowing the bridge between academia and practice. For this I am truly thankful.

For Tracey, it has been an honour to work with the amazing array of women involved in this project. What has been striking about each of the contributors has been the common elements uniting them – an extraordinary depth of character, compassion, determination and 'fire in the belly' about a topic that can be at once horrifying while also providing a unique lesson in the human capacity for forgiveness, heroism and ingenuity in the face of violence and terror. The opportunity to work closely with Helen has been a dream and I remain deeply grateful for her trust, guidance and ability to constantly inspire. She is a true friend and mentor. Friends and family have been incredibly supportive throughout this endeavour – most particularly and most gently, Doug Merlino. Thank you.

Helen Durham – Sydney, Australia
Tracey Gurd – New York, United States

Part I

Listening to Women's Voices

The first section of this book listens to the personal experiences of women during armed conflict. Sometimes women's stories surprise us. This is particularly so when they tell of experiences that seem outside of the 'box' usually reserved for women during war, or when they speak of the complex, multifaceted and sometimes contradictory roles women play during and after armed conflict. Sometimes the voices we hear scream with pain or cry with compassion. Sometimes the words women say are not things we like (or expect) to hear. Sometimes women's words are the only things that keep societies – and families – together. The voices in each of these chapters speak of all these things.

This section starts with the horrific and courageous story of Jan Ruff-O'Herne. Here, the Australian grandmother writes of her experience as a sex slave for the Japanese army in Indonesia during World War II. Jan's chapter is followed by Mimi Doretti's. Mimi, a forensic anthropologist, writes of the heartbreaking work of exhuming mass graves in the wake of armed conflict and of returning the remains to victims' families. In this chapter, she tells of the personal connection she made with the wife of a 'missing' man exhumed in Ethiopia many years after his disappearance.

The next two pieces give us an on-the-ground perspective of armed conflict – the first from a soldier stationed in Iraq and the second from a humanitarian operationalist. Penny Cumming is an Australian army lawyer who recently returned from active duty in Baghdad. She tells of life in a Middle Eastern war zone and the issues she grappled with as a woman involved in combat operations. Charlotte Lindsey then provides an overview of the International Committee of the Red Cross' (ICRC's) recent global study on women and war, outlining some of the ways in which women experience armed conflict around the world and highlighting how the ICRC has attempted to assist and protect women.

This section then turns to the voices of women activists who have taken on non-traditional roles during and after armed conflict. The first is Neela Marikkar, founder of Sri Lanka First – an initiative devoted to using economic power and business strategies to promote peace in Sri Lanka. She talks of the way in which business has been creative in working towards peace in a country wracked by civil war for many years. The next is by Luz Méndez. A member of a revolutionary movement in Guatemala from a young age, Luz went on to become one of the only women at the negotiating table when peace talks began in her country. Luz symbolizes the fluid and shifting roles women take on before, during and after armed conflict.

The inclusion of such stories in this book is based on the philosophy that the development of international humanitarian law can only benefit from gaining an understanding of women's real-life experiences, perspectives and stories of armed conflict. It is only through listening to the voices of women such as these that we, as an international community, can more deeply reflect and understand the ways in which war impacts upon women. This will help us to work towards formulating legal and practical responses that can reduce women's suffering and engender empowerment.

Fifty Years of Silence: Cry of the Raped

Jan Ruff-O'Herne*

My experience as a woman in war is one of utter degradation, humiliation and unbearable suffering. During World War II, I was a so-called 'Comfort Woman' for the Japanese Military, a euphemism for military sex slave. I was born in Semarang (Java) and had a most wonderful childhood until my life was torn apart by the war.

I was nineteen years old when, in 1942, Japanese troops invaded the former Netherlands East Indies (Indonesia). Together with thousands of other women and children I was interned in a Japanese prisoner of war camp for three and a half years.

Many stories have been told about the horrors, insults, brutalities, suffering and starvation of the Dutch women in Japanese prison camps. But one story was never told: the most shameful story of the worst human rights abuse committed by the Japanese during World War II. The story of the 'Comfort Women' and how these women were forcibly seized, against their will, to provide sexual services to the Japanese Imperial Army. The world ignored these atrocities for almost fifty years. It has taken fifty years for these women's ruined lives to become a human rights issue.

Why did it take so long? Perhaps the answer is that these violations were carried out against women. Women are always the victims in war. We have all heard it said: they are only women, this is what happens to women during war. Rape is part of war, as if war makes it right. Rape in war is a power game. It is used as a reward for the soldiers. In some countries like Bosnia, Rwanda and Kosovo, rape is also used as a weapon and a means to genocide.

It was February 1944. I had been interned in Ambarawa prison camp together with my mother and two young sisters for two years. I was returning to my barrack from one of my heavy camp duties. Suddenly there was a great commotion in the camp. A number of Japanese military arrived in army trucks. We were expecting to be called for roll call. However this time the order was given: all single girls from seven-

---

* Jan Ruff-O'Herne lives in Adelaide, South Australia, and has spent the last ten years working tirelessly to support the plight of the Asian 'Comfort Women' and the protection of women in armed conflict. She travels the world giving presentations on this topic and has received numerous awards including a knighthood from the Queen of the Netherlands; ANZAC Peace Prize; 'The Order of Australia' and a Papal Honour from Pope John Paul 'Dame Commander of the Order of St. Sylvester'.

Helen Durham and Tracey Gurd (eds.), Listening to the Silences: Women and War, *pp. 3–8.*
© *2005 Koninklijke Brill BV. Printed in The Netherlands.* ISBN 90 04 14365 3.

teen years and up were to line up in the compound. We did not like this command and immediately became suspicious.

There was an air of fear throughout the camp and some girls tried to hide. We were assembled in a long line and we trembled with fear as a number of high-ranking Japanese military walked towards us. We did not like the look of these Japanese. It was the way they looked us up and down. The way they laughed among each other and pointed at us. The young girls stood there frightened, heads down, not daring to look up. The Japanese paced up and down the line. At times our chins would be lifted so they could see our face.

Up and down they marched, sneering, pointing, touching. After some discussion among themselves, half the girls were sent away. I was left standing with still a long line-up of girls. My whole body was trembling with fear. The selection process continued until ten girls were ordered to step forward. The others could go back to their anxious waiting mothers. I was one of the ten. I could hear the crying and shouting of the women as they tried to pull us back, fighting bravely with the Japanese.

Through our interpreter we were told to pack a small bag of belongings and report immediately to the front gate where the trucks were waiting to take us away. We were not told any details. The girls and their mothers – and indeed the whole camp – protested with all their might. The entire camp was in uproar, screaming, crying, fighting.

It was all in vain. Oppressed and bullied by the enemy, broken and enslaved helplessly by a brutal force, we were sheep for the slaughter. The guards stood over us as we packed a few things. I packed my Bible, prayer book, crucifix and rosary beads. At that moment, they seemed to me the most important things. Like weapons, they would keep me safe and strong.

Flanked by the guards, we were taken to the front gate. We had to say goodbye to our mothers and loved ones. My mother and I could not find words to speak. We looked into one another's eyes and threw our arms around each other. There, in that moment, it seemed as if we both died in each other's arms.

By this time all the girls were crying, as we were forced into the trucks. We huddled together like frightened animals. We had no idea where we would be taken. We soon realised that we were travelling on the main road to Semarang. As we came closer to the city, we drove through the hillside suburb of Semarang. The truck stopped in front of a large house. Seven girls were told to get out. I was one of them. We were soon to find out what sort of a house we were forced to live in. Nervously we kept together as we were ushered into the house by the Japanese officer who seemed to be in charge. Each girl was shown her own bedroom. I could not sleep that night and neither could the other girls. We ended up all together in the one big bed, huddled together in fear and finding strength in prayer.

The next day some more Japanese came to our house and we were all called to the living room. We were made to understand that we were here for the sexual pleasure of the Japanese. In other words, we found ourselves in a brothel. We were to obey at all times. We were not allowed to leave the house. In fact, the house was guarded and trying to escape was useless. We were in this house for only one purpose: for the Japanese to have sex with us. We were enslaved into enforced prostitution. My whole body trembled with fear. My whole life was destroyed and collapsing from under my feet.

We protested loudly that we would never allow this to happen to us, that it was against all human rights, that we would rather die than allow this to happen to us. The Japanese stood there laughing, saying that they were our captors and they could do with us as they liked, and, if we did not obey our families would suffer. They produced papers for us to sign, written in Japanese, which we could not understand. We refused to sign. We were beaten, but did not sign.

The following day we saw the front room of the house being turning into a reception area. We were ordered to have our photographs taken. We all looked at the camera angrily or with sad expressions on our face. The photos were then placed on a pin-up board in the reception area. We were given Japanese names and flowers were put in our bedrooms.

A Japanese woman arrived at the house. 'At last, a woman,' I thought. 'A woman would understand and help us, surely.' But the woman showed no pity either. In the meantime, the whole house was being geared up to function as a brothel.

Opening night arrived. We were all terrified and we huddled together in the dining room. We were all virgins and none of us knew anything about sex. We were all so innocent and we tried to find out from each other what to expect and what was going to happen to us.

As we sat there waiting, fear had completely overpowered our bodies. Even up to this day I shall never forget that fear. In a way, it has been with me all my life. I knew that the only thing that could help us now was prayer. I opened my prayer book and led the girls in prayer.

As we were praying we could hear the arrival of more and more military to the house: the crude laughter and boots treading the floor, the excitement among the officers. We were ordered to each go to our own rooms, but we refused to go. We stayed closely together, clinging to each other for safety. My whole body was burning up with fear. It is a fear I can't possibly describe, a feeling I shall never forget and never lose. Even after more than fifty years I still experience this feeling of total fear going through my body and through all my limbs, burning me up. It comes to me at the oddest moments. I wake up with it in nightmares and still feel it just lying in bed at night. But worst of all, I felt this fear every time my husband was making love to me. I have never been able to enjoy intercourse as a consequence of what the Japanese did to me.

The house was filling up with Japanese. We sat waiting in fear, huddled together till the time had come and the worst was to happen. One by one, the girls were dragged into their bedrooms crying, protesting. They pleaded, they screamed, they kicked and fought with all their might. This continued until all the girls were forcefully taken to their rooms.

After a while I hid under the dining-room table. I could hear the crying coming from the bedrooms. I could feel my heart pounding with fear. I held tight to my wooden crucifix that I had tucked into my belt around my waist. I had been wearing the crucifix like this continually. I though that wearing it might convey some message and it would keep me strong.

Eventually I was found and dragged out from under the table. A large Japanese officer stood in front of me, looking down at me, grinning at me. I kicked him on the shins. He just stood there laughing. My fighting, kicking, crying and protesting made no difference. I screamed, 'Don't! Don't!' and then in Indonesian, 'Djangan, djangan'. He pulled me up and dragged me into my bedroom, he closed the door and I ran into a corner of the room. I pleaded with him in a mixture of English and Indonesian and tried to make him understand that I was here against my will and that he had no right to do this to me.

I curled myself up in the corner like a hunted animal that could not escape. 'O God, help me.' I prayed, 'Please God, don't let this happen to me'.

The Japanese officer was in total control of the situation. He had paid a lot of money for opening night and he was obviously annoyed. Consequently he became very angry. He took his sword out of its scabbard and pointed it at me, threatening me with it. I told him that he could kill me, that I was not afraid to die and that I would not give myself to him. I repeated again and again, 'Djangan, djangan, don't, don't'. But he kept pointing the sword at me, touching my body with it, threatening to kill me. I pleaded with him to allow me to say some prayers before he would kill me. While I was praying he started to undress himself and I realised that he had no intention of killing me. I would have been no good to him dead. He was getting impatient by now and he threw me on the bed. He tore at my clothes and ripped them off. He threw himself on top of me, pinning me down under his heavy body.

I tried to fight him off, I kicked him, I scratched him, but he was too strong. The tears were streaming down my face as he raped me. It seemed as if it would never stop.

I can find no words to describe this most inhuman and brutal rape. To me it was worse than dying. My whole body was shaking when he eventually left the room. I gathered what was left of my clothing and ran off to the bathroom. I wanted to wash all the dirt, the shame and hurt off my body.

In the bathroom I found some of the other girls. We were all in shock and crying, not knowing what to do, trying to help each other. We washed ourselves as if it could wash away all that happened to us. I dared not go back to the dining room and decided to hide myself. I hid in a room on the back verandah. My whole body was shaking with fear. 'Not again, I can't go through this again,' I thought.

But after a while the angry voices and footsteps came closer and I was dragged out of my hiding place. The night was not over yet. There were more Japanese waiting. The terror started all over again. I never realised suffering could be so intense as this. And this was only the beginning.

At the end of that first horrific night, in the early hours of the morning, seven frightened, exhausted girls huddled together to cry over lost virginity, to give each other comfort and strength. How many times was each one raped that night? What could we do? We were so utterly helpless. How could this have happened to us?

In the daytime we were supposed to be safe, although the house was always full of Japanese coming and going, socialising, eyeing us up and down. Consequently we were often raped in the daytime as well. As soon as it was getting dark, the house would be 'opened' and a terrible fear would burn up my body. Each evening I tried to hide in a different place, but I was always found then dragged into my room, after severe beatings.

One morning I decided to cut off all my hair to make myself look as unattractive as possible. I cut my hair until I was quite bald. 'No one would want me like this,' I thought. But of course, it did not help me one bit. The rumour spread that one of the girls had cut off all her hair and it turned me into a curiosity object.

As the months passed all of us girls lost weight. We hardly touched our food. We shared our fears and our pain and humiliations. We were exhausted and our nerves were stretched to the limit. Continually we put in a protest to any high ranking officer that visited the brothel, but it always fell on deaf ears.

Always and every time the Japanese raped me I tried to fight them off. Never once did any Japanese rape me without a violent struggle and fight. Often they threatened to kill me, often they severely beat me.

During the fights I hit out strongly and delivered mighty blows and kicks and scratches. I injured the Japanese quite often. Because of this and because of my persistent fights, I was told that if I did not stop the fighting they would move me to a brothel down town for soldiers – a brothel with native girls where conditions were worse.

One day a Japanese doctor arrived at our house. Immediately I thought that he would be able to help us. Surely, as a doctor he would have compassion for us. I requested to speak to the doctor. But he showed no interest, no signs of compassion or apology. Instead, the doctor ended up raping me on the first day of his visit.

In the days leading up to the doctor's visit, gynaecological type of equipment had been installed in one of the rooms on the back verandah. From now on we were to be examined for any possible diseases. Each time the doctor visited us he raped me in the daytime. The door of the doctor's examination room was always left open. To humiliate us even more, any other Japanese in the house were allowed to look on while we were being examined. They would come into the room or stand at the open door to look at us while we were being examined. This humiliation was unbearable and as horrific as being raped.

More anxiety came when I realised that I was pregnant. I was absolutely terrified. How could I give birth to and love a child conceived in such horror? Like pillars of strength, the girls gave me their support and they advised me to tell our Japanese woman guard that I was pregnant. I approached the woman and as an answer to the problem she produced a bottle full of tablets. I could not kill a foetus, not even this one. I continued to refuse the tablets. Eventually they were forced down my throat. I started my period shortly after.

During the time in the brothel, the Japanese abused me and humiliated me. I was left with a body that was torn and fragmented everywhere. There was not an inch of my body that did not hurt. The Japanese had ruined my young life. They had stripped me of everything. They had taken everything away from me: my youth, my self-esteem, my dignity, my freedom, my possessions, my family. But there was one thing that they could never take away from me. It was my Faith and my love for God. This was mine, it was my most precious possession and nobody, nobody could take that away from me. It was my deep Faith in God that helped me survive all that I suffered at the brutal, savage hands of the Japanese.

I have forgiven the Japanese for what they did to me, but I can never forget.

When the war was over, the atrocities done to me would haunt me for the rest of my life. I could not talk about it to anyone, the shame was too great. I had no counselling and I had to get on with my life as if nothing had happened. After seeing the Korean 'Comfort Women' on TV, I decided to back them up in their plight for an apology and for justice and compensation. In December 1992, I broke my 50 years of silence at the international public hearing on Japanese war crimes held in Tokyo and revealed one of the worst human rights abuses to come out of World War II. It is by telling my story that I hope these atrocities against women in war will never be forgotten and will never happen again.

2

The Roses

Mimi Doretti *

Someone sent me flowers at the hotel in London where I was spending a few days before leaving for Ethiopia. I love flowers, but not really roses. Yet these roses were so incredibly beautiful, so fresh and such a deep, dark red, that at the last minute, I cut off three of them from the vase where they were about to be abandoned and took them with me to Addis Ababa. This was in May 2002 – but this story starts many years earlier.

I   Addis Ababa 1993

We arrived in Ethiopia to support the work of the Special Prosecutor's Office (SPO) of Addis Ababa. This office was set up in 1992 to investigate the crimes committed by the previous regime of Colonel Mengistu Haile Marian.

I'm an anthropologist and part of the Argentine Forensic Anthropology Team (EAAF in Spanish), which, for the last 20 years, has applied forensic anthropology and archaeology to the investigation of human rights cases. Our work is requested by human rights and judiciary organisations around the world to investigate cases, exhume and analyse human remains – mostly bones – belonging to victims of human rights abuses. We try to identify them so that the remains can be returned to the families and can provide information about the victim's cause and manner of death (a gun shot wound, for example; and whether it was a homicide, a suicide or an accident). We write a report for the person or entity in charge of the investigation and sometimes testify about our findings before special commissions of inquiry, courts and international tribunals.

*   Mimi Doretti is a co-founder and full time researcher of the Argentine Forensic Anthropology Team (EAAF). Since 1992, she has coordinated EAAF's office in New York. She remains grateful to Leslie Carson and Arshes Anasal for their editorial assistance while writing this chapter. Mimi also wishes to thank the individuals named in this piece – Mr. Ato Girma Wakjira, Dr. Clyde Snow, Ms. Anahí Ginarte and most particularly Ms. Tirfinesh Kahsay – for allowing their real names to be used and their experiences to be shared.

Helen Durham and Tracey Gurd (eds.), Listening to the Silences: Women and War, *pp. 9-14.*
© *2005 Koninklijke Brill BV. Printed in The Netherlands.* ISBN 90 04 14365 3.

Weeks before, while preparing for EAAF's first visit to Ethiopia, I called Addis Ababa from New York to ask one of the lawyers working for the SPO to describe the pattern of human rights violations during the Mengistu regime. 'What do you mean?' he said. 'Well, in Argentina it was primarily the disappearance of people. It would help us to understand what we are facing here if you could brief us about it.' He replied, sounding slightly irritated and trying to be patient at the same time, '*Every* possible violation was committed here and in large scale – disappearances, torture, extra-judicial executions, summary executions, rape, famine as a weapon of war. You should read *Evil Days. Thirty Years of Famine and Repression in Ethiopia* by Human Rights Watch.' 'Okay. Excuse my ignorance,' I said. I bought the book.

We stayed in Ethiopia for three weeks, trying to learn as much as possible about the country, the SPO, the recent past conflict and to see whether, and in what cases, the team could assist the SPO with forensic work. We also gave presentations about forensic anthropology and archaeology to judges, Supreme Court members, prosecutors and lawyers who were setting up a public defence office.

II   Addis Ababa 1994

We returned for four months in 1994. One of the cases that the SPO asked us to investigate involved the disappearance of 30 political prisoners, all men, while in custody. The chief of the office, Ato Girma Wakjira, gave us basic information about the background of the case. The men who disappeared were from different political groups and regions of Ethiopia, imprisoned at different times in two main prisons. One of the prisons was called Makalawi, located in Addis Ababa. The other one was the Combolcha prison in the Wollo province. One day in October 1979, the men's relatives were stopped when trying to leave their daily packages of food and clean clothing for their loved ones inside the prison. 'He is no longer here. Your food is no longer necessary. No further information is available,' each of them was told.

For fifteen years, the relatives of these 30 men could not find out any information about the fate of their family members, whether they had been transferred to another prison, or if they were dead or alive. In fact, the families of the Combolcha prisoners did not even know that their disappearance was connected with that of the other prisoners from Makalawi.

Finally, in 1994, the SPO asked us to dig up a grave inside a military intelligence compound in the outskirts of Addis Ababa. In a clearing inside a small eucalyptus forest, behind several short buildings, the SPO lawyers marked a place. It was an oblong, almost rectangular, depression. Underneath a layer of heavy rocks, lime and blankets, approximately two metres from the surface, we found 30 male skeletons with green nylon ropes around their necks.

We worked at this site for several weeks, slowly removing the skeletons and the associated evidence which mostly included clothing and personal effects. We rarely saw anybody other than the guards and people behind windows that we would occasionally see in some of the several buildings in the compound still used by the military intelligence. The place looked deserted. When taking a break from the work, we made jokes about being inside of a 1960 very cold, Cold War movie. None of the Ethiopian doctors that worked with us on other cases were allowed to work with us this time. No presumed relatives of the victims were allowed either, as we had not yet confirmed the identities of the remains. The only people who joined us at the site were lawyers from the SPO. At the compound, guards and designated helpers – people who we later learned where the ones who originally buried the remains – worked with us. Some days a military man dressed in civilian clothing would visit the site and bring us coffee and sweets, which his assistants would hand down into the grave to us on trays with delicate china coffee cups.

Once the exhumation was advanced enough, the SPO decided to open the site and the grave to the local and international press, religious leaders and the diplomatic community for a day. We were asked to say a few words about what people were seeing – though the scene was quite eloquent in itself. The Coptic patriarch, a high religious official, blessed the grave.

The investigation continued. The SPO provided us with a list of 30 names thought to correspond to the ones who disappeared in 1979 from the two prisons and were suspected to be in that grave. We interviewed the relatives of the victims to ask them for ante mortem information – that is, physical information about the victims when they were alive: age at time of death, sex, height, ancestry, which hand they used, dental information, old fractures, diseases that could have affected bones, photos. All of this information was later compared with the information coming from the analysis of the skeletal remains in order to make identifications.

Because the reported victims in this case had been held in custody for several years in some instances, we also interviewed men who were formerly imprisoned with the people thought to be the buried at the intelligence compound. We thought they could share information about injuries or physical changes that may have occurred while the men were in prison. Torture, ill treatment and beatings are often common in human rights cases. Sometimes knowledge of these abuses can offer important information about the physical data that we need to add to the pre-mortem information, such as broken ribs, noses and teeth.

The SPO and our investigation showed that the prisoners who 'disappeared' while in custody were indeed the 30 men found at the military compound grave. Interviews with former prisoners confirmed that one night, 20 prisoners from the Combolcha prison were taken in a truck to Makalawi. It was a cold night and they were wearing blankets over their shoulders – blankets that we later found in the grave. Other witnesses told us that the men were seen by other prisoners when they arrived at the Makalawi prison. One survivor even recognised a friend among the group. The men were put into cells next to the prisoners we interviewed. The next morning they were called one at a time by the guards every ten minutes or so and were never seen again. Another ten prisoners from the Makalawi prison shared the same fate. By the early afternoon, there were rumours among the prisoners that the whole group had been executed.

The interviews strongly suggested that the connection between the two groups listed as victims from Makalawi and Combolcha was solid. Later, the identification at the laboratory of eight of the bodies found in the grave reconfirmed this link and proved that the list of victims corresponded with the remains found at the site.

III   Tirfinesh

Among the relatives that we interviewed before digging the grave was the wife of one of the missing men. Ms. Tirfinesh Kahsay was in her late thirties, slim, attractive, with long brown hair and almond brown, very bright, eyes. By Ethiopian standards, she was probably a middle class woman. When we finished the laboratory work, we called Ms. Kahsay to meet us in the SPO office. The head of the office, Ato Girma, authorised us to speak with each of the families and explain the findings to them. He participated in most of these meetings, explaining and translating the findings and providing comfort to the relatives. None of us spoke Amharic, the official language in Ethiopia, but Ms. Kahsay spoke enough English for us to understand each other. We told her that we identified her husband among the victims from the grave. She started crying. She said this was the moment she has been waiting for years; it was both the happiest and the saddest. 'I loved this man dearly. I loved him so much. We were so happy together.' Finding his remains was the end of the hope of finding him alive, she continued. Somewhere deep inside, she knew he had been killed but she could not bring herself to declare him dead and stop searching for him without concrete evidence. All of these years her life was frozen, paralysed. Now, she said, she will finally be able to start a new life again. Maybe she would even remarry.

A few days later, Ms. Kahsay invited us for tea at her house in the afternoon. Three or four of us went. We sat in her living room while she showed us photographs of herself and her husband together. As we went through the albums, I looked at her and the things around the room. It was a quite large and neat space with a soft afternoon light coming in through a small window. The house was small, too. It wasn't luxurious but it was just fine. Somehow there, her solitude was bigger. Waiting. An unconfirmed widow, I thought.

'Do you want to see the remains?' we asked her at a certain point, as we always do with all relatives in such cases. 'Yes,' she said assertively.

Ms. Kahsay came to the Black Lion Hospital the next morning. We were working at the morgue facilities, consisting basically of one big room with white tiles and windows on the top of one wall, sinks in one corner and three or four autopsy tables in the middle. A small room was annexed to this one, where we kept the remains under 24-hour custody. By then, we had some experience in what to do at these moments, though no concrete rules apply. We laid out the bones in anatomical position on an autopsy table, just as a body would look if the flesh had been still there. Everything was clean. No other skeletons were displayed on the other tables. We put the clothing that he was wearing when we found him next to his bones.

She asked how we knew it was him and how he died. Several things resulted in his positive identification. Among them, we showed her a photo of him smiling while having dinner, revealing very characteristic frontal upper teeth. We showed her those exact features on the skull we had in front of us. She nodded. As for the cause of death, we told her very likely they had all been strangled, but that we had not finished our study regarding that issue.

Over the years, we more or less had learned how to answer the impossible questions that family members ask while standing before the skeleton of their relative. We try to go as far as the questions go; not beyond, not short. We do not want to hide information but also do not want to go where they are not asking us to go.

There were no more questions. She was crying, more and more. We stepped away from the table, unable to keep ourselves from silently crying with her. She touched his skull several times and said words in Amharic. My face was full of tears, but I was looking straight towards her and the scene, as if crying for me was an unavoidable accident but out of place. I felt it was only her mourning – not ours – which should take place there. The pain for the pain of others.

She sat next to his remains and asked to be left alone. We left the room and waited outside. After a while, she called us back. She seemed more recovered. She even smiled a bit, while taking some flowers out of her bag. 'I brought these roses. I would like to put them in the box with his remains until the reburial.' We looked at each other, a bit disconcerted. 'Of course,' we said and sealed the box with two roses inside.

IV   2002

Eight years had passed when we received a call in our New York office from the Chief Prosecutor of the SPO in Addis. He asked us to come back and testify in the case which was finally going to be heard in court.

Dr. Clyde Snow, a world leading forensic anthropologist, pioneer in the application of forensic anthropology to human rights investigations and our mentor, worked with us in the case in 1994. His expert testimony would be vital in court. Dr. Snow, Anahí Ginarte (an EAAF Argentinean anthropologist who also worked on this case in 1994) and I met in Ethiopia in May 2002.

My roses survived the trip from London. As soon as I arrived to Addis, I put them on a glass on my night table at the hotel room.

The next day, we met again with Ato Girma, who was still head of the SPO. He asked us to display the skeletons of the 13 individuals from the case that had been identified on tables in the courtroom. (Between 1994 and 2002, five more individuals had been identified using DNA analysis). He said physical evidence had never been used in the courts before in Ethiopia, so the three-judge panel and the defence lawyers may not be sure that the slides we wanted to show them actually corresponded to the skeletons we exhumed. We understood his point but we were also worried about creating a sensationalistic courtroom 'show' by actually bringing the skeletons. 'Could we meet with the relatives of the identified victims? If they agree, we'll do it,' we offered. Girma agreed.

We went back to the hotel. I entered my room and the roses had disappeared. Instead, some orange, unidentifiable flowers were on my night table. I rushed out of the room and asked a maid in the corridor if she was the one that made up my room. She was, and said she took the flowers away because they were wilting and she thought I would be happier with new flowers. 'Is there a way to recover them?' I asked, despairingly. No, it was too late. I went back to my room feeling helpless, disturbed.

Several days later, we met at the SPO offices with the relatives of the people identified in the case. Ms. Kahsay came along with the group. She was a bit older, still slim, with the same nice smile and sparkling eyes. Anahí and I embraced her. She was fine, she said. I didn't dare ask her if she had remarried – there was not much time and there were people around – though it was on my mind all the time. It was also that I wasn't sure if I could ask her about it. There was a clear current of affection between us – a strong and peculiar bond. But I did not really know this woman. In fact, still today I know extremely little about her. This is part of our work. We often share extremely intense, private moments with people we hardly know and then we rarely see each other again. From both ends, I guess the memory that binds us is too painful to stay in contact.

Ato Girma called us into his office. He explained to the relatives that we needed their opinion about the display of the remains in court. Each of the relatives spoke about their case. Almost all cried as they talked, followed by long pauses. Waiting for the translation was difficult. I looked at their hands, their clothing, their faces. They all agreed that we should show the skeletons in court. Even if it would be very hard for them to watch, everything should be done to achieve justice. There were many silences in the conversation and a feeling of some dignity in the room. The next discussion was if they were going to be present or not. An old lady said she would not be able to watch it; she would faint if she had to. Ato Girma offered her and the others transcripts of the session if they could not attend. Ms. Kahsay said she would think about it.

The day before testifying, the Court allowed us to bring the boxes with the remains and the rest of the evidence to accommodate them on tables in the courtroom. We displayed the 13 identified skeletons in a shell shape, between the panel of judges and the defendants, their lawyers and the public. We put the ropes and clothing found with each individual next to their bones. Anahí and I opened the box of Fatima's husband's remains and found one rose still there, withered and dried. We had completely forgotten about the roses. We put it between his bones on the table in court.

The next day, the court was full of people. It was a very large room within the huge court compound, quite simply furnished with wood benches occupying most of the space. Dr. Snow testified about the laboratory findings. Skeleton by skeleton, he explained with the help of slides and a translator how each person was identified and how they died. When he reached Ms. Kahsay's husband's table, he first picked up a long bone, looked at it and did not say much. Then, he picked up the rose and held it as if it was a bone for a few seconds. He then turned to the public, looked for a brief moment at it and put the rose back. In the back row of the courtroom, I saw Ms. Kahsay nodding slowly.

3

Combat Operations in Iraq:
An Australian Soldier's Perspective

*Penny Cumming**

The hardest thing about going to war was leaving my children. At the time they were aged five, four and one – too young to understand what was going on. My kids were relatively familiar with me or my husband going away for periods of time – but the concept of one of us leaving for six months, or even nine months, was well beyond them. All they knew – all that I could explain – was that I was going on a 'work' plane for a long, long time to live in the desert.

They did not fully understand that I was going until I got to the airport. The look of terror on their faces as they realised that Mummy was going tore my heart to shreds. I had to pry their fingers from my legs so that I could get free and walk away from them – the accusation in their eyes so very clear to me – how can you leave us? It was only after I returned home that my husband told me how my two older children turned to him as I left and beat his legs, 'I hate you Daddy, I hate you Daddy!'

I spent the next two days crying my heart out.

Seven months later and safely back home, the pain of remembering is still almost as intense. Having being through the most recent armed conflict in Iraq and having seen and heard of some of the most awful atrocities, personally, the hardest thing for me still was leaving my children. I also believe I am exceptionally lucky in being able to say that.

So what was my war like? I am a legal officer with the Australian Army. I deployed to another country in the Middle East approximately five weeks before combat operations commenced against Iraq to work with the Australian National Headquarters as part of a legal team. Our role was to provide advice to the Australian commanders on the laws of armed conflict. After combat operations ceased in Iraq, I moved forward with the advance party of the Australian Headquarters to Baghdad. I spent two months there as the legal officer on the forward headquarters before spending my final month working with the Coalition Headquarters for Iraq, also based in Baghdad.

---

*   Penny Cumming is a Legal Officer with the Australian Army. The views expressed in this paper are the views of the author only and are not attributable to the Australian Army, the Department of Defence or the Commonwealth of Australia.

Helen Durham and Tracey Gurd (eds.), Listening to the Silences: Women and War, *pp. 15-20.*
© *2005 Koninklijke Brill BV. Printed in The Netherlands.* ISBN *90 04 14365 3.*

Combat operations in Iraq, for me, appeared to be conducted by remote control. Being geographically located away from the fighting meant that I was distanced from the war. The fighting was watched on CNN or computer screens and could have been watched from anywhere in the world. Legal issues associated with the war came and went. I worked long hours, but it all retained a surreal and distant feel because, to my mind, there was no immediate and personal threat, no danger. I needed to constantly remind myself that this was not just 'another exercise'; that the targets reviewed today would be struck tonight in Baghdad – I could even watch it on television. Was this different from any other war movie?

The only exception to this was my concern for my friends who were deployed into more dangerous locations. For the first few weeks, I would anxiously scan reports each night when I began my shift to ensure there had been no Australian casualties. We were lucky. We had no casualties – but always at the back of my mind was a need to know that my 'mates' were okay.

At night, I would stand outside in the empty desert listening to the sounds of the bombers taking off and returning from their raids. Some nights, I would be able to watch on CNN the impact of rounds dropped from bombers which had taken off a few hours before. What was I thinking? Was I thinking of the safety of fellow coalition defence members, my brothers-in-arms? No. I was thinking of the mothers of small children – some one like me who just happened to be born an Iraqi rather than an Australian. How do you protect your children from something like that? How do you make sure that it is not your child that is killed when the building is hit? You can't. It becomes a matter of luck, fate, God, Allah – something – but it made me all the more determined to never allow my children to be placed in such a situation. It also made me appreciate how lucky I am to have the ability to say that: to be able to choose where I go and what I do. Inside my mind, did this then mean that I was more determined to 'fight for Iraqi freedom'? I don't know. I don't think so. But I do know that it made me want to help those Iraqi mothers and their children.

My real experience of the war began when I arrived in Baghdad. In the Australian Army, all members of the army receive basic training as soldiers: that is, learning how to fight. I thought I would have to use those basic fighting skills when I went to war – however, it was only when I got to Baghdad and had a weapon in my hand that I felt that I was involved in any type of conflict. Instead of fighting by remote control, I was now on the ground and was in a position to the see the direct consequences of my actions. There was a real threat that we could be targeted for attack each time we moved outside the compound where we lived. Coalition vehicles had been destroyed by mines only a short distance from the front gate of our compound. At night, it was common to hear small arms fire – and occasionally heavy machine gun fire – from incidents occurring on the perimeter of our compound.

One of the frequent questions asked of me when I got home was, 'Did you ever feel really afraid?' It took me a while to think of the right answer the first time I was asked the question. In an objective sense, I was in a dangerous environment. In a subjective sense, though, I was not afraid: rather, I felt prepared. What I did find interesting was my change in mindset and the need to 'psych' myself up each time I was on a task that entailed leaving the compound. I found that I would be pumped on adrenalin and would generally become more aggressive. Upon reflection, I believe that this is a necessary part of the need to be prepared to use lethal force to protect yourself or your fellow soldiers.

I recall one day driving back from central Baghdad to our compound. I was travelling in the backseat of our vehicle behind the driver. I was watching out my side of the vehicle with my weapon. I noticed a small child, about eight- or nine-years-old, standing in the driveway of a house. An older male, probably in his mid teens, was standing with him. Before I knew it, the child had raised a stick and pointed it at the driver of our vehicle. I knew it was a stick but immediately thought to myself that it could have been a weapon. I could have shot that child for pointing a stick. My next thought was, 'What on earth is his mother doing letting him out on the street behaving like that? He will get himself killed!'

Is this an Australian soldier thinking? Is this a woman soldier thinking? Is it a mother thinking? I can't divorce myself into these separate entities to answer the question. I am all three rolled into one. What did this teach me? That if I had to, I would kill a child to protect myself or a fellow soldier. I knew if I could kill a child, I could kill a man or a woman just as easily. Was I proud of myself for finding that out? Did I take pleasure in this new-found knowledge? No. But it did give me a sense of confidence in knowing that I would be capable of doing my job if it came to it – in the same way that I am satisfied when I reach the summit of a hill that has taken five hours to climb. It is merely the satisfaction of knowing you can do something if you have to. From that, I have become a bit more confident.

As a 'girl' soldier in Baghdad, I was a novelty to the local population. The security environment meant that there were limited opportunities to mix with the locals, but on a couple of occasions, I got to speak (as best I could) with the Iraqi people living in the neighbourhood of the Australian Embassy in Baghdad. I will never forget the delight on the faces of the family that lived in a house nearby when they realised that I was a girl. The women of the house were laughing and pointing at me when I first walked by. I looked just like every other soldier. When I then removed my helmet, they laughed even harder – not out of jest, but more out of surprise. They were very keen to talk with me and were pleased to hear I had a family of my own back in Australia. I felt a bond between us – however slight – purely from being women. I believe this type of connection did not exist – and never would exist – between the local men and the male Australian soldiers.

I received very different responses in two other incidents. The first occurred at a government building in Baghdad. I was walking through a courtyard when I noticed a lady nearby, walking with her daughter who was about the same age as one of my own children. Having had very little contact with children while away – and missing my own – I wanted to say hello. Through broken and very bad Arabic, I said hello and introduced myself. I didn't think about the scary picture I must have presented. I was wearing full combat body armour, helmet, webbing and carrying a loaded weapon. The little girl was very apprehensive, but I removed my helmet and smiled. When she realised I was a girl she relaxed, as did her mother. We introduced ourselves and 'chatted' as best we could. We parted with handshakes and smiles.

A few days later at the same building, I noticed a number of women waiting outside the offices. Putting on my warmest smile, I greeted them in Arabic only to be met by a look of pure hatred and disgust from one of the women. To me, it felt like a slap in the face. It really made me sit back and think about who I was and what I was doing. Initially it was hard not to take it personally. Why did she hate me? What had I done to her? Thinking more about it, I could not take it personally. I reconciled it with the thought that if I was in Australia and foreign soldiers had moved into my country – maybe even dropped bombs that had killed one of my family – then why on earth would I want to smile at them? I would hate them.

But what of my fellow sisters-in-arms? I had the pleasure of sharing a tent with approximately 60 other women for the first three months of my deployment – seven Australian girls with the remainder American. There were no special bonds. The normal tiffs that occur when too many people try to live in a confined space happened on a regular basis. The bond of sisterhood did not extend to our Coalition counterparts in my experience.

It did, however, exist in a very real and strong sense between my fellow Aussies. Being girls, we were all accommodated together and living in close confinement when we were based outside Iraq. This also occurred in Baghdad. To my mind at least, there is almost a sort of assumption among Australian Army girls that we will all get on well. My approach, wrongly or rightly, is that we will be sympathetic to each other's causes and supportive when another is having a bad day. That has been my experience throughout my military career, whether in barracks or on exercise. There are exceptions – there always will be – but I think the willingness to get along together stems from being a minority. Working and living in a male-dominated and physically demanding environment means you become more 'blokey'. But it is only another girl who understands the need to paint your toenails hot pink in the middle of a desert during a war where you are wearing your GP boots 18 hours out of every 24. It is only in the girls' tent that you find the stack of fashion magazines, the gossip magazines, the home magazines and numerous photographs and cards from friends, family, children, partners – all the touches that transforms an austere military environment into a semblance of homeliness. To put it simply and in military parlance – it was a 'chick' thing and I honestly believe that many of the guys missed that feeling of homeliness. This is not to say that the females were an exclusive club and kept to ourselves. Of the good friends that I made while deployed, only one was a woman. The other four were male.

Another image that sits clearly in my mind was the day of the 'Free Undies'. Again through the female network and friendships, the Australian girls were invited to attend the 'free underwear' gala that some US soldiers had organised. A company in the US had donated a number of boxes of bras and knickers of various sizes. By this time, many of the American girls had been living in the field for up to six months. We had been in the field for about ten weeks. Out of curiosity more than necessity, I attended with three other girls from the Australian contingent. After driving around for 20 minutes looking for the right unit, we finally found it in a dust bowl – a series of tents under camouflage netting. It was summer so it was about 50 degrees Celsius (approximately 120 degrees Fahrenheit). The sight still brings a smile to my face.

A row of boxes set out in the dirt, filled to the brim with underwear of ridiculous proportions. Some bras were big enough to hold at least two watermelons. We figured they must have been dual-use weapons – catapulting boulders being the primary role! But nonetheless, in the middle of the heat and the dust was a scene that resembled any good department store sale. Girls of all ranks and sizes sorted through the boxes looking for the miracle bargain! It was refreshing to see – if only for the knowledge that the normalcy, for which we all lusted, had not gone. Two days later, I noticed one of the 'boulder-holders' flapping in the breeze, tied to the entrance of the Australian stores tent.

In barracks – and even in the compound in Baghdad – the overwhelming feeling between the Australians was, in my mind, teamship. For me, the Australians deployed with me became my surrogate family. There were some that I liked more than others, some I disliked, some I had fallings out with. But they were my family and the bond could not be broken whether I wanted it there or not. I was fortunate when it came time for me to leave Baghdad, as many of those who had deployed with me had already gone or were going. When I left, I grieved for the loss of my new 'family', but was helped by the knowledge that this family no longer existed in Baghdad.

What I have found, instead, is that a special bond exists between those of us who were deployed. Since I returned, I have had brief encounters with a few people who were deployed at the same time as me, but worked in different regions. We greet each other as old friends. I suspect, though, that this bond is hollow and will whittle away with time. The 'common bonds' we found during conflict fade in the overwhelming presence of day-to-day life.

My time working with the Australians was a professionally rewarding experience. My time working with the Coalition headquarters was better. It was here that I finally felt that I was making a real contribution to help the Iraqi people. My work entailed assisting with the restoration of Iraqi courts. I do not think that my efforts resulted in tangible benefits to the Iraqi people, but it was an area in which my skills could best be used. I believe that contributing to the reconstruction of Iraq was – and still is – very important to me in coming to terms with the 'war'. Is this a compensator in my own mind for the destruction inflicted during combat operations? Or as a woman, is it my need to create something rather than destroy? I don't know.

An insensitive fellow visiting Australian troops in the Middle East asked me about the war. I remember his exact words: 'It must have been great fun, blowing all those things up'. I was repulsed by his enthusiasm. I had never regarded my involvement with the combat aspects of the conflict as 'fun'. Instead I can still recall the puzzlement that dawned on me the day I realised that what I was doing was real. It was almost with a shock that I accepted that the combat missions – being planned and conducted each day – were real and that consequences were life and death.

The significance of going to war did not really dawn on me until I got home. For the last six months I had simply been doing my job. When I got home, I found that I had 'been to war'. The terms 'war veteran' and 'returned soldier' are being used about me but do not sit well with me. It was a shock when, on my third day back in Australia, my husband introduced me to a Vietnam veteran he had just met. The veteran shook my hand and looked me in the eye and said, 'Welcome back. No one ever said that to me – I want to say it to you'. With those words, I felt I had been brought into an exclusive club – that I was now a veteran too, recognised by those who had also been to war. My problem is that I don't feel that I deserve that honour. I do not feel that I placed my life on the line, that I fought for my country – that I went to war. I just did my job.

4

The Impact of Armed
Conflict on Women

*Charlotte Lindsey**

This chapter aims to draw attention to the multifaceted ways in which women experience armed conflict and, to a limited extent, to some of the activities carried out by the International Committee of the Red Cross (ICRC) to assist and protect women.

The ICRC is continuously striving to assess the impact of armed conflict on its victims. Listening to the people affected by conflict is a significant part of these efforts. In 1998, the ICRC initiated a study aimed at improving its understanding of the specific impact that armed conflict has on women. This study, entitled *Women Facing War*, was published in October 2001 and investigates the needs of women in times of war, the protection accorded to women by international humanitarian law (IHL) and ICRC activities on behalf of women in its' worldwide operations.

In recent years, much attention has been devoted in academic debate and the media to sexual violence, particularly rape, inflicted upon women and girls during war. Articles in legal reviews have also focused attention on the protection afforded to women under IHL, especially since the establishment of the International Criminal Tribunals for the former Yugoslavia (ICTY) and for Rwanda (ICTR). Placing increased attention on the situation of women in wartime is fully warranted. However, the focus has generally been on sexual violence and women as refugees, to the exclusion of many of the other ways women are affected by armed conflict.

Today, the vast majority of armed conflicts occur within a State's borders. Such internal conflicts have a devastating impact upon civilian populations. With respect to civilian women, there used to be a perceived security – a sense that as a woman, and particularly as a mother, one would be spared the excesses of warfare. Recent and present armed conflicts show that this perception often does not correspond to reality. On the contrary, women are targeted and suffer violations of IHL precisely because they are women. War has also had an enormous impact on civilian men. Men in war

---

*   Charlotte Lindsey is currently Deputy Director of Communication at the ICRC Headquarters in Geneva and has undertaken a broad range of missions in the field with the ICRC. She has a Masters of Science in Communication Management from the University of Swiss-Italy. Charlotte was, at the time of writing this chapter, Head of the ICRC's Women and War Project. This chapter is a personal contribution.

Helen Durham and Tracey Gurd (eds.), Listening to the Silences: Women and War, *pp. 21-35.*
© *2005* Koninklijke Brill BV. Printed in The Netherlands. ISBN 90 04 14365 3.

are generally characterised as protagonists – combatants actively engaged in the armed conflict. Yet many men, including men of military conscription age, do not take up arms and fight. These civilian men may suffer enormously – targeted because they are men of fighting age, irrespective of the fact that they are civilians. It is also necessary to recognise that women take up weapons as members of the armed forces in many armed conflicts and thus are not always civilians.

Women have tended to be classified within a single category: 'women and children' and, consequently, as 'vulnerable'. Yet women are not necessarily vulnerable and certainly have needs, experiences and roles in situations of armed conflict that differ from those of children whom they are so often categorised alongside. Women often display remarkable strength as evidenced by the roles they assume in wartime to protect and support their families.[1] The assumption that women are vulnerable overlooks the fact that women are more and more frequently taking up arms.[2]

I   Women Taking Part in Hostilities

Women are actively engaging in many armed conflicts around the world and have played a part in wars throughout history.[3] In the Second World War, women took part primarily in reservist or support units (including work in munitions factories) in the German and British forces and, in the case of the Soviet Union, participated directly in the fighting as members of all services and units.[4] Since then, women have assumed a much greater role and are more frequently joining the armed forces, voluntarily and involuntarily, performing both support and combatant roles. To give a few examples, in the United States military, 'overall, 14 percent of active duty personnel are women' and of the US forces who served in the 1990-1991 Gulf War, 40,000 were women.[5] In the war in Iraq in 2003, women constituted approximately 15 percent (or one in seven) of the US military personnel.[6] It is estimated that a fifth of the Eritrean armed forces were female[7] and up to a third of the fighting forces of the Liberation Tigers of Tamil Eelam (LTTE) involved in the civil war in Sri Lanka were women.[8] The role of female 'suicide bombers' in Sri Lanka, Israel and the Russian Federation also underscores the

---

1   ICRC, *Women Facing War* (2001) 28.

2   Children have also taken part, and continue to take part, in armed conflict, but this is a very different situation and constitutes a clear violation of IHL.

3   ICRC, above n 1, 23.

4   See Françoise Krill, 'The Protection of Women in International Humanitarian Law' (1995) 249 *International Review of the Red Cross* 337-363.

5   Greg Siegle, 'Women Critical to Success of US All-Volunteer Force' (1999) 31(23) *Jane's Defence Weekly* (23 June 1999).

6   Shauna Curphey, '1 in 7 U.S. Military Personnel in Iraq is Female', *Women's E-news* (2 April 2004).

7   David Hirst, 'Ethiopia: Human waves fall as war aims unfold', *The Guardian* (Great Britain) 18 May 1999.

8   Dexter Filkins, 'Sri Lanka Women at War', *International Herald Tribune* (France) 13 March 2000.

extent to which women are prepared to take action and that women are as capable as men of perpetrating extreme violence.

Despite such examples of women's participation in armed conflict, some countries and cultures still exclude women from active participation in combat roles in the armed forces. The majority of women still experience the effects of armed conflict as members of the civilian population. Civilian status affords them protection in conflicts of both an international and non-international character.

II Women as Members of the Civilian Population

As members of the civilian population, women (and girls) are subjected to innumerable acts of violence during situations of armed conflict. They often suffer the direct or indirect effects of the fighting, enduring indiscriminate attacks as well as a lack of food and other essentials needed to ensure their healthy survival. Women invariably have to bear greater responsibility for their children, their elderly relatives and often the wider community, when male family members have left to fight, are interned or detained, missing or deceased, internally displaced or in exile. The very fact that many of their menfolk are absent often heightens the insecurity and danger for the women and children left behind. It exacerbates the breakdown of the traditional support mechanisms upon which the community – especially women – previously relied. Increased exposure to armed conflict, threat of injury or attack, as well as a loss of means for economic survival, often causes women and children to flee. It is common knowledge that women and children constitute the majority of the world's refugees. But what of the women who do not flee?

Ironically, women often do not flee the fighting or the threat of hostilities because they and their families believe that the very fact that they are women (often with children) will afford them a greater measure of protection from the warring parties, sometimes in the belief that their socially constructed gender role will protect them. Therefore, some women stay behind to protect the family's property and livelihood; to care for the elderly, young and sick family members who cannot flee as they are less mobile; to keep their children in school (as education is such an important factor for many families and their future); to visit and support family members in detention; to search for their missing family members; and even to assess the level of insecurity and danger in order to decide whether it is safe for displaced family members to return. Some may argue that in doing so, women are extending the gender roles that existed pre-conflict in times of war: the fact that women remain as caretakers is a continuation of the pre-war status quo. In fact, this perceived protection – that as a woman you will be safe – is often not the reality. On the contrary, women have been targeted precisely because they are women, for example, because they are perceived as symbolic bearers of the future of their cultural and ethnic identity and as responsible for future generations of their community. The ICRC assisted, for example, large numbers of mostly elderly and frail women left behind in the former United Nations Protected Areas in Croatia (UNPAs, frequently referred to as the 'Krajinas'). They had been left by their fleeing family members to protect the property and/or could not or would not leave their homes. Even these elderly, often incapacitated, women were not free from harassment and attack.

Women's exposure to indiscriminate attack is particularly acute in non-international armed conflict due to the proximity of the fighting. They have also been forced to harbour and feed soldiers, thus being exposed to the risk of reprisals by the opposing forces and placed in difficult and inappropriate situations: having another mouth to feed on scant resources coupled with a serious threat to the personal safety of the woman and her children. As one peasant woman in El Salvador eloquently stated in the *People on War* survey, '[it] was terrible, because if you didn't sell tortillas to the guerrillas, they got mad, and if you didn't sell to the soldiers, they got mad, so you had to collaborate with both sides'.[9]

Owing to the proximity of the fighting and/or the presence of arms bearers, women invariably have to restrict their movements. This severely limits their access to supplies of water, food and medical assistance (of all types) and their ability to tend their animals and crops, to exchange news and information and to seek community or family support. Limited access to medical assistance can have an enormous impact on women, especially in terms of reproductive and maternal health. Childbirth complications, arguably more likely in the stressful conditions of war, can lead to increased child and maternal mortality or illness. Reproductive health care is vital to save lives and prevent and reduce illnesses and disabilities due to complications during pregnancy, labour and after giving birth. In addition to obtaining care for themselves, women have an important role in promoting and maintaining the health of their family and community. They know, or can learn, how to prevent illnesses and care for sick family members and should be supported and assisted in these efforts.

Women are all too often harassed, intimidated and attacked in their homes, while moving around their village and its environs and when passing checkpoints. A lack of identity documents – a problem experienced by many women who have lost them or were never previously issued with documentation in their own right – severely affects the personal safety and freedom of movement of women, increasing their risk of abuse.

Women are also endangered because of their presence amongst the armed forces or armed groups despite being there completely against their will – abducted to provide sex, food and cleaning in their camps. During the period of their abduction, and often afterwards, these women and girls can face considerable danger from attack by the opposing forces as well as their abductors. The best known wide-scale example of such abductions was that of the so-called 'comfort women' in the Far East during the Second World War – a term which in no way encompasses the horrific nature of the ordeal to which these women were subjected[10] – as demonstrated in Jan Ruff O'Herne's moving account of her experiences in this book. But the abduction of women in war-

---

9   ICRC, *People on War Report: ICRC Worldwide Consultation on the Rules of War* (1999) (available on request from the ICRC website <www.onwar.org>). To mark the 50th anniversary of the 1949 *Geneva Conventions*, the ICRC launched a consultation in 17 countries, 12 of which were or had been at war, giving the general public a chance to express their opinions on war.

10   ICRC, above n 1, 25.

time is not just a thing of the past. In contemporary armed conflicts, women and girls continue to be abducted by armed groups in countries such as Uganda.[11]

III   Sexual Violence in Armed Conflict

As Maggie O'Kane describes in her chapter later in this book, the armed conflict in Bosnia and Herzegovina drew the world's attention to the issue of the rape of women as a method of warfare. People were horrified to hear accounts of women being abducted and detained in order to be raped, sometimes with the aim of impregnating them. In many conflicts women have been systematically targeted for sexual violence – sometimes with the broader political objective of 'ethnically cleansing' an area or destroying a people. During the *People on War* survey undertaken by the ICRC in countries which had been, or are still at war, one in nine of all respondents reported that they knew somebody who had been raped. Nearly as many reported that they knew somebody who had been sexually assaulted.[12]

Rape, forced prostitution, sexual slavery and forced impregnation are violations of IHL and are now an everyday part of the vocabulary of war. It must, however, be emphasised that they are not 'new' crimes. Who didn't learn in their history lessons of marauding armies entering conquered towns on a rampage of 'looting and raping'? Yet few of us were probably taught that 'rape' was a crime which can never be justified as a means of warfare or display of power, nor as a reward for the victorious army or as a lesson to the vanquished 'enemy' unable to protect their womenfolk.[13]

It is not possible to give anything but estimates as to the number of victims of sexual violence (female or male, adult or child). Not all victims survive and the majority of victims will never report the violation against them. Reliable statistics are not easy to obtain and those available are often based on the numbers of victims seeking medical help for pregnancy, sexually transmitted infections (STIs) or termination of pregnancy. The numbers of women seeking such assistance often become the basis upon which statistics are extrapolated. However, many women are generally too afraid to speak of their experiences for the very real fear of ostracism or retaliation by their family or community. Many also believe that they are beyond help once they have been violated. Moreover, the worst atrocities against the civilian and detainee or internee populations (groups which are expressly protected under IHL) all too often occur when international organisations are not present to witness, and attempt to put an end to, the violations. This was the case in Kosovo (during the period of the NATO air strikes), in Chechnya during the Russian military campaign, in rural areas of Sierra

---

11   Human Rights Watch, *Uganda – Abducted and Abused: Renewed Conflict in Northern Uganda* (2003) Volume 15, No 12(A); Thalif Deen, 'Africa: Abduction of Women, Children Growing in Warzones', UN InterPress Service (29 January 2004) UN website <http://www.un.org>.

12   ICRC, above n 9.

13   On rape in war see in general Susan Brownmiller, *Against Our Will: Men, Women and Rape* (1975). Note that 'looting and raping', one a property crime and the other a direct and violent attack on a person, are often linked together as violations in times of war. Also see ICRC, above n 1.

Leone and in numerous other conflict situations around the world. While recognising that statistics on the numbers of victims of a crime like rape are invaluable in order to ensure effective support and assistance (the right help in the right places), statistics should not become the main issue. One person raped is one too many.

Sexual violence is a particularly brutal act against its victim. The ICRC has long considered sexual violence as a war crime and a serious violation of IHL.[14] At the 27th International Conference of the Red Cross and Red Crescent in Geneva during 1999, the ICRC reiterated its concern at the occurrence of sexual violence in armed conflict. It pledged to States and components of the International Red Cross and Red Crescent Movement that it would place specific focus on making known to parties to armed conflicts the protection accorded to women by IHL, with particular emphasis on the issue of sexual violence.[15] The full implementation of IHL must become a reality. The prime responsibility for achieving this rests with parties to an armed conflict. Parties to an armed conflict have a duty to ensure the protection of, and respect for, all civilians and persons no longer taking part in hostilities. They must observe the rules and take necessary action so that violations, such as sexual violence, do not occur. If such crimes are committed, they must bring the perpetrators to justice.

It is important to note the significant work of the ICTY and ICTR, both of which have prosecuted and convicted perpetrators of sexual violence against women. In addition, the Rome Statute of the International Criminal Court also explicitly mentions sexual violence as a war crime.[16] These are significant developments in the battle against impunity and for the realisation of more effective mechanisms for enforcing international law.

---

14   See in particular ICRC, *Statement before the Commission for Rights of Women, European Parliament* (Brussels) 18 February 1993: 'Le CICR a dénoncé la pratique du viol commis par toutes les parties au conflit, comme les autres exactions commises à l'encontre des civils. Le viol est considéré comme un crime de guerre et il est grand temps de trouver des solutions permettant de mettre un terme à ces pratiques inacceptables'. Resolution 2 B of the 26th International Red Cross and Red Crescent Conference (Geneva, 1995): '[The Conference] (a) expresses its outrage at practices of sexual violence in armed conflicts, in particular the use of rape as an instrument of terror, forced prostitution and any other form of indecent assault; ... (c) strongly condemns sexual violence, in particular rape, in the conduct of armed conflict as a war crime, and under certain circumstances a crime against humanity, and urges the establishment and strengthening of mechanisms to investigate, bring to justice and punish all those responsible'. ICRC Update on the Aide-Memoire on rape committed during the armed conflict in ex-Yugoslavia, of 3 December 1992: 'As never before in its history, the ICRC has spoken out forcefully against systematic and serious abuses committed against the civilian population in Bosnia-Herzegovina, such as... rape, internment, deportation, harassment of minority groups...' The act of rape is an extremely serious violation of international humanitarian law. Article 27(2) of the *Fourth Geneva Convention* states: 'Women shall be especially protected against any attack on their honour, in particular rape, enforced prostitution, or any form of indecent assault'.

15   This pledge was announced by the President of the ICRC at the 27th International Red Cross and Red Crescent Conference (Geneva, 1999). See ICRC web site <www.icrc.org/eng/women>.

16   *Rome Statute of the International Criminal Court* (1998) UN Doc A/CONF 183/9, Article 8(2)(xxii).

IV   Missing Persons and Widowhood

The conflict in Bosnia and Herzegovina put the plight of women and the survivors of sexual violence onto the world agenda. Besides sexual violence, this war (like many others before and since) was characterised by the separation of men from women and children – both a voluntary and involuntary separation. Men took up fighting roles, fled to third countries and safe areas, or were rounded up and detained and/or killed in large numbers. Often women stayed behind to try to ascertain the fate and whereabouts of their male relatives – or to protect their property – initially believing that the war would not last long and that they would be spared. However, all sides in this conflict failed to protect and spare the lives of civilian men, women and children. Although the majority of the dead or missing were men (and mostly men of military age, though many were not part of the armed forces), women were also killed or remain unaccounted for. There are still 17,232 persons,[17] reported by their families to the ICRC, considered missing long after the end of the conflict. Of these, 92 percent are men and eight percent are women.

The very fact that many women survive conflicts in which their menfolk have died or disappeared has enormous implications. The wars in the former Yugoslavia and the genocide in Rwanda have highlighted the plight of widows and women desperately trying to ascertain the fate of their loved ones. The survivors of these wars – and others throughout the world – are now struggling to cope not only with the difficulty of providing an immediate livelihood or means of survival for themselves and their family, but also with the additional trauma and uncertainty of not knowing what will happen to them in the absence of their menfolk.[18] Widows and relatives of missing men – fathers, sons and husbands – may well be left without entitlement to land, homes and inheritances, social assistance and pensions, or the right to sign contracts. They and their children can be subjected to violence and ostracism as a result of their status.[19]

All over the world, tens of thousands of women are searching for news about the fate of missing relatives. This search often endures long after a conflict has ended. The inability to mourn and bury their loved ones has an enormous impact on the survivors and the coping mechanisms they adopt.[20] IHL recognises the need and right of families to obtain such information.[21] The ICRC endeavours to find out about persons

---

17   In addition to these persons reported missing, the Bosnia-Herzegovina authorities believe that there are a further 10,000 persons unaccounted for.

18   See, for example, Mercedes Doretti's chapter, 'The Roses', earlier in this book describing the impact of the 'missing' on individual women left behind after war.

19   See ICRC website <www.icrc.org> for report on ICRC workshop on 'Widowhood and Armed Conflict' held in November 1999, Geneva. See also Radhika Coomaraswamy's chapter 'Sexual Violence During Wartime' in this collection.

20   The specific needs of women were recognised by the 'International Conference of Government and Non-Government Experts on the Missing', held by the ICRC in Geneva, February 2003.

21   *Protocol Additional to the Geneva Conventions of 12 Aug 1949, and relating to the Protection of Victims of International Armed Conflicts*, 7 December 1978, 1125 UNTS 3 ('*Protocol I*') Article 32.

missing in relation to armed conflicts through the Red Cross family news network, visits to places of detention, enquiries in response to tracing requests and representations to the warring parties to clarify their fate. But all too frequently, parties to an armed conflict do not do enough in this regard, thereby prolonging the agony of war for years after the fighting has ceased. As one mother, whose son has been missing since 1991 as a result of the conflict in the former Yugoslavia, so tragically exclaimed: 'There used to be a saying around here that the worst thing which can happen to someone is to bury their own child. It seems nowadays that there is something far worse – not knowing what happened to him at all'.[22]

Women often display enormous courage and resilience as survivors and as heads-of-households – a role for which many of them had little or no preparation and which is made more difficult by the social constraints often imposed on women. Many women have taken up this challenge and resolutely set aside their trauma in order to go on living for their children.

V   Displaced Women

It is widely stated that women and children make up the majority of the world's refugees,[23] but to this, internally displaced persons can also be added. Fleeing and living in displacement creates numerous problems for women around the world and often exposes women to enormous risks. Women generally flee taking few possessions with them and many become separated from family members. Displacement may force women to become reliant on support from the local population in the area to which they are displaced, or on assistance from international and non-governmental organisations. They often have to travel long distances in their search for water, food, firewood and for traditional foods and herbs for medicines for themselves and their families. During this search, women frequently risk attack and injury due to the fighting, mines and unexploded ordnance, as well as sexual abuse, especially rape.[24]

Women display tremendous strength and resourcefulness in the coping mechanisms they adopt in trying to ensure their own survival and that of their family. However, women in camps for displaced persons may be particularly vulnerable, especially when they are heads-of-household, widows, elderly women, pregnant women or mothers with small children, for they have to shoulder all the daily responsibilities for survival which consume enormous amounts of time and energy. Furthermore, they may be overlooked by camp authorities and organisations providing assistance. This is due to the fact that in many cultures women are rarely in the public sphere and thus are not included in assessments and needs evaluations. As such, their special needs may not be taken into account. For example, pregnant women need greater

---

22   Quoted from ICRC, *Special Report: The Issue of Missing Persons in Bosnia and Herzegovina, Croatia and the Federal Republic of Yugoslavia* (1998).

23   See, for example, United Nations High Commission on Refugees (UNHCR), *Sexual and Gender-Based Violence Against Refugees, Returnees and Internally Displaced Persons: Guidelines for Prevention and Response* (May 2003).

24   See ICRC, above n 1, 66.

access to health services and larger food rations. Women may prefer to receive specific foodstuffs for the preparation of household meals: grains or beans, for example, that do not require soaking (minimising the need for water where it is scarce) or cooking times (reducing the amount of firewood needed). Women in situations of displacement also invariably lack the privacy needed to maintain their personal hygiene and dignity. They may have to share living quarters, washing and toilet facilities with many people. As these facilities are frequently easily accessible to men, many women are forced to choose between maintaining personal hygiene and maintaining their dignity and safety. For these reasons, women need to be actively included in the planning, implementation and evaluation of activities carried out and assistance distributed in their favour.

In countries where the ICRC is present, it works to protect and assist persons displaced by armed conflict. In many of these countries, women have been specifically consulted by the ICRC as to what assistance should be distributed and to whom to find out, for example, what would best meet the needs of households headed by women. To prevent the abuse and exploitation of women beneficiaries, women need to be actively included in the planning, implementation and evaluation of activities carried out and assistance distributed.

VI   Women Deprived of their Freedom

Detention in wartime conjures up images of men languishing behind bars or barbed wire. The detention of women is rarely portrayed in media images, yet women are also deprived of their freedom as a result of conflict. In 2002, the ICRC visited 448,063 persons deprived of their freedom in relation to armed conflicts around the world, including some 6,352 women. The majority of these women and girls were detained in relation to an armed conflict or situation of internal disturbance.

Around the world, the majority of persons deprived of their freedom are men. This means that there are few prisons or places of detention solely for women. This may mean that women are detained in worse conditions than men. In many cases, women detainees are consequently housed in the men's prison. Since the women are fewer in number, their section is usually the smallest and may lack adequate sanitary and other facilities. However, the existence of a separate prison for women can also pose problems. As women generally constitute only a minority of detainees, the few prisons built specifically for them may be situated far from their home. Being sent there means being separated from their family and the support that families provide.

People deprived of their freedom often rely heavily on their relatives to visit them and bring additional food and other items (including medicines, clothes and toiletries). Women often suffer from a lack of family visits and therefore are deprived of their family's emotional and material support. There are many reasons for this: the remoteness of the place of detention, insecurity for visitors, relatives may be unwilling or unable to come (because they are displaced, have disappeared or are missing), or may lack money to pay the travel costs.

Women deprived of their freedom often have the added concern of their children's well-being, either because young children are detained with them and are being raised in difficult conditions, or because they have been separated from their children and are uncertain as to who is raising them and how. Even where a family member has taken over responsibility for the children, this enforced separation can be very difficult for women to bear.

Women also have specific needs that they find difficult to meet in detention. For instance, women and girls of menstruating age often have problems in obtaining suitable sanitary protection, regular access to sanitary facilities (toilets and washing areas) and appropriate clothing to deal with their menstruation in a manner that preserves their health and dignity.

Both men and women are often subjected to maltreatment, including sexual violence, while deprived of their freedom. For women, there is a serious risk of pregnancy and gynaecological problems. Many women fear the consequences these may have both for their life in detention and after their release when they return to their families and communities.

As a general rule, the ICRC registers persons deprived of their freedom in relation to an armed conflict or internal disturbance. It visits them (speaking to them in private without the presence of guards or authorities) to assess their conditions of detention and treatment. With the consent of the detaining authorities, it provides non-food assistance in the form of sanitary and hygienic requisites, such as sanitary protection for women, clothes, buckets, cooking pots and recreational items, as well as medical supplies (to the medical services). The ICRC also makes confidential reports to the detaining authorities regarding the conditions of detention and the treatment of persons deprived of their freedom with the aim of improving their situation and putting an end to any violations.[25]

VII   Protection of Women in International Humanitarian Law

Since its inception, IHL has accorded women general protection equal to that of men.[26] At the same time, the law recognises the need to give women specific protection according to their specific needs. This protection is enshrined in the four *Geneva Conventions of 12 August 1949 for the Protection of War Victims* and their two *Additional Protocols* of 8 June 1977.[27] The *Conventions* and *Protocols* protect women (and men) as

---

25   See in general Krill, above n 4.

26   International humanitarian law is not the only body of law relevant to situations of armed conflict, human rights law is also applicable. These two bodies of law should not be seen as mutually exclusive; their methods of implementation should be viewed as complementary.

27   *Geneva Convention for the Amelioration of the Condition of the Wounded and the Sick in Armed Forces in the Field*, 12 August 1949, 75 UNTS 31 ('*First Geneva Convention*'); *Geneva Convention for the Amelioration of the Condition of Wounded, Sick and Shipwrecked members of the Armed Forces at Sea*, 12 August 1949, 75 UNTS 85 ('*Second Geneva Convention*'); *Geneva Convention Relative to the Treatment of Prisoners of War*, 12 August 1949, 75 UNTS 135 ('*Third Geneva Convention*'); *Geneva Convention Relative to the Protection of Civilian Persons in Time of War*, 12 August 1949, 75 UNTS 287 ('*Fourth Geneva Convention*'). All entered into force 21 October 1950; *Protocol Additional to the Geneva Conventions of 12 Aug*

members of the civilian population not taking part in an armed conflict. Women (and men) as members of the armed forces or armed groups are also protected through provisions that lay down limitations on permissible means and methods of warfare and when they are captured by the enemy and deprived of their freedom. This contribution does not aim to deal exhaustively with the legal regime established by IHL to protect women as this topic is covered later in the book by authors such as Helen Durham and Judith Gardam. However a brief overview in this context may be useful.

A   *The Law of International Armed Conflicts*

Women who have taken an active part in hostilities as combatants are entitled to the same protection as men when they have fallen into enemy hands. The *Third Geneva Convention relative to the Treatment of Prisoners of War* stipulates that prisoners of war (POWs) shall be treated humanely at all times. Besides this general protection, women are also afforded specific protection based on the principle that 'women shall be treated with all the regard due to their sex'.[28] This principle is followed through in a number of provisions which expressly refer to the conditions of detention for women in POW camps. The principle of differentiated treatment for women also resulted in provisions relating to the separate confinement of women from men and the immediate supervision of women by female guards.[29]

Women (and men) who, as members of the civilian population, are taking no active part in hostilities are afforded protection under the *Fourth Geneva Convention relative to the Protection of Civilian Persons in Time of War* and under *Additional Protocol I*. Women are in general protected against abusive treatment by the parties to the armed conflict and also against the effects of the fighting. They are entitled to humane treatment, respect for their life and physical integrity and to live free from torture, ill-treatment and harassment. In addition to this general protection, women are afforded specific protection under the *Fourth Geneva Convention* and *Protocol I*, which stipulate that 'women shall be especially protected against any attack on their honour, in particular against rape, enforced prostitution or any form of indecent assault'.[30]

IHL also lays down provisions for pregnant women and mothers of small children (generally considered to be children under seven years of age to ensure that they are adequately provided for). Women are also protected, as members of the civilian population, against the effects of the hostilities and by rules which impose limits on the use of force. In the conduct of hostilities, the parties to an armed conflict must 'at all times distinguish between the civilian population and combatants and between

---

1949, and relating to the Protection of Victims of International Armed Conflicts, 7 December 1978, 1125 UNTS 3 ('*Protocol I*') and *Protocol Additional to the Geneva Conventions of 12 Aug 1949, and relating to the Protection of Victims of Non-International Armed Conflicts*, 7 December 1978, 1125 UNTS 609 ('*Protocol II*').

28   *Third Geneva Convention*, above n 7, Article 14(2).

29   Ibid, Articles 97 and 108; *Protocol I*, above n 7, Article 75(5).

30   *Fourth Geneva Convention*, above n 7, Article 27(2). See also *Protocol I*, above n 7, Articles 75 and 76.

civilian objects and military objectives and accordingly shall direct their operations only against military objectives'.[31]

B   *The Law of Non-International Armed Conflicts*

Persons who take an active part in hostilities in the course of a non-international armed conflict do not have POW status when they fall into enemy hands. However, in such a case they are entitled to the fundamental guarantees afforded by Article 4 of *Additional Protocol II relative to the Protection of Victims of Non-International Armed Conflicts*. Women are entitled to the same protection as men, but also have a right to particular protection.

Persons not taking part in such a conflict are protected by Article 3 common to the four *Geneva Conventions*. While it contains no special provision on the protection of women, this rule establishes fundamental guarantees for the treatment of all persons not taking part in the hostilities. Furthermore, *Additional Protocol II* stipulates in general terms that 'outrages upon personal dignity, in particular humiliating and degrading treatment, rape, enforced prostitution and any form of indecent assault' are forbidden.[32] *Additional Protocol II* also provides for special treatment of women who are arrested, detained or interned in relation to the hostilities. In such cases, 'except when men and women of a family are accommodated together, women shall be held in quarters separated from those of men and shall be under the immediate supervision of women'.[33]

Women as members of the civilian population are also protected against the effects of hostilities in non-international conflicts. *Additional Protocol II* stipulates that 'the civilian population as such, as well as individual civilians, shall not be the object of attack'.[34]

C   *Honour in International Humanitarian Law*

Article 27 of the *Fourth Geneva Convention* uses the term 'honour' when referring to the specific protection conferred by IHL on women against attacks like 'rape, enforced prostitution, or any form of indecent assault'. In recent years, some writers have voiced concern about the use of the word 'honour' in relation to sexual violence, claiming that it fails to recognise the brutal nature of rape and uses instead a 'value-laden' term to define the interest warranting legal protection, rather than the woman herself, and for embodying the notion of women as property.[35]

---

31   *Protocol I*, above n 7, Article 48.
32   *Additional Protocol II*, above n 7, Article 4(2)(e).
33   *Ibid.* Article 5(2)(a).
34   *Ibid.* Article 13.
35   See in particular Catherine N. Niarchos, 'Women, War and Rape: Challenges Facing the International Tribunal for the former Yugoslavia' (1995) 17 *Human Rights Quarterly* 671-676; and Judith Gardam, 'Women, Human Rights and International Humanitarian Law' (1998) 324 *International Review of the Red Cross* 421-432.

The question of 'honour' – a term which is also used in other articles of the *Geneva Conventions* and not only those pertaining to women – demands greater examination than it can be afforded in such a general chapter covering many aspects of women and war. To briefly touch upon this issue, honour is a code by which many men and women are raised, and by which they define and lead their lives. Therefore, the concept of honour is much more complex than merely a 'value' term. But to a certain extent, the concerns outlined above are valid. It is unfortunate that the language adopted by States fifty years ago, when the *Geneva Conventions* were written, links violations of a sexual nature with a woman's honour. This could lead to questions such as whether it is the honour of the woman that IHL wants to protect, or whether it is the woman herself? The answer is clearly the latter.

If one looks at Article 27 as a whole, it is clear that the law grants 'protected persons, in all circumstances, respect for their persons (...) They shall at all times be humanely treated, and shall be protected especially against all acts of violence or threats thereof ...'. This protection is conferred upon men and women, adults and children. It was intended to be as broad as possible encompassing all acts of violence and threats thereof. The second paragraph of this provision, referring to special protection for women, aims to strengthen this protection by highlighting sexual violence. Linking sexual violence and honour, however, has made it seem to some that this provision is less about physical protection for women and more about the social value traditionally attached to a woman's chastity. Since the *Geneva Conventions* were drafted, law and language have evolved, as Article 76 of *Additional Protocol I* clearly shows. The 160 States Parties to this *Protocol*[36] attest to its universality. Article 76 provides protection to women in the power of a party to the conflict (a broad field of application). It states 'women shall be the object of special respect and shall be protected in particular against rape, forced prostitution and any other form of indecent assault'. There is no mention of the term 'honour'.

In conclusion, the *Geneva Conventions* and *Additional Protocols* stipulate that women must be respected and protected against rape, enforced prostitution or any form of indecent assault. In order to strengthen their protection, this part of the law must be emphasised, disseminated and enforced during situations of armed conflict.

VIII   Recent ICRC Initiatives

The ICRC study, initiated in 1998, aimed to better identify the ways in which women are affected by armed conflict and to determine whether its own response could be improved. The study aimed to:
(1)   identify the needs of women, including their access to basic goods and services such as food, water, shelter and health care;
(2)   draw up a realistic and comprehensive picture of ICRC activities in favour of women affected by armed conflict, and assess whether these activities adequately respond to the needs identified; and

---

36   ICRC, *Annual Report: 2002* (2003) 417.

(3)   examine international law, in order to assess the extent to which it provides adequate coverage of the needs identified.

Following a request to provide periodic reports regarding ICRC activities carried out on behalf of women, information was provided by ICRC delegations around the world. Visits were made to ICRC delegations to gather information and hold discussions with ICRC personnel. During these visits, discussions were arranged with women affected by armed conflict in camps for displaced persons, places of detention, hospitals and orthopaedic centres, with beneficiaries of ICRC programs and with women's organisations. Information was gathered from ICRC personnel returning from the field and also from ICRC publications, documents and training materials. First-hand information from war-affected women, collected as part of the *People on War* survey, added an invaluable dimension to the study.[37]

On the basis of the study's findings, the ICRC published a *Guidance Document*[38] to enhance the protection and assistance of women affected by armed conflict. This initiative was supported at the 27th International Red Cross and Red Crescent Conference in Geneva, 1999, by States Parties to the *Geneva Conventions* and by the International Red Cross and Red Crescent Movement.[39]

Furthermore, the ICRC's pledge on women and war made at the 27th International Conference renewed the ICRC's commitment to the effective protection of women.[40] This pledge was intended not only to promote the respect to be accorded to women and girls affected by armed conflict, but also to make sure that their specific needs are appropriately assessed in the ICRC's own operations. ICRC delegations around the world have been instructed to focus increased attention upon the needs of women affected by armed conflict and to adapt where necessary the ICRC's activities and programmes to ensure that they are met. The *Guidance Document* is part of this process.

The ICRC study, *Guidance Document* and pledge comprise part of a long-term commitment to better addressing the needs of women in situations of armed conflict. The ICRC hopes that these initiatives will lead to a more effective operational response by the ICRC to the needs of women affected by armed conflict, as well as to increased respect for and implementation of the protection conferred upon women by international law. The prime responsibility rests with the parties to an armed conflict, namely to observe the rules and to ensure respect for the rules – and also with States to bring individuals who violate these rules to justice. The study also aimed to motivate

---

37   ICRC, above n 9.

38   ICRC, *Addressing the Needs of Women Affected by Armed Conflict: An ICRC Guidance Document ('Guidance Document')* (2004).

39   *Resolution 1: Plan of Action for the Years 2000-2003*, 27th International Red Cross and Red Crescent Conference (Geneva, 1999). At the 28th International Red Cross and Red Crescent Conference, an outline of the 'Guidance Document' was presented.

40   The ICRC committed itself to increasing its dissemination of knowledge of the protection which should be accorded to women and girl children, especially with regard to sexual violence, among parties to armed conflicts throughout the world.

others involved in conflict situations – whether directly or indirectly – to seek ways of preventing and alleviating the suffering of women in war.

IX Conclusion

War, whether international or non-international, causes extreme suffering for those caught up in it. Women experience war in a multitude of ways – from taking an active part as combatants to being targeted as members of the civilian population specifically because they are women, for example, through rape. But the impact of war on women must be recognised as more than sexual violence. War also means separation, the loss of family members and of the very means of existence. War means injury and deprivation. War forces women into new roles and necessitates the development of new coping skills.

It is also important to rethink the categorisation of women as automatically 'vulnerable' and 'victims' in times of war. Women are politicians, community leaders, partners in assistance operations in their communities and activists for reconstruction, reconciliation and peace. Women are not necessarily 'vulnerable' and 'victims', although many women have been placed particularly at risk in situations of armed conflict. Women display tremendous resourcefulness in the coping mechanisms they have developed as survivors of wars, as participants in humanitarian programmes and as heads-of-households. One of the greatest challenges for the humanitarian community is to improve the plight of women who should be better supported, protected and assisted when confronted by war.

States and parties to armed conflict must do their utmost to ensure respect for the safety and dignity of women in wartime. Women themselves must be more closely involved in all measures taken on their behalf. Every State bound by the treaties of IHL has the duty to promote and implement the rules and, should crimes occur, to bring the perpetrators to justice. If women have to bear so many of the tragic effects of armed conflict, it is not because of any shortcomings in the rules protecting them, but because these rules are all too often not observed. The general and specific protection to which women are entitled must become a reality. Constant efforts must be made to increase knowledge of, and compliance with, the obligations of IHL. Responsibility for improving the plight of women in times of war must be shared by everyone.

5

Sri Lanka First: The Business of Peace

*Neela Marikkar**

I   Introduction

This is a story of how a group of business people, tired of witnessing the destruction of a country through conflict, organised for the 'silenced voices' of those in favour of peace to be heard. While the business context in Sri Lanka is predominately male, I never felt that being a woman was a disadvantage. Our bonds as business leaders were deeper than issues of gender. As a woman, I am extremely committed to peace. In Sri Lanka, like many places, women have lost more than 65,000 fathers, husbands, sons and brothers to war. As other chapters in this book will explore, women are left as widows, looking after families without the support needed and deeply mourning the loss of their children. Women need resolution to violence within their homes, families, communities and countries. Women also need ways to communicate their messages of peace and outlets for their views on these matters. Sri Lanka First provided this in a simple and effective way.

II   Background

Sri Lanka has been subjected to a long and violent 20-year ethnic conflict. The war was fought mainly in the North and East of the country where the people lived the war day in and day out. While the families of the armed forces would have felt the impact of the war, for those living in the southern part of the country – other than the occasional bomb that would go off – the war did not affect us on a daily basis. We even had continuous GDP growth of between three and four percent per annum right throughout the years of conflict. Yes, there were check points in parts of the city and

*   Neela Marikkar is the president of Sri Lanka First, a group of business leaders who advocate for a negotiated settlement between the Government of Sri Lanka and the Liberation Tigers of Tamil Eelam (LTTE). She has worked with the United Nations Development Programme (UNDP), the Sri Lankan Government and the Sri Lankan Chamber of Commerce with the aim of reviving the economy and increasing foreign investment. Ms. Marikkar is Managing Director of Grant McCann-Erickson (a member of the international network McCann-Erickson Worldwide, USA) and has worked in advertising, promotions and public relations for more than 20 years.

Helen Durham and Tracey Gurd (eds.), Listening to the Silences: Women and War, *pp. 37–42.*
© 2005 *Koninklijke Brill BV. Printed in The Netherlands.* ISBN 90 04 14365 3.

that was uncomfortable, a sense of unease prevailed, yet on the whole life proceeded as normal.

On 24 July 2001, things changed dramatically. For the first time the whole country was affected. Sri Lanka had her own devastating terrorist attack on the country's International Airport. This time, the implications for the country's economy were far reaching. The ease with which the terrorists were able to penetrate this highly secure environment seemed incredible. Overnight Sri Lankan Airlines, the national carrier, lost half its fleet. The air force lost eight of its eleven aircraft which were on the ground at that time. Sri Lanka suddenly became an extremely dangerous place. Foreign missions advised citizens, tourists and businesspeople to refrain from visiting Sri Lanka as it was now considered a high risk country. Until then, the high risk classification had only been in the North and the East. The rest of Sri Lanka was considered relatively safe.

III   Impact

Becoming a high risk nation meant high risk insurance premiums were imposed on every aspect of business, starting with tourism. Every aircraft that landed in Sri Lanka was charged an additional US$150,000 as a war risk premium. Every passenger who got off was charged an additional US$80. The fear that the next terrorist attack would be on the national port meant that Sri Lanka's Port was classified as a high risk zone as well. Any ship that called was levied an additional war risk premium of US$100,000. This meant ships stopped calling and aircrafts stopped landing. Airlines flying daily to Sri Lanka cut down their flights to once a week and some others pulled out completely. Ships started bypassing Sri Lanka. We could not get our exports out or our imports in. For the first time, the war had really reached home. It deeply affected the entire country and we – in the South – began to feel the impact very quickly. The tourism industry was the first affected. Prior to the attack, occupancy rates in hotels in the South were close to 100 percent. Afterwards, the occupancy rate dropped to five percent. The industry started laying off hundreds of employees.

IV   Action

It was at this time that I joined a group of others working in the communication field along with members of the tourism industry. We volunteered our time to assist the Tourist Board and the Government in managing the negative media fall out. While working in this group, I participated in a committee which looked into the actual events that happened at the airport itself. The more that we worked on this particular aspect of the attack, the more we began to realise that even if we were to increase security, it was not the answer. Bringing in an international security company to guard the airport or putting a ten-foot electrical fence around the perimeter of the entire airport was not a long-term solution. I think the realisation came to us that the only way to secure the country against the terrorists' acts was to end the war. This was the only way that we could ensure that we would never have to experience another attack of this nature. We realised that the country could not withstand one more serious attack like this. Further, we could not guarantee that even with increased security at the airport and the Port that the terrorists would not hit other vital areas such as power and water supply systems. The possibilities were endless.

I took the initiative to get a group of business leaders and business organisations together who were members of the Chamber of Commerce and who shared the same view: that the business community should step in to do something to end this war. I think many of us had individually done different things on a company basis, but collectively there had not been an initiative that was singularly focused on a peaceful resolution to ending the war. One of the key factors to finding a political settlement to this crisis was to develop a way of managing the acrimony between the two main Southern political parties. Their hatred for each other was greater than their hatred for the terrorists and this made it extremely difficult to advance the issue. This has been evident over the last 50 years. The division on this particular ethnic issue has been used by the two main political parities in the South for selfish political gains. In fact, it has been one of the most serious causes of the conflict and one of the greatest obstacles to the resolution of the peace process.

Given this situation, our core group of business leaders decided that the time had come to find a way to bring these two political parties together to find a long-term political solution to the ethnic crisis. To do this we also recognised that political parties and politicians listen only to their voters. They go the way they feel the voters want them to go. Before the airport attack, the pro war lobby appeared to be very strong. They got all the media coverage, they were the people who created the noise and because they shouted the loudest, the media sensationalised them. This was despite the fact the moderates, who were by far the larger majority in the country, were for peace. Our belief was that we had to empower the moderate voice in civil society, even among politicians within their own political parties.

The airport attack had left a huge war-weariness among civil society. There was a sense of hopelessness and desolation that the military was unable to prevent such a massive attack on the airport. The realisation that this war could not be won militarily gave us the opportunity to actually approach people. For the first time, members of civil society were willing to listen. They were prepared to consider a non-military solution. The business leaders realised that it was crucial to get civil society on board to influence the political leadership. This gave rise to a non-political business initiative for peace. In order to achieve our objective, the business community decided to have an extensive communication campaign on every available media – not only mainstream media but also at a grass-roots level. We worked with several non-governmental organisations, the members of which went out to rural villages to explain what the war had cost the country, what it would continue to cost and why we wanted our political leaders to come together to negotiate a final peaceful resolution to end the war. One of the components of this campaign was to have a visible show of strength and support for a peaceful resolution to the political leaders. We asked civil society to demonstrate whether it really wanted a peaceful resolution to the war and if it really wanted political leaders to come together to end this war. We asked people to come out of their homes and offices on 19 September 2001 at 12 noon to hold hands for peace for 15 minutes. This was a very unique instruction because Sri Lankans, as a rule, do not like to get involved in this type of demonstration. We believed it was important for us, though, to establish just how much people wanted peace. We also wanted to demonstrate to our political leaders what the majority of the people wanted. We were confident that the majority of the people wanted a peaceful resolution to the war. Many of us took time to explain to our staff that if there were to be one more attack of this magnitude that none of the businesses would survive. From all this, Sri Lanka First was born. We all recognised that it was time to put the country first – not our own individual needs, not our business needs.

The mass communication campaign we ran was extensive. We had hard hitting, graphic but simple messages about what this war had cost. The campaign was extremely effective because it was focused. It just gave simple facts and every fact had a solution. The solution was linked to a peaceful resolution of the war. On television, the campaign was different. It was much more emotional. It showed people of all ethnic communities coming together, lending weight to the idea that we can live together and work together as one nation in peace and harmony. At grass-root levels, we went out with leaflets. We used several marketing companies, both multi-national and local, to distribute posters into their distribution channels so that the posters could be found in the remotest villages in all the little stores and retail outlets. We were able to penetrate the entire country, even the north that was a strong hold of the LTTE. Even there, we were able to carry out the campaign in the Tamil newspapers in the north and get posters out as well.

In the midst of all this were the terror attacks of 11 September 2001 in New York and Washington DC. This was not something that we ever anticipated. When 9/11 happened, the entire world turned against terrorists and we came under severe criticism here in Sri Lanka by the media. When the world was asking that terrorists be wiped out, we were doing the reverse. We were asking the government and our political leaders to stop the war and to talk to the terrorists and try to resolve this in a peaceful manner. The print media were extremely critical of us but we decided that we would not stop our campaign because we really believed that after 20 years of war, we could not fight terrorism. We also recognised that terrorism had root causes and if we didn't get to those roots and resolve them at that level, we would never have a solution.

When 19 September dawned, I remember waking up that morning thinking 'O my God! What if nobody comes out? What if nobody holds hands? What if this whole campaign fails?'

V   Result

It didn't fail. When I stepped out of my office building with my staff of 140 at 11.45am that morning, there was hardly anybody on the road. I walked to the main road. As we lined up along the street, we began to see other people coming out of other buildings from offices, shops, restaurants, from hospitals and before long – within the next ten to 15 minutes – the street that we were on (one of the main roads of the city of Colombo) was filled with people. On the centre island of the road, there was a row three deep of people holding hands. There were two rows on either side of the road.

There were some areas where there were rows five people deep. It was an amazing sight. The media reported that we had over one million people who came out and stood for peace right across the country. Even in the north, in Jaffna, the media reported that there were thousands of people who came out and held hands for peace.

There were pockets where nobody came. There where places were those who were anti-peace had done a lot of work to prevent people coming out, in particular in certain rural areas. By and large, though, the turn out was unprecedented. I remember standing there and I felt tears roll down my face – just watching the people coming out and feeling that I had something to do with this – it was a sense of great joy. We believe it was the turning point in the conflict. For the first time, the political leaders saw for themselves that the majority of people wanted peace. What this demonstration had done was empower the moderates in large numbers. It was a simple demonstration, a simple show of support. It did not mean that we had to carry placards or make a noise – you came very quietly out of your home or out of your office and you just stood out there and held hands with strangers for 15 minutes and went back in. It was a peaceful demonstration and the impact of that demonstration was profound.

A few weeks later, the government was dissolved and the President called for fresh elections. The politicians themselves realised that what people wanted was a peaceful solution to the ethnic conflict and that became the political platform for all the major political parties in the run-up to the elections. During the election campaign we ran more campaigns telling voters to vote for candidates who stood for peace, irrespective of their political party. We wanted to ensure that people voted for candidates who would support an end to the war through a political solution.

On 5 December 2001 a new government was elected to office on the peace mandate. Within one week, the terrorists declared a cessation of hostilities and held out an olive branch to the new government. They said that for the first time, they really believed the people of Sri Lanka wanted peace. On Christmas Eve 2001, the new government of Sri Lanka reciprocated and ceased hostilities. In February 2002 the Government of Sri Lanka and the LTTE signed a ceasefire agreement brokered by the Royal Norwegian government. In September 2002 the first round of peace talks began.

VI   Conclusion

Sri Lanka First continues its role in educating civil society on the need to find a peaceful resolution to the ethnic conflict. They continue with their media campaign to educate civil society on the causes of the conflict and possible solutions. For my part, I was proud of the hard won achievements, but aware that there continues to be much that is needed to be done to advance peace. I strongly advise women – whether they are professionals, academics, in business or homemakers – to get involved in issues that affect their nation. What affects our nation will always affect our families, our children and us. Standing aside because we feel helpless only weakens us. If we stand up for what we believe in and use our specific skills – whether individually or collectively – we can make a difference. Women have the power to influence. Even if we do not have direct or formal power we are mothers, wives, sisters, daughters. Our families can listen to us. Even Presidents, Prime Ministers and terrorist leaders have mothers, wives and daughters. Change that can influence a nation and its people can start from the home.

6

Women's Role in Peacemaking:
Personal Experiences

Luz Méndez*

For more than three decades, Guatemala endured a protracted armed conflict which originated from, and was sustained by, abysmal socio-economic inequalities, a lack of political liberties and ethnic discrimination against indigenous peoples. In the 1950s, a progressive, elected government had implemented economic and political reforms to remedy those injustices and promote development in the country. The overthrow of this government by a US-led armed intervention – and the return of military dictatorships – opened the door for armed conflict in the early 1960s, which continued through to the 1990s.

In December 1996, after 36 years of internal armed conflict, the Government of Guatemala and the Guatemalan National Revolutionary Unity (URNG) signed the *Agreement on a Firm and Lasting Peace*. The negotiations, which lasted more than five years, were moderated by the United Nations. The signing of the final peace accords meant not only an end to war, but also the enactment of a group of articulated agreements addressing the main political and socio-economic inequalities and ethnic discrimination that had plagued Guatemala. The peace accords provide the most comprehensive platform for socio-economic development and democratisation in the country's history, defining a new vision of the Guatemalan nation for the mid and long terms.

Women have traditionally been excluded from peace negotiations and their specific needs ignored as a result of discrimination against women and unequal gender relationships. For this reason, the inclusion of gender equality provisions in the Guatemalan peace accords were particularly important, adding an extra dimension of meaning and value to the agreements while also increasing their legitimacy. Aimed at the elimination of discrimination against women; the promotion of women's political participation; and improving women's access to education, health, housing and other resources, these provisions also incorporate the creation of institutions to promote gender equality. The inclusion of gender commitments in the accords is the result of women's participation and influence in the peace process.

---

*   Luz Méndez is President of the Advisory Board of the National Union of Guatemalan Women, a former member of the UNIFEM team of gender experts to the Burundi Peace Talks, a Member of the Policy Commission of Women Waging Peace, Member of the

Helen Durham and Tracey Gurd (eds.), Listening to the Silences: Women and War, *pp. 43–49.*
© *2005 Koninklijke Brill BV. Printed in The Netherlands. ISBN 90 04 14365 3.*

I   Women's Participation in the Guatemalan Peace Negotiations

A   *How Did I Get Involved in the Peace Negotiations?*

I became committed to social justice and democracy in my country at an early age, as one of thousands of young Guatemalan people who joined the social and revolutionary movements in the 1970s. We realised that we were living in a country where the majority of the population lacked the basics for a dignified human life – running water, electricity, schooling and even basic literacy. At the same time, the young people of my generation had lived in an authoritarian political atmosphere our whole lives. Unions and opposition parties, along with peasant and other grassroots groups, had been forbidden since 1954. The successive military regimes used political repression as a method of governance – killing, torturing and 'disappearing' social and political leaders.

It seemed nearly every family had at least one murdered or 'disappeared' relative – including my own. One of my close uncles was kidnapped by the security forces and vanished without a trace. His mother looked for him year after year, making countless trips to the morgue, trying to find his body among the mutilated corpses that appeared in a steady stream. Her life and her sanity were destroyed by what she saw. Tens of thousands of Guatemalan families can tell the same story.

My first involvement in a social movement occurred when I was 16-years-old. I was elected president of my high school student government. We organised and advocated for students to have desks, blackboards and even a library. Later, I was elected international secretary of the executive committee of the University Students Association. Through this, I not only advocated for students' rights, but also became involved in the political life of my country. As opposition parties were banned, social organisations had to play the role of denouncing and opposing the military regime.

In those years, many women joined the revolutionary movement, acting either as political militants, armed combatants or logistics supporters. The struggle for social change became the highest priority in our lives. Many had to leave their families – even their children – to go to the mountains to fight. No matter the type of activities we were doing, we all knew we were putting our lives at risk. Many women died, including my best and dearest friend.

When I was 22-years-old, I joined the Workers Party. This party was operating in secret and years later became part of the Guatemalan National Revolutionary Unity (URNG). When the peace negotiations began, I was appointed as a member of the URNG's Political-Diplomatic Team. Simultaneously, this team was asked to take part in the peace negotiations. I had been a political militant for 15 years when the peace negotiations began.

Advisory Board of Global Fund for Women and a former member of the Guatemalan National Revolutionary Unity's delegation to the table of peace negotiations. Ms. Méndez would like to thank Annemarie Brennan of the Hunt Alternatives Fund for her editorial assistance with this chapter.

When I first joined the negotiating team in 1991, I was not conscious of gender inequalities. Soon after, I became aware of this social dimension. From my personal experience – and with the support of a women's association that I joined – I realised that women, irrespective of their socio economic status, ethnic backgrounds and political beliefs, face a specific type of inequity: gender oppression. This awareness was a turning point in my life. I committed myself to the cause of women's rights and gender equality. I immediately began to consider the need to include a gender perspective into the URNG's program and the peace accords. I started to look for ways to integrate these issues.

The five years I spent participating in the peace negotiations represents one of the most satisfying – and most challenging – times of my life. For several years, I was the only woman at the peace table, among about ten people in each party's delegation. I confronted problems deriving from gender discrimination, feeling alone in a world of men. The support of members of the women's group to which I belonged, as well as the encouragement I felt in 1995 while attending the Fourth World Conference on Women in Beijing, were invaluable sources of strength as I worked towards the goal of achieving the peace accords.

B   How Did Women from Civil Society Take Part in the Peace Negotiations?

In the midst of the negotiations, the format was changed to give representatives of civil society the opportunity to take part in the peace process. The URNG supported and promoted this idea. As a result, the Assembly of Civil Society was created as a parallel table of dialogue. As a forum for the organised sectors of the Guatemalan society – including trade unions, peasants, indigenous groups, academics, human rights advocates, religious groups and women's organisations – the assembly's mission was develop consensus proposals on substantive issues of the peace agenda. The resulting proposals were presented as recommendations to the parties at the negotiating table, who defined the content of the peace accords and signed the agreements.

The experience of Guatemalan women's organisations in the Civil Society Assembly can serve as a model for the inclusion of civil society organisations in other national peace processes. First, the women's organisations succeeded in being accepted as a sector inside the Assembly of Civil Society. After that, women's groups were able to achieve a common platform for the peace negotiations. Finally, their representatives advocated inside the Civil Society Assembly for the inclusion of women's proposals in the recommendations the Assembly delivered to the government and URNG.

When those Civil Society Assembly recommendations were analysed at the negotiating table, I felt empowered looking at the inclusion of the women's proposals. The circumstances under which the negotiations were taking place did not permit me to establish direct communication with the leaders of the women's groups. Notwithstanding, I made a tacit commitment to them to support their points at the negotiating table. I studied their recommendations carefully, trying to find ways to make them more acceptable to both parties and to the moderator. I developed other points and advocated for them all at the table. As a member of the Political-Diplomatic Team, I was not expected to speak up in the plenary meetings of the negotiations. But

I did – to advocate for the inclusion of specific gender equality provisions in the agreements. It is also necessary to say that after the Beijing conference, the UN moderating team at the Guatemalan negotiations had a more supportive attitude towards the inclusion of these topics in the agreements.

C   *The Results*

The conjunction of all those efforts resulted in the inclusion of gender-specific commitments into the accords. They include legal reforms, public policies and the creation of institutions for the promotion of gender equality. Among them are:
–   the fulfilment of the *United Nations Convention on the Elimination of all Forms of Discrimination against Women*;
–   a review of the national legislation to remove or alter laws that discriminate against women;
–   the participation of women in decision making at local, regional and national levels;
–   provisions for women's equal access to education and training, including programs to eradicate discrimination against women;
–   women's access to housing, credit, land and other productive resources;
–   a national program on women's health;
–   the criminalisation of sexual harassment;
–   the creation of the Office for the Defence of Indigenous Women; and
–   the creation of the National Women's Forum.

All of these topics have been further developed by the women's movement in the years after the peace agreements. One strong message remains, however: gender issues must be taken seriously and they deserve to be included in peace agreements.

For the women's movement in Guatemala, the provisions about gender equality included in the peace agreements have helped to support our demands and proposals. Almost all of the processes prompted by women's organisations during these years have found a base of legitimacy in the peace agreements.[1]

D   *The Implementation Stage*

The Guatemala peace negotiations have been seen as a successful process. In many senses it was: a comprehensive peace agenda made possible the discussion and approval of a platform for socio-economic development and democratisation. The format allowed the involvement of civil society groups in the discussion of substantive issues. The deployment of the UN human rights verification mission during the negotiations contributed to the conclusion of the negotiations. The political atmosphere in the country began to improve even during the negotiations. The war ended

---

[1]   After the signing of the peace agreements I became actively involved in the Guatemalan women's movement, as the General Coordinator of the National Union of Guatemalan Women (UNAMG).

completely. The disarmament and demobilisation processes were successful. For the first time in decades, there was openness for the participation of all political and social actors with diverse ideological and political tendencies.

Nevertheless, seven years after the signing of the peace accords, the most significant provisions – including the electoral, fiscal and rural-development reforms – have not yet been implemented. The economic and social conditions have deteriorated and the political gains are also at risk. The economic and political ruling forces have looked with fear upon – and, in fact, opposed – the due implementation of the agreements. On the other hand, political and social organizations underestimated the effort needed to implement these agreements. Few of them were prepared to accomplish the big task of building peace. It is hopeful, however, that during the last year, the support for the accords by diverse social and political sectors has increased and many of them are honestly looking for ways to recover the path.

Since the signing of the peace agreements, significant progress has been made in establishing a new legal and institutional framework that favours gender equality, including the Law for the Comprehensive Advancement of Women, the National Women's Policy and Equal Opportunity Plan, the Women's Presidential Secretariat, the Office for the Defence of Indigenous Women and the National Women's Forum. The role of the women's movement has been decisive in the creation of this framework, contributing to the whole process of democratisation and peace building. Despite these achievements, women continue to be marginalised from elected bodies and high-level appointed positions. The results of the 2003 electoral process evidence a negative tendency in women's representation in the parliament. Stronger measures, including affirmative actions, are needed to remove the significant structural and institutional obstacles for women's full participation in the electoral process and political sphere as a whole.

II   Advocating for Women and Peace in the World

By the end of the 1990s, the international political situation had changed dramatically. While the armed conflicts were over in Central America, several new internal conflicts had emerged in other regions of the world. As a result of women's advocacy, the international community began to pay attention to the specific effects of armed conflict on women and the exclusion of women from peace negotiations and post-conflict reconstruction processes. Since 1999, I have taken part in international initiatives aimed at women's full participation in peace negotiations and peace building, as well as the incorporation of a gender perspective into peace accords. I have had the opportunity to meet with diverse leaders and women's representatives at different stages of peace processes.

As part of the efforts made by non-governmental organisations, I have advocated for the UN to create an international framework that protects women and girls during armed conflict and which would remove obstacles to women's participation in peace processes. I was a speaker at the first informal meeting that the UN Security Council held with women's organisations to discuss these topics, preceding the approval of Resolution 1325 on Women, Peace and Security in 2000.

At the same time, I have taken part in UN teams aimed at supporting gender equality in peace processes. I was vice-chairperson of the 2004 Expert Group Meeting on *Enhancing Women's Participation in Electoral Processes in Post-Conflict Countries,* which made recommendations supporting the incorporation of gender perspectives and women's full and equal participation in post-conflict electoral processes.

I was a member of the Gender Experts Team to the Burundi peace talks, convened by UNIFEM in 2000. This team comprised three women and one man who had participated in peace processes in South Africa, Uganda, Eritrea and Guatemala. During one round of negotiations in Arusha, Tanzania, we held meetings with the international Facilitation Team[2] and each of the 19 negotiating parties. We shared our experiences about the participation of women in the peace negotiations and post-conflict reconstruction efforts in our own countries, addressing both best practices and lessons learned. We also advocated for the inclusion of Burundian women and a gender perspective into the Burundi peace accord. Following our work with them, the negotiating parties supported the proposal of UNIFEM and the Tanzanian Mwalimu Nyerere Foundation to call an All-Party Burundi Women's Peace Conference during the next round of negotiations. This Conference was a remarkable opportunity for Burundi women, who had demanded for several years, without success, to take part in the negotiations. Hutu and Tutsi women were able to overcome their differences and build a common women's platform for the peace talks. I have an intense memory of the historic meeting when this platform was presented by Burundian women to Facilitator Nelson Mandela, who committed to support it. I have also a vivid recollection of the moment when more chairs were brought to the negotiating room, allowing women to take a seat beside the chiefs of their own party delegations during the meeting in which women presented their common proposals to the negotiators. When the accord was signed in August 2000, all but one[3] of the proposals made by women were included in the agreement. This remarkable experience, which brought together a variety of strategies and key people, deserves to be taken into account for future peace initiatives. I hope, at the same time, that complete peace can be achieved soon in Burundi.

I have also taken part in international initiatives aimed at strengthening women's civil society organisations which advocate for peace processes in their own countries or regions. These initiatives have also aimed to achieve women's full participation in peace processes and post-conflict reconstruction. I have had the opportunity to be part of missions to, and meetings with, women from Colombia, the Middle East, Iraq and several other regions or countries living in conflict or post-conflict stages.

When meeting with Colombian women who lead civil society groups involved in peace advocacy efforts, I have always admired their strength and creativity in mobilising women in favour of peace. I also marvelled at their ability to overcome their differences in crucial moments.

---

2   The Facilitation Team, lead by former South African President Nelson Mandela, was made of 18 members, representing African and European countries as well as international and regional bodies.

3   A 30 percent representation for women in decision-making bodies.

As part of a Women Waging Peace mission, I met with Israeli and Palestinian women in Jerusalem who have been working for peace in their region. It is striking to listen to their stories and see their suffering, as well as the resilience and energy of these women, who live in such harsh conditions. In Amman, Jordan, I addressed a group of Iraqi women who are striving for an equal place in the future reconstruction of their country.

Among the main insights I have shared in all of these international activities are:

–   Peace negotiations and post-conflict reconstruction provide a unique opportunity for advancing towards democratisation, socio-economic development and gender equality. To ensure women play an influential role in these processes, special measures must be included in the format of the negotiations. It is indispensable to assure women a place where the decisions are made.

–   The participation of women in peace negotiations is absolutely necessary, not only as a principle of gender equality, but because of the themes that women bring to the negotiating table. Experience has demonstrated that the foremost concerns, needs and demands of women are included in peace agreements when women – equipped with a gender perspective – participate in, and influence, peace processes.

–   Negotiations are only the first part of the peace process. The post-conflict peace building stage can be even more crucial and difficult. In order to guarantee the equal participation and leadership of women during this period, clear provisions must be included in the accords, establishing quotas or reserved seats for women's representatives in all the bodies in charge of the implementation of the agreements. We need women at the peace table, but we also need women – empowered women – in the post-conflict stage. It is vital that the international community support women in this period.

III   Final Reflections

During the long years of the Guatemalan peace negotiations, I never imagined that international instruments would be created in favour of integrating a gender perspective and promoting women's full participation in peace processes. It is remarkable to see how the efforts made by women at the international arena have succeeded to such a great extent. The United Nations system has responded by creating an international framework for the protection of women and girls during armed conflicts and the inclusion of gender perspectives in peace and security issues. The challenge that remains is this framework's due implementation.

We also have a bigger challenge. In order to create a better and safer world for us – and for the coming generations – the root causes of wars must be understood and tackled. Only by doing that would we be able to prevent the emergence of more armed confrontations and build a global, lasting peace and security for women and men everywhere.

Part II

How Does Law and Practice Affect How We Hear Women's Voices?

This second section of the book aims to review the factors that operate to liberate and obscure the voices of women, in law and in practice, when dealing with issues relating to armed conflict. In all the articles, women talk about their professional (and at times personal) response to suffering during times of armed conflict. These writers, in raising issues of concern, expose in a variety of fields what should be, and is being, done to address the impact of war and conflict upon women.

The section commences with an article by the former United Nations Rapporteur on Violence Against Women, Radhika Coomaraswamy, who examines the issue of sexual violence and armed conflict and the steps to be taken both in law and within communities to combat this issue. Next Jeanne Ward, an International Rescue Committee officer, writes about issues of gendered violence occurring in refugee and internally displaced persons (IDP) camps and provides case studies outlining the ways in which the matter is being dealt with on the ground and the extent to which women's voices are being heard and acted upon. Maggie O'Kane, a war correspondent, then talks about both theoretical and personal issues related to being a woman reporter in such environments.

The section then focuses upon the law with Helen Durham, an international lawyer, outlining the relevant international legal norms aimed at protecting women during times of armed conflict. Judith Gardam, international legal academic, then provides a broad critique of these principles within the international legal regime. Kelly Askin, Senior Legal Officer for the Open Society Justice Initiative's international justice division, follows with a review of the jurisprudence arising from the *ad hoc* international criminal tribunals and the issues for consideration in the prosecution of gendered crimes in other international and hybrid courts.

Finally, this section turns to look at other voices involved in the search for truth and justice. As the ICTY Gender Adviser, Patricia Viseur-Sellers considers the responses of investigators and interpreters in international criminal legal proceedings dealing with violence against women. This is followed by Georgina McEncroe, member of an NGO, writing about the activities and passion of civil society in responding to atrocities committed against women. In conclusion Hayli Miller, an academic, writes about the unique experiences of women during their participation in Truth Commissions.

7

Sexual Violence during Wartime

*Radhika Coomaraswamy**

I Introduction

Violence against women during wartime has been one of history's great silences. Though other aspects of war have received detailed consideration over the last few centuries, violence against women during armed conflict was an invisible issue, often seen as a necessary cost of war. In recent times, due to activism of women's groups around the world, the international community has begun to outline standards and prosecute perpetrators. This has led to a great deal of research and activism at the international level on issues pertaining to the situation of women during armed conflict. This chapter attempts to summarise these developments while drawing on the personal experience of the author during her appointment as the United Nations Special Rapporteur on Violence Against Women.

Part II of the paper will discuss the debates relating to the causes of violence against women during wartime. Part III will look at how women are affected by war and how they are both victims and agents in a military context over which they rarely exercise control. The fourth section will deal with issues of law and accountability, discussing international standards for the accountability of perpetrators. The fifth section will look at the humanitarian consequences of war. Part VI will analyse certain special issues that have arisen in recent times with regard to armed conflict and discuss the need to outline these concerns for the international community. Finally, this chapter will look at examples from around the world where women have resisted war and have taken an active part in the rehabilitation of their societies. In conclusion, this piece sets out a range of recommendations to deal more effectively with the horror of sexual violence against women during wartime.

II Causes of Violence against Women during Wartime

Many authors have speculated on the causes of violence against women during wartime. Scholars such as Catharine MacKinnon locate the cause of this violence in

---

* Radhika Coomaraswamy is the Director of the National Human Rights Commission of Sri Lanka. Between 1994 and 2003, she was the United Nations Special Rapporteur on Violence Against Women.

Helen Durham and Tracey Gurd (eds.), Listening to the Silences: Women and War, *pp. 53–66.*
© 2005 *Koninklijke Brill BV. Printed in The Netherlands.* ISBN 90 04 14365 3.

patriarchy and male attempts to dominate and subjugate the female.[1] Other writers, such as Susan Brownmiller, see sexual violence during wartime as an aspect of the communication between males. In this analysis, men rape women to dominate and humiliate other men who are seen as their enemy.[2] In Latin America, feminists argue that rape, sexual violence and murder are required acts to socialise military recruits and to permanently separate the recruits from the civilian population. It is a means of brutalisation to harden soldiers for battle and to bond men with one another.[3] In ethnic wars, some commentators argue that sexual violence is a means of asserting and marking boundaries between ethnic groups, reinforcing the tension and animosity among communities.[4]

Whatever the philosophical roots of violence against women during wartime, certain patterns of sexual violence are discernible if one studies the conduct of war in different parts of the world. In some wars, such as in the former Yugoslavia, evidence before the International Criminal Tribunal for the former Yugoslavia (ICTY) appears to show that sexual violence was used as a tactical weapon to intimidate and terrorise the population of the 'other side'. Commanders encouraged and used it as part of their military operations. Rape as a conscious instrument of war has been a factor in many wars throughout the years. Rape and sexual violence are also used to punish certain women who may be close to leading male figures of the other side. In Haiti, in what is termed 'political rapes', wives and daughters of dissident political leaders were systematically raped.[5] The same was true in East Timor. Wives and relatives of suspected guerrilla leaders were subject to rape.[6] With regard to women prisoners, rape is often used as a means of interrogation. In Peru, women suspected of supporting the Shining Path were often raped while in custody as part of the interrogation process. Other Latin American wars have recorded similar experiences. Women are also raped or sexually harassed by fellow activists and men from the same political group. In Colombia, many ex-combatants have spoken about being raped or sexually harassed by their male superiors as a first step in initiation.[7] Finally, armed conflict creates an atmosphere

1   See for example Catherine A MacKinnon, 'Sex Equality: – On Difference and Dominance' in Catharine A MacKinnon, *Toward a Feminist Theory of the State* (1989).

2   Susan Brownmiller, *Against Our Will: Men Women and Rape* (1975).

3   Cynthia Enloe, 'All the Men are in The Militias, All the Women Are Victims:- The Politics of Masculinity and Femininity in Nationalist Wars' in Lois Ann Lorentzen and Jennifer Turpin (eds) *The Women War Reader* (1998) 50.

4   Darius M Rejali, 'After Feminist Analyses of Bosnian Violence' in Lorentzen and Turpin, above n 3, 31.

5   *Report of the Special Rapporteur on Violence Against Women, its Causes and Consequences: Report on the Mission to Haiti*, 56 UN ESCOR, UN Doc E/CN.4/2000/68/Add.3 (2000) [*Mission to Haiti*].

6   *Report of the Special Rapporteur on Violence Against Women, its Causes and Consequences: Mission to Indonesia and East Timor on the Issue of Violence Against Women*, 55 UN ESCOR, UN Doc E/CN.4/1999/68/Add.3 (1999) [*Mission to Indonesia and East Timor*].

7   *Report of the Special Rapporteur on Violence Against Women, its Causes and Consequences: Mission to Colombia*, 58 UN ESCOR, UN Doc E/CN.4/2002/83/Add.3 (2002) [Mission to Colombia].

of impunity and lawlessness. Many men take advantage of this situation to rape and commit acts of sexual violence against women. The impunity attached to their actions encourages them to commit these acts without fear of being arrested or prosecuted.

In ethnic wars, rape and sexual violence take on an added dimension. Work on the India-Pakistan partition by scholars, as well as research on the war in the Former Yugoslavia, points to ethnic factors that increase the vulnerability of women. In such contexts, rape and sexual violence are seen as attacks on a woman's honour. Raping her shames and humiliates the whole community.[8] Vindicating women's honour, then, becomes the battle cry of the other side. In addition, rape and talk of sexual violence is used to mark boundaries between communities, especially in the context of highly mixed populations. By raping the other, one searches for purity, certainty and distance from the other, who then becomes merely the object of violence. Research has shown that rape was highest in situations of mixed populations, where public rapings, along with public murder, were an aspect of forcing differentiation and distance.[9]

During wartime, sexual violence is not usually a private crime. It is often committed in public, in front of fellow soldiers and the family of the victim. This public spectacle is aimed at instilling terror among the population, but it also strengthens bonds and comradeship among fellow soldiers or militias. The public acts are meant to harden the warrior and to create shared experiences among the men. Studies into the lives of perpetrators have clearly shown that this element of male bonding is an essential aspect of rapes during wartime.

III   How Women Are Affected by War

Women are affected by armed conflict in myriad ways. They are often direct victims of violence, either being killed, maimed, or subject to sexual violence. This direct violence is often severe and of the 'shock the conscience' variety. Women are often gang-raped and killed, usually in front of their families.[10] They are sexually mutilated and sometimes their bodies are tattooed. They are paraded naked through the streets and some are forced to dance nude on tables.[11] They are made to become sexual slaves as

---

8   Ritu Menon and Kamla Bhasin, *Borders and Boundaries: Women in India's Partition* (1998).

9   Silva Meznaric, 'Gender as an Ethno-Marker: Rape, War and Identity Politics in The Former Yugoslavia' in Valentine M Moghadam (ed) *Identity, Politics, and Women: Cultural Reassertions and Feminisms in International Perspective* (1994).

10   See *Report of the Special Rapporteur on Violence Against Women: Report of the Mission to Rwanda on the Issues of Violence Against Women in Situations of Armed Conflict*, 54 UN ESCOR, UN Doc E/CN.4/1998/54/Add.1 (1998) [*Mission to Rwanda*]; *Report of the Special Rapporteur on Violence Against Women: Mission to Sierra Leone*, 58 UN ESCOR, UN Doc E/CN.4/2002/83/Add.2 (2002) [*Mission to Sierra Leone*]; *Mission to Indonesia and East Timor*, above n 6; *Mission to Colombia*, above n 7. For the Former Yugoslavia, see Alexandra Stiglmayer (ed) *Mass Rapes: The War Against Women in Bosnia Herzegovina* (1994).

11   See *Prosecutor v. Kunarac, Kovac and Vukovic (Foca)* (Judgment) Case No. IT-96-23-T and IT-96-23/1-T, 22 February 2001 <http://www.un.org/icty/foca/trialc2/judgement/kun-tjo 10222e.pdf>.

well as domestic slaves and they are sometimes forcibly impregnated.[12] Human rights groups have documented the nature and scale of this sexual violence in many countries throughout the world. They convey a pattern of brutality and humiliation that is often unimaginable for those living in peacetime.

In addition to being direct victims, women suffer violence as refugees or internally displaced persons (IDPs). While the men go to war, women are usually displaced with their children, trying to eke out a life in a refugee camp. They are often victims of sexual violence in flight and harassed once they are in the camps. If they are with their husbands, women are often subject to increased rates of domestic violence. Some scholars have argued that women often make use of the refugee status to acquire agency over their lives, having escaped the structures of patriarchy. But for many women, being a refugee and an IDP is a state of victimhood in which they are subject to sexual violence and discrimination as a matter of course. In addition, they are denied basic economic and social amenities and often have to survive in subhuman situations.

During wartime, the presence of large armies and unattached males often leads to a demand for prostitution. This demand is often met by trafficking women from across borders or from the countryside. Lured by job offers and other enticements, many of these women end up in brothels in terrible conditions. The Japanese army's 'comfort women' of World War II are the best known victims of these practices. They were often lured by job offers and in some cases, such as Jan Ruff O'Herne's, they were forcibly removed from their families. The women were then kept in brothels run by the Japanese army. There, they were raped 40 times a day in little bed cubicles and were subject to extraordinary violence and humiliation. After the war, many returned home with terrible scars and an inability to make a new life.[13] Today, trafficking continues, though private owners run the brothels. In recent times, the presence of large numbers of UN peacekeepers has led to trafficking and prostitution in areas adjoining their camps. This has caused a great deal of unhappiness among local populations and new efforts are being made to curb these activities and to raise awareness among the peacekeepers.

Women are also affected by war in the sense that many of them become war widows. Their husbands may have been killed in combat or lost in displacement. These women take on the burden of being single-parent families, trying to make a living in new places and new contexts. They are often at the bureaucratic mercy of state institutions and international humanitarian agencies. Many complain of sexual harassment and difficulty while living in the community. Many others turn to prostitution to make ends meet. They have to find food, clothing and shelter for their children – as well as education – and this is often an uphill struggle. In some countries, widows are denied inheritance rights. When a woman's husband dies, ownership of his prop-

---

12   See Rhonda Copelon, 'Surfacing Gender: Re-Engraving Crimes Against Women in Humanitarian Law' (1994) 5(2) *Hastings Women's Law Journal* 243.

13   *Report of the Special Rapporteur on Violence Against Women, its Causes and Consequences: Report on the Mission to the Democratic People's Republic of Korea, the Republic of Korea and Japan on the Issue of Military Sexual Slavery in Wartime*, 52 UN ESCOR, UN Doc E/CN.4/1996/53/Add.1 (1996) [*Mission to Korea and Japan*].

erty reverts back to his family, leaving the widow at the mercy of her male in-laws.[14]
As will be discussed in more detail below, the lack of inheritance rights makes war
widows into paupers. If they have no male children, they are denied any right to the
husband's property.

Women can be sexually exploited during armed conflict. In some wars, pornography plays an important role. In the Bosnian war, some of the rapes were publicly performed and videotaped. The tapes were then sold as pornographic material. Women
victims were ordered to pose in certain positions and pictures were taken for pornographic magazines. This exploitation of women's bodies during war, with strikingly
modern technology of video cameras and hi-tech props, was one of the great horrors
of the war in the former Yugoslavia. The Serbs directing the films used sophisticated
modern methods, props and even dubbed the dialogue. This cynical and dehumanis-
ing use of women is a new contribution to the depravity of war.[15]

Women are also victims in another sense. Many of them become armed combatants, especially in recent times. As female combatants, they are entitled to the protection of the *Geneva Conventions*. In practice, however, they are often not afforded
the special treatment and care to which they are legally entitled. Women in guerrilla
movements are particularly vulnerable to rape from the other side. If they are captured, they are invariably raped during interrogation. For this reason, the female fighters of the Liberation Tigers of Tamil Eelam take cyanide capsules rather than endure
capture. In addition, many of these women are subject to sexual assault from their
own colleagues. In Colombia, ex-combatants spoke of sexual abuse by commanders and colleagues, as well as a ban on pregnancy, that often made them leave the
movement. The control of reproductive rights often goes hand-in-hand with the presence of female fighters. Though some women would argue that the right to take up
arms is the right of women as resistance fighters, the spectre of armed women cadres
raises disturbing issues about women, non-violence and women's role in peace movements. Many argue that belonging to an armed movement is an act of empowerment.
Whether participation at the lower echelons of a military chain of command can be
truly liberating for women, however, is one of those interminable debates within the
women's movement.

Women are often compelled to work in munitions and production factories
preparing uniforms, shells and other military equipment needed for war. In Britain,
making ammunition for the troops was seen as a patriotic duty for the female muni-
tion factory worker during World War II. Women in guerrilla villages have sewed and
made clothing for their troops. The entrance of women into public life as workers who
assisted men during wartime – only to return to the home after the war ends – is a
well known pattern in the conduct of war. It is also true that women play a major part
in peace efforts. But their presence in the 'war machine' cannot be overlooked. Many
women play an important part in the conduct of war.

---

14   For an extensive discussion of these issues, at least in the South Asian context, see gener-
     ally Bina Agarwal, *A Field of One's Own* (1994).

15   Catharine M. MacKinnon, 'Turning Rape into Pornography: Post Modern Genocide' *Ms.*
     (Washington DC) July/August 1993, 24-30.

Perhaps the greatest, but least quantifiable, impact of war on women is in the process of militarisation. Militarisation re-inscribes certain masculine values and lifestyles. These lifestyles may condone violence and a measure of aggression, often resulting in greater violence in the home and greater violence in the community. Army deserters, young men with guns, the climate of impunity and the celebration of martial valour all help to create a context where violence becomes acceptable. This has many consequences for women. They are often the first victims of this tolerance for the violent lifestyle and the last to benefit from the largesse of the state toward its military apparatus.

IV   International Standards of Accountability

There are two conflicting approaches on how history treats violence against women in wartime. Many scholars have argued that such crimes have been invisible and that history has no recollection of these horrible events. Seen as a necessary consequence of war, violence against women in armed conflict has been ignored by recorded history and those involved in making and implementing international standards. These scholars feel that patriarchal notions of sexual violence and the invisibility of women in the international law-making process led to the complete neglect of sexual violence during wartime. Such violence is rarely named as a terrible crime and there are few provisions in international law that deal with these acts.

It is often pointed out that the *Hague Convention*, the first document of the twentieth century to deal with crimes of war, has no provision with regard to sexual violence during wartime and only mentions a general notion of 'family law'. It is also pointed out that though Article 27 in the *Fourth Geneva Convention* clearly states that crimes against women's 'honour' are prohibited, sexual violence is not mentioned as one of the crimes that constitute a 'grave breach' of the *Geneva Conventions* triggering individual criminal responsibility and universal jurisdiction. Cast in the language of 'honour', these crimes have a very patriarchal ring to their language and tenor. The Statute of Nuremberg is also silent with regard to sexual violence. Such acts do not explicitly constitute war crimes or crimes against humanity in its provisions. It is only in the 1990s with the international tribunals in The Hague and Arusha that sexual violence has been treated as a serious war crime and a crime against humanity.

Another school of thought, usually emanating from the office of prosecutors around the world, is the belief that sexual violence against women has always been seen as a prohibited act of war. Pointing to the chivalry codes of the medieval ages, the provisions on honour in the *Hague Conventions*, the provisions of *Control Council Rule No. 10 of the Occupying Powers of Germany*, the trial of Japanese Commanders for sexual violence in Nanking, these prosecutors argue that sexual violence against women has always been seen as a crime of war. They also point out that the general clauses on torture and wilful killing that mark the language of the *Geneva Conventions'* provisions on grave breaches were meant to include acts of sexual violence and assault. They argue that the prohibition against sexual violence during wartime is so universal that it is an aspect of customary international law.[16] These arguments set the framework for the legal argument about the accountability of perpetrators for sexual violence during wartime.

Most countries of the world are signatories to the *Geneva Conventions* and are therefore bound by these provisions. Jurists and courts have held that the principles contained in the *Geneva Conventions* are so universally recognised that they constitute customary international law and states are bound regardless of whether they have signed relevant treaties. The universality of the *Conventions* makes them still the most important documents when it comes to dealing with individuals who have committed crimes during wartime.

Some states have gone beyond the *Geneva Conventions* and signed the *Rome Statute* on the International Criminal Court. The *ICC Statute* is 'the state of the art' document on international war crimes and crimes against humanity. It is far-reaching in its treatment of sexual violence and there is explicit language with regard to sexual violence and gender discrimination. Individuals are held criminally responsible for the prohibited acts and can be brought before the international court. Most states have not ratified the *ICC Statute* to date and with active lobbying by the United States against it, the likelihood that there will be many signatories during the first few years is slim. The *Geneva Conventions*, therefore, still remain the most important documents with regard to binding provisions of international humanitarian law.

The nature of international norms and standards have evolved rapidly in the last decade because of the terrible wars that took place in the Former Yugoslavia and Rwanda. These wars, both internal and external, so shocked the conscience of the world – with effective media coverage and international mobilisation – that there was rapid development of international capacity with regard to the prosecution of war crimes and crimes against humanity. Over the last decades, the ICTY and the International Criminal Tribunal for Rwanda (ICTR) have made some far-reaching judgements that have resulted in people being prosecuted and convicted at the international level for war crimes and crimes against humanity. Sexual violence has been an important part of their considerations. Their pronouncements are important because they interpret the law to cover actual fact situations and therefore give depth and meaning to the law. The law is in the process of evolving, but significant milestones have already been reached. These milestones will be discussed more fully in Kelly Askin's chapter below.

V   The Humanitarian Consequences of Conflict

Sexual violence during wartime has enormous consequences for women living in war zones. Many women flee their homes with their children because of the possibility of sexual violence. It is often said that women and children comprise 80 percent of the refugees or the internally displaced in any given context. Men may have become combatants or prefer to risk staying behind. Women and children, on the other hand, go

---

16   This is the argument of the prosecutors at the International Criminal Tribunal for the former Yugoslavia (ICTY) and the International Criminal Tribunal for Rwanda (ICTR).

in large numbers to refugee shelters. In most areas of the world, agriculture or fishing is the main livelihoods of communities. Becoming a refugee often implies a complete break with livelihood cycles and an absolute dependence on humanitarian agencies for basic survival.

Women who leave their homes often have to walk long distances for water, food or medical help. During these long journeys, women are often attacked and raped. These cases have been documented among many refugees and have received international attention with regard to Somali refugees in Kenya. Women fleeing the Vietnam conflict by boats were often raped by pirates at sea. Sexual violence during flight occurs regularly and is often a major consequence of war. Women in flight are extremely vulnerable and are often asked for sexual services in return for bureaucratic or military favours.

When women reach refugee camps, they are often subject to sexual harassment by camp officials and soldiers guarding the camp. The structure of the camp is extremely important: women activists have insisted that women be consulted when camps are designed. Where toilets are far away and secluded, women often experience sexual violence. Women often have to offer sexual services to receive placement in the camp, or for any provisions or privileges in the camp. Sexual services sometimes become a negotiating point for receiving even the most basic of services.

Research in refugee and IDP camps points to a dramatic increase in domestic violence in camps where families flee together. Research done in West Timor shows a startling increase in domestic violence in the camps, as men vent their frustrations on the women in their families.[17] This has been confirmed by experiences in many refugee camps and interviews with women internally displaced. The social frustrations and disempowerment that populations face when they are displaced has terrible implications for women in the family. Husbands, brothers and sons often use domestic violence as a means of expressing displeasure at circumstances beyond their control. At the same time, some research points to the fact that women who come as single parent units to the camps are seemingly empowered. They are suddenly given the right to make decisions about their lives and the lives of their children. They become important people in the camps, negotiating their rights and entitlements.[18]

In the armed conflict areas, even without flight, women face great difficulties. In many societies, women are responsible for the procurement of food and water. During war, traditional systems of food distribution break down. It becomes imperative that alternative systems are put in place to ensure access to food. Economic sanctions against enemy-held territories often result in dramatic increases in malnutrition and food-related diseases. In this context, international humanitarian agencies often assist in the granting of food to these areas with the consent of governments. But many foodstuffs are left out and the payment of commissions and levies to local residents

---

17   Report submitted to the Special Rapporteur on Violence Against Women by the Asia Pacific Forum on Women Law and Development (copy on file with author).

18   Dharini Rajasingham-Senanayake, 'Ambivalent Empowerment: The Tragedy of Tamil Women in Conflict' in Rita Manchanda (ed) *Women, War and Peace in South Asia* (2001) 102.

result in less food at a higher price reaching the target population. As women are often the heads of single-parent households in war zones, this attempt to meet basic food needs occupies a great deal of their time. They spend hours trying to get the necessary permits from bureaucrats. In addition, they often have to pay a price to the local soldier or operative on the ground to deliver the food. Once they get the food and return home, in some contexts, some of the food is taxed by the local guerrilla commanders and the women end up with only a small portion of their entitlement. The lack of accountability creates a great deal of hardship and survival becomes very difficult.

In many societies, women engage in subsistence agriculture and it is their main means of livelihood. In a war zone, this livelihood is often disrupted. During war, women are in grave danger when they try and carry on with day-to-day living. They are often the individuals asked to bring water and firewood, as well as work on the land. They may be caught in the crossfire, or they may step on uncleared mines. They are unable to graze cattle or continue performing any daily tasks because of these realities. In some cases, women and children are forcibly evicted from the land by local commanders or invading troops. This forced eviction is another aspect of warfare that takes a terrible toll on women.

Women's access to land is a major problem even after conflict. In many societies, widows are denied inheritance and if they do not have male heirs, they can be sent off the land by their husband's relatives. This leaves many war-widows in a precarious position. Women often become paupers and begin begging in the streets during and after war. This pauperisation of women because of the legal system and the exigencies of war is a serious problem. In Afghanistan, begging became the only means of survival during the Taliban regime when women were refused the right to work. Women had no option but to beg in the streets, always accompanied by their young sons who were their required male escort.

Another serious concern is health care for women during wartime. Women and children living in war zones risk suffering from communicable diseases, epidemics and very poor nutrition. They also have limited access to health care. This is particularly the case with regard to reproductive health care. Women rarely have access to family planning resources in war-affected areas or in refugee camps. Pregnant women in those areas are rarely given pre-natal or post-natal care. Most importantly, they have limited access to emergency obstetric care.

Women who have experienced sexual violence have even more serious health and health care problems. They are rarely given effective medical treatment immediately after being sexually assaulted. In addition, they suffer terrible wounds. In both Sierra Leone and Rwanda, their vaginal areas were often ripped apart and this can be a life-threatening situation, especially for very young girls. These rape victims require special surgery to help them regain a semblance of a normal sexual life. In most societies, there are very few gynaecologists trained to deal with these complicated cases. In Rwanda just after the war, with a large number of women who had suffered sexual violence, there were only five gynaecologists who could give treatment for the women concerned.[19] Women had to tend to their own wounds or rely on herbal medicine.

---

19   *Mission to Rwanda*, above n 10.

Many of these women had contracted HIV/AIDS because of the sexual violence. In Rwanda, some women said that men infected with HIV/AIDS deliberately had sex with women from the other ethnic group to infect them with the disease as part of the war.[20] In war zones and refugee camps, the risk of contracting HIV/AIDS is extremely high, as many women have to give sexual services so that they can survive. Besides HIV/AIDS, other sexually transmitted diseases can have grave consequences for women, including infertility, inflammation, abortion and infection.

With little access to health care, women often suffer these conditions in silence. In some countries, such as Afghanistan, women could not be treated by male doctors and this often led to high rates of female mortality. In other countries, women do not travel long distances because of cultural reasons, so unless it is a terrible emergency, women do not seek out medical services. Hospitals in war zones are often undersupplied and understaffed, especially since health professionals are likely to leave the war zone for safer areas. There is a dearth of drugs and embargoes imposed by the other side can lead to the complete denial of important medicines for the civilian population. This, in turn, can lead to epidemics or the prevalence of certain kinds of illnesses such as cholera and malaria that, in other circumstances, can usually be brought under control by health professionals.

One of the worst problems in war zones, which receives little attention, is the socio-psychological issues that often paralyse women and make them incapable of dealing with their own lives. In Rwanda, psychologists estimate that 80 percent of the women who survived the war were suffering from major psychological problems and needed treatment.[21] Yet few societies have the resources or the strategies to deal with these psycho-social issues. According to psychiatrists working in these areas, fear is a central element in people's lives. This fear often leads to severe depression on the part of women. It also includes psychosomatic manifestations such as chronic stomach problems, palpitations, nausea, insomnia and a loss of appetite and sexual energy. Thoughts of suicide and acts of self-mutilation are also very common. In this context, only a concerted and planned intervention will help alleviate many of the issues faced by these women. In most societies, mental health does not receive even minimal attention. It is therefore often left to the international community to raise these concerns and assist in setting up programs for their development. This will be discussed in more detail in the following chapter by Jeanne Ward.

The problems faced by so-called 'children of hate' also deserve some attention and are often neglected. Because East Timor and Rwanda are both Catholic countries women who became pregnant as a result of rape refused to have abortions. Sometimes the children born of rape were given to orphanages, but often the children are brought up by the affected mother. The psychological manifestations of this relationship are often evident from the beginning and are often unhealthy for both the women and the children. The women and their children are in need of a great deal of support and counselling to help them deal with these problems, but they rarely get any assistance from the state.

---

20 *Ibid.*
21 *Ibid.*

VI   Other Problems Relating to Violence against Women during War Time

The problem of the girl child caught up in a zone of armed conflict is a special topic that requires separate attention. Girl children, like women, are killed and maimed during war. It is argued that women and girl children suffer landmine casualties, for example, in greater numbers, since fetching water and firewood are often their traditional labour.[22] In addition, there are now many girl child combatants fighting for different causes around the world. In Sierra Leone, girl children as young as ten were often kidnapped, then injected with a substance and sent into battle. After battle they were required to provide sexual services to the male cadres and commanders. Finally, there are international and national networks of trafficking that pick up girl children from war zones and offer them a life away from the war. These networks traffic the girl children for prostitution or domestic services where they sometimes live out unconscionable lives.

Another increasing problem relates to the UN peacekeeping forces. Members of these forces, sent in to protect civilian populations, sometimes engage in acts of sexual violence. Such cases have been recorded in Mozambique, Somalia, Cambodia and Sierra Leone.[23] There has also been increased trafficking of women to areas where peacekeepers are stationed, whether in Kosovo or Sierra Leone or East Timor. Attitudes of some UN officials have not ameliorated the situation. The Head of the UN Mission to Cambodia, when questioned about sexual abuse and trafficking, replied 'I am not a puritan: 18-year old, hot-blooded soldiers had a right to drink a few beers and chase after beautiful things of the opposite sex'.[24]

The attitude toward women by peacekeepers is accentuated by the fact that sometimes there is a lack of women in the peacekeeping operations. From 1957-1991, women accounted for 5 to 25 percent of the international civilian staff supporting peacekeeping operations. Today, in most peacekeeping operations, women comprise about one-third of the peacekeeping civilian staff. It was only after 1994 that the UN asked member states for female soldiers, but women in combat roles in peacekeeping operations is less than 10 percent.[25] The presence of women in peacekeeping operations has led to a strengthening of the bonds with local communities and has allowed women from the communities more access to peacekeepers.

In many of the societies at war, there are also many women's groups that are in the forefront for the struggle for peace. It would be an overstatement to say that women are by nature supporters of peace. There are many women who see themselves as mothers of warriors, many who have worked in munitions factories and many who have screamed for war in the violent rhetoric that often underpins the political side of

---

22   Carol Nordstrom, 'Girls Behind the (Front) Lines' in Lorentzen and Turpin, above n 3, 85.

23   Jennifer Turpin, 'Many Faces: Women Confronting War' in Lorentzen and Turpin, above n 3, 6.

24   *Ibid.*

25   *Ibid.* 143.

military mobilisation. Women leaders such as Margaret Thatcher and Indira Gandhi led their nations to war without the slightest hesitation. And yet, it is empirically true that women are present in large numbers in peace movements, often taking the lead in organising for peace.

In recent times, one has seen the phenomenon of women's groups being actively involved in the peace process. In Northern Ireland, the Women's Coalition for Peace got elected and took part in the peace negotiations, often creating a channel of communication with the male members. In Burundi and Somalia, women have been present at the peace talks. In other countries, women's movements for peace create the conditions for peace agitation and peace activism. The Women in Black in Israel, the Naga Mothers' Front, the Women for Peace movement in Sri Lanka and countless others have asked for the cessation of violence. Women are also in the forefront of the demand for accountability with regard to war crimes and crimes against humanity. The Mothers of the Plaza in Peru, South African women and The Mothers' Front in Sri Lanka were movements aimed at demanding accountability for the loss of their sons. Peace and accountability for human rights violations have been twin themes in women's peace movements around the world. In some contexts, these women remain the only hope in a context of protracted war and ethnic conflict.

VII   Recommendations

1. The system of accountability for sexual violence as war crimes and crimes against humanity should be strengthened. Countries should be encouraged to sign the *Rome Statute* for the International Criminal Court and to amend their national laws to recognise the different types of sexual violence as war crimes and crimes against humanity. Prosecutors and investigators around the world should be supported in bringing such cases before international or national tribunals and before truth and reconciliation commissions. It is important to ensure that everyone recognises that these crimes are unacceptable and that those who commit these crimes will be prosecuted and punished.

2. UN peacekeeping operations should be sensitive to the problems of the local female population. They should implement effective measures to protect the female population from sexual abuse and exploitation. Special internal mechanisms should be instituted to ensure that those who violate such codes will be punished or transferred. There should be more women at all levels of peacekeeping operations.

3. International and national humanitarian agencies should make violence against women during wartime a high priority. In this sense, there should be systematic attempts to:

    a. make combatants and civilians aware that sexual violence during wartime is an international crime against humanity. This should be done by ensuring that troops are properly trained and guerrilla groups properly informed by agencies such as the ICRC.

    b. protect women living in the war zones from sexual violence and disruption of their livelihood through strict adherence to the *Geneva Conventions.*

c. provide women in war zones and refugee camps with minimum services, including:

 I. *the right to food.* Food should not become a hostage of war. Food to the civilian population, either through humanitarian efforts or through protection of livelihood, should be guaranteed. There should be no economic embargoes that affect the right to food and water.

 II. *health care.* Health care should be provided to women living in war zones and women should have access to medical personnel with special expertise in wounds resulting from sexual violence. International and national surgeons specialising in v-section operations for women, as well as gynaecologists skilled in diseases relating to the reproductive system, should be an integral part of any medical team sent by the national or international health authorities. In this context, treatment for HIV/AIDS and programs to educate the population about HIV/AIDS should also be a part of any health strategy in war zones.

 III. *psycho-social support.* Trained counsellors and community workers should be included in any such team at refugee camps or hospitals in and around war zones.

 IV. *mobile units of health professionals in contexts where access to health services is limited.* Mobile humanitarian services assisting both sides will be of great assistance in the context of war.

 V. *the opportunity for women to participate in the decision-making processes at refugee and IDP camps.* Women should be involved in all decision-making with regard to refugee and IDP camps and in the management of such camps. The same should be true with regard to local-level leadership involved in individual projects.

 VI. *the prevention of bureaucratic exploitation of women.* It must be recognised that when services are given to the general population, at the lower level of these bureaucratic establishments women are often asked to provide sexual services in return for the provisions. It is important to ensure an implementing strategy that prevents this type of exploitation.

 VII. *an environment in which sexual harassment and domestic violence is not accepted.* Sexual harassment and domestic violence in refugee camps and community centres are often major problems. The management of these camps and centres should make it clear that these practices will not be tolerated. There should be a committee from the camp or centre – in which women actively participate – to look into these matters.

 VIII. *education and awareness-raising about mines and de-mining projects.* Women and girls should be specially targeted for this education, since they are often the individuals who fetch the water and the firewood.

 IX. *economic security.* Inheritance laws and other impediments that prevent women's access to land and livelihood during and after conflict should be amended so that war widows are given economic security and some assistance.

x.   *programs specifically focussed on women-headed households.* Special programs for female-headed households in war zones should be implemented to ensure that these widows are not left at the mercy of local level bureaucrats and commanders. Programs in awareness-raising, skills training, trauma counselling and child management will be of great assistance to these women.

xi. *special protection for the girl child.* The girl child should not be neglected in the context of armed conflict. Special programmers should exist to reintegrate women and girl children who have been combatants in war. Their needs are different from male combatants. There should also be programs to prevent girl children from being trafficked from war zones to slavery-like situations where they must engage in prostitution or other activities. Trafficking of women and girl children should be a serious concern for military authorities and humanitarian agencies working in war zones.

8

Gender-Based Violence among Conflict-affected Populations: Humanitarian Program Responses

*Jeanne Ward**

I Introduction

In the previous chapter, the former Special Rapporteur succinctly characterises sexual violence against women during wartime as 'one of history's great silences'. In giving voice to the nature and scope of violence suffered by women and girls during and following armed conflict, Radhika Coomaraswamy refers to the 'humanitarian implications' of that violence – enumerating risk factors and outcomes in terms of women's and girls' morbidity, mortality, human rights and development and detailing recommendations to limit the extent and impact of violence. Taking into account some of the recommendations for field-based health, psycho-social and protection services outlined by Ms. Coomaraswamy, this chapter will outline the development of programmatic initiatives spearheaded by the humanitarian community[1] within the last ten years, focusing especially on challenges for field-based programs to address the legal rights of survivors.

Starting with an introduction to the terminology of 'gender-based violence' (GBV), which is the most common idiom of the humanitarian field in describing violence against women and girls, the chapter will then provide a brief account of the historical antecedents that brought GBV within the scope of humanitarian assistance, identifying some of the lessons learned in early programming strategies and highlighting resources developed thus far to inform and improve programming. A current standard for response will be articulated, with considerations of the extent to which

---

* Jeanne Ward is currently based in Nairobi, Kenya, where she works for the Reproductive Health for Refugees Consortium (RHRC) on a global project to improve programming to address gender-based violence among conflict-affected populations. She is the author of *If Not Now, When?: Addressing Gender-Based Violence in Refugee, Internally Displaced and Post-Conflict Settings* (2002). She gratefully acknowledges the research assistance of Meghan O'Connor of the International Rescue Committee.

1 'Humanitarian community' is a term used informally in this chapter to include local, national and international organisations and institutions whose shared mandate is the care and protection of people affected by armed conflict, including refugees, internally displaced persons (IDPs) and returnees.

Helen Durham and Tracey Gurd (eds.), Listening to the Silences: Women and War, *pp. 67-87.*
© 2005 *Koninklijke Brill BV. Printed in The Netherlands.* ISBN 90 04 14365 3.

the humanitarian community is adequately acting as a bridge between survivors' legal needs and local legal structures. Recent initiatives will be briefly outlined, highlighting in particular two examples of projects representing the vanguard in identifying and responding to legal issues related to violence against women.

A   Evolution of Terms

The very earliest humanitarian programming addressing violence against conflict-affected women focused on exposure to sexual violence and was primarily based in refugee camps. In 1996, the International Rescue Committee (IRC) introduced a project entitled the 'Sexual and Gender-Based Violence Program' – the project's title as well as its activities advanced the concept of gender as elemental to violence. The term 'sexual and gender-based violence' (SGBV) gained favour within the humanitarian community because it could be used generally to reference multiple forms of violence – such as sexual violence, domestic violence and harmful traditional practices. In that way it was more applicable to projects that were operating in increasingly diverse settings (that is, displaced camps and returnee communities as well as refugee settings) and with increasingly broad mandates to address multiple forms of violence.

The SGBV phrasing is widely used by UNHCR, the rationale for which is explained in a somewhat confounding manner in their 2003 *Sexual and Gender-Based Violence Against Refugees, Returnees and Internally Displaced Persons: Guidelines for Prevention and Response*. Though sexual violence is defined within the Guidelines as a form of gender-based violence, preference is given within the guidelines and in UNHCR's work to the term 'sexual and gender-based violence' because the term 'recognises that, although the majority of victims/survivors are women and children, boys and men are also targets of sexual and gender-based violence.'[2]

To avoid the confusion illustrated in the Guidelines, the Reproductive Health Response in Conflict (RHRC) Consortium[3] has advocated for and uses the term 'gender-based violence' (GBV), of which sexual violence is considered one component. In so far as the term implies that issues of gender underlie virtually all forms of violence against women and girls that humanitarian programs seek to address, the term has important theoretical and practical implications: the language speaks to the

---

2   United Nations High Commissioner for Refugees, *Sexual and Gender-Based Violence Against Refugees, Returnees and Internally Displaced Persons: Guidelines for Prevention and Response* (2003) 10.

3   RHRC Consortium members represent a mix of advocacy, development, humanitarian relief, research and training organisations. Four members of the RHRC Consortium – the American Refugee Committee, CARE, the International Rescue Committee and Marie Stopes International – focus on working with international and local NGOs, UN agencies, target populations and host country governments to provide direct reproductive health services to persons affected by armed conflict. JSI Research and Training Institute and Columbia University's Heilbrunn Department of Population and Family Health are primarily involved in project research, staff training and technical assistance. The Women's Commission for Refugee Women and Children, as an expert resource and advocacy organisation, serves as coordinator of the Consortium.

necessity of examining the societal and relational contexts in which violence against women and girls occurs and therefore begs the inclusion of men, women, boys and girls in any efforts to reduce violence.

Despite the fact that the terminology is useful in underlining the gendered dimensions of violence against women and girls, application of the term in GBV programming that exclusively targets women and girls is misleading. In its fullest sense, GBV encompasses violence against men and boys that results from gender roles or gender-role expectations (for example, forced conscription based on the expectation that males fight in wars) and yet GBV programs have not evolved to address these concerns. The term is also easily misunderstood to suggest that gender, when applied to women and girls, is synonymous with victimisation. Notions of 'gender-based empowerment' then seem counterintuitive – if not wrong – and women as direct and indirect perpetrators of violence is an issue not widely acknowledged or investigated in humanitarian work. Finally, 'gender' is not a term that is easily adaptable to other languages, resulting in many field staff using the acronym GBV without fully grasping its meaning. To address this need, GBV programs have avoided using the terminology in project components that are visible to the community. For example, a GBV project in Kosovo operates a 'Women's Wellness Centre' and a GBV project in Sierra Leone runs a sexual assault referral centre that is known to the community as the 'Rainbo Centre'.

As GBV programming continues to evolve, the language used will anticipate programmatic progress – as in the case of increasing male involvement in initiatives to reduce GBV and recognising men and boys as vulnerable to GBV – and with that progress language will be modified to reflect lessons learned. For the purposes of this chapter, the term GBV will be used generally to mean violence against women and girls.

II Background

Humanitarian attention to the issue of war-related violence against women and girls is in its relative infancy. In fact, the United Nations High Commissioner for Refugees (UNHCR) has formally recognised the distinct needs of women and children affected by armed conflict only in the last fifteen years. Following the *Third World Conference on Women* in Nairobi in 1985, the first working group on refugee women was convened to advocate for the needs of women affected by conflict. The working group's lobbying activities resulted in the 1989 appointment of a Senior Coordinator for Refugee Women to UNHCR. In 1990, UNHCR adopted a policy on refugee women's protection, from which evolved UNHCR's 1991 *Guidelines on the Protection of Refugee Women*. By highlighting the general protection needs of women affected by conflict (as distinct from men), the guidelines set the stage for standardising programming that specifically target women. The guidelines explicitly acknowledged exposure to sexual violence as a vulnerability of refugee women and called upon the humanitarian community to address it within its protection mandate.

Reproductive health activists were at the forefront of responding to this call. In 1994, the Women's Commission for Refugee Women and Children released a ground-breaking study, *Refugee Women and Reproductive Health: Reassessing Priorities*.

This study revealed that even the most basic reproductive health services – including those to address GBV – were not available to women displaced by war. At the 1994 International Conference on Population and Development in Cairo, responding to GBV was identified as one of four basic pillars of reproductive health programming.[4]

At this same conference, minimum health standards for refugees were expanded to include reproductive health services and, by extension, treatment for victims of sexual violence. The need for these services was reinforced by media coverage in Bosnia and Rwanda, illustrating for the world the extent to which women and girls were targets of sexual violence during war and stimulating donor attention to the issue. Reproductive health in general – and sexual violence in particular – was officially on the agenda of donors and humanitarian agencies charged with responding to the needs of the conflict-affected.

In 1995, the RHRC was established to promote the institutionalisation of reproductive health services in refugee settings worldwide and has since developed programs in communities affected by armed conflict, working in all phases of emergencies (from the initial crisis to reconstruction and development).[5] While other organisations and institutions[6] have made significant financial, technical and programming contributions to support the evolution of GBV theory and practice in conflict-affected settings, few parallel the RHRC Consortium's broad sweep of GBV-related service delivery, training, technical assistance, advocacy and resource development. As programs have evolved, the RHRC Consortium has attempted to move beyond the initial medical model that defined early projects to address the broader protection needs of GBV survivors, including the provision of legal services. A brief overview of this evolution is described below.

III   GBV Program Development

Prior to the Cairo conference, the few projects that existed around the world to address violence against women in conflict were more often led by dedicated local, national or international women's health and rights organisations. These groups often worked independently of the resources and support of the larger humanitarian com-

---

4   The three other pillars are safe motherhood, including emergency obstetric care, family planning and treatment for sexually transmitted infections (STIs), including HIV/AIDS.

5   The evolution of humanitarian programming and resources to address GBV described in this chapter primarily focus on the individual and collaborative activities of member organisations within the RHRC Consortium. This bias towards outlining the activities of the RHRC Consortium in part reflects the fact that the author has been directly working with RHRC Consortium members for the last four years. It also reflects the fact that since its inception, the RHRC Consortium has been the global leader in designing and implementing a range of projects to address GBV in settings affected by conflict.

6   These institutions and organisations include, but are certainly not exclusive of, UNHCR, the United Nations Population Fund (UNFPA), the United Nations Development Fund for Women (UNIFEM), the World Health Organisation (WHO), the International Committee of the Red Cross (ICRC), Medicins Sans Frontier (MSF), Physicians for Human Rights (PHR), International Medical Corps (IMC), Oxfam, Save the Children, the Christian Children's Fund (CCF) and Mercy Corps.

munity. Many of those organisations are still operational today and offer lessons to the humanitarian world in sustainability of programming.

After the Cairo conference, the expansion of reproductive health programming for refugee populations created channels of communication within and among the humanitarian community regarding the nature and scope of GBV. This communication resulted in increased understanding and acceptance among humanitarian aid providers of the pervasiveness of violence against women in conflict, in turn stimulating increased global attention to the issue. The intersection of the fields of reproductive health and GBV also allowed for a greater understanding of the physical and mental health impacts of violence against women, including STIs, reproductive tract trauma, unwanted pregnancy and complications associated with unsafe abortions, somatic complaints, depression and suicide.

In 1995, UNHCR published *Sexual Violence Against Refugees: Guidelines on Protection and Response*, which highlighted some of the major legal, medical and psycho-social components of prevention and response to sexual violence. Also in 1995, UNHCR and the United Nations Population Fund (UNFPA) collaborated to form an Inter-Agency Working Group (IAWG) of expert international reproductive health organisations. A year later, IAWG produced an inter-agency field manual, *Reproductive Health in Refugee Situations*, which includes information about the prevention and management of GBV from emergency to stable phases of displacement. While both these resources were critical to advancing basic knowledge regarding GBV, they did not articulate detailed methodologies for developing specialised field-based programs or protocols to tackle GBV.

Reproductive health specialists working in refugee contexts often had limited or no professional preparation in addressing GBV. Despite their commitment to meet a spectrum of reproductive health needs – as well as to support rights of women and girls to be free from violence – activities targeting violence were frequently limited to training health care workers in basic concepts of violence and providing remedial services to survivors. In the early days of GBV programming, support for the expansion of GBV-related services was additionally restricted by a general reluctance in the humanitarian community to impose 'western' belief systems regarding issues of violence against women. Many maintained that responding to acts of violence against women was the preserve of culture and therefore outside the scope of humanitarian intervention. Thus, most early GBV services were limited to remedial care: emergency contraception and treatment for STIs. Programs whose specific orientation was to address violence against women were the exception. Yet these early specialised programs have provided lessons and resources that are the foundation of current initiatives. To the extent that these early programs have educated the international community about the needs and rights of survivors, they have also helped to reduce the reluctance of humanitarian actors to address GBV in conflict-affected settings.

A   Dadaab, Kenya

Among the first UNHCR-supported projects specifically designed to address violence against women refugees was a 'Women Victims of Violence Project' instituted in

1993 in refugee camps in northern Kenya. Reflecting the prevailing approaches at that time, the project's initial objectives included responding to sexual violence through the provision of reproductive health and psycho-social services to women identified as victims, coordinating anti-violence activities through an inter-agency Anti-Rape Committee and decreasing the incidence of rape. The project also paid the salary of a female lawyer whose role was to encourage and support survivors in prosecuting their attackers. Notably, the exclusive orientation was to rape cases. Service design and delivery was 'top down'– initiated and provided by staff of international organisations (as well as one national Kenyan organisation). The stated objective of the project was to lower the number of rape cases despite the fact that instituting effective programming was bound to increase the numbers of women reporting rape.

In 1995, program management was transferred to CARE. Renamed the 'Vulnerable Women and Children Project', activities were expanded to acknowledge other types of risks and risk groups. CARE also instituted participatory processes in project redesign and implementation, outlined in their *Assessment Report of Issues and Response to Sexual Violence: Dadaab Refugee Camp, Kenya,*[7] resulting in a significant increase in refugee participation through anti-rape committees and security and justice committees. In part, this participatory process was reflective of CARE's long-standing commitment to promote locally-based initiatives. In this particular instance, it was also a strategy born of financial necessity: a decrease in UNHCR funding during the mid-1990s resulted in significant staff layoffs, including the lawyer and the majority of CARE employees responsible for providing social support to rape survivors.

One of the findings of CARE's participatory assessment was that 90 percent of reported rapes or attempted rapes occurred when women refugees were collecting firewood outside the camps. In an effort to reduce the incidence of rape, UNHCR initiated a firewood distribution project. Though unsustainably costly, a UNHCR evaluation of the project determined that the incidence of rape related to firewood collection was significantly reduced in the period following distribution. The evaluation also noted, however, that incidence of rape dramatically increased in other locations. This project, then, had the unfortunate outcome of promoting refugee dependency on international assistance while also failing to impact the overall prevalence of rape.

B   Kibondo, Tanzania

A second major initiative to address violence against refugee women was launched in 1996 by the International Rescue Committee (IRC) in camps in Tanzania. This 'Sexual and Gender-Based Violence Program' provided the humanitarian community with some of the first data on violence against refugee women. This data was published by IRC in *Pain Too Deep For Tears: Assessing The Prevalence Of Sexual And Gender-Based Violence Among Burundian Refugees In Tanzania.*[8] Its findings indicated that 27 percent

---

7   CARE, *Assessment Report of Issues and Response to Sexual Violence: Dadaab Refugee Camp, Kenya* (1998).

8   IRC, *Pain Too Deep For Tears: Assessing The Prevalence Of Sexual And Gender-Based Violence Among Burundian Refugees In Tanzania* (1997).

of women interviewed had been exposed to sexual violence since becoming refugees. Importantly, the assessment process was used to engage the refugee population in examining the issue of GBV and defining how to respond to survivors and implement preventive actions. The programming outcomes were later detailed in *A Safe Space Created By And For Women: Sexual And Gender-Based Violence Program Report,*[9] which describes how IRC staff worked with women refugee leaders to design specific GBV intervention strategies. A primary activity was the development of refugee-staffed drop-in centres, located near maternal and child health clinics to reduce the visibility, potential for stigmatisation and risks associated with survivors visiting the centres. The drop-in centres were also the site of meetings of women leaders in the community, who gathered together to sing, dance and discuss issues in their communities.

As with the Dadaab program, the initial orientation of the project was toward the reduction of sexual violence experienced by refugee women. During the early stages of programming, however, support services were expanded to address domestic violence, sexual harassment and the abduction and early marriage of girls. As increasing numbers of girls sought assistance at the drop-in centres, staff developed special approaches to interview children and address their needs. Other program developments included recruiting male leaders to disseminate information about violence issues to men in the camps and building the capacity of women leaders.

In the 1998 summary report of the project, staff burn-out was identified as a major issue. Visibility in the community and their role in protecting survivors resulted in staff members being threatened and harassed, especially those who worked and lived in the camps. Not only did staff suffer the risk of violence associated with their work, some had themselves been victims of sexual or domestic violence. Despite these significant stress factors, no professional services were available to staff for psychological support. There was also little in the way of judicial process for cases of domestic violence, such that case workers struggled to combat issues to which the larger system did not respond. An evaluation published by Human Rights Watch in 2000, four years after implementation of GBV programming, highlighted the fact that there were no policies or procedures for protecting women refugees from domestic violence. It also noted that traditional justice systems promoted systems of patriarchy that often exploited rather than assisted survivors.[10]

The Dadaab and Kibondo initiatives illustrate several principles that remain central to current programming. One of the most important principles is the use of participatory approaches in assessment, project design and implementation. While participation is critical in all types of humanitarian intervention, the fact that it is generally more time-consuming and costly (at least in the short run) can discourage the application of participatory processes. In the case of addressing GBV programming, however, lack of community support and trust can have enormous consequences

---

9   IRC, *A Safe Space Created By And For Women: Sexual And Gender-Based Violence Program Report* (1998).

10   Human Rights Watch, *Seeking Protection: Addressing Sexual and Domestic Violence in Tanzania's Refugee Camps* (2000) 55-81.

in terms of survivor and worker safety, stigmatisation of those seeking help and ulti-mately, capacity to generate behavioural change required to reduce violence.

Both programs also illustrate the value of using baseline participatory research to introduce concepts and provide education about violence-related issues, as well as to identify leaders in the community who are interested in addressing or are already addressing the issue of GBV. Other standards illustrated by the programs include designing inter-agency teams for collaboration and mutual support; reaching beyond rape to tackle other forms of violence to which women and girls are exposed; pro-moting the safety and care of GBV staff; designing methods for addressing the needs of children; engaging men directly in project activities and as targets in community education; and developing strategies to improve the general conditions of women and girls, such as promoting female leadership and improving access to education and income-generating projects.

These early case studies also demonstrate – most clearly through the Dadaab firewood distribution project – that it is critical not to confuse factors that contribute to violence with those that cause violence. Looking at contributing factors, such as points of vulnerability within camps where violence more often occurs, may be valu-able in terms of decreasing cases of violence in that particular instance. This approach alone, however, does not acknowledge the underlying factors that will continue to per-petuate violence. If humanitarian programming seeks to address contributing factors to violence as the ultimate goal, gains (if any) will likely be short-term only.

Finally, both programs reveal the challenges of instituting legal services, espe-cially when programs are operating on limited budgets and have little power to inform institutional change. In the case of Dadaab, the lawyer was a temporary solution to a pervasive problem. While there is no evaluative data about the impact of her work, it is likely that her capacity to effect change within a judicial system with inadequate legal protections for GBV was limited, thus raising the question of the ethics of pursuing prosecution for clients. Her position was also unsustainable given budget fluctuations. In the case of Kibondo, the effort to support traditional leadership – among both men and women – was a challenge in the case of traditional justice which was based on systems that blamed the victim. As the Human Rights Watch report illustrates, even several years after program implementation, the legal process for survivors of domestic violence was more likely to result in further victimisation. Again, this raises the ques-tion of the ethics of introducing efforts to identify and intervene in GBV crimes if legal protections are not available to the survivor.

The lessons learned through these and other early programming efforts were reviewed at an international conference on GBV sponsored in 2001 by UNHCR and attended by international and field-based UNHCR personnel, as well field staff working in (or on behalf of) GBV programs. Conference activities culminated in the publication of *Prevention and Response to Sexual and Gender-Based Violence in Refugee Situations, Inter-Agency Lessons Learned Conference Proceedings*[11] in which the multi-sectoral approach was determined to be fundamental to combating GBV. To date, this

---

11   UNHCR, *Prevention and Response to Sexual and Gender-Based Violence in Refugee Situations, Inter-Agency Lessons Learned Conference Proceedings* (2001) 33-7.

multi-sectoral model forms the 'best practice' for prevention and response to GBV in refugee, IDP and post-conflict settings.

A basic premise of the multi-sectoral approach is that GBV cannot be satisfactorily addressed through the provision of services within a single sector. As outlined above, early GBV programs primarily focused on health care. Efforts to provide legal services were limited or, more often, non-existent. In part because of programs' severely restricted abilities to meet the full spectrum of survivors' needs, the humanitarian community began to identify services and systems that should be in place to promote prevention and response to GBV. Examples include: collection of forensic evidence by health providers; appropriate investigation and documentation of cases by security personnel and judicial processes that guarantee fair and just resolution of cases. If even one component of these services is unavailable, there is the likelihood that, at minimum, a survivor will not be able to access justice or worse; failures in the system will result in further harm to the survivor.

Under the multi-sectoral model, legal support to survivors is a fundamental component, as is ensuring comprehensive protective legislation and access to due process. According to the multi-sectoral model, members of the legal sector are charged with: reviewing and revising laws that reinforce GBV and gender-discrimination; providing free or low-cost legal counselling and representation to survivors; conducting on-going training to members of the judiciary to apply laws and carry out judicial proceedings privately, respectfully and safely; instituting provisions for monitoring court processes and collecting and analysing data on cases; and conducting broad-based community education on the existence and content of anti-GBV laws.

At the heart of the multi-sectoral model is coordination with the population being served: women and girls who have been victimised or are at risk of GBV. At the programmatic level this means that, at least theoretically, women and girls are included from the outset of GBV program design and continue to play an active part in monitoring, evaluation and on-going program development. In some instances this strategy of community involvement is achieved by international NGOs linking directly with existing women's organisations to build their capacity to address GBV. In other instances this strategy involves recruiting women from the target community to work for a project that is run by an international NGO. In still other instances, volunteer women's groups are formed to identify the needs of their own and to work directly with the local or international NGOs that are providing GBV-related services. Whatever the case (and these are very general models, to which there are many exceptions) all those working on behalf of women's rights and the prevention of GBV are, according to the multi-sectoral approach, responsible for participating in coordination meetings in which data can be shared and action plans and programs developed.

At the individual level, the centrality of women and girls within the multi-sectoral model means that the rights and needs of survivors are pre-eminent, in terms of access to respectful and supportive services, guarantees of confidentiality and safety and the ability to determine the course of action for addressing the GBV incident. Efforts should be made to reduce potential stigma to the survivor through broad-based community education as well as through the provision of confidential services. Survivors should be informed of their options at every step of case management. They should be able to exercise a right to choose the course of action in terms of medical and psycho-social treatment, police intervention and legal assistance. This orientation to the rights of survivors cuts across all sectors and is the foundation of ethical service.

IV   Current Programming

While the broad outline of roles and responsibilities within the multi-sectoral model provides a general framework for combating GBV, the implementation of the model remains weak in virtually every humanitarian setting around the world. In 2001, the RHRC Consortium initiated a global assessment of the major types of GBV occurring in conflict-affected settings, related programming and gaps in programming. This assessment represented an attempt to articulate some of the common challenges to addressing GBV in conflict-affected settings and to provide broad-based recommendations for advocacy and action. Those findings and recommendations were detailed in *If Not Now, When?: Addressing Gender-Based Violence in Refugee, Internally Displaced and Post-Conflict Settings.*[12] Research for the report involved interviews with GBV survivors, local service providers, representatives of national ministries and administrators of international NGOs. The conclusions of the global report detail some of the key limitations in GBV prevention and response in humanitarian settings. Foremost among those limitations is the failure – at both the international and national levels – to prioritise GBV as a major health and human rights concern, resulting in a lack of financial, technical and logistical resources necessary to implement comprehensive plans and policies to address GBV. Most programs investigated in the report maintained similar basic principles and goals but each were acting relatively independently of one another and without the benefit of field-tested methodologies and tools. Their participatory methods, however important in engaging and empowering women, were undermined by entrenched and institutionalised systems of gender inequality that actively promoted or implicitly condoned GBV.

In the face of entrenched systems that endorse or ignore GBV, even if programs have the desire and, importantly, the means to provide legal services, their capacity is more often limited by the absence of laws relating to GBV crimes or – where laws exist – inadequate judicial systems. The most glaring examples come from countries such as Thailand and Pakistan, where many refugees (Burmese and Afghan, respectively) are not recognised under the 1951 *United Nations Convention Relating to the Status of Refugees* and therefore have no legal rights, least of all to pursue prosecution of GBV crimes that are committed against them by, for example, military and police within the host country. UNHCR has not yet widely assumed the important task of advocating to host governments for improved protections against GBV crimes. In other examples, GBV policies are not born out in practice. Colombia, for example, has model legislation and yet GBV is a pervasive and largely ignored problem, not only among Colombia's IDP population, but also in the population at large. In

---

12   RHRC, *If Not Now, When?: Addressing Gender-Based Violence in Refugee, Internally Displaced and Post-Conflict Settings* (2002).

Kosovo, where several key anti-GBV initiatives were implemented during the influx of humanitarian assistance that followed the NATO intervention in 1999, the Office for Security and Cooperation in Europe (OSCE) reviewed the judicial process. In a scathing report published in 2001, OSCE detailed biases within the judicial system that severely limited prosecution of GBV crimes. The limitations of judicial systems is even more alarming in settings where the decision to press criminal charges is at the discretion of the State – as is often the case with sexual violence committed against a victim by someone other than her intimate partner – so that a survivor has no choice but to enter a system which is not prepared to protect her rights.

If – hypothetically, in most cases – protective legislation exists and judicial systems are prepared to prosecute cases efficiently and respectfully, evidentiary requirements mean that health care providers must be able to collect forensic evidence in a timely manner and be prepared to present that evidence at a trial. Police or relevant security forces must be trained to investigate and appropriately document their findings. Psycho-social assistance must be on-going, especially should the survivor's case be brought to trial. The frustrating reality for many survivors of GBV crimes in conflict-affected settings around the world – as well as for organisations developing GBV programming – is that systems do not exist to ensure basic protections to survivors, least of all survivors' access to justice.

Despite the limitations of programs, increased attention to GBV is allowing for progress in the field. An expanding international donor base has led to the development of a number of GBV projects in humanitarian settings worldwide, including Congo-Brazzaville (1998, IRC), Kosovo (1999, IRC), East Timor (2000, IRC), Pakistan (2001, IRC), Eritrea (2001, CARE), Zambia (2001, CARE), Rwanda (2002, IRC), Uganda (2002, IRC), Thailand (2003, ARC and 2004, IRC) and Côte d'Ivoire (2003, IRC). There is increasing communication among projects about methodologies and challenges and each is providing new insights regarding best practices for addressing GBV in conflict-affected settings. While participatory approaches and multi-sectoral coordination are at the heart of all current programming, strategies vary according to setting and donor demands and resources. Several projects are operating from a basic service delivery and community education model; others are functioning as 'umbrella projects', providing financial and technical support to improve local projects' ability to address GBV. Still others are working at the national level to influence government policies and create standards for GBV prevention and response. Some projects include components of all these approaches.

A significant shift in recognition of GBV issues by the humanitarian community was hastened by a report released in 2002 by Save the Children-UK and UNHCR detailing abuses committed in West African refugee camps by employees of humanitarian organisations. The report, implicating specific international organisations and institutions, received global media coverage. UNHCR, as well as many international organisations, responded to the allegations with unprecedented (in terms of GBV issues) rapidity. An inter-agency task force was designated by the UN with responsibility for creating staff codes of conduct and protocols for reporting abuses. Several international organisations have independently developed their own internal codes of conduct and reporting mechanisms and are currently instituting them in programs throughout the world. The efficiency of action by the humanitarian community reflects the capacity of organisations to address GBV when and if there is sufficient motivation. Because of the revelations of sexual exploitation and the subsequent response, GBV is gaining increased attention in conflict-settings throughout the world, systems of reporting are being strengthened and more efforts are being directed at prosecution and prevention of violence.

There are several projects that have taken the lead to try and improve legislation and legal services for survivors, including GBV projects in Sierra Leone and Guinea. The Guinea program illustrates the challenges of instituting legal assistance for a refugee population that typically is not well-protected by host government laws. The Sierra Leone program demonstrates the challenges of providing an array of services to survivors that supports their access to justice within a system that is only beginning to develop broad-based programming to address GBV.

V   Examples from the Field

A   Sierra Leone[13]

1   Background

For over a decade, Sierra Leone has been plagued with civil war. Beginning on a large-scale in 1991, opposition to successive military and civilian regimes by an armed rebel group, the Revolutionary United Front (RUF), caused mass internal displacement of Sierra Leoneans, as well as their exodus into the border countries of Côte d'Ivoire, Liberia and Guinea. The UN estimates that the civil war forced 400,000 Sierra Leonean refugees to flee to neighbouring countries, left 450,000 people internally displaced, 50,000 dead, 100,000 mutilated and over one quarter of a million women raped. Following the declaration of the end of the war in January 2002, the UN facilitated the disarmament of 45,000 male and female combatants.[14]

The conflict in Sierra Leone makes evident the violence to which women are subjected during war and its aftermath. Recorded rates of sexual violence in the war in Sierra Leone have led it to be characterised as the 'war against women'. Throughout the civil conflict, rape, sexual assault and sexual slavery were used as weapons of war. Girls as young as eight years old were abducted, gang-raped and forced to remain with or marry into militia groups. RUF fighters used women as human shields.[15] In a comprehensive prevalence survey of 991 IDP women and their family members conducted by Physicians for Human Rights (PHR) in 2001, almost all households (94

---

13   Written by Meghan O'Connor of the International Rescue Committee with the assistance of Beth Martin IRC Sierra Leone GBV Coordinator.

14   UNIFEM. 'Gender Profile of the Conflict in Sierra Leone – Introduction' (2004) *WomenWarPeace.org* website, <http://womenwarpeace.org/sierra_leone/sierra_leone.htm> [2].

15   UNIFEM. 'Gender Profile of the Conflict in Sierra Leone – The Impact of the Conflict on Sierra Leonean Women' (2004) *WomenWarPeace.org* website, <http://womenwarpeace.org/sierra_leone/sierra_leone.htm> [2].

percent) reported some exposure to war-related violence and 13 percent reported incidents of war-related sexual assault. Extrapolating from their findings, PHR estimates that approximately 50,000 to 64,000 IDP women may have histories of war-related assault.[16] High rates of rape and sexual assault resulted in a large number of unwanted pregnancies and subsequently unsafe abortions, STIs including HIV/AIDS and other negative health outcomes.[17]

2   Overview of the GBV Program

The IRC GBV program in Sierra Leone grew out of an initial assessment conducted by IRC in 1999 in IDP camps in the Kenema district, which exposed the need for reproductive health (RH) treatment for war-related sexual assault. After services were implemented for IDPs, survivors from the host communities also started coming forward for treatment. Women and girls were reporting multiple forms of GBV, such as domestic violence and non-conflict related rape – including marital rape, sexual exploitation and forced marriage. Consequently, the IRC GBV program extended its services to address varying types of GBV. Operating in Freetown, Kenema, Kailahun and Kono districts (as well as in nine refugee[18] and IDP camps) the GBV program provides psycho-social counselling, referral and advocacy services to survivors of GBV.

Early in programming, IRC GBV program staff recognised a need to build the capacity of the community, government and local institutions to respond to GBV. In addition to providing direct services and referrals, the IRC GBV program trains local institutions and the community through awareness-raising campaigns and GBV seminars. It also coordinates GBV prevention and response with the government of Sierra Leone (the Ministry of Social Welfare, Gender and Children's Affairs, the Ministry of Health and Sanitation, the Ministry of Justice and the Sierra Leone Police/Family Support Unit). This institution-building is reflected in IRC's Sexual Assault and Referral Centre (SARC) Project, which was developed to provide comprehensive and quality services for survivors of sexual assault and implement an effective referral system through which survivors could receive appropriate follow-up care and attention. Under this project, IRC has established two of three proposed sexual assault centres (one in Freetown in March 2003 and one in Kenema District in November 2003). Operating within government medical institutions, IRC has trained a small cadre of local medical staff to provide comprehensive post-sexual assault treatment in accordance with the World Health Organisation's protocols for clinical management of rape survivors. Medical staff of SARC is also trained on protocols for evidence collection and information recording to ensure information is admissible in court. In addition, IRC trains the Police/Family Support Unit on police roles and responsibilities in

---

16   Physicians for Human Rights, *War-Related Sexual Violence in Sierra Leone: A Populations-Based Assessment* (2002) 3.

17   IRC, *GBV Lessons Learned and Critical Issues* (2003) 33-4.

18   As Sierra Leone's civil war concluded, a two-decade long conflict was escalating in Liberia. Until Liberia's cease-fire in 2003, Sierra Leone continued to receive refugees from across the Liberian border, resulting in almost 10,000 Liberians in refugee camps in Sierra Leone.

cases of sexual assault and encourages the officers to make referrals to the SARCs. Since March 2003, the Police/Family Support Unit has referred 98 percent of the clients that have presented for treatment at the SARC Freetown. The SARCs' services include the provision of immediate medical care, forensic exams, psycho-social assistance, legal referral and testimony for court cases.

3   Establishing a Legal Component

While developing the SARC project, the IRC GBV program staff recognised that the IRC GBV clients typically have little or no awareness of their legal rights. To address this, the project incorporates a legal referral and services component that has afforded GBV clients – survivors, their families and witnesses to GBV – a confidential forum through which they can seek legal counsel and representation. This legal aspect of GBV programming has necessitated that IRC's GBV staff (at the management and community level) understand the justice system in Sierra Leone, as well as Sierra Leone's laws relating to GBV and the protection of women and girls.

There are two systems of law in Sierra Leone. One is a combination of statutory and common law. The other is customary ('tribal' or 'community') law. Under the Constitution of 1991, each system is guaranteed a place in the legal structure of the country. The statutory law consists of laws passed by various acts of the Parliament and the common law is based on British common law introduced under British colonial rule. Within the statutory law system, two courts – the Magistrate and High Court – hear and try cases. Even though the statutory and common law are supreme, customary law long predates the Constitution of 1991 and is widely practiced throughout the country by various tribes.[19]

Sierra Leone does not have laws tailored specifically to women and children. Its connection to British common law, however, has provided the courts with significant legal powers with which to punish gender-based crimes. With the exception of cases of early forced marriage, FGM (rarely prosecuted) and 'less severe' domestic violence, the High Court is the only court in the country with jurisdiction to hear most GBV cases. The reality is that customary law is more accessible and more commonly followed by the majority of the population of Sierra Leone. There is a paucity of lawyers outside of Freetown,[20] so that statutory law courts see only small fraction of GBV cases, usually the most brutal. More often, tribal chiefs exercise authority over GBV cases. Decisions imposed by these chiefs are often idiosyncratic, varying from wide-ranging fines to requiring a child rape victim to marry the perpetrator.

In 2002, the Special Court for Sierra Leone was established to try those that bear the greatest responsibility for committing violations of international humanitarian law and crimes against humanity in Sierra Leone since 30 November 1996. The Special Court has allowed rape, sexual slavery, enforced prostitution and forced preg-

---

19   National Forum for Human Rights, *The Law People See* (2002) 8.

20   After the war, High Court sittings have been infrequent, especially outside of Freetown. For example in Kenema, the High Court has been in session only five times from February 2002-December 2003.

nancy to be considered crimes against humanity, providing another system through which survivors of war-related GBV can prosecute perpetrators.

Since sexual assault in Sierra Leone is a state offence, prosecution of sexual assault cases is the responsibility of the Law Officer's Department of the Ministry of Justice. Using legal aid outside of the Law Officer's Department is a duplication of services that is not sustainable. Therefore, the SARC project is focusing its efforts on improving the systems already in place.

4   Provision of Legal Services

The SARC psycho-social staff advise survivors, families and witnesses to GBV on their legal rights. Currently the IRC GBV program is developing a training module, entitled *Access to Justice,* to enhance staff's ability to communicate legal information to clients and counsel them on the best options for pursuing legal action. The module will also train staff to facilitate discussions about community members' understanding of and access to justice.

Building upon a case management model, clients are first provided with information about the options available to them for legal redress through the Magistrate, High Court, or, for wartime acts of GBV, the Special Court. Clients are informed about what to expect if legal action is pursued. Current law requires that at the High Court level an adult victim (16 years or older) and a child (under 16 years old) give evidence at the trial in an open court and be subjected to cross-examination by the defence. The testimony must be explicit. Before the case reaches the High Court, the survivor must also give her evidence in a preliminary hearing at the Magistrate Court level, which at the discretion of the Magistrate Court, can be given 'in camera'. The same rules apply to a child (under 16 years old). Clients are also informed of the frequent delays and adjournments in hearings with Magistrates and High courts and the cost of transport to and from court. (In many instances the victim and witnesses must travel long distances to testify. As a result, witnesses who do not have something directly at stake in the outcome of the case are much less likely to testify.)

IRC's GBV clients who wish to pursue legal action are referred to the Law Officer's Department. During the course of prosecution, the SARC staff liaises with the Family Support Unit officers and with the Law Officer's Department to ensure that cases are dealt with promptly and appropriately by the police and judiciary. Since March 2003, of the approximately 600 clients who received services from the SARCs, the majority requested that legal action be taken against their perpetrators. SARC staff has accompanied most of these clients to court appearances. By April 2004, 21 cases have been filed in the High Court and a further 354 have been filed in the Magistrate Court in Freetown. In Kenema 24 cases have been filed in the Magistrate Court. While only a small number of these cases have reached the end of prosecution, all have resulted in convictions.

The success rate allows for optimism, but the reality is that women are still reluctant to utilise these systems. The cultural stigma associated with GBV fosters reticence in most survivors. The majority do not come forward unless they have a specific physical health need. Even when informed of their legal rights, many women are still not likely to pursue a case legally – most likely because of the arduous, often shameful process associated with prosecution.

5   Legal Capacity and Institution Building

Training, public sensitisation and advocacy are key to improving survivors' access to justice. The IRC collaborates with the Law Officer's Department to implement training and awareness-raising activities for the partners and communities with whom IRC works. In order to familiarise the SARC medical and psycho-social staff with the Sierra Leone High Court proceedings and expectations, the Law Officer's Department trains SARC staff to provide expert testimony. IRC GBV staff, along with lawyers from the Law Officer's Department, hold sensitisation activities throughout villages in the western area of Sierra Leone. These awareness-raising campaigns have informed community chiefs and elders that collaborating with perpetrators is an offence as well as an injustice to the client. In most local communities in the Western Area, chiefs and elders now collaborate with the police to ensure that perpetrators are detained and charged.

IRC GBV staff and partners meet regularly with the Director of Public Prosecutions, lawyers from the Law Officer's Department, and the Sierra Leone Chief of Justice to discuss procedural reform. The issues discussed include the problems of frequent adjournments and open court hearings, as well as the need to assign specific court days and more prosecutors for GBV cases. Legislative reform is also a priority. Meetings are held with the Law Reform Commissioner to address national laws that discriminate against women and children and lobby for changes to these laws.

Recently, the SARC project staff met with the Vice President of Sierra Leone to introduce the project and share information with him about the numbers of cases of sexual assault treated by SARC. The Vice President has pledged his support and has spoken with the Minister of Social Welfare, Gender and Children's Affairs about his concerns. Although there is much work to be done to ensure legislative reform, the government of Sierra Leone's positive response to the SARC project's activities is promising.

B   Guinea[21]

1   Background

Guinea, one of the world's poorest countries, has for more than fifteen years accommodated nearly one million refugees fleeing civil wars in Liberia and Sierra Leone. Refugees from Liberia began arriving in Guinea in 1989, followed by the arrival of Sierra Leonean refugees in the early 1990s. Although the repatriation of Sierra Leonean refugees began in 2002, increased conflict in Liberia between 2002 and 2003 swelled the number of Liberian refugees in Guinea. Despite the cease-fire in June 2003 and the current disarmament process, Liberia still faces bouts of violence and political instability, resulting in a protracted refugee situation. Renewed fighting in

---

21   Written by Meghan O'Connor of the International Rescue Committee with the assistance of Gina Paulette, ARC Guinea GBV Program Coordinator.

Côte d'Ivoire, previously a haven to Liberian refugees but now itself a producer of refugees, is placing an even larger burden on Guinea.[22]

Tension within these countries has created widespread regional instability, each country accusing the other of supporting rebel activity. Cross border attacks between neighbouring countries' insurgent groups and the Guinean military (occurring most frequently in border towns in which the refugee camps are located) have left an estimated 20,000 Guineans displaced and have threatened the security of the refugee camps. The Guinean government has held the refugee population responsible for the cross border attacks, often responding with military action targeting the refugee communities. In 2001, the Guinean government forced refugees living in the host communities to return to the refugee camps.[23]

Insecurity as well as a general sense of despair has fostered a hostile, often violent environment in the camps. Various forms of GBV are rampant in the refugee and host communities. Domestic violence is considered a 'normal' practice, forced or early marriages are particularly widespread and refugee women's groups maintain the practice of FGM.[24] Tacit acceptance of GBV penetrates the larger community – including government and non-governmental aid workers, healthcare providers, local business owners, local law enforcement personnel and refugee protection personnel. In 2002, the UNHCR and Save the Children UK released a report that revealed the magnitude and scope of sexual exploitation and abuse in the region of West Africa, documenting high numbers of humanitarian aid workers and peacekeepers as perpetrators of sexual abuse and exploitation against conflict-affected women and girls.

2 Overview of the GBV Program

The GBV program in Guinea evolved, similar to the program in Sierra Leone, from an emergency RH program. During an RH assessment in 1999 conducted by the IRC, many refugee women in the targeted camps expressed concerns about reproductive health problems that were linked to GBV. Consequently, IRC initiated a GBV program to provide basic health and psycho-social services to refugee survivors of GBV. Working with the community, local health and social service providers, the government, law enforcement and humanitarian organisations to coordinate response and prevention measures, the program gradually expanded to meet the needs of survivors of GBV among the host communities. The program also expanded to include American Refugee Committee (ARC) as an implementing partner. Currently, the program operates in three regions – Kissidougou, N'Zerekore and Dabola – and has served approximately 150,000 Liberian refugees, 5,000 Ivorian refugees, 30,000 Sierra Leonean refugees and Guinean women and children survivors of GBV.

By providing direct services and referrals, the program addresses the psychosocial, medical, legal and security-related needs of survivors. Community educators

---

22   US Committee for Refugees. 'Information By Country: Guinea', *World Refugee Survey Report 2003*, <http://www.refugees.org/world/countryindex/guinea.cfm> [10]-[36].

23   Human Rights Watch, 'Profile of Guinea'. (2002) <http://hrw.org/doc/?t=africa&c=guinea>

24   IRC, above n 17, 11-14.

work closely with camp leaders, local authorities, UNHCR and other NGO partners to develop community-based systems of response, to advocate on behalf of the needs of survivors and to coordinate referrals and services for survivors. A Women's Centre has been created in each camp in which direct services are provided and activities for women are organised. Advisory boards, comprised of members of the refugee communities and representatives of local organisations, are tasked with identifying GBV cases and organising night patrols to ensure safety for women.

Capacity and institution-building are important components of the GBV program. The IRC/ARC staff have conducted a variety of educational activities and trainings to increase the communities' and beneficiaries' understanding of GBV issues in the form of workshops, discussions, home visits, community meetings, dramas and role-plays, cultural performances, marches and sport competitions. Guinean authorities, camp enforcement personnel and other NGO partners have participated in the trainings. IRC/ARC is encouraging these institutions to incorporate gender awareness into all levels of their operations.

3   Establishing a Legal Component

In March 2003, the ARC developed a legal aid clinic to provide legal services and legal rights education to refugee women and to implement community-wide education and advocacy campaigns on GBV and women's rights. The Legal Aid for Women (LAW) clinic, based in N'Zerekore and travelling to refugee camps, educates the refugee community on Guinean laws related to GBV, including sexual and physical violence, as well as paternity and child support. It provides free legal advice to refugee survivors of GBV, legal assistance, local court representation, reviews GBV-related legislation and proposes revisions to improve women refugees' protection.

While articles within the Guinean constitution pertain directly to GBV (that is, laws concerning rape, sexual assault, paternity and child support) and while Guinea has ratified various international conventions that should reinforce women's protection, the reality is that most GBV cases are rarely prosecuted, authorities do not hold perpetrators accountable and survivors have little access to the legal system. The LAW clinic prosecutes cases under Guinean statutory law. In addition, cases presented to the N'Zerekore court may also include references to international documents and covenants that have been adopted by Guinea. In December 2002, members of the N'Zerekore court agreed that all international documents that have been ratified by Guinea should be accepted as law and applied as such in Guinean courts.

4   Provision of Legal Services

The clinic is staffed with three Guinean lawyers, one of whom is the lead lawyer responsible for interpreting the law and pleading cases. Two assistant lawyers write up the complaints and negotiate with the Guinean justice officials, but cannot plead cases. Bilingual (French/English) refugee staff, trained as legal assistants, act as the first point of contact for clients. This is intended to create a setting in which refugee women can come forward freely and feel understood and well received. The legal assistants conduct the first intake, act as translators and assist the lawyers in dealing with the justice system.

Most of the clients the N'Zerekore clinic receives are walk-ins rather than referrals. In the camps, however, the IRC GBV program is the main conduit through which the clinic receives clients. To increase women's access to the clinic, the LAW staff travel to each of the camps at least once a week to receive cases, provide follow-up and conduct awareness campaigns. The camps' Women's Centres serve as a base of operations for LAW. Because the Women's Centres host a range of activities, it is not likely that a woman seeking legal services would be easily identified as such, thus reducing the fear and stigmatisation associated with being a survivor of GBV. The Women's Centres also function as safe spaces, so that if a client is threatened or feels unsafe during the course of the prosecution, she can retreat to the centre. The broad reach of the Women's Centres' activities and services helps to create a sense of community and build a support network among women in the community.

Engaging clients in understanding the legal process and promoting their control over the legal process are both priorities for LAW. The client intake procedure, including a consent form and a confidentiality statement, stresses that clients are the primary decision-makers for pursuing prosecution and have the right to drop their cases at any time. After receiving information on their rights and their options for recourse, the clients must authorise written consent for the clinic to take action. Also included in the intake are authorisation forms for the clinic to refer clients to UNHCR and other NGO partners that may provide further protection or medical and psychological treatment. If the client requests that charges be filed, the team accompanies the client through the steps of pressing charges and/or filing a case at the local court in N'Zerekore. The clinic's legal team then works closely with the justice officials and NGO partners to collect and/or present evidence and arguments to the court. To monitor the progress of cases, client follow-up forms are completed and a legal assistant provides status reports to the client on a weekly basis. Throughout these legal procedures, the clinic ensures that the client understands each step and how it relates to her rights and protection.

Since March 2003 to April 2004, LAW has processed 118 cases, provided free legal counselling and mediation in 75 cases and assisted in court actions in 43 cases. The range of cases processed includes domestic violence, sexual assault, paternity and child support issues. An evaluation of the clinic, conducted by an independent consultant, is currently underway. Clients have provided feedback via focus group discussions held periodically by the clinic to ascertain client satisfaction with the services, to document any challenges encountered during the legal process and to request recommendations for improving the clinic's services. During weekly women's group meetings, women are encouraged to discuss openly any issues regarding the clinic and/or any other services that are provided to them. The feedback received from clients has, in general, been positive. Women claimed that the clinic has made a positive impact on their self-perception and their perception and treatment within the community. Some of the responses include, 'I now have somebody to fight for me', 'I've gotten my self-esteem', and 'I am gaining respect and courage'. Clients have communicated that the clinic offers and symbolises the protection, care and guidance one should receive from family members. Despite this positive feedback, the clients have also complained that the clinic has not been useful in helping them cope with day-to-day problems such as finding work, vocational training and schooling.

5   Legal Capacity and Institution Building

The LAW clinic has initiated community-wide education efforts to encourage refugees' and local authorities' understanding of GBV and women's protection rights. It aims to deter would-be GBV offenders and build the capacity of local NGOs to address legal needs. Community education activities and refugee radio programs provide a forum through which LAW can advertise the clinic's services and promote awareness of the legal repercussions of GBV. The clinic trains staff, beneficiaries and implementing partners on Guinean law and international conventions and declarations pertaining to refugee rights, reproductive rights, women's rights, children's rights and human rights. For example, one national women's legal aid NGO 'Association Femme Justice Aide', which conducts legal training courses nationwide, has been trained by LAW and now replicates the trainings independently. The clinic's 'Country Wide Trainer', along with the legal staff, provides trainings to local justice system workers (judges, prosecutors, and court clerks) and those involved in the direct protection of refugees such as the National Bureau for Refugees (BCR), the police and the paramilitary National Gendarmerie (a branch of the armed forces). The legal assistants hold at least one mass sensitisation campaign per month targeting the aforementioned groups and conduct numerous smaller-scale sensitisation campaigns in the refugee camps and refugee schools. In collaboration with IRC, law enforcement officers and those involved in apprehending and prosecuting perpetrators are trained in relation to their role in the legal process, while medical and social service providers receive training as it relates to the importance of physical evidence and detailed, accurate record keeping. Engaging the government, NGO service providers and law enforcement personnel has helped to reinforce the referral network among these partners so that survivors of GBV can be systematically referred for appropriate health, psycho-social and legal services.

Women and children remain inadequately protected under Guinean law. Moreover, the domestic laws of Guinea are inconsistent with many of the international conventions Guinea has signed and ratified. To overcome these obstacles, the clinic has begun a review of existing legislation to explore the potential for improved protection of refugees, particularly women and their children. In collaboration with the government, the clinic hopes to draft proposals for legislative reform. The revisions will incorporate international conventions ratified by Guinea and institute penalties for violations of women's rights.

VI   Conclusion

The humanitarian community has only begun to trace the outlines of an approach for improving prevention and response to GBV in conflict-affected settings around the world. However, the multi-sectoral model offers a valuable theoretical springboard from which to develop comprehensive services. Most important within the multi-sectoral approach is the right of survivors to self-determination; that is, survivors should be able to make informed choices about accessing assistance and managing their recovery from GBV. Informed choice requires, first and foremost, options for assistance, ranging from health care, to counselling, to police protection, to legal aid. Though recognised even in the earliest GBV programs as an important component of service delivery, the challenges of providing legal aid touch virtually all sectors providing GBV services: in order for the judicial process to be efficient and effective, health, psycho-social and security sectors must each contribute their expertise. Thus, developing legal processes requires a broad-based approach aimed at capacity-building multiple sectors at multiple levels.

The Sierra Leone and Guinea case studies illustrate, in comparison to the earlier Dadaab and Kibondo projects, how humanitarian programming to address GBV has evolved in a just few years. On the other hand, the limited numbers of women coming forward for legal and other assistance in the Sierra Leone and Guinea programs illustrates how much further GBV programs have to go in terms of reaching those their programs intend to serve. As a broader net of GBV prevention and response programming is developed in Sierra Leone and Guinea, as well as in other conflict-affected settings around the world, the greater the possibility that the humanitarian community can progress in its mandate to protect women and children affected by armed conflict. The experiences and needs of these women and children must continue to be the basis for any humanitarian action to address GBV: it is only with their participation and through their leadership that GBV programming will continue to progress.

9

Reporting on Women during Armed Conflict: A War Journalist's Perspective

*Maggie O'Kane**

In 1992, Maggie O'Kane arrived in Bosnia to start her award-winning coverage of the Yugoslav conflict for London's Guardian *newspaper. There, she exposed stories that made an enormous impact on the international community's understanding of crimes against women during armed conflict. She uncovered, among other things, the existence and location of 19 rape camps in Bosnia. Through her stories, she provided a forum for the voices of women who had been held captive in these factories, schools, sawmills and furniture stores. That year, she won the prestigious* Journalist of the Year *award for her reporting. Since then, Maggie has reported as a Special Correspondent for the Guardian on wars in Chechnya, Kosovo, East Timor and most recently, Iraq. She won the* Amnesty International Joint Foreign Correspondent of the Year *award in 1993 and the* James Cameron Memorial Trust Award for Journalism *in 1996. In 2002, Maggie was named the* European Journalist of the Year *for her documentary* Looking for Karadzic, *which chronicled her search for former Bosnian Serb leader and alleged war criminal, Radovan Karadzic. Here, Maggie talks about the process of locating rape camps during the war in Bosnia, the importance of women reporters 'in the field' during armed conflict, embedded reporting, the interaction between journalists and international criminal tribunals and the impact motherhood has had on her work.*

Q: Maggie, you were recognised for the quality of your reporting in Bosnia, particularly your coverage of the systematic crimes perpetrated against women. Could you talk about the process you underwent in uncovering the stories in Bosnia – particularly the systematic abuses against women in the rape camps – and what obstacles you faced in bringing the stories and the voices of these women to light?

A: The first time I heard about these rape camps was in a place which I call the Goražde valley. It was an area held by Bosnian forces and included people who had

---

* Maggie O'Kane is the Editorial Director of Guardian Films, the documentary unit of the London Guardian newspaper. This is an edited transcript of a phone interview conducted in February 2004.

Helen Durham and Tracey Gurd (eds.), Listening to the Silences: Women and War, *pp. 89–93.*
© *2005 Koninklijke Brill BV. Printed in The Netherlands. ISBN 90 04 14365 3.*

been ethnically cleansed from areas like Višegrad which – as we now know – was one of the areas where a lot of the rape atrocities took place. While I was in the Goražde valley, people talked about the camps which, at that time, were located in the area occupied by the Bosnian Serbs. It was incredibly dangerous to physically get to where they were. I wasn't able to go and see these camps. But throughout the year or two when I first started reporting, I kept hearing reports about rape.

The breakthrough came when, in one of the central Bosnian towns called Zenica, a centre was established to encourage people to report what had happened to them during the war. I went to this centre and discovered files of women who either claimed to have been raped themselves, or people who had heard accounts from relatives or friends about being raped. I decided to employ four students from the local college to go through the files with me and together we categorised them.

The methodology was to separate them into different piles: those which recorded eyewitness accounts of women who were victims and who described what had happened to them. Another pile was for second-hand accounts of people who hadn't been raped, but had knowledge of rapes or had heard reports of them. The third pile was one in which we tried to cross-reference the information from the previous two piles in an attempt to pinpoint the particular rape locations – a furniture factory in one town, a school in another town. We spent about four days working on all of this information with a number of people – usually three, four or five others.

Using this information and a map – I published this in the *Guardian* at the time with the map – we identified between 15 and 17 locations where women consistently reported being brought to and raped. We wrote up a fairly comprehensive picture of what had happened, mainly because the details – when they were cross-referenced – were entirely consistent of where the rapes took place and the descriptions of the people who perpetrated them. Through the Zenica Resource Centre, I then located women refugees who had fled to Zenica and were still living there. I interviewed them directly as well as using the paperwork to substantiate the work.

Q: How did you get in touch with the women that you spoke to, and what were their responses?

A: My translator's mother worked as a doctor with these women. Through my translator, I asked her mother to approach women who might be interested in talking about it. The doctor was a member of the community, you know, an older woman in her late 50s or early 60s who had been dealing with the raped women. There were lots of women who were reluctant – for a lot of obvious reasons – to talk about their experiences. But there were also women who, like the women who had testified about rape in The Hague, felt that they needed to bear witness.

Q: Since you uncovered this story, some scholars have argued that these types of gender-based human rights abuses – like the operation of the rape camps – were more widely reported in Bosnia because there were more women reporters in the field than in previous wars – do you agree with that argument?

A: Yes, I do actually. I remember a male colleague of mine said to me that you could only have done this story if you were a woman. I would say, on the one hand, it was easier – certainly – to talk to the women who had directly experienced [the rapes]. But in terms of actually investigating the material that already existed, you could have done that if you were a man. But I think there is an element of rape in war that is almost taken for granted. Perhaps it's women's horror about the crime of rape that made us more determined to pursue it as a story. I'm always reminded of a rugby song – I remember hearing it being sung on a bus years ago in Dublin:

> And the officers crossed the Rhine – da-dum, da-dum,
> They raped the women and drank the wine, da-dum, da-dum

I remember that it really struck me. This was being sung by school boys coming back from a march! So in a strange way, perhaps we lived in a world where rape was taken as a by-product of war. Something, in a sense, that wasn't really worthy of being examined in its own right with the same degree of intensity that we would approach other subjects. When you consider there was no such thing as rape within marriage 20 years ago, then you just look at how we see rape today – for example, why we find it difficult to recognise that prostitutes can be raped – it's a complex issue. I think it is an issue about which women feel more acutely and that it is an issue that women are more interested in. Maybe the fact that there were more female reporters in that war reflected the fact that it became more of an issue.

Q: In the other armed conflicts that you have covered in Kosovo, East Timor, Chechnya and most recently, Iraq, you've told the stories of women as refugees, as rape survivors, as activists – women taking on a whole range of roles during armed conflict – so I'm wondering why you chose to seek out and listen to these voices?

A: My approach to stories is simple: if it is on the wire services, I'm not interested. That's my criteria for the day. I go out to try and find ways of telling a story which is left and right, but that you're not going to read on the wires. That's what I feel is my brief. So, for example, if I am in Sarajevo and I am in a café and the woman at the next table, a young girl, is writing a love letter to her boyfriend – who is at the front and whom she hasn't seen for a couple of months – and she is describing life in the city and how she misses him, I'll write from her perspective. It's a very graphic way of illustrating life under siege, their fears, the way people live, in a way that's told very close to the writer because she's writing to him, but the story is written through the prism of a newspaper. By putting it into a newspaper, you are offering people an insight. Or if I'm going to talk about mass killing in Kosovo, I will try to give a voice to a woman who was at the scene. There was one particular story about the massacre of an extended family in a pizzeria in a place called Suva Reka. In order to describe the horror of that scene, I wrote in the voice of a woman who survived, describing the horror of running and trying to protect your children and then discovering that you are the only one that survives on the back of a truck that is full of dead bodies – including the dead bodies of your children. That's the voice of a woman who can explain what it's like when there's a pogrom against a people.

Q: Since you first started reporting in Bosnia – what sort of changes if any have you noticed in the ways that women's voices and experiences have been perceived and covered by the international media during armed conflict?

A: I think because there are more women writing, issues like rape have become a bigger concern. I think that there's a changing style – particularly in the British media – in terms of the subjects that we write about, the way we write about them and the conventional mode of reporting. The conventional stories about strategy and politics have been added to with a more personal take.

Q: Do you think that the emergence of embedded reporting of the type and scale that we saw in Iraq has an impact on the ability of women's voices to be heard by the media and hence the international public during conflicts like the war in Iraq?

A: It's a disaster for all kinds of voices – not just women's voices, but men's voices, for everybody's voices. It's an effective form of censorship which is about military propaganda and, of course, that will not reflect the voices of the people. The tragedy of the Second Gulf War, and even the first one, was that the actual voices of the people who suffered were drowned out in a military cacophony and it's a tragedy for good reporting.

Q: What kind of relationship, if any, do you think journalists should have with the international criminal tribunals, particularly in the light of the *Randall* decision which held that journalists should only be compelled to testify at the ICTY under exceptional circumstances? Could you comment with particular reference to the prosecution of crimes against women?

A: Well I agree with *Randall* – I think that if there were exceptional circumstances where I could make the difference regarding whether or not the person who I believed was involved in committing crimes against humanity would be sentenced, I think I would have a very difficult decision to make. In exceptional circumstances I would testify – however, I think that very, very, very rarely, journalists are actual eyewitnesses to an event like a killing or a rape, so therefore our testimony can be of only limited value. If you balance that against the importance of journalists in the field actually recording the first draft of history, I think they can be seen as people who have a very important role as observers rather than participants. Once you become part of the prosecution procedure then you become a participant and therefore you are vulnerable to attack. In the case of the journalists who uncovered the massacre at Srebrenica or journalists like myself who were traveling around when the rape camps were discovered at Prijedor or Sušica, our testimony could help to create a legitimate case for combatants in future conflicts to say 'well, let's take them out as well'. There's the issue of personal safety, but there's also the issue of placing us in a position where we can't do our work effectively and it's very important that journalists can do their work effectively. There are a lot of negatives to journalists testifying. Sometimes I wonder if there's a bit of a cult of personality that us journalists were flattered to be asked to testify in The Hague. Some people do it in a very high profile way. I think it's the wrong thing to do. I personally have, in a subtle and a discreet way, given all the assistance I can to investigators if they were looking for any further information on what I had already written, or any further contacts or leads. I'm very happy to give information to them, but to become a high profile witness doesn't serve journalism very well, doesn't serve the truth very well and actually we're also not very high quality witnesses. Relying on journalists is kind of a lazy way out, sometimes, for the prosecutors.

Q: If you feel comfortable, would you like to make any comments on the impact that being a mother has had on your work as a war journalist?

A: I think that it has made me understand the intensity of the suffering of people who are caught up in a war situation – for example, the mothers in Cambodia under the Khmer Rouge who were housed in detention centers like Tueng Sleng, where they knew their children were to be executed. The instinct to protect as a mother is so overwhelming that to be in a position in which you are not able to protect your children is a huge, huge extra burden of pain that I had never anticipated before. The idea of not being able to protect my children, as many women find themselves in Sarajevo or Cambodia and Congo, is an aspect of suffering that I have never really understood until I became a mother. That, in a way, helps me to understand the intensity of the situation. I think some of my work, like in Suva Reka where this family was massacred, was definitely informed by my own feelings of motherhood. I think that probably helped me to write about it in a better way. On a more practical level, being a mother makes it more difficult for me to leave my children for long periods of time. Now I'm the Editorial Director of Guardian Films – which is the Guardian's Documentary Unit – and that was a decision taken partly because of the fact that I now have two children and I found it very difficult to leave the second one in the same way that I felt compelled to leave the first one. It's a very hard job to keep doing when you've got kids. For women who are soldiers who are sent off for six months on a tour of duty it's really, really painful. I think being a mother makes me more understanding of other people's suffering, basically.

10

International Humanitarian Law and the Protection of Women

*Helen Durham**

I   Introduction

This contribution intends to expose the reader to the range of provisions found in International Humanitarian Law (IHL) relating to the protection of women. The aims and background of IHL will be explored and then an examination will be undertaken on the general and specific provisions within IHL that focus upon women. Topics dealt with include the requirement of equality of treatment within IHL for protected persons; the provisions relating to prohibition of sexual violence against women; the elements of the treaties dealing with the women as expectant and nursing mothers, as internee and as Prisoners Of War (POW). The paper then focuses upon the laws of war relating to the methods and means of warfare and notes that this area has specific relevance to the well being of women. A review of the general legal norms contained in this area, as well as specific issues such as weapons and conduct of hostilities, is undertaken. In concluding, the author notes that while certain elements of IHL are products of their time and written in an archaic manner, the relevance of IHL today is still high. Like all areas of law, IHL unfortunately does not ensure that inhumane activities are eradicated. It is, however, a powerful and useful tool for working towards the protection of women during times of armed conflict.

II   Aims of IHL

IHL is a highly specialised area of international law (*lex specialis*) that devotes itself to the reduction of suffering during times of armed conflict by protecting victims and regulating the methods and means of warfare. IHL is limited in its applica-

---

*   Helen Durham is admitted as a Barrister and Solicitor of the Supreme Court of Victoria and has a combined Law/Arts degree as well as a Doctorate of Judicial Science from The University of Melbourne. She is currently Legal Adviser to the International Committee of the Red Cross (ICRC) Regional Delegation for the Pacific. The views expressed in this article are those of the author and are not necessary those of the ICRC.

Helen Durham and Tracey Gurd (eds.), Listening to the Silences: Women and War, *pp. 95-107.*
© 2005 *Koninklijke Brill BV. Printed in The Netherlands.* ISBN 90 04 14365 3.

tion and only applies in time of war (a term for international conflict) and internal armed conflict. Unlike some legal norms found in international human rights law, there are no elements of IHL that can be 'suspended' by a State.[1] The basic principles of IHL are found predominately in the *Four Geneva Conventions of 1949*[2] and their *Additional Protocols of 1977*,[3] however numerous other treaties, especially those dealing with restriction of specific weapons, continue to evolve.[4] Furthermore, as well as the *Geneva Conventions* and their *Additional Protocols* there is a range of other treaty law such as the *Hague Conventions* and a raft of customary international legal principles which also deal with the conduct of hostilities and the protection of victims of armed conflict.[5] For the purposes of this chapter, the author will limit examination to the *Geneva Conventions* and their *Additional Protocols*.

IHL does not involve itself in pronouncements relating to the legality, or lack thereof, of the resort to armed conflict. Rather the regulations relating to the use of force (*jus ad bellum*) are a matter for the United Nations Charter. Not surprisingly, debates surrounding *jus ad bellum* are complex and often inherently political, as matters such as the distinction between self-defence and aggression have no simple answers. IHL, on the other hand, attempts to remain free from controversy and its provisions apply to all sides of an armed conflict, irrespective of the reasons for the conflict itself. Thus IHL, or the law in war, (*jus in bello*) aims to protect all war victims, no matter to what party they belong or the *rationale* for the fighting. It is of crucial importance to the integrity and respect of IHL that *jus ad bellum* be kept distinct from *jus in bello*.

---

1   For further discussion on the distinction between human rights law and IHL see Louise Doswald Beck and Sylvain Vité, 'International Humanitarian Law and Human Rights Law' (1993) 293 *International Review of the Red Cross* 94.

2   *Geneva Convention for the Amelioration of the Condition of the Wounded and the Sick in Armed Forces in the Field*, 12 August 1949, 75 UNTS 31 ('*First Geneva Convention*'); *Geneva Convention for the Amelioration of the Condition of Wounded, Sick and Shipwrecked members of the Armed Forces at Sea*, 12 August 1949, 75 UNTS 85 ('*Second Geneva Convention*'); *Geneva Convention Relative to the Treatment of Prisoners of War*, 12 August 1949, 75 UNTS 135 ('*Third Geneva Convention*'); *Geneva Convention Relative to the Protection of Civilian Persons in Time of War*, 12 August 1949, 75 UNTS 287 ('*Fourth Geneva Convention*'). All entered into force 21 October 1950. As of April 2004 there are 191 State Parties.

3   *Protocol Additional to the Geneva Conventions of 12 Aug 1949, and relating to the Protection of Victims of International Armed Conflicts*, 7 December 1978, 1125 UNTS 3 ('*Protocol I*') and *Protocol Additional to the Geneva Conventions of 12 Aug 1949, and relating to the Protection of Victims of Non-International Armed Conflicts*, 7 December 1978, 1125 UNTS 609 ('*Protocol II*'). The *Additional Protocols to the Geneva Conventions of 12 August 1949*, were opened for signature on 12 December 1977 and entered into force 7 December 1978. As of April 2004 there are 161 State Parties to *Protocol I* and 154 to *Protocol II*.

4   See Tim McCormack, 'The Relationship Between International Humanitarian Law and Arms Control' in Helen Durham and Timothy McCormack (eds) *The Changing Face of Conflict and the Efficacy of International Humanitarian Law* (1999) 65.

5   For a more detailed discussion on IHL see the ICRC publication by Frits Kalshoven, *Constraints on the Waging of War* (2001).

Within the IHL framework, attempts to 'humanise' armed conflict have at times been met with a range of criticisms. Some scholars argue that IHL merely legitimises rather than restrains violence.[6] Feminist legal scholars have expressed frustration at IHL's lack of analysis of matters such as systemic gender inequalities. They argue that this contributes to IHL's inability to move beyond a 'male norm' when dealing with the impact of armed conflict upon women.[7] Many of these criticisms highlight the tension between the pragmatic and limited aims of IHL and the range of expectations often placed upon this area of law. IHL, as discussed above, neither makes judgements on the use of force nor attempts to place any regulations upon the basis of social structure before, or after, the conflict. Its limited application during the most extreme circumstance society can encounter, and its limited aim (to ensure the survival for as many people as possible), leaves no room for just war theories or deeper social analysis of inherent inequalities required by feminist legal theory. Such debates are not the focus of this contribution. However such analysis is important and must continue to ensure that a review of the relevance of IHL to the protection of women is constantly undertaken.[8]

III   Protection for Women Found in IHL

A   IHL Relating to Women: General Principles

IHL is based upon equality of protection. Numerous provisions within the *Geneva Conventions* and their *Protocols* state that treatment is to be 'without adverse distinction found on sex ...'[9] Other articles clearly express that women should benefit from treatment 'as favourable as that granted to men'.[10] Thus women are clearly entitled to the same protections as that granted to men, as civilians, combatants or those not longer taking part in hostilities. This notion of equality is a fundamental tenant of IHL.

Yet this non-discriminatory principle is tempered by the acknowledgement within IHL that women have specific needs and that a 'blanket' application of protection is not adequate. In this sense, IHL could be deemed to prohibit discrimination against

---

6   See Chris af Jochnick and Roger Normand 'The Legitimation of Violence: A Critical History of the Laws of War' (1994) 35 *Harvard International Law Journal* 49.

7   This issue is raised in the article written by Judith Gardam in this section. See also Judith Gardam and Michelle Jarvis, who write 'IHL takes a particular male perspective on armed conflict, as a norm against which to measure equality. In a world where women are not equals of men, and armed conflict impacts upon men and women in a fundamentally different way, a general category of rules that is not inclusive of the reality for women cannot respond to their situation' in their *Women, Armed Conflict and International Law* (2001) 93.

8   For a further discussion on this topic see Helen Durham 'Women, Armed Conflict and International Law' (2002) 84 *International Review of the Red Cross* 656.

9   *First Geneva Convention*, above n 2, Article 12; *Second Geneva Convention*, above n 2, Article 12; *Third Geneva Convention*, above n 2, Article 16; *Fourth Geneva Convention*, above n 2, Article 27; *Protocol I*, above n 3, Article 74; and *Protocol II*, above n 3, Article 4.

10   *Third Geneva Convention*, above n 2, Article 14.

women if it results in unfavourable treatment. It does allow, as will be discussed, preferential or beneficial treatment in certain circumstances.

B   Specific Protections: Sexual Violence

Sexual violence during times of armed conflict is not an atrocity suffered exclusively by women. However, as has been clearly discussed by Radhika Coomaraswamy in a previous chapter, a vast number of victims of this crime are female. Often females are victims of sexual violence during conflict for the gendered reason that they are women and thus 'symbolic' bearers of their culture. Often they are placed in vulnerable positions, defending families and communities without normal social infrastructure for protection. The *Geneva Conventions* and *Additional Protocols* have special provisions relating to the prohibition of sexual crimes during times of international and internal armed conflict. Article 27 of the *Fourth Geneva Convention* states 'Women shall be especially protected against any attack on their honour, in particular against rape, enforced prostitution, or any form of indecent assault'. As Charlotte Lindsey notes in her earlier article, though the term 'honour' has been criticised and must be seen as a product of the terminology of the drafting of late 1940s, it does create a binding legal norm that prohibits such attacks upon women. With the opportunity in 1977 to revisit these crimes, *Additional Protocol I* supplements the regulations dealing with international armed conflict. Article 75(b) expressly prohibits against either sex:

> outrages upon personal dignity, in particular humiliating and degrading treatment, enforced prostitution and any form of indecent assault.

This is complemented by Article 76, which repeats the protections articulated for women in the *Four Geneva Conventions*, without using the term honour. Instead the article requires that women 'shall be the object of special respect and shall be protected in particular against rape, forced prostitution and any other form of indecent assault'.

In relation to non-international armed conflicts, *Additional Protocol II* requires humane treatment of all persons not, or no longer, taking direct part in hostilities irrespective of whether they are detained, without any adverse distinction. In particular, Article 4(e) prohibits the range of crimes found in Article 75 (b) of *Additional Protocol I*. While Common Article 3 to the *Four Geneva Conventions* – the only protection provided in the *Conventions* for non-international conflicts – does not specifically mention rape, it does forbid 'outrages upon personal dignity, in particular humiliating and degrading treatment'.[11] Similarly, while the provisions in the *Geneva Conventions* dealing with 'grave breaches' unfortunately do not specifically mention rape or sexual violence, these crimes are implicitly covered in terms such as 'inhuman treatment... wilfully causing great suffering or serious injury to body or health'.

Despite at times clumsy and archaic terminology, the *Geneva Conventions* and their *Additional Protocols* leave no doubt that sexual violence against women (children and men) is a serious crime. Indeed, as Kelly Askin expresses in her chapter later

---

11   *Four Geneva Conventions*, above n 2, Common Article 3(1)(c).

in this book, prosecutors at international criminal institutions have found a range of ways to prosecute, and increasingly convict, individuals for sexual violence using a plethora of international crimes and articles within international law, including IHL. Askin notes that at times, there are benefits to the victim/survivor being able to prosecute gendered crimes in a more 'neutral' manner (through, for example, torture provisions) due to cultural issues of shame and isolation. Recent legal developments, such as the statute for the International Criminal Court,[12] adopt a more precise and concise definition of such atrocities. This is a welcomed and necessary development. It is essential to clearly articulate the sorts of horrific crimes relating to sexual violence that have been perpetrated against women during times of armed conflict and then 'silenced' over many years. Sadly the law is not always obeyed. The prohibitions against gendered and sexual violence during armed conflict and war are not new, however, and consistently need to be enforced.

C   Specific Protections: Pregnant Women and Mothers of Young Children

In numerous societies around the world, women are required during times of armed conflict to care for communities and protect vulnerable elements of the population including children, the sick and elderly. Criticisms have been levelled at IHL for the identification of women in terms of their relationship to 'others' and the overtly numerous references to women in their role as child-bearers. On the other hand, IHL pragmatically acknowledges the difficulties in providing for unborn or young children during armed conflict. Thus, IHL creates a range of preferential measures for women who find themselves in this situation. In general terms, Articles 38 and 50 of the *Fourth Geneva Convention* state that pregnant women and mothers of children under seven years shall be granted preferential treatment (to the same extent as the nationals of the State concerned) and that the Occupying Power shall not hinder the application of such treatment that may have been previously granted. In this *Convention,* the capacity for parties to a conflict to create hospital and safety zones specifically refers to, among others, the protection for expectant mothers and mothers of children under seven.[13] Provisions within *Additional Protocol I* also refer to the need to give pregnant women and new-born babies the same protection as that accorded to the sick and wounded.[14]

In relation to interned civilians during international armed conflict, Article 132 of the *Fourth Geneva Convention* requires the Parties to a conflict to:

> conclude agreements for the release, the repatriation, the return to places of residence or the accommodation in a neutral country...in particular children, pregnant women and mothers with infants and young children ...

---

12   *Rome Statute of the International Criminal Court,* opened for signature 9 October 1998, UN Doc. A/CONF.183/9 (1998), 37 ILM 999 (1998) (entered into force 1 July 2002) ('*ICC Statute*').

13   *Fourth Geneva Convention*, above n 2, Article 14.

14   *Protocol I*, above n 3, Article 8.

Article 89 of this *Convention* requires that interned expectant and nursing mothers (as well as children under 15 years) to 'be given additional food, in proportion to their physiological needs'. In relation to medical attention for maternity cases interned, Article 91 deals with the requirement of 'adequate treatment … and shall not receive care inferior to that provided for the general population'. In both the *Fourth Geneva Convention* (Article 23) and then expanded in *Protocol I* (Article 70), expectant and nursing mothers are given priority in relief action. The wording of Article 23 in the *Fourth Geneva Convention* appears outdated by referring to 'tonics', however the meaning of this requirement obviously relates to materials pertaining to the maintenance of good health.

Furthermore pregnant women and mothers of dependent infants who are 'arrested, detained or interned for reasons relating to the armed conflict' are required to have their cases considered with the utmost priority pursuant to *Protocol I*.[15] In relation to judicial guarantees, Article 76(3) of this *Protocol* also provides that Parties to the conflict 'to the maximum extent feasible' shall avoid pronouncement of the death penalty for an offence related to the armed conflict and not execute such sentences on pregnant women or mothers having dependent infants. The laws relating to internal armed conflict found in *Protocol II* prohibit absolutely the death penalty to be carried out on pregnant women or mothers of young children.[16]

D   *Specific Protections: Women as Civilian Internees*

Women are deprived of their freedom during times of armed conflict for various reasons. Women can be placed in detention as prisoners of wars, civilian internees, security detainees or for reasons unrelated to the conflict. In an earlier chapter of this book, Charlotte Lindsey has raised the unique and substantial problems relating to women in detention. Furthermore, the section above has outlined a number of the legal norms relating to women detained as expectant or nursing mothers.

In general, IHL contains a number of regulations relating to detention in connection to armed conflict. The major themes found in the *Geneva Conventions* and their *Additional Protocols* in this area relate to the classification of individuals detained and the basic conditions of internment. In addition, irrespective of whether a person is interned as a prisoner of war or a civilian, the location of places of detention must be safe.[17]

In relation to specific provisions relating to women as civilian internees in international armed conflict, Article 75 (5) of *Protocol I* states:

> Women whose liberty has been restricted for reasons related to the armed conflict shall be held in quarters separated from the men's quarters. They shall be under the immediate supervision of women. Nevertheless, in cases where families are detained

---

15   *Ibid.*, Article 76(2).

16   *Protocol II*, above n 3, Article 6(4).

17   *Fourth Geneva Convention*, above n 2, Article 83 and *Third Geneva Convention*, above n 2, Article 23.

or interned, they shall, whenever possible, be held in the same place and accommodated as family units.

The *Fourth Geneva Convention* notes that if, as an 'exceptional and temporary measure', women are interned with men who are not members of their family 'the provision
of separate sleeping quarters and sanitary conveniences' shall be obligatory.[18] Article
97 of this Convention states that 'a women internee shall not be searched except by a
woman'.

In relation to disciplinary punishments, Article 119 of the *Fourth Geneva
Convention* states that account shall be taken of a number of factors, including the
internee's sex.

The obligations of detaining women in separate quarters from men and being
under the immediate supervision of women also pertain during non-international
armed conflicts and are found in *Protocol II*, Article 5.

E   Specific Protections: Women as Prisoners of War

As noted previously, women prisoners of war are required to benefit from the general
protection accorded to all prisoners of war 'as favourable as that granted to men' and
discrimination based on sex is prohibited. Similar to the obligations of the Detaining
powers relating to civilians interned, women prisoners of war under the *Third Geneva
Convention* require 'separate dormitories' from men,[19] 'separate conveniences'[20] and to
be treated with 'all regard due to their sex'.[21] There are distinctions made between the
treatment of female prisoners of war and civilian internees, however, due to the different nature of the reasons for detention. Female combatants are often taken and placed
in detention in a less organised and more dangerous manner than their civilian counterparts and are likely to be carrying weapons. In this sense, there are no restrictions on
men searching female prisoners of war, nor is there the strict requirement of completely
separate quarters, with the focus being merely upon dormitories and conveniences.

In the area of prisoner of war labouring for the Detaining Powers, due account
must be given to the sex of prisoner when identifying tasks.[22] In relation to disciplinary measures, punishments for female prisoners of war are not to be more severe than
that accorded to males.[23] When undergoing disciplinary or penal punishment, women
are to be confined in quarters separate from men and under the immediate supervision of women.[24]

---

18   *Fourth Geneva Convention*, above n 2, Article 85.
19   *Third Geneva Convention*, above n 2, Article 25
20   *Ibid.*, Article 29.
21   *Ibid.*, Article 14.
22   *Ibid.*, Article 49.
23   *Ibid.*, Article 88.
24   *Ibid.*, Articles 97 and 108.

IV   Impact of the Methods and Means of Warfare on Women

An area that is often overlooked in reviewing the protections afforded to women under IHL is that relating to the limitations on the methods and means of warfare. Such limitations have been agreed upon by States in order to protect civilians from the effects of hostilities as well as provide certain protections for combatants, such as in the area of the use and development of weapons. Originally located in the *Hague Conventions* of 1899 and 1907, the majority of these regulations are now encoded in *Protocol II* and much of their substance has crystallised into customary international law.[25]

A   Conduct of Hostilities: General Principles

The basic rule in relation to the conduct of hostilities in international armed conflict is found in Article 48 of *Protocol I* and states:

> In order to ensure respect for and protection of the civilian population and civilian objects, the Parties to the conflict shall at all times distinguish between the civilian population and combatants and between civilian objects and military objectives and accordingly shall direct their operations only against military objectives.

Furthermore, Article 51 of this *Protocol* prohibits indiscriminate attacks, defined as those not directed at a specific military objective. Attacks are also prohibited which are not proportional and cause incidental loss of civilian life 'excessive in relation to the concrete and direct military advantage anticipated'. Similar, but more limited, obligations apply in internal armed conflict with Article 13 of *Protocol II* requiring:

> The civilian population as such, as well as individual civilians, shall not be the object of attack. Acts or threats of violence the primary purpose of which is to spread terror among the civilian population are prohibited.

Other areas of consequence found in *Protocol I* are those regulations that specifically protect civilian objectives;[26] objects indispensable to the survival of civilian population;[27] the natural environment[28] and works and installations containing dangerous forces.[29] Finally, it is important to observe that IHL also contains rules relating to limitations on weapons. Article 35 of *Protocol I* states that the choice of methods and means of warfare to Parties are not unlimited and that it is prohibited to employ weapons that cause 'superfluous injury or unnecessary suffering'.[30]

---

25   Françoise Krill 'The Protection of Women in International Humanitarian Law' (1985) *International Review of the Red Cross* 13.

26   *Protocol I*, above n 3, Article 52.

27   *Ibid.*, Article 54.

28   *Ibid.*, Article 55.

29   *Ibid.*, Article 56.

30   For further information on the conduct of hostilities, see the ICRC publication by Marco Sassoli and Antoine Bouvier, *How Does Law Protect in War?* (1999) 159-185.

Unfortunately the treaty based laws found in Protocol II relating to internal armed conflict are not as well developed as those applicable during international armed conflict. Yet Article 14 of *Protocol II* deals with the protection of objects indispensable to the survival of the civilian population and specifically prohibits the starvation of civilians as a method of combat.

B   Relevance to Women

While obviously not specifically mentioning women, these rules are substantially relevant when dealing with the issue of the protection of women during times of conflict. This is noted in the International Committee of the Red Cross (ICRC) Guidance Document 'Addressing the Needs of Women Affected by Armed Conflict':[31]

> As women are not generally recruited to fight, they remain largely unarmed and unprotected at times when traditional forms of moral, community and institutional safeguards have disintegrated and weapons abound.

As the major part of the civilian population during times of conflict; as the ones often left to care for the young, elderly and sick; as the ones left struggling to find clean water, food and essential household items and as the ones trying to hold communities together – women are greatly affected by the rules relating to the conduct of hostilities. With the destruction of infrastructure, such as sewage systems and electricity, women die of dysentery and have to fight harder to keep their families alive with limited health care available. With the destruction of the natural environment, women have difficulties ensuring there is fire-wood to cook with and that crops can be grown. If the laws relating to the conduct of hostilities are neither known or obeyed, the impact upon women both during and post-conflict is devastating. History has shown that deaths of civilian post-conflict due to disease, starvation and lack of infrastructure can be high and 'silent', in the sense that the international community loses interest believing the fighting, and thus danger, is over. In reviewing the protections provided for women in IHL, it is essential to understand and continue to advocate for regulations in the area of the methods and means of warfare to be applied and broadened.

V   Weapons and Women

As previously noted, during times of conflict women are significant members of the civilian population and often left undefended. The use of particular weapons, such as those which continue to maim and kill after the conflict, is a matter of concern. From the basic principles discussed, a range of treaties relating to individual weapons continue to be developed. Some of this treaty law, such as the Conventional Weapons Convention (CWC) Protocols banning blinding laser and incendiary weapons,[32] are

---

31   ICRC, *An ICRC Guidance Document: Addressing the Needs of Women Affected by Armed Conflict* (2004) 20.

32   *Convention on Prohibition or Restrictions on the Use of Certain Conventional Weapons Which May Be Deemed To Be Excessively Injurious or To Have Indiscriminate Effects*, opened for

not of specific relevance to women. However this section will outline a few areas in IHL having an impact upon women and needing reflection and examination.

A   Anti-personnel Landmines

In the late nineties, the international community rallied behind the concept of a treaty to ban the use, transfer and stockpiling of anti-personnel landmines.[33] The development of the Ottawa Treaty was a result of a number of progressive governments, and a mass of civil society, outraged at the limited existing provisions within IHL dealing with these deadly and indiscriminate weapons.[34] While women do not necessarily make up the majority of the statistics of victims of anti-personnel landmines, they are amply represented and anti-personnel landmines have a significant impact upon women's lives. Women suffer directly by having these weapons put their personal safety in jeopardy during and after conflict. They suffer by the presence of anti-personnel landmines making the tasks they have to undertake, such as collecting firewood and water, even more difficult and dangerous. Furthermore, women suffer by losing the male members and children of their communities to these weapons, thus having to take on extra burdens of caring for victims and providing for families. Even today, in places as such Afghanistan, the ICRC has noted an increase in post-conflict injuries and death of women in the community from anti-personnel landmines post-conflict. This is due to the new freedoms and lack of restrictions women experience today compared to under the previous regime. With greater opportunity to move more freely, but not the experience or understanding of devastation of anti-personnel landmines, it is essential to directly target women in Afghanistan in landmine awareness today.[35] Although IHL treaties have been developed and implemented to help protect civilians from danger, there is yet more work to be done. In developing and implementing IHL treaties, the work to protect civilians from dangers is not completed. The protection of women also requires active and constant dissemination and education.

B   Explosive Remnants of War

Unfortunately anti-personnel landmines are not the only weapons that continue to kill long after the conflict is over. Explosive Remnants of War (ERW) are increas-

---

signature 10 October 1980, 1342 UNTS 137, 19 *1523* (entered into force 2 December 1983) ('CWC').

33   *Convention on the Prohibition of the Use, Stockpiling, Production and Transfer of Anti-Personnel Landmines and on Their Destruction,* opened for signature 18 September 1997, 36 ILM 1507 (entered into force 1 March 1999) ('*The Ottawa Treaty*').

34   For a discussion on this topic see Maxwell Cameron, Robert Lawson and Brian Tomlin (eds) *To Walk Without Fear: The Global Movement to Ban Landmines* (1998) and John English 'The Ottawa Process: Paths Followed, Paths Ahead' (1998) 52 *Australian Journal of International Affairs* 121.

35   ICRC, 'Afghanistan: new freedoms, new dangers' (2003) ICRC Website <http://www.icrc. org/Web/eng/siteengo.nsf/iwpList74/A6D46AF01E386465C1256DD0003CA01E> (copy on file with author).

ingly found to destroy the lives of civilians and limit re-construction efforts post-conflict. The development of the most recent *Protocol* to the CWC dealing with ERW is a significant advancement in IHL that will have an impact on the lives of countless women throughout the world. ERW include unexploded or abandoned artillery shells, hand grenades, cluster bombs, sub-munitions and other similar ordinance. The *Protocol* to the CWC places a number of obligations upon State Parties, including the requirement to clear the explosive remnants of war in the territory it controls after a conflict; to take all feasible precautions to protect civilians from the dangers of explosive remnants, and to record information on the use and placement of these weapons to provide to organisations involved in clearing unexploded weapons. This is a positive advance in ensuring that women are protected during and after war and armed conflict.

C   Small Arms

The increasing availability and movement of small arms before, during and post armed conflict, has a significant effect upon civilians. Studies by the ICRC indicate a dramatic increase in morality rates when small arms, such as revolvers, pistols, rifles and sub-machine guns are available in communities post-conflict.[36] Small arms have also been seen to contribute to increased deaths in situations of domestic violence and lead to an increase risk of sexual violence.[37] While there is currently no multi-lateral treaty in international law relating specifically to the regulation of these weapons, numerous regional initiatives on this topic are emerging and should be encouraged.[38] Women in regions such as the Pacific have been specifically involved in encouraging warring factions to relinquish small arms to advance community peace and stability.[39] This is an area within the context of armed conflict that needs more analysis when considering the safety of women.

VI   International Criminal Prosecutions

As previously noted, there have been significant advances in the area of international criminal prosecutions of those accused of sexual violations against women during times of armed conflict. The statutes for the two international criminal *ad hoc* Tribunals for

---

36   ICRC, *Arms Availability and the Situation of Civilians in Armed Conflict* (1999).

37   *Ibid.*, 23.

38   Such initiatives include *Guidelines on Conventional Arms Transfers* set by the European Union; *the Inter-American Convention Against Illicit Manufacturing of and Trafficking in Firearms, Ammunition, Explosives and other Related Materials*; a moratorium on the production and import of small arms among West African States and a *Regional Action Plan* by the States of the Southern African Development Community. See ICRC, above n 36, 54-57.

39   Mary-Louise O'Callaghan, 'Tell men to disarm, women urged' *The Australian* (Sydney) 7 August 2003 (copy on file with author).

the Former Yugoslavia (ICTY)[40] and Rwanda (ICTR)[41] articulate such crimes in a limited manner.[42] As Kelly Askin writes in her article, however, this has not restricted these international legal instruments producing strong jurisprudence relating to the serious nature of such crimes at international law. Also as discussed by Askin, the ICC greatly enhances the opportunities for the pronouncement of prohibition on a broader and more fulsome range of sexual and gender based crimes. Added to this, the ICC's Statute has clear requirements within the organs of the Court itself, and the experts employed, to take note of gender.[43] Such advances cannot be underestimated. Yet there are a range of crimes that the *ICC Statute* did not advance or develop which, as discussed above, greatly impact upon women.

The provisions found within the *ICC Statute* relating to the prohibition of use of certain weapons are very weak. In international armed conflicts, the only specific weapons prohibited are poisoned weapons;[44] asphyxiating, poisonous gases, liquids or similar materials;[45] and expanding bullets.[46] There is a generic article which allows for amendments to be added once specific weapons are the subject of a 'comprehensive prohibition'.[47] This process is a complex one, however, and there is no guarantee that State Parties will be willing to 'add to' the subject matter jurisdiction of the ICC in the future. There could also be considerable debate surrounding the determination of a weapon that has been comprehensively prohibited. For example, despite wide ratification, it is unlikely that treaties such as the *Ottawa Treaty* or the *Protocol dealing with Explosive Remnants of War* will receive universal ratification. This may result in such weapons never being prohibited pursuant to the ICC. It is important to note that there is no prohibition of any weapons within the sections of the ICC dealing with non-international armed conflict. This is a conservative approach to the potential cus-

---

40   SC Res 827, UN SCOR (3217th mtg.) UN Doc. S/827/1993 (1993) (Statute contained in UN Doc. S/25704, Annex (1993), attached to the 'Report on the Secretary-General Pursuant to Paragraph 2 of Security Council Resolution 808'), 32 ILM 1159 (1993) ('*ICTY Statute*')

41   SC Res 955, UN SCOR, (3453d mtg.) UN Doc S/INF/50 Annex (1994), 33 ILM 1598 (1994) ('*ICTR Statute*').

42   *ICTY Statute*, above n 40, Article 5 as Crime Against Humanity and *ICTR Statute*, above n 41, Article 4 as a violation of Article 3 common to the *Four Geneva Conventions*, above n 2, and of *Protocol II* above n 3.

43   For a further discussion on this topic see Cate Steains 'Gender Issues' in Roy S. Lee (ed) *The International Criminal Court: The Making of the Rome Statute: Issues, Negotiations, Results* (1999) 357.

44   *ICC Statute*, above n 12, Article 8(2)(xvii).

45   *Ibid.*, Article 8(2)(xviii).

46   *Ibid.*, Article 8(2)(xix).

47   *Ibid.*, Article 8(2)(xx). This article states in full 'Employing weapons, projectiles and material and methods of warfare which are of a nature to cause superfluous injury or unnecessary suffering or which are inherently indiscriminate in violation of the international law of armed conflict, provided that such weapons, projectiles and material and methods of warfare are the subject of a comprehensive prohibition and are included in an annex to this Statute, by an amendment in accordance with the relevant provisions set forth in article 121 and 123'.

tomary developments of IHL. As most conflicts are non-international in nature, is a great limitation on the protective capacity of the ICC.

In relation to the conduct of hostilities, the ICC also is more restricted on the legal norms it articulates. While in international armed conflicts the majority of the important elements found in *Protocol I* are identified, this is not the case with the articles dealing with non-international conflicts. Crucial rules such as those dealing with the protection of objects indispensable to the survival of the civilian population, including the prohibition of starvation as a method of combat[48] and the protection of works containing dangerous forces[49] are missing from the ICC. These and other similar legal norms under IHL have a significant impact upon civilians and particularly women.

The ICTY and ICTR have made limited references to the area of international law dealing with the conduct of hostilities in indictments. Thus while some cases have dealt with these issues, to date there have been no substantive judgements or developments of jurisprudence in this area.[50] Yet women (as well as men and children) continue to perish as 'collateral damage' and from the lack of essential foodstuffs and medical assistance during times of conflicts. The maturing of this specific area of IHL will eventually occur, but must be understood and continually advocated for by those dedicated to improving the plight of women in war.

VII Conclusion

IHL, like all areas of international law, must be consistently reviewed and revisited to ensure that it accords with the realities that it attempts to modify. Women continue to be victims and survivors of great atrocities during times of armed conflict. To address this issue, it is necessary to take a broad view of the international laws aiming to limit suffering during times of conflict, and in particular that which applies specifically and generically to women. The existing legal framework, which at times is a product of the era in which it was drafted, contains a range of significant and often complex regulations, to protect women. There is no doubt that many areas in IHL need development. In particular, this author would argue, in relation to the regulations placed upon warring parties during non-international armed conflict. However there is much work to do within the existing legal framework to ensure that important elements of IHL are included in international prosecutions; are understood by the military, arms bearers and authorities; and incorporated into domestic legislation. The major advances made at an international legal institutional level cannot be underestimated and must be greatly welcomed. Concurrently, efforts must be continued and increased to ensure that within the domestic realm the protection of women during times of armed conflict is deemed of utmost importance.

---

48 *Protocol II*, above n 3, Article 14.

49 *Ibid.*, Article 15.

50 For some legal reasoning on this topic see *Prosecutor v. Martic (Decision on the Review of Indictment pursuant to Rule 61 of the Rules of Procedure and Evidence)*, Case No. IT-95-11-R61, 8 March 1996, ICTY website, <www.un.org/icty>.

Women and Armed Conflict: The Response of International Humanitarian Law

*Judith Gardam**

I Introduction

The last decade has witnessed increasing recognition of the distinctive experiences of women during times of armed conflict. A number of major studies have comprehensively documented the impact of armed conflict on women.[1] For example, in 2001, the International Committee of the Red Cross (ICRC) published *Women Facing War* (hereafter ICRC study) that identifies the needs of women during periods of armed conflict and examines the extent to which international law (in particular international humanitarian law (IHIL) address these needs.[2] The study, discussed by Charlotte Lindsey in an earlier article, provides the basis for the future operational response of the organisation to the situation of women in armed conflict.[3] The United Nations has also conducted its own investigations into the impact of armed conflict on women. Security Council Resolution 1325 of 31 October 2000 called on the Secretary-General to 'carry out a study on the impact of armed conflict on women and girls, the role of women in peace-building and the gender dimensions of peace processes and conflict resolution'.[4] The resulting study entitled *Women, Peace and Security* (hereafter UN

---

* Dr. Judith Gardam is a Reader in Law at the University of Adelaide Law School, Australia. She teaches in the area of public international law and has specific expertise in the use of force by States, International Humanitarian Law and Feminist Legal Theory. Dr Gardam has an LLB (WA and Monash), an LLM and a Ph.D.(Melbourne). She is widely published and is co-author of *Women, Armed Conflict and International Law* (2001).

1 See also the comprehensive description of the ways in which women are affected by armed conflict in Judith Gardam and Michelle Jarvis, *Women, Armed Conflict and International Law* (2001) 19-52 and Judith Gardam and Michelle Jarvis, 'Protecting Women in Armed Conflict: The International Response to the Beijing Platform for Action' (2000) 32 *Columbia Human Rights Law Review* 1.

2 ICRC *Women Facing War* (2001) ('*ICRC study*').

3 ICRC, *Addressing the Needs of Women Affected by Armed Conflict: An ICRC Guidance Document* (2004).

4 SC Res 1325, 55 UN SCOR (4213th mg), UN Doc S/Res/1325 (2000).

Helen Durham and Tracey Gurd (eds.), Listening to the Silences: Women and War, *pp. 109-123.*
© *2005 Koninklijke Brill BV. Printed in The Netherlands.* ISBN 90 04 14365 3.

study) was presented by the Secretary-General in 2002.[5] The Security Council initiative is of particular significance as an indication that the issue of women and armed conflict is perceived as relevant to the maintenance of international peace and security and is consequently being addressed at the highest levels.

A further positive development is the emergence of a broad approach to the issue of women and armed conflict. Until recently, the focus of investigations of the impact of armed conflict on women – and the majority of the concrete advances for their protection – have been in the area of sexual violence.[6] However, there is now widespread acknowledgment that these activities, although of epidemic proportions, are just part of the full picture of the reality of armed conflict for women.

The growing acknowledgment that women experience armed conflict in different ways to the remainder of the population inevitably calls for a response to this phenomenon from the various actors and agencies whose mandate concerns the victims of armed conflict. The aim of this paper is to consider the extent to which law reform has been perceived to be a relevant strategy for responding to the challenges of improving the situation of women in times of armed conflict. The focus of the discussion is primarily IHL, the development of which is the special responsibility of the ICRC.[7] Specifically, I consider the challenges posed by the situation of women in armed conflict to the fulfilment of the mandate of IHL to address, without discrimination, the humanitarian problems arising from armed conflict. The humanitarian objective of IHL is reflected in the definition of IHL adopted by the ICRC that refers to:

---

5   See *Women, Peace and Security, Study Submitted by the Secretary-General Pursuant to Security Council Resolution 1325 (2000),*57 UN SCOR, UN Doc S/2002/1154 (16 October 2002) ('*UN Study*'). See also Elisabeth Rehn and Ellen Johnson Sirleaf, *Women, War and Peace: The Independent Experts' Assessment on the Impact of Armed Conflict on Women and Women's Role in Peace-building* (2002), UNIFEM website <http://www.unifem.undp.org/resources/assessment/index.html>.

6   In the context of law, the major developments have been in relation to the enforcement of re-interpreted norms of IHL so as to better deal with sexual violence against women. The majority of this work has been undertaken by the two UN ad hoc war crimes tribunals: the International Criminal Tribunal for the Former Yugoslavia (ICTY) and the International Criminal Tribunal for Rwanda (ICTR). The ICTY was established in 1993 by the UN Security Council. See SC Res 827, 48 UN SCOR (3217th mtg at 29), UN Doc S/827/1993 (1993) (Statute contained in UN Doc. S/25704, Annex (1993), attached to the 'Report on the Secretary-General Pursuant to Paragraph 2 of Security Council Resolution 808'), 32 ILM 1159 (1993). The ICTR was established in 1994 by the UN Security Council. International Criminal Tribunal for Rwanda, SC Res 955, 49 UN SCOR (3453d mtg at 15), UN Doc S/INF/50 Annex (1994), 33 ILM 1598 (1994). In a continuation of this trend, the Rome Statute of the International Criminal Court, adopted in 1998, recognises rape and a range of other gender specific crimes as offences over which the Court will have jurisdiction. *Rome Statute of the International Criminal Court*, UN Doc A/CONF.183/9 (1998) 37 ILM 999 (1989), opened for signature 9 October 1998, entered into force 1 July 2002. The Statute was adopted by the United Nations Diplomatic Conference of Plenipotentiaries on the Establishment of an International Criminal Court on 17 July 1998.

7   For the role of the ICRC, see the *Statutes of the International Committee of the Red Cross of 24 June 1998*, reprinted in (1998) 324 *International Review of the Red Cross* 537.

international rules established by treaties or custom, which are specifically intended to solve humanitarian problems directly arising from international or non-international armed conflicts and which, for humanitarian reasons, limit the right of parties to a conflict to use the methods, and means of warfare of their choice, or protect persons and property that are, or may be, affected by conflict.[8]

The discussion proceeds as follows. I commence by describing in a general way the protections offered to women by IHL and other relevant areas of international law. I then critically examine the findings of the ICRC and the UN studies (and other UN initiatives) as to the adequacy of the existing legal regime that protects women in times of armed conflict. It is apparent from such an investigation that law reform is not seen as having a role to play in ameliorating the situation of women and armed conflict. My aim overall is to demonstrate that this complacency in relation to the law is misplaced. There is the need for an international initiative that focuses solely on the place of law reform in strategies to improve the position of women during times of armed conflict. It may be that the international legal regime in relation to women and armed conflict is as satisfactory as its proponents suggest. Justice, however, demands that this claim be subjected to rigorous scrutiny.

II   The Legal Regime for Women during Times of Armed Conflict

Modern IHL can be conveniently divided into those rules that govern the conduct of hostilities and those that deal with the protection of victims of armed conflict.[9] Theoretically, women benefit from all the provisions of IHL.[10] In common with the civilian population, they enjoy the rules of IHL which provide protection against the effects of hostilities[11] and when they are in the hands of an adverse party to the con-

---

8   Jean Pictet et al (eds) *Commentary on the Additional Protocols of 8 June 1977 to the Geneva Conventions of 12 August 1949* (1987) xxvii.

9   See generally Dieter Fleck (ed) *Handbook of Humanitarian Law in Armed Conflict* (1995). For a comprehensive description of IHL as applicable to women in times of armed conflict, see Gardam and Jarvis, above n 1.

10   The most relevant treaty rules for the purposes of this article are *Geneva Convention for the Amelioration of the Condition of the Wounded and the Sick in Armed Forces in the Field*, 12 August 1949, 75 UNTS 31 ('*First Geneva Convention*'); *Geneva Convention for the Amelioration of the Condition of Wounded, Sick and Shipwrecked members of the Armed Forces at Sea*, 12 August 1949, 75 UNTS 85 ('*Second Geneva Convention*'); *Geneva Convention Relative to the Treatment of Prisoners of War*, 12 August 1949, 75 UNTS 135 ('*Third Geneva Convention*'); *Geneva Convention Relative to the Protection of Civilian Persons in Time of War*, 12 August 1949 75 UNTS 287 ('*Fourth Geneva Convention*'). All entered into force 21 October 1950; *Protocol Additional to the Geneva Conventions of 12 Aug 1949, and relating to the Protection of Victims of International Armed Conflicts*, 7 December 1978, 1125 UNTS 3 ('*Protocol I*') and *Protocol Additional to the Geneva Conventions of 12 Aug 1949, and relating to the Protection of Victims of Non-International Armed Conflicts*, 7 December 1978, 1125 UNTS 609 ('*Protocol II*'). The Additional Protocols were opened for signature on 12 December 1977 and entered into force on 7 December 1978.

11   See for example, *Protocol I*, above n 10, Part V.

flict.[12] As combatants, they are covered to the same extent as men by the provisions relating to the legitimate means and methods of combat[13] and those in favour of prisoners of war,[14] the wounded and the sick.[15]

The four 1949 *Geneva Conventions* and the two *Protocols* of 1977 establish a system of equality in the sense that no adverse distinction can be drawn between individuals on the basis of, *inter alia*, sex.[16] Differentiation on the basis of sex is thus permissible as long as its impact is favourable. This interpretation of equality allows for the rules providing specific protections for women that are contained in all of the four 1949 *Geneva Conventions* and both the *Protocols*. The starting point of the system of special protection for women is the provisions that deal with the 'regard' or 'consideration due to women on account of their sex', and require that they be accorded special respect and protection.[17] These provisions are described as having the purpose of preserving the 'modesty' and 'honour' of women and to take account of their 'weakness'. For example, in the context of Article 14 of the *Third Geneva Convention*, the phrase, '[w]omen shall be treated with all the regard due to their sex …', has been explained in the following terms: '[i]t is difficult to give any general definition of the 'regard' due to women. Certain points should, however, be borne in mind; these points are the following:

A. **Weakness.** – this will have a bearing on working conditions … and possibly on food;
B. **Honour and modesty.** – The main intention is to defend women prisoners against rape, forced prostitution and any form of indecent assault …
C. **Pregnancy and childbirth.** – If there are mothers with infants among the prisoners, they should be granted early repatriation … women who have given birth should be repatriated with their child, while pregnant women should either enjoy special treatment, or, if their state of health permits, should also be repatriated.[18]

---

12   See for example, the *Fourth Geneva Convention*, above n 10; *Protocol I*, above n 10; and *Protocol II*, above n 10.

13   See for example, *Convention (II) with Respect to the Laws and Customs of War on Land and Annexed Regulations*, signed at The Hague, 29 July 1899 and *Convention (IV) with Respect to the Laws and Customs of War on Land, and Annexed Regulations*, signed at The Hague, 18 Oct 1907, (1910) and *Protocol I*, above n 10.

14   See for example, the *Third Geneva Convention*, above n 10.

15   See for example, *First Geneva Convention*, above n 10 and the *Second Geneva Convention*, above n 10.

16   See *Second Geneva Convention*, above n 10, Article 12; *Third Geneva Convention* above n 10, Articles 16 and 88; and *Protocol II*, above n 10, Article 2(1).

17   See for example, *First Geneva Convention*, above n 10, Article 12; *Second Geneva Convention*, above n 10, Article 12; *Third Geneva Convention*, above n 10, Article 14; and *Protocol I*, above n 10, Article 76.

18   Jean Pictet et al (eds), *Geneva Convention Relative to the Treatment of Prisoners of War* (1960) 147-148. See also commentary on common Art 12 of the *First* and *Second Geneva Convention*, Jean Pictet et al (eds), *Geneva Convention for the Amelioration of the Condition of Wounded, Sick and Shipwrecked Members of Armed Forces at Sea* (1960) 92.

Standing alone, the provisions in relation to 'regard', 'consideration' or 'special respect', are statements of general principle and impose no concrete obligations. They are supplemented by more detailed rules. For example, women prisoners of war and internees are entitled, where feasible, to separate quarters, sanitary conveniences and supervision by women.[19] Other provisions are designed to directly protect women from sexual assault.[20] Pregnant women and mothers of young children are the beneficiaries of a number of provisions dealing with such matters as early repatriation, priority in medical care, emergency relief and the provision of food and medical supplies.[21] Overall, the rules are designed to either reduce the vulnerability of women to sexual violence,[22] directly prohibit certain types of sexual violence or protect women when pregnant or as mothers of young children.

The restricted coverage of IHL is ameliorated, to some extent, by human rights norms. Human rights norms, to a limited degree, mirror the protections for women in IHL and thus are particularly significant in the context of non-international armed conflicts where the provisions of IHL are rudimentary. For example, in common with IHL, human rights norms prohibit the imposition of the death penalty on pregnant women.[23]

Protocol II to the four 1949 *Geneva Conventions* recognises the complementary nature of human rights norms. Its Preamble refers to the fact that international instruments relating to human rights already offer a basic protection to the human person. Of particular significance to women is the *Convention on the Elimination of all Forms of Discrimination Against Women*, which expressly addresses issues such as trafficking in women and the exploitation of prostitution of women, which may occur in times of armed conflict.[24]

The provisions of international refugee law also provide some degree of protection for women during times of armed conflict – particularly in the aftermath of armed conflict. The United Nations High Commissioner for Refugees (UNHCR) has

---

19   For example, *Third Geneva Convention* above n 10, Article 25 requires that: '[i]n any camps in which women prisoners of war, as well as men, are accommodated, separate dormitories shall be provided for them'. See also *Third Geneva Convention*, above n 10, Articles 29, 97 and 108 (in relation to prisoners of war) and *Fourth Geneva Convention*, above n 10, Article 124; and *Protocol II*, above n 10, Article 5(2)(a) (in relation to internees). See also *Fourth Geneva Convention*, above n 10, Article 76 (in relation to protected persons).

20   See for example, *Fourth Geneva Convention*, above n 10, Article 27(2); *Protocol I*, above n 10, Articles 75 (2) and 76; and *Protocol II* , above n 10, Article 4 (2)(e).

21   See for example, *Fourth Geneva Convention*, above n 10, Articles 17, 18, 23, 89, 91, 127; and *Protocol I*, above n 10, Articles 70, 76(2) and 76(3).

22   The link between the provision of separate quarters and the vulnerability of women to sexual violence, is made explicit in Claude Pilloud et al, *Commentary on the Additional Protocols of 8 June 1977 to the Geneva Conventions of 12 August 1949* (1987) 1390.

23   *International Covenant on Civil and Political Rights*, opened for signature 19 December 1966, 999 UNTS 171, Article 6(5), (entered into force 23 March 1976 ('*ICCPR*')).

24   See *Convention on the Elimination of all Forms of Discrimination Against Women*, opened for signature 17 July 1980, 1249 UNTS 13, Article 6 (entered into force 3 September 1981) ('CEDAW').

been markedly pro-active in addressing the distinctive experiences of women refugees, a large number of whom have been forced to leave their homes as a result of armed conflict.[25]

III   The Adequacy of the Legal Regime for Women in Times of Armed Conflict

There is the widely held perception that the rules of IHL for women are adequate and that what is needed is better enforcement.[26] This same assumption, as to the satisfactory nature of the existing rules of IHL relevant to women, is reflected in a range of initiatives dealing with the issue of women and armed conflict. For example, in March 1994 the Commission on Human Rights appointed a Special Rapporteur on Violence against Women, including its Causes and Consequences.[27] From the commencement of her work, the Special Rapporteur made it clear that 'all violations of the human rights of women in situations of armed conflict, and in particular, murder, systematic rape, sexual slavery and forced pregnancy ...' would be covered by her mandate.[28] Accordingly, the Special Rapporteur has considered the topic of armed conflict as part of her work on violence against women perpetrated or condoned by the State. In her Preliminary Report, the Special Rapporteur focused, *inter alia*, on the issue of sexual violence during armed conflict, including the treatment of refugee women.[29] In 1998, the Special Rapporteur compiled a more detailed report, specifically on violence perpetrated or condoned by the State with a significant focus on the issue of sexual violence against women during armed conflict; while in custody; and against refugee and internally displaced women.[30]

Despite identifying the serious humanitarian problem of what happens to women in armed conflict and proposing strategies to deal with these events, the Special Rapporteur does not suggest that IHL is in any way deficient and confines herself to a recommendation that the four 1949 *Geneva Conventions* should be 're-examined

---

25   See for example, UNHCR, *Sexual and Gender-Based Violence Against Refugees, Returnees and Internally Displaced Persons, Guidelines for Prevention and Response* (2003).

26   Cf however, Hilaire McCoubrey, *International Humanitarian Law* (2nd ed) (1990), (acknowledging that 'the provision made for women in the humanitarian laws of armed conflict can, in some respects, be argued to be both inadequate and outdated').

27   *Questions of Integrating the Rights of Women into the Human Rights Mechanisms of the United Nations and the Elimination of Violence Against Women*, UN Doc E/CN/.4/RES/1994/45 (1994). The mandate of the Special Rapporteur was extended for a further three-year period in 1997. See *CHR Res 1997/44*, ESCOR Supp. (No. 3) UN Doc E/CN.4/1997/44 (1997). See also *Final Report of the Special Rapporteur on the Situation of Systematic Rape, Sexual Slavery and Slavery-like Practices During Periods of Armed Conflict*, 50 UN ESCOR, UN Doc E/CN.4/Sub.2/1998/13 (1998) and *Update to the Final Report of the Special Rapporteur on the Situation of Systematic Rape, Sexual Slavery and Slavery-like Practices During Periods of Armed Conflict*, 52 UN ESCOR, UN Doc E/CN.4/Sub.2/2000/21 (2000).

28   *Preliminary Report of the Special Rapporteur on Violence Against Women, its Causes and Consequences*, 50 Un ESCOR, UN Doc E/CN.4/1995/42 (1994) [7].

29   *Ibid.*, [310 (c)] and [310(d)].

30   *Report of the Special Rapporteur on Violence Against Women, its Causes and Consequences*, 54 UN ESCOR, UN Doc E/CN.4/1998/54 (1998) [1].

and re-evaluated so as to incorporate developing norms against women during armed conflict'.[31] The 2001 report of the Special Rapporteur considers in particular the juris-prudential and structural developments in the system of enforcement of norms pro-hibiting sexual violence. The report is critical of some aspects of the Statute of the International Criminal Court, such as the definitions of forced pregnancy and gender. Once again however, the emphasis of the recommendations is on the issue of enforce-ment of existing norms.[32]

Other UN initiatives, including the Beijing Platform for Action, have not ques-tioned the extent to which IHL provides adequate protection for women, or raised law reform as a serious possibility.[33] At the Beijing Conference, women and armed conflict was identified as one of the 12 critical areas of concern to be addressed by Member States, the international community and civil society. Paragraph 44 of the Beijing Platform for Action, calls on '[g]overnments, the international community and civil society, including non-governmental organisations and the private sector'… 'to take strategic action', *inter alia*, in relation to the '[t]he effects of armed or other kinds of conflict on women, including those living under foreign occupation'. Nevertheless, the only reference to IHL in the Platform is in the context of achieving the reduction of the 'incidence of human rights abuse in conflict situations'.[34] Here, the Platform calls for the upholding and reinforcement of the norms of IHL and human rights law in relation to these offences against women and the prosecution of all those responsible for breaches thereof.

Silence on the issue of reassessing the adequacy of IHL for women continued at the special session of the UN General Assembly entitled *Women 2000: Gender Equality, Development and Peace for the Twenty-First Century*, held in June 2000 to review the progress made towards implementation of the Platform for Action in the five years following the Beijing Conference. The outcome document adopted by the General Assembly identifies developments taking place in the context of the two UN ad hoc war crimes tribunals and the Statute of the ICC, as among the examples of achievements in the critical area of women and armed conflict.[35] There is, however, no recognition of the need to assess whether the existing provisions of IHL are adequate to address the needs of women.

Security Council Resolution 1325 has been hailed as a groundbreaking initiative in the movement to improve the position of women in times of armed conflict and is discussed in detail later in this book. The Council, while calling for a study of the impact of armed conflict on women and girls, reiterated the need for all parties to

---

31 *Ibid.*, [22].

32 *Report of the Special Rapporteur on Violence Against Women, its Causes and Consequences*, 57 UN ESCOR, UN Doc E/CN.4/2001/73 (2001) [18], [19], [66].

33 Fourth World Conference on Women, Action for Equality Development and Peace, Beijing Declaration and Platform for Action, UN Doc A/Conf.177/20 (1995) (hereafter *Beijing Platform for Action*).

34 *Beijing Platform for Action*, above n 33, 'Strategic Objective E 3'

35 See *Unedited Final Outcome Document, Further Actions and Initiatives to Implement the Beijing Declaration and Platform for Action*, 10 June 2000 [12].

armed conflict to 'respect fully international law applicable to the rights and protection of women and girls, especially as civilians' and emphasized the significance of prosecuting war crimes of sexual violence against women and girls.

The legal regime relevant to women and girls in times of armed conflict was not specifically included in the mandate for the UN study. A chapter of the study, however, is devoted to an overview of IHL, human rights law and refugee law as 'complementary strands of international law'. The treatment of the legal regime in the study is descriptive in nature, outlining the relevant provisions of IHL, human rights law and refugee law. The study points out that the provisions of IHL are granted to all without discrimination and that additional protection is provided to pregnant mothers and mothers of young children. Reference is then made to the complementary protections available in human rights instruments and refugee law.

In conclusion the study 'call(s) upon all parties to adhere at all times to their obligations under principles of international humanitarian law, human rights law and refugee law' and 'to prosecute all perpetrators of crimes of gender-based and sexual violence directed against women and girls and ensure wide knowledge of international humanitarian law and human rights law'. Nowhere is it suggested that law reform may be called for as a strategy to overcome the situation of women in times of armed conflict.

This view as to the adequacy of the legal regime in relation to women and armed conflict is shared by the ICRC. In its opinion the 'tragic plight of women does not primarily result from a lack of humanitarian rules to protect them but rather from a failure to coherently interpret and implement existing rules'.[36] The ICRC study is comprehensive in its treatment of the legal regime protecting women in times of armed conflict. However, a similar conclusion is reached as to the adequacy of the law: 'on the whole – subject to minor exceptions set out below – the law does adequately cover the needs of women in situations of armed conflict. But this is true only if one considers all the applicable bodies of law simultaneously, in particular international humanitarian law and human rights law'.[37] Moreover, according to the study, the law is adequate in both international and non-international armed conflict. Some gaps are acknowledged: 'the more substantive of which appear to relate to the issue of return after arbitrary displacement and the question of personal documents'.[38] The study isolates the challenge for improving the position of women in times of armed conflict as one relating to 'ensuring respect for an implementation of the existing rules'.

The one exception to this general trend is the Women, War and Peace study completed by UNIFEM in 2002. Although the UNIFEM study does not consider the adequacy of the law in detail, it raises the possibility that existing international law is insufficient to address women's needs. Accordingly, the Independent Experts, who prepared the study, call upon the Secretary-General to 'appoint a panel of experts to

---

36   See ICRC, *'Advancement of Women and Implementation of the Outcome of the Fourth World Conference on Women: Statement by the ICRC to the UN General Assembly'*, 53 UN GAOR, Third Committee, (15 October 1998) available at <http://www.icrc.org>.

37   *ICRC study*, above n 2, 213.

38   *Ibid.*, 214.

assess the gaps in international and national laws and standards pertaining to the protection of women in conflict and post-conflict situations and women's role in peace-building'.[39]

There are several aspects to the treatment of the legal regime by the UN and ICRC study on which I wish to comment in support of my argument that an examination of the adequacy of the law regulating the treatment of women during times of armed conflict is necessary. First, in relation to the methodology adopted by the studies, both commence with a detailed consideration of the impact of armed conflict on women and girls.[40] It might be expected that the description of the law that follows might be linked in some way to what has come before. However, this is not the case with the UN study. There is no indication that the authors of the report have taken the events that they have identified and considered in what way existing international law address these phenomena. In fact, the study identifies many distinctive experiences of women during times of armed conflict that are not regulated in any way or quite superficially by the existing legal provisions.[41]

In contrast to the UN study, the explicit methodology adopted by the ICRC study is to identify the needs of women during times of armed conflict and then determine to what extent the existing legal regime addresses these needs. The operational response of the organisation is then evaluated and key points identified. For example, the reality of arbitrary displacement for women during times of armed conflict is documented followed by a review of the applicable law and how the ICRC deals with this phenomenon in the field.[42] From this perspective, the ICRC study makes an impressive contribution to improving the understanding of what happens to women during times of hostilities and the applicable law. The methodology of this study, therefore, is sound, even if one can criticise some of its conclusions.

Secondly, the UN study purports to use a 'gender analysis as the basis for understanding what happens to women and girls in armed conflict and to develop effective operational responses'.[43] This approach has the beneficial result of leading to the recognition of many hitherto unacknowledged ways in which women are affected by armed conflict. The recognition of the way in which gender influences how women experience armed conflict is particularly marked in the study's assessment of the socio-economic dimensions of armed conflict.[44] Despite the fact that gender is the preferred methodology in examining the reality of armed conflict for women, however, the examination of the law that follows makes no attempt to rely on the insights that gender can provide. The applicable law is accepted uncritically and no suggestion is made that its provisions may, in fact, reflect an outdated and distorted view of women.

39   Rehn and Johnson Sirleaf, 'Independent Experts' recommendations for full implementation of Security Council Resolution 1325 (number 12)', above n 5.

40   See 'II Impact of Armed Conflict on Women and Girls' in *UN study*, above n 5, 13-32.

41   See for example *UN study*, above n 5, 65-73 (discussing the socio-economic dimensions to armed conflict for women).

42   See *ICRC study*, above n 2, 65-73.

43   *UN study*, above n 5, 14.

44   *Ibid.*, 22-5.

The ICRC study focuses on 'women', a term that is used as a 'biological and as a socially or culturally based reference (to gender)'. It is a significant advance for the organisation to recognise the existence of gender as a factor in the way women experience armed conflict. For many years, there was considerable resistance within the ICRC to the idea that the impact of armed conflict on women may be determined, to some extent, by their socially-constructed roles. The study, however, explicitly states that the 'impact of war on women is not only a result of biological differences, but also of the different constraints and opportunities arising from their role in society (gendered roles)'.[45] There is, however, an assumption that the gendered and biological woman constitutes two distinct categories. The study envisages a biological category of woman, whose needs flow naturally from this condition. It is well recognised, however, among feminist scholars that the category of biological women is also constructed. There is no such entity as the pre-ordained women with her special needs. A woman's needs resulting from her biology are just as determined by how these functions are perceived in the society of which she is a part. To illustrate this point – the study refers to the special needs of women being related to their need for privacy. Is this natural, or imposed on women?[46] Nevertheless, the reliance on 'privacy' as being the basis for many of the provisions relating to women is certainly a welcome advance on the traditional use of the concept of a woman's honour in such contexts. To ignore the influence of gender in relation to women's biological needs, however, is to run the risk of further entrenching a limited vision of women. Disappointing as this may be to those who take the view that without an acknowledgment of gender there is very little the regime can do to effectively to address the experience of women in times of armed conflict, the study in many instances acknowledges the gendered impact of armed conflict on women. This is particularly marked in the section dealing with the vulnerability of women, a discussion that, in fact, represents an explanation for women's experience in armed conflict that is based on gender.[47]

A failure to investigate the gendered assumptions that underlie IHL must call into question whether enforcement of a flawed regime is the way forward for women. Accepting, for the sake of argument, the limitations of IHL and, moreover, recognising the restricted role that law can play in regulating an activity that some say defies regulation, would the situation improve for women with better enforcement of the existing provisions of IHL, or is something far more fundamental required to achieve this goal? In order to ensure an effective regime to protect women in armed conflict, it is essential to isolate not only the symptoms of their vulnerability, but its underlying cause. The major underlying cause of the particular vulnerability of women in armed conflict – namely the endemic discrimination that exists against women in all societies – is consistently overlooked in any discussion of IHL and is not addressed in its provisions. The key to moving ahead is not only the acknowledgment of this factor but ensuring that its impact on the existing legal regime is investigated.

---

45   *ICRC study*, above n 2, 36.
46   *Ibid.*, 21.
47   *ICRC study*, above n 2, 28-30.

IHL certainly recognises, to some extent, the vulnerability of women in armed conflict. This acknowledgment of women's situation is of great significance. IHL, however, assumes the underlying cause of their vulnerability to be attributable to their child-bearing functions and to their role as sexual objects. Women do need special consideration in these contexts and the existing provisions of IHL are important. Moreover, compliance with these provisions would improve the situation for many women in armed conflict today. However this is only part of the picture of the extent of the vulnerability of women in armed conflict and its underlying cause.

Women are vulnerable to the effects of armed conflict and experience it differently to other members of the population. This is not only because they have distinctive biological characteristics, but also because of the underlying systemic discrimination that exists against women in all societies. The nature and impact of this discrimination varies widely between cultures, but all women experience it at some level.

Nowhere are women full participants in society.[48] Women are disadvantaged in access to education and health care. They are considerably less mobile because of their traditional role in caring for others. Seventy percent of the world's population living in poverty are women.[49] Their work remains grossly unpaid, unrecognised and undervalued.[50] In addition, women's political opportunities are severely limited. They are generally denied access to power structures and participation in decision-making at all levels and this exclusion carries through into the context of armed conflict.[51] Therefore, women are unable to draw attention to the particular difficulties they experience in conflict situations and, moreover, are powerless to recommend any preventative action in response.

The low status of women in society is reflected in their treatment by the law, in property rights, rights of inheritance, laws related to marriage and divorce and rights to acquire nationality or property or seek employment. Given this lack of full participation in society – and their gender and biological roles – it is inevitable that armed conflict impacts extremely harshly on women. Women, moreover, lack the resources, education or skills to deal with the conditions that result from armed conflict.

---

48   See generally UNDP, *Human Development Report* (1995).

49   The feminisation of poverty was a key area of concern at the Beijing Conference, see *Beijing Platform for Action*, above n 33 [49]-[59]. See also *African Platform for Action Adopted by the Fifth Regional Conference on Women* held at Dakar from 16 to 23 November 1994, UN Doc E/CN.6/1995/5/Add.2, (1994) [25]; *Second Review and Appraisal of the Implementation of the Nairobi Forward-Looking Strategies for the Advancement of Women*, Report of the Secretary General, UN Doc E/CN.6/1995/3/Add.1 (1995) [92].

50   See UNDP, *Human Development Report* (1995) 97 (estimating women's invisible annual contribution to the global economy at eleven trillion dollars).

51   See for example, in the context of Palestinian women, Hilary Charlesworth, 'International Human Rights Law: Prospects and Problems for Palestinian Women', in Stephen Bowen (ed), *Human Rights: Self Determination and Political Change in the Occupied Palestinian Territories* (1997),79, 81-85; see also 'Stop Press: Emergency Appeal, Women in Somalia' (1992) 3/4 *Changing the World* 8 and Tosca Looby, 'Women in Bougainville', (1992) 42 *Refractory Girl* 66, 67.

So it is not only the better enforcement of the provisions of IHL that is the key to improvements in the legal protections for women in armed conflict. It needs to be recognised that IHL operates on a false assumption: namely, that apart from their roles as mothers and in the context of sexual violence, women not only share the same experience of armed conflict as other members of the population but are able to avail themselves equally of the existing protections offered by IHL. This is not the case.

It is of undoubted significance that recent studies of women and armed conflict accept the premise that the major contributing factor determining the impact of these events on women is the endemic discrimination that women experience globally. However, it is to be regretted that these initiatives have failed to apply this insight to their analysis of the law in order to determine whether the legal regime responds to this phenomenon or merely reproduces and, in some respects, exacerbates its effects.

The final aspect of the two recent studies of women and armed conflict that warrants comment is the fact that both studies place a great deal of confidence in the ability of human rights norms to complement the provisions of IHL.[52] Since the adoption of the United Nations Charter in 1945, IHL has been undergoing a subtle, but pervasive, change. The regime of IHL, initially primarily utilitarian in nature, is now frequently seen as allied to, or even as part of, the developing regime of human rights. The nature of the relationship alleged to exist between the two regimes varies, depending on the context, but the trend is well developed to treat IHL and human rights as sharing common values and as directed to the same ends.[53] In both the *Nicaragua Case* and the *Nuclear Weapons Advisory Opinion*, the International Court of Justice recognised this evolving relationship.[54]

The major impetus for the increasing focus on the protection of human beings in armed conflicts is that human rights norms provide a mechanism for confronting the appalling reality of non-international armed conflicts in today's world. These conflicts have dominated the international scene for many decades. They are almost uniformly conducted without any restraint in relation to the means and methods of combat used by the warring factions and the treatment of the civilian population. The rules of IHL developed primarily as a response to international armed conflict. The effectiveness of Common Article 3 to the four 1949 *Geneva Conventions*, sometimes referred to as the 'mini-convention on non-international armed conflicts', has been severely limited by the reluctance of states to accept that its threshold of applicability had been reached. Moreover, *Protocol II* adopted in 1977 has a high threshold before its provisions come into operation.[55] Apart from these conventional provisions, for many years IHL had

---

52   See *UN study*, above n 5, 36-8 and *ICRC study*, above n 2, 22-3.

53   See for example, Raúl Emilio Vinuesa, 'Interface, Correspondence and Convergence of Human Rights and International Humanitarian Law', 1998 *Yearbook of International Humanitarian Law* 69 (1999).

54   *Military and Paramilitary Activities in and against Nicaragua (Nicaragua v. US)* (Merits) [1986] ICJ Rep 14, and *Legality of the Threat or Use of Nuclear Weapons, (General Assembly)* Advisory Opinion, [1996] ICJ Rep 26.

55   *Protocol II* applies to armed conflicts 'that take place in the territory of a High Contracting Party between its armed forces and dissident armed forces or other organized armed groups which, under responsible command, exercise such control over a part of its territory

little to offer by way of protections for victims of these savage and intractable conflicts. Human rights norms, in contrast, are designed to address the mistreatment of individuals within the borders of a state and are consequently more readily adaptable than IHL to situations involving internal armed conflict.[56]

The importance of human rights in armed conflict is now a very common theme in a variety of venues, including those that deal with the enforcement of international criminal law. Moreover, increasingly there is a tendency to attribute considerable importance to the ability of human rights norms to compensate for the deficiencies of IHL. Although there is undoubtedly ongoing erosion of the boundaries between human rights law and IHL, as things stand at present, there are significant limitations on the ability of human rights law to provide protection to individuals in times of armed conflict. Traditionally, the two regimes were not intended to be complementary. As Christopher Greenwood explains '[h]uman rights law is designed to operate primarily in normal peacetime conditions, and within the framework of the legal relationship between a state and its citizens. International humanitarian law, by contrast, is chiefly concerned with the abnormal condition of armed conflict and the relationship between a state and the citizens of its adversary ...'.[57]

Consequently, the human rights regime does not necessarily address in any meaningful detail the particular challenges that individuals, specifically women, face in times of armed conflict. The provisions of human rights are not crafted to cover situations of conflict where societal structures have broken down. The issues with which these norms deal take on new forms in the midst of the disruption caused by armed conflict, a factor that is not reflected in their content. For example, to what extent can it be realistically argued that instruments such as the *International Convention on the Elimination of all Forms of Racial Discrimination* and the *International Covenants on Civil and Political Rights* and *Social, Economic and Cultural Rights* of 1966, provide any degree of significant protection for women in times of internal armed conflict? Those who argue that human rights norms can compensate for the gaps of IHL often refer to very general norms, such as the right to an adequate standard of living and the right to enjoy 'the highest attainable standard of physical and mental health'.[58] Even in times of peace, these norms are so vague and permissive in content as to provide only the most general level of protection. During the exigencies of conflict, they cannot effectively resolve the rights and entitlements of various categories of war victims to humanitarian assistance.

A particular characteristic of the human rights regime that contributes to its limited ability to supplement the norms of IHL is that except for a basic core of

---

as to enable them to carry out sustained and concerted military operations and to implement this Protocol.' The Protocol expressly does not apply to 'situations of internal disturbances and tensions, such as riots, isolated and sporadic acts of violence, and other acts of a similar nature, as not being armed conflicts.' *Protocol II*, above n 10, Article 1.

56   See Theodor Meron, *Human Rights in Internal Conflicts: Their International Protection* (1987) 2–70.

57   See Christopher Greenwood, 'Scope of Application of Humanitarian Law,' in Deiter Fleck (ed), above n 9, 102.

58   See for example, *ICRC study*, above n 2, 106, 109, 116.

rights, parties can derogate from many human rights norms during armed conflict.[59] Moreover, even non-derogable rights, such as the right to life, must yield precedence in times of armed conflict to the regime of IHL and take their content from what is permissible in that regime.[60] In contrast, there is no similar concept of derogability in IHL.

It is, therefore, necessary at all times to distinguish between human rights norms that are also reflected in the provisions of IHL – such as those in Common Article 3 to the four 1949 *Geneva Conventions* – and those that are not. Those human rights norms that are not also reflected in the provisions of IHL are subject to derogation and are limited in their ability to supplement IHL. It is instructive to consider the norms that are included in the Secretary-General's 2002 study as complementing the protections available to women and girls in times of armed conflict, particularly internal armed conflict. Amongst those referred to are the right to life and freedom from torture and other inhuman and degrading treatment.[61] The conventional and customary norms of IHL however, already proscribe murder, torture and other inhuman and degrading treatment.[62] Human rights norms that have not been recognised in the specific provisions of IHL, therefore, have limited ability to overcome the gaps of IHL.

In a sense, the very point of IHL is that it sets the limits of derogability in relation to the treatment of human life in times of armed conflict. Therefore, it is of critical importance to have a body of IHL that adequately reflects the distinctive experiences of women facing armed conflict and not to delegate responsibility for addressing the humanitarian problems that women face to the human rights regime.

IV   Conclusion

To date the overwhelmingly preferred strategy of the international community for addressing the impact of armed conflict on women has been to improve compliance with, and enforcement of, the relevant existing legal provisions. There is no doubt that emphasis on these activities is an important and worthwhile strategy. If the provisions

---

59   The non-derogable human rights include the right to life; freedom from torture and other inhuman or degrading treatment or punishment; freedom from slavery; and the non-retroactivity of penal laws. See Raúl Emilio Vinuesa, above n 303, 87-90 (for a discussion of non-derogable human rights). See also *General Comment No 29, States of Emergency* (Article 4), CCPR/C/21/Rev.1/Add.11 (2001).

60   See the discussion of this issue in the context of the right to life by the International Court of Justice in *Legality of the Threat or Use of Nuclear Weapons Advisory Opinion*, above n 54. Compare, however, the criticism of the Court's treatment of the relationship between human rights and IHL in Vera Gowlland-Debbas, 'The Right to Life and Genocide: The Court and an International Public Policy', in Laurence Boisson de Chazournes and Philippe Sands (eds) *International Law and the International Court of Justice and Nuclear Weapons* (1999) 315.

61   *UN study*, above n 5, 36.

62   See for example, Common Article 3 to the *Four Geneva Conventions*, above n 10; Article 12, *Second Geneva Convention*, above n 10; Article 32, *Fourth Geneva Convention*, above n 10; Article 75, *Protocol I*, above n 10.

of IHL (and other areas of international law) are, in fact, adequate to deal with the situation of women in times of armed conflict, then this is the most that can be expected. My argument is that this assumption has not been subjected to careful scrutiny.

It may be that IHL does not hold the future for the regulation of armed conflict. Perhaps the regime is too conservative, ancient and too closely associated with the military to be flexible enough to respond to the challenges facing it – not only from women, but also children, combatants and civilians generally. It is true that the current boundaries of IHL also restrict what can be achieved by its provisions, although these are not immutable.[63] Its contemporary relevance has also not been assisted by the decision of the International Court of Justice in the *Nuclear Weapons Advisory Opinion*,[64] or by its failure to protect civilians from the devastating consequences of the campaigns of aerial bombardment that characterised the Persian Gulf conflict (1990-91)[65] and Kosovo conflict (1999).[66]

Nevertheless, IHL has undergone a remarkable renaissance in the context of international criminal law, including crimes of sexual violence against women. The two ad hoc criminal Tribunals have adopted creative, new interpretations of existing legal provisions so as to cover of acts of sexual violence against women during times of armed conflict. There is scope for other provisions of IHL, of particular relevance to women, to be enforced: for example, those that criminalise indiscriminate bombardment of the civilian population, of whom women make up a large percentage.[67] For the considerable variety of ways in which women are affected by armed conflict, however, there are no provisions of IHL to be reinterpreted and enforced. This silence on so many of the wartime experiences of women poses a continuing challenge to IHL to fulfil its humanitarian mandate.

---

63 See Gardam and Jarvis, above n 1, 122-8 (for a critical analysis of the boundaries of IHL).

64 *Legality of the Threat or Use of Nuclear Weapons*, above n 54. In this case the ICJ appears to accord pre-eminence to the right of self-defence of States over the limitations of IHL, see Judith Gardam, 'The Contribution of the International Court of Justice to International Humanitarian Law' (2001) 14 *Leiden Journal of International Law* 349 for a discussion of this issue.

65 For the impact on civilians of the Coalition allies' actions against Iraq, see Human Rights Watch, *Needless Deaths in the Gulf Conflict* (1991).

66 For the impact of the NATO actions in Kosovo on the civilian population, see *Report on the Human Rights Situation involving Kosovo*, 54 UN ESCOR, UN Doc IIC/K304 (1999); and Human Rights Watch, *Civilian Deaths in the NATO Air Campaign* (2000).

67 See ICTY cases *Prosecutor v. Djukic*, (Indictment), Case No. IT-96-20, 29 February 1996, <http://www.un.org/icty/indictment/english/dju-ii960229e.htm>, and *Prosecutor v. Blaskic*, (Judgment) Case No. IT-95-14, 3 March 2000 <http://www.un.org/icty/blaskic/trialc1/judgement/bla-tj000303e.pdf>. See generally, William Fenrick, 'Attacking the Enemy Civilian as a Punishable Offence' (1997) 72 *Duke Journal of Comparative & International Law* 539.

12

The Jurisprudence of International War Crimes Tribunals: Securing Gender Justice for Some Survivors

*Kelly D. Askin**

The International Criminal Tribunals for the former Yugoslavia (ICTY) and Rwanda (ICTR) were established by the United Nations Security Council in 1993 and 1994 to prosecute war crimes, crimes against humanity and genocide committed during armed conflicts in the Balkans in the 1990s and in Rwanda in 1994.[1] Since then, dozens of indictments have been issued by these Tribunals, charging the accused with individual or superior responsibility for various forms of sexual violence. Several ICTY/R Judgments have confirmed many of the allegations by holding individuals criminally responsible for conduct consisting of rape, sexualised enslavement, sexualised torture, gender and sex persecution, forced nudity and other forms of sexual violence.[2] The permanent

---

*   B.S., J.D, Ph.D (law). Senior Legal Officer, International Justice, Open Society Justice Initiative; Fellow, Yale Law School; 2004-2005 Fulbright Global Scholar.

1   International Criminal Tribunal for the former Yugoslavia, SC Res 827, 48 UN SCOR (3217th mtg at 29), UN Doc S/827/1993 (1993) (Statute contained in U.N. Doc. S/25704, Annex (1993), attached to the 'Report on the Secretary-General Pursuant to Paragraph 2 of Security Council Resolution 808'), 32 ILM 1159 (1993); International Criminal Tribunal for Rwanda, SC Res 955, 49 UN SCOR (3453d mtg at 15), UN Doc S/INF/50 Annex (1994), 33 ILM 1598 (1994).

2   See especially *Prosecutor v. Jean-Paul Akayesu*, (Judgment), Case No. ICTR-96-4-T, 2 September 1998, <http://www.ictr.org/default.htm> ('*Akayesu* Trial Chamber Judgment'); *Prosecutor v. Zejnil Delalić et al.*, (Judgment), Case No. IT-96-21-T, 16 November 1998, <http://www.un.org/icty/celebici/trialc2/judgement/cel-tj981116e.pdf> ('*Čelebići* Trial Chamber Judgment'); *Prosecutor v. Anto Furundžija* (Judgment), IT 95 17/1-T, 10 December 1998 <http://www.un.org/furundzija/trialc2/judgement/fur-tj981210e.pdf> ('*Furundžija* Trial Chamber Judgment'); *Prosecutor v. Dragoljub Kunarac et al.* (Judgment), IT-96-23-T & IT-96-23/1-T, 22 February 2001 <http://www.un.org/icty/kunarac/trialc2/judgement/kun-tj010222e.pdf >('*Kunarac* Trial Chamber Judgment'); *Prosecutor v. Miroslav Kvočka et al.* (Judgment), IT-98-30-T, 2 November 2001 <http://www.un.org/icty/kvocka/trialc/judgement/kvo-tj011002e.pdf> ('*Kvočka* Trial Chamber Judgment'). See also Kelly D. Askin, 'Prosecuting Wartime Rape and Other Gender-Related Crimes Under International Law: Extraordinary Advances, Enduring Obstacles' (2003) 21 *Berkeley Journal of International Law* 101-164; Kelly D. Askin, 'Sexual Violence in Decisions and Indictments of the Yugoslav and Rwandan Tribunals: Current Status' (1999) 93 *American Journal of International Law* 97-123.

Helen Durham and Tracey Gurd (eds.), Listening to the Silences: Women and War, *pp. 125-153.*
© 2005 *Koninklijke Brill BV. Printed in The Netherlands.* ISBN 90 04 14365 3.

International Criminal Court, which came into force on 1 July 2002, has jurisdiction to prosecute rape, enforced prostitution, sexual slavery, forced pregnancy, enforced sterilisation and other forms of sexual violence of comparable gravity.[3] Furthermore, hybrid or internationalised tribunals, composed of both international and local judges, prosecutors and defence attorneys, have authority to adjudicate similar crimes in East Timor, Sierra Leone, Kosovo and eventually Cambodia. The result is a much improved effort and concept to end impunity for crimes committed exclusively or disproportionately against women and girls. Nonetheless, enormous obstacles and challenges remain.

This paper will examine the current jurisprudence relating to gendered crimes, particularly sexual violence, from the Yugoslav and Rwanda Tribunals and consider how this jurisprudence can be used to prosecute sex crimes under the terms of the respective Statutes in the ICC and in the hybrid courts of East Timor, Sierra Leone and Cambodia. Focusing upon the various crimes in a thematic manner, this paper will also review the conceptualisation of the crimes themselves within international law, noting the various impacts that terminology of crimes and prosecutorial strategies can have upon victims-survivors. While the process and the outcome are indisputably imperfect, great strides have nevertheless been made in understanding, conceptualising, defining, prosecuting and punishing various forms of sexual violence.

I   Overview: Current and Future Challenges – Changing the Framework

Despite the fact that rape is a serious crime in domestic criminal codes in every region of the globe, the crime is largely ignored worldwide. Impunity is especially prevalent during periods of armed conflict or repressive regimes. Whether committed during wartime or so-called peacetime, impunity is due to a number of factors. Most of these factors are related to deeply entrenched patriarchal stereotypes that regard gender abuses as private issues or insignificant crimes, or worse, suggest that the women deserved the abuse (typically because of some behaviour, dress, real or perceived indiscretion or 'immoral' behaviour). Thus, sex crimes are often not genuinely investigated or rigorously prosecuted. Even when it is indisputable that sexual violence was inflicted and it was directed against women and girls simply because of their sex/gender, survivors of sexual assault are still typically treated as tainted, dishonoured or unmarriageable because of the sexual nature of the abuse. Such harmful stereotypes and stigmas serve as strong deterrents for reporting the crime, particularly when complaints are unlikely to secure redress and reporting the crime will heap *additional* violations on the survivor. Thus, as in other crimes, there needs to be some incentive to report the crime, such as having the complaint taken seriously, investigated and prosecuted. Throughout most of the world, there is not only very little incentive, but actually strong disincentives, to reporting sex crimes. Consequently, there is little incentive for not committing sex crimes, particularly when it is against women of the opposing side during armed conflict and the harm inflicted is broad and collective.

---

3   *Rome Statute of the International Criminal Court,* opened for signature 17 July 1998, UN Doc. A/CONF.183/9 (1998), 37 ILM 999 (1998) (entered into force 1 July 2002) (*'ICC Statute'*) Articles 7(1)(g), 8(2)(b)(xxii), 8(2)(e)(vi).

In the context of war, sex crimes have become common weapons of terror and destruction. All sides of the conflict abuse women and girls during conflict. Men rape women to humiliate them and the armies who failed to protect them. Men rape women to express superiority or conquest. Men rape women to avenge the rape of their own women. Men rape women to release tension and anxiety. Men rape women because they are members of the enemy group. Men rape women to satisfy their own depraved cravings. Men rape women to energise them for combat. Men rape women because they are angry or scared. Men rape women because they are producers of children. Men rape women for countless other reasons and purposes. Some women encourage or otherwise participate in the rape of women in order to persecute and otherwise harm enemy women. Regardless of the intent or the purpose behind the violence, the result is typically the same: physical, mental, sexual and social injury to the victim; and mental harm to those associated with the victim. Until the misconceptions and stereotypes change, and until men take a more prominent role in denouncing sex crimes and the perpetrators of these crimes, sexual violence will remain exceedingly common and will remain underreported and underprosecuted.[4]

II Prosecuting Gender-related Crimes in International/ised Courts and Tribunals

When committed in the context of armed conflict or mass atrocity, gender-related crimes can be prosecuted in many ways, including as war crimes of rape, torture and outrages upon personal dignity; as rape, torture, enslavement, persecution and inhumane acts constituting crimes against humanity; and as instruments of genocide. The jurisprudence of the ICTY and ICTR has been limited by the terms of the applicable Statutes, the charges brought by the Prosecution and the evidence presented at trial. Thus, the jurisprudence is somewhat selective and restrictive and in no way precludes additional developments of the law. The Statute of the ICC, the UNTAET Regulations for East Timor[5] and the Statute of the Special Court in Sierra Leone[6]

---

4   Many of these themes have been expanded upon in Kelly D. Askin, 'Comfort Women – Shifting Shame and Stigma from Victims to Victimizers' (2001) 1 *International Criminal Law Review* 5, 29; Kelly D. Askin, 'The International Criminal Tribunal for Rwanda and Its Treatment of Crimes Against Women' in John Carey et al. (eds) *International Humanitarian Law: Origins, Challenges & Prospects – Vol II* (2004); Kelly D. Askin, *War Crimes Against Women: Prosecution in International War Crimes Tribunals* (1997).

5   See especially East Timor Regulations promulgated by the United Nations Transitional Administration in East Timor (UNTAET), Reg. 2000/11 *On the Organization of Courts in East Timor*, 6 March 2000 (Section 10, Exclusive Jurisdiction for Serious Crimes); UNTAET/REG/2000/14, *Amending Regulation No. 2000/11*, 10 May 2000; UNTAET/REG/2000/15, *On the Establishment of Panels with Exclusive Jurisdiction Over Serious Criminal Offences*, 6 June 2000.

6   *Statute of the Special Court for Sierra Leone*, 16 January 2002, established by *Report of the Secretary-General on the Establishment of the Special Court for Sierra Leone* (the Statute is contained in the report's Annex – an *Agreement between the United Nations and the Government of Sierra Leone pursuant to Security Council resolution 1315 (2000)* of 14 August 2000), UN Doc. S/2000/915 (2000), UN website, <http://ods-dds-ny.un.org/doc/UNDOC/GEN/N00/661/77/PDF/N0066177.pdf?OpenElement>.

greatly expand the explicit enunciation of gender-related crimes from those identified in the ICTY and ICTR Statutes. The statutes of these more recent courts allow
many of the crimes to be prosecuted as a named crime and not under an obscure or
less appropriate term (such as outrages upon personal dignity, cruel treatment or inhumane acts). The broader and more vague terms should, in general, be reserved for times
when the act does not fall within a specifically enumerated crime or the elements do
not satisfy the more universally recognised crimes, such as rape and torture.

According to Articles 7 and 8 of the ICC Statute and Sections 5 and 6 of
UNTAET Regulation 2000/15, the courts are entitled to prosecute the war crimes and
crimes against humanity of rape, sexual slavery, enforced prostitution, forced pregnancy, enforced sterilisation or any other form of sexual violence of comparable gravity. Article 2 of the Special Court for Sierra Leone authorises prosecution of crimes
against humanity for essentially the same crimes – although 'enforced sterilisation'
is not expressly listed, the Statute does specify that 'any other form of sexual violence' can also be prosecuted. Of these crimes, only 'rape' is explicitly included within
the jurisdiction of the Yugoslav and Rwanda Tribunals as crimes against humanity.
'Rape' and 'enforced prostitution' are also included as war crimes within the terms of
the Rwanda and Sierra Leone Statutes. Although there is no jurisprudence in the
ICTY or ICTR redressing crimes explicitly prosecuted as sexual slavery, forced pregnancy and enforced sterilisation, suggestions on how these crimes might be prosecuted are included in the discussion below. In addition, the ICC Statute, UNTAET
Regulations and the SCSL Statute also grant the courts' authority over other crimes
which have been used to prosecute sex crimes, including torture, enslavement and
persecution. While the Statute of the proposed Extraordinary Chambers for prosecuting Khmer Rouge leaders in Cambodia initially regressed by explicitly including only rape as a crime against humanity, the superseding Agreement between the
Cambodian Government and the United Nations authorises prosecution of the same
crimes against humanity as are listed in the ICC Statute.[7]

The ICC, the Serious Crimes Panels in East Timor and the Extraordinary
Chambers of the Khmer Rouge Tribunal in Cambodia also have jurisdiction to hear
cases involving 'other forms of sexual violence of comparable gravity.' Article 2 of the
Statute for Sierra Leone simply authorises prosecution of 'any other form of sexual
violence' without specifying that the other sex crimes must entail comparable gravity.
The crimes of sexual mutilation, forced marriage and forced abortion were cited in the

---

7   *Law on the Establishment of Extraordinary Chambers in the Courts of Cambodia for the
     Prosecution of Crimes Committed During the Period of Democratic Kampuchea*, 10 August 2001,
     NS/RKM/0801/12, Article 5, crimes against humanity. The Law/Statute is supplemented
     and superseded by the *Agreement between the United Nations and the Royal Government of
     Cambodia Concerning the Prosecution Under Cambodian Law of Crimes Committed During
     the Period of Democratic Kampuchea*, 6 June 2003, article 9. Gender crimes committed
     during the Khmer Rouge regime were scarcely documented, so prior to extensive investi-
     gation and evidence-gathering, it is premature to assume that other forms of sexual vio-
     lence, particularly forced marriage, were not committed.

Kvočka Trial Chamber Judgment as crimes entailing serious sexual violence and can also be explicitly prosecuted as named crimes in each of the above courts.[8]

By and large, sexual slavery and enforced prostitution cover largely the same acts and, especially taking into account the survivor's views, sexual slavery is the preferred and more appropriate term to use when attempting to redress such crimes.[9] The term 'enforced prostitution' was retained and included within the scope of the ICC Statute primarily because of its historical significance, namely its explicit inclusion in the 1919 War Crimes Commission Report and in the 1977 *Additional Protocols*. Particularly in light of the fact that victim-survivors find the term offensive, 'enforced prostitution' is given only cursory treatment in the discussion below. In most cases, when the elements of enforced prostitution are established, the crime should more appropriately be prosecuted as sexual slavery.

Certain crimes, such as persecution and torture, and some terms, including 'gender', have been defined in the ICC Statute or ICC Elements of Crimes, as well as in the UNTAET Regulations and Sierra Leone Statute. The ICC Elements are guidelines[10] and some of the elements of crimes negotiated by states are incompatible with contemporary norms.

Whenever possible in the prosecution of sex crimes – particularly when there are multiple viable options for prosecuting a particular crime – the victim-survivor should be informed of the alternatives and consulted as to which charge is preferable. The particular crime charged in the indictment may have significant consequences for the survivor. For many women, it may be easier to marry or continue in a relationship if the crime committed against them is legally classified as, for example, torture instead of rape. For others, it will be imperative that the sexual violation committed against them be publicly identified and legally classified as rape and that the perpetrator be convicted of a sex crime.

The specific crimes charged may have other impacts as well. For example, the *Kvočka* Trial Chamber has held that if a series of crimes such as murder, torture and rape are charged separately and also jointly as persecution for the same acts, persecution subsumes the other crimes. Thus, if this finding is upheld by the Appeals Chamber, in the ICTY a person could not be convicted of both rape and persecution as crimes against humanity for the same underlying acts. Under the cumulative conviction scheme of the Yugoslav and Rwanda Tribunals, however, one could be convicted of both rape and torture as crimes against humanity for the same underlying act. Furthermore, one could be convicted of persecution as a crime against humanity

---

8   *Kvočka* Trial Chamber Judgment, above n 2 [180] fn 343.

9   See for example, Women's International War Crimes Tribunal '"Comfort Women" Judgment: Transcript of Oral Judgment Delivered on 4 December 2001' Women's Caucus for Gender Justice website <http://www.iccwomen.org/archive/tokyo/summary.htm> [604] and [634] ('"Comfort Women" judgment') (noting the 'vehement objection of many survivors to classifying the crimes committed against them as forced prostitution' and emphasising that '[n]otwithstanding that forced prostitution involves essentially the same conduct as sexual slavery, it does not communicate the same level of egregiousness.')

10   *ICC Statute*, above n 3, Article 9(1) stating that the Elements of Crimes 'shall assist the Court in the interpretation and application' of the justiciable crimes.

and rape as a war crime.[11] Clearly, charging an accused with additional and alternative crimes may be crucial prosecutorial strategies.

One of the benefits of the ICC Statute, UNTAET Regulations, Khmer Rouge Tribunal law and Sierra Leone Special Court Statute's explicit enunciation of a number of gender-related crimes is that it allows more terminological accuracy as to which precise crime has been committed than that available in the ICTY/R charges. Accuracy is particularly important for reasons of legal clarity, deterrence and the stigma that may be associated with a crime. Nonetheless, there may be significant overlap in many of the crimes. There are also a number of crimes, such as forced nudity, forced marriage or sexual humiliation, which can be prosecuted under the broader proscriptions that capture crimes not explicitly enumerated elsewhere in the Statutes or Regulations. This will be particularly useful when prosecution under 'other forms of sexual violence' is not available in the authorising Statute.

A   Rape

Rape can be prosecuted under the ICTY, ICTR, ICC, Sierra Leone and Cambodia Statutes and UNTAET Regulations in a number of ways. It can be prosecuted explicitly as a crime against humanity. The *actus reus* of rape can also be prosecuted as a crime against humanity under the enslavement, torture, persecution and inhumane act provisions. If genocide was deemed present during the time and place of the crimes charged and committed with the requisite intent by the accused, rape can also be prosecuted under the genocide provision (especially sub-articles (b) and (d) (causing serious bodily or mental harm and imposing measures intended to prevent births within a group)). During the course of an armed conflict, the Statutes and Regulations provide means for prosecuting rape in both international and non-international armed conflicts, although the nature of the conflict would have to be established. Depending upon the situation, the *actus reus* of rape can also be prosecuted as a war crime under some of the more vague proscriptions, such as 'willfully causing great suffering', 'outrages upon personal dignity', 'violence to life and person', 'cruel treatment', or the torture and inhuman treatment provisions.

The definition of rape articulated in *Akayesu* entails 'a physical invasion of a sexual nature, committed on a person under circumstances which are coercive'.[12] The elements, most recently refined in *Kunarac*, which built upon and expanded the *Furundžija* elements, were also endorsed by the *Kvočka* Trial Chamber. The elements of rape most recently advanced and supported, could be considered to consist of the following elements:[13]

11   *Kvočka* Trial Chamber Judgment, above n 2 [233]-[234]. For the cumulative convictions scheme of the ICTY, see especially the extensive discussion in *Prosecutor v. Delalic* (Appeals Judgment), Case No. IT-96-21-A, 20 February 2001, <http://www.un.org/icty/celebici/appeal/judgement/cel-aj010220.pdf> ('*Čelebići* Appeals Chamber Judgment').

12   *Akayesu* Trial Chamber Judgment, above n 2 [688].

13   *Kunarac* Trial Chamber Judgment, above n 2 [460], [495].

A. the sexual penetration, however slight:
    (i) of the vagina or anus of the victim by the penis of the perpetrator or any other object used by the perpetrator; or
    (ii) of the mouth of the victim by the penis of the perpetrator;
B. the sexual activity must:
    (i) be accompanied by force or threat of force to the victim or a third party; or
    (ii) be accompanied by force *or* a variety of other specified circumstances which made the victim particularly vulnerable or negated her ability to make an informed refusal; or
    (iii) occur without the consent of the victim.

The elements of rape contained in the ICC and UNTAET documents[14] provide somewhat similar requirements, which also import the protections afforded in ICTY/ R Rule 96:
A. The perpetrator invaded the body of a person by conduct resulting in penetration, however slight, of any part of the body of the victim or of the perpetrator with a sexual organ, or of the anal or genital opening of the victim with any object or any other part of the body.
B. The invasion was committed by force, or by threat of force or coercion, such as that caused by fear of violence, duress, detention, psychological oppression or abuse of power, against such person or another person, or by taking advantage of a coercive environment, or the invasion was committed against a person incapable of giving genuine consent.[15]

In interpreting the elements ultimately determined to apply during periods of mass violence, the *Čelebići* Trial Chamber found that coercive conditions are inherent in situations of armed conflict.[16] The *Furundžija* Trial Chamber stressed that 'any form of captivity vitiates consent'.[17] The *Akayesu* Trial Chamber noted that '[t]hreats, intimidation, extortion and other forms of duress which prey on fear or desperation may constitute coercion, and coercion may be inherent in certain circumstances, such as armed conflict or the military presence' of combatants among the refugees.[18] The Judges have therefore implicitly recognised that situations of armed conflict or mass

---

14   *ICC Elements of Crimes*, UN Doc PCNICC/2000/1/Add.2 (2000); UNTAET Regulation 2001/25, above n 5, Section 34.
15   *ICC Elements of Crimes*, above n 14, Article 7 (provisions pertaining to crimes against humanity elements not included above). Two footnotes to these elements explain that the 'concept of "invasion" is intended to be broad enough to be gender-neutral;.and '[i]t is understood that a person may be incapable of giving genuine consent if affected by natural, induced or age-related incapacity'. The *ICC Elements* import into the elements most of the language used in ICTY/R Rule 96 and UNTAET Reg. 2001/25, amending Reg. 2000/30 at Section 34.3, evidence in cases of sexual assault. Note that SL Rule 96 is quite different than ICTY/R Rule 96.
16   *Čelebići* Trial Chamber Judgment, above n 2 [495].
17   *Furundžija* Trial Chamber Judgment, above n 2 [271].
18   *Akayesu* Trial Chamber Judgment, above n 2 [688].

violence create conditions that make women especially vulnerable to sexual violence. Wartime conditions, such as the breakdown of law and order, an atmosphere of impunity and violence and situations in which unprotected women are held singly or collectively in detention by opposing armed forces, should be taken into account. There is also an implicit awareness that evidence which may be available in the case of domestic rape, such as sperm, fingerprints or bruises are rarely available after sustained periods of lawlessness.

The *Kvočka* Trial Chamber noted that rape is not only prohibited by Common Article 3 to the Geneva Conventions, it is also 'a crime explicitly protected against by Article 27 of the *Fourth Geneva Convention*, Article 76(1) of *Additional Protocol I*, and Article 4(2)(e) of *Additional Protocol II*. Rape is a war crime under these provisions as well, and not solely under Common Article 3 of the Conventions'.[19] *Furundžija* also recalled that rape can constitute a war crime or crime against humanity, be used as an instrument of genocide or be a means of torture.[20] Thus, there is explicit recognition that rape is an international crime of multiple dimensions.

The *Čelebići*, *Furundžija* and *Kunarac* Judgments convicted the accused of torture committed by means of rape. The *Akayesu* Judgment concluded that rape was committed as an instrument of the genocide in Rwanda. The *Akayesu* and *Kunarac* Judgments found that in Rwanda and the Balkans, rape was committed as part of a widespread and systematic attack against civilian populations, constituting a crime against humanity. The *Kvočka* and *Krstić* Judgments found that when rape is committed with a persecutory intent against a protected group, it may be classified as persecution.

It is important to note that while the Yugoslav and Rwanda Tribunals protect against persecution on political, racial and religious grounds, the ICC Statute extends these grounds. It authorises prosecution of '[p]ersecution against any identifiable group or collectivity on political, racial, national, ethnic, cultural, religious, gender ... or other grounds that are universally recognised as impermissible under international law, in connection with any act referred to in this paragraph or any crime within the jurisdiction of the Court.'[21] Gender is defined in the ICC Statute as 'the two sexes, male and female, within the context of society'.[22] While not wholly satisfactory or elucidating, the mere fact that 'gender' was included in the Statute represents a progressive development of the law.[23]

There are a number of considerations that should be taken into account before prosecuting rape under other applicable provisions, such as torture or persecution. The most obvious implication is that prosecuting the crime under other provisions typically obscures the sexual nature of the crime. This has both positive and negative

---

19   *Kvočka* Trial Chamber Judgment, above n 2 [234] fn. 409.

20   *Furundžija* Trial Chamber Judgment, above n 2 [172].

21   *ICC Statute*, above n 3, Article 7(1)(h).

22   *Ibid.*, Article 7(3).

23   For more discussion on this issue, see Cate Steins, 'Gender Issues' in Roy S. Lee (ed) *The International Criminal Court: The Making of the Rome Statute, Negotiations, Results* (1991) 357–390.

aspects. A survivor may prefer the sexual nature of the crime not be advertised, but the potential deterrent effects of convicting for torture versus rape may not be as strong if the language does not indicate that the crime punished was rape, especially given the historical neglect and impunity afforded to rape crimes.

B   Enslavement and Sexual Slavery

Enslavement and rape, but not sexual slavery, are expressly listed as crimes against humanity in the Yugoslav and Rwanda Statutes. Rape committed during the course of enslavement has been successfully prosecuted as a crime against humanity in the Yugoslav Tribunal for conduct essentially constituting sexual slavery. Sexual slavery is an explicitly listed crime within the ICC, Sierra Leone and Cambodia Statutes and the UNTAET Regulations.

There may be select instances when a prosecutor would prefer to charge enslavement and rape instead of sexual slavery. Thus, these crimes, while having clear overlap, will be treated together here.

The ICC Statute follows and elucidates the definition of slavery in the Slavery Convention by defining enslavement as 'the exercise of any or all of the powers attaching to the right of ownership over a person and includes the exercise of such power in the course of trafficking in persons, in particular women and children'.[24]

In the ICTY *Kunarac* trial, the Chamber also followed the Slavery Convention and held that enslavement consists of the exercise of any or all the powers attaching to the right of ownership over a person.[25] The *actus reus* is the exercise of any or all of the powers attaching to the right of ownership over a person. The *mens rea* consists of intentionally exercising such powers.[26]

The *Kunarac* Trial Chamber found that indicia of enslavement include 'elements of control and ownership; the restriction or control of an individual's autonomy, freedom of choice or freedom of movement; and, often, the accruing of some gain to the perpetrator. The consent or free will of the victim is absent ... . Further indications of enslavement include exploitation; the exaction of forced or compulsory labour or service, often without remuneration and often, though not necessarily, involving physical hardship; sex; prostitution; and human trafficking'.[27] It stressed that consent or free will was 'often rendered impossible or irrelevant by, for example, the threat or use of force or other forms of coercion; the fear of violence, deception or false promises; the abuse of power; the victim's position of vulnerability; detention or captivity, psychological oppression or socio-economic conditions'.[28]

---

24   *ICC Statute*, above n 3, Article 7(2)(c). UNTAET Regulation 2000/15, above n 5, Section 5.2(c) defines it identically.

25   *Kunarac* Trial Chamber Judgment, above n 2 [539].

26   *Ibid.*, [540].

27   *Ibid.*, [542].

28   *Ibid.*

Yet indicia are not requirements – rather they are indicators which help determine the existence of enslavement. Thus, such indicia could be applicable to determining the presence of sexual slavery if indicia of enslavement are combined with activity of a sexual nature.

The ICC Elements of sexual slavery are comprised of the following:

1. The perpetrator exercised any or all of the powers attaching to the right of ownership over one or more persons, such as by purchasing, selling, lending or bartering such a person or persons, or by imposing on them a similar deprivation of liberty.
2. The perpetrator caused such person or persons to engage in one or more acts of a sexual nature.[29]

The 'Comfort Women' Judgment forcefully rejected the element of sexual slavery put forth in paragraph 1 of the ICC Elements. Instead it agreed with the elements recommended by the UN Special Rapporteur on rape, sexual slavery and slavery-like practices during armed conflict and those adopted by the *Kunarac* Trial Chamber. The 'Comfort Women' Judgment states that it views the ICC Elements as 'inconsistent with a proper recognition of the breadth of factors that constitute enslavement and the relationship of sexual slavery thereto as a matter of customary international law'. It also suggests that the ICC Elements Annex reflect an unreasonably narrow construction that seemingly limits the crime to 'situations involving commercial exchange' and thus the elements 'do not adequately reflect the crime under international law'.[30]

The *Kunarac* Trial Chamber explicitly recognised that commercial activity is not a requirement, although it is an example of treating someone as disposable property: 'The 'acquisition' or 'disposal' of someone for monetary or other compensation, is not a requirement for enslavement. Doing so, however, is a prime example of the exercise of the right of ownership over someone.'[31]

Duration is an indicia but not a required element of slavery. The *Kunarac* Trial Chamber recognised that 'its importance in any given case will depend on the existence of other indications of enslavement'.[32] Duration may help in determining when multiple instances of rape become sexual slavery. Evidence of ownership is demonstrated through such acts as possessing, using, loaning, trading or selling of women. Although every single rape can be considered as the perpetrator demonstrating an exercise of ownership over the victim's body, as a practical and legal matter it is not useful to classify every rape as an exercise of ownership and thus as sexual slavery. If a woman is abducted and subjected to sexual violence, it would likely constitute sexual

---

29   *ICC Elements of Crimes*, above n 14 [7] (crime against humanity elements not included here). The footnote to this text states: '[i]t is understood that such deprivation of liberty may, in some circumstances, include exacting forced labour or otherwise reducing a person to a servile status as defined in the Supplementary Convention on the Abolition of Slavery, the Slave Trade, and Institutions and Practices Similar to Slavery of 1956. It is also understood that the conduct described in this element includes trafficking in persons, in particular women and children'.

30   'Comfort Women' Judgment, above n 9 [628]-[629].

31   *Kunarac* Trial Chamber Judgment, above n 2 [542].

32   *Ibid.*

slavery. However in some such instances, a woman may be raped multiple times and it would more accurately be characterised as multiple rapes, not sexual slavery. In other instances, even without abduction or confinement, multiple rapes may be more accurately classified as sexual slavery.

Controlling a person's activities, or using someone while being able to prevent others from using them too, or being able to loan your possession to others are typical exercises of ownership over another. If a woman is knowingly held in detention and continually raped, it may be that the persons responsible for holding her in captivity for sexual access are guilty of sexual slavery. Yet the individuals who violate her sexually are likely to be guilty of rape, not sexual slavery, if they knowingly take advantage of the situation. Thus, for example, if they would be punished if they released or killed the victim, they are likely not the ones exercising the ownership powers. Another example can be found in the situation of the former 'comfort women'. In this instance, it would be the Japanese military and government authorities who established and facilitated the 'comfort system' and others who maintained the 'comfort stations' who would be guilty of sexual slavery. The common soldiers who visited the facilities would be guilty of rape if they knew that the women were not there voluntarily, but, arguably, they would probably not be guilty of sexual slavery in most instances.

Mistreatment is not an element of the crime of enslavement (and hence sexual slavery), although it is almost always present. Yet, as the *Pohl* case emphasised in the post World War II trial:

> Slaves may be well fed, well clothed, and comfortably housed, but they are still slaves if without lawful process they are deprived of their freedom by forceful restraint. We might eliminate all proof of ill-treatment, overlook the starvation, beatings, and other barbarous acts, but the admitted fact of slavery ... would still remain. There is no such thing as benevolent slavery. Involuntary servitude, even if tempered by humane treatment, is still slavery.[33]

Exercise of ownership over a person can occur even under relatively humane conditions, as the test is exercising rights of ownership, not mistreatment. Indeed, it is often beneficial to treat one's property well if one intends to continue use of or benefit from their possession. The 'comfort women' held for sexual servitude to Japanese officers were sometimes treated better than the women held for usage by the common soldier, in that they may have been given more food, more comfortable living quarters, makeup or clean clothes. Yet they were still sex slaves.

Supporting the holdings in the *Kunarac* Judgment, the 'Comfort Women' Judgment of the Peoples' Tribunal gave its findings of the essential elements of sexual slavery as:

---

33   *US v. Oswald Pohl and Others*, Trials of War Criminals Before the Nuremberg Military Tribunals under Control Council Law No. 10 – Vol V (1949) [958], [970], <http://www. yale.edu/lawweb/avalon/imt/pohl/pohl.htm>. The Nuremberg Judgment also convicted Speer in connection with the Nazi slave labour program, despite his insistence 'the slave labourers be given adequate food and working conditions so that they could work efficiently'. IMT Judgment, <http://www.yale.edu/lawweb/avalon/imt/imt.htm> [579].

'[T]he *actus reus* of the crime of sexual slavery is the exercise of any or all of the powers attaching to the right of ownership over a person by exercising sexual control over a person or depriving a person of sexual autonomy. Thus, we consider that control over a person's sexuality or sexual autonomy may in and of itself constitute a power attaching to the right of ownership. The *mens rea* is the intentional exercise of such powers. [34]

The UN Special Rapporteur on rape, sexual slavery and slavery-like practices during armed conflict defined sexual slavery as 'the status or condition of a person over whom any or all of the powers attaching to the right of ownership are exercised, including sexual access through rape or other forms of sexual violence'. She explains that '(s)lavery, when combined with sexual violence, constitutes sexual slavery'.[35] The Special Rapporteur noted that '(w)hile the most commonly recognised form of slavery involves the coerced performance of physical labour or service of some, again, this is merely a factor to be considered in determining whether a 'status or condition' exists which transforms an act, such as rape, into sexual slavery. It is the status or condition of being enslaved which differentiates sexual slavery from other crimes of sexual violence, including rape'.[36]

The 'Comfort Women' Judgment asserted that sexual access does not need to be the primary reason for the enslavement: 'We find that the control of a person's sexuality itself indicates a power attaching to the right of ownership, which is the defining aspect of the *actus reus* of the crime of sexual slavery. This is so regardless of whether the sexual coercion occurs as incidental to or alongside other conditions that independently constitute enslavement'.[37]

In instances where enslavement exists, but the victim is 'only' raped once or comparatively rarely, sexual slavery could still be charged under the ICC Element's formulation of sexual slavery (which refer to perpetrating 'one or more acts of a sexual nature'). However, in most such circumstance, it may nonetheless be more appropriate to charge the crimes as enslavement and rape and to reserve the sexual slavery charge for instances when the sexual aspect of the enslavement plays a more dominate role – when the sexual access is 'a' (not necessarily 'the') motivating factor behind the enslavement or when any form of sexual violence has a significant presence during the enslavement. An opportunistic or isolated instance of rape during enslavement would not necessarily turn the enslavement into sexual slavery.

Although the threat and fear of rape usually remains constant during many periods of enslavement, it is necessary to make distinctions between crimes and to charge and convict an accused of the crime that most accurately (legally and factually) reflects the crimes that were committed. If held in enslavement for three months and raped once during this period, most victims would not classify the crime committed against

---

34   'Comfort Women' Judgment, above n 9 [618].

35   *Contemporary Forms of Slavery: Systematic Rape, Sexual Slavery and Slavery-like Practices During Armed Conflict: Update to the Final Report Submitted by Ms. Gay J. McDougall*, 52 UN ESCOR, Doc. E/CN.4/Sub.2/2000/21 (2000) [47].

36   *Ibid.*, [50].

37   'Comfort Women' Judgment, above n 9 [631].

them as sexual slavery, unless the threat of rape was a real and significant presence during the enslavement. Consequently, rape and enslavement would likely be the most appropriate charges. As to how many times during a three-month period a person would need to be raped or subjected to other forms of sexual violence before the acts should be classified as sexual slavery would depend on the facts of each case, how the sexual aspect of the enslavement ensued and the perceptions of the victims.

Similarly, a woman could be held for a relatively short period of time, such as a few days, and repeatedly raped. Those acts clearly constitute multiple rapes, and they might also constitute sexual slavery, depending on the circumstances. Intent, treatment, exclusivity, duration, exercise of ownership and other factors should be considered in determining the most appropriate charges. In sexual slavery, the adjective 'sexual' should be indicative of a form or nature of the slavery, although not necessarily the exclusive or dominant form or nature. It is also important to emphasise that the presence of domestic labour should in no way detract from the sexual aspect of enslavement if both domestic and sexual services are demanded. Here, again, it might be useful to solicit input from the survivors as to which charges are most appropriate.

C   Torture

In the ICTR *Akayesu* case and the ICTY *Furundžija* case, Trial Chambers reproduced the definition of torture found in the *Torture Convention* and defined the essential elements as follows:

(i)   The perpetrator must intentionally inflict severe physical or mental pain or suffering upon the victim for one or more of the following purposes:
   (a)   to obtain information or a confession from the victim or a third person;
   (b)   to punish the victim or a third person for an act committed or suspected of having been committed by either of them;
   (c)   for the purpose of intimidating or coercing the victim or the third person;
   (d)   for any reason based on discrimination of any kind.
(ii)   The perpetrator was himself an official, or acted at the instigation of, or with the consent or acquiescence of, an official or person acting in an official capacity.[38]

To constitute a crime against humanity, the torture would of course need to be committed as part of a widespread or systematic attack directed against any civilian population. The Appeals Chamber for the ICTY affirmed the definition of torture put forth by the *Furundžija* Trial Chamber, thus retaining the state action requirement.[39]

Finding the above definition too restrictive in the context of international crimes, however, the *Kunarac* Trial Chamber concluded that the definition provided for in the *Torture Convention* is meant to be applied only in the context of the *Convention* and is intended to be directed against state obligations, not individuals. The Trial Chamber suggested that the victim should be entitled to benefit from other interna-

---

38   *Akayesu* Trial Chamber Judgment, above n 2 [594].
39   *Furundžija* Appeals Chamber Judgment, above n 2 [111].

tional instruments that might afford a broader protection.[40] It found that the definition of torture under international human rights law and international humanitarian law differed and state action was not required in international humanitarian law. More specifically, 'the presence of a state official or of any other authority-wielding person in the torture process is not necessary for the offence to be regarded as torture under international humanitarian law.'[41] The UNTAET Regulations similarly do not impose a state actor requirement.[42] The *Kvočka* Trial Chamber also agreed with the *Kunarac* Trial Chamber's analysis and found that 'the state actor requirement imposed by international human rights law is inconsistent with the application of individual criminal responsibility for international crimes found in international humanitarian law and international criminal law.'[43] International human rights law primarily regulates states whereas international criminal law and international humanitarian law focuses more on individual responsibility and accountability.

The *Kunarac* Trial Chamber held that the elements of torture under the customary international laws of war entail:

(i)   The infliction, by act or omission, of severe pain or suffering, whether physical or mental.

(ii)   The act or omission must be intentional.

(iii) The act or omission must aim at obtaining information or a confession, or at punishing, intimidating or coercing the victim or a third person, or at discriminating, on any ground, against the victim or a third person.[44]

Both objective and subjective criteria are relevant in assessing the requisite gravity of harm necessary to constitute 'severe' pain and suffering.[45] It has been widely recognised that sexual violence causes severe pain and suffering to be inflicted upon the victim. The *Furundžija* Trial Chamber found that being forced to witness rape also inflicted severe pain and suffering[46] and the *Kvočka* Trial Chamber opined that having one's rape watched would also result in severe pain and suffering.[47] The *Kvočka* Trial

---

40   *Kunarac* Trial Chamber Judgment, above n 2 [473] and [482].

41   *Ibid.*, [496].

42   UNTAET Regulation 2000/15, above n 5, defining torture in Section 5 as a crime against humanity as 'the intentional infliction of severe pain or suffering, whether physical or mental, upon a person in the custody or under the control of the accused; ...' at Section 5.2(d), and defining torture in Section 7, as an 'ordinary crime', as 'any act by which severe pain or suffering, whether physical or mental, is intentionally inflicted on a person for such purposes as obtaining from him/her or a third person information or a confession, punishing him/her for an act he/she or a third person committed or is suspected of having committed, or humiliating, intimidating or coercing him/her or a third person, or for any reason based on discrimination of any kind... .'.

43   *Kvočka* Trial Chamber Judgment, above n 2 [139].

44   *Kunarac* Trial Chamber Judgment, above n 2 [497].

45   See *Kvočka* Trial Chamber Judgment, above n 2 [143]. See also discussion in *Čelebići* Trial Chamber Judgment, above n 2 [461]-[469].

46   *Furundžija* Trial Chamber Judgment, above n 2 [267].

47   *Kvočka* Trial Chamber Judgment, above n 2 [149].

Chamber also found that the sheer threat or fear of rape and other forms of sexual violence may inflict severe pain and suffering on vulnerable detainees in a concentration camp, constituting torture.[48]

As to the purposive requirements, the Yugoslav Tribunal has recognised that the list provided in the *Torture Convention* – namely obtaining information or a confession, to punish, intimidate, coerce or discriminate against a victim or other person – was not intended to be exhaustive but merely representative.[49] The *Furundžija* Trial Chamber added 'humiliation' to the list of expressly prohibited purposes.[50]

The *Čelebići* Trial Chamber stressed that the prohibited purpose did not need to be the sole or primary purpose of inflicting the pain or suffering.[51] The *Kunarac* Trial Chamber reached the same conclusion, noting: 'There is no requirement under customary international law that the conduct must be *solely* perpetrated for one of the prohibited purposes of torture, such as discrimination. The prohibited purpose need only be part of the motivation behind the conduct and need not be the predominant or sole purpose'.[52]

While there is some inconsistent treatment in the case law in identifying the elements of torture, the Appeals Chamber is generally remedying the discrepancies. Unless required for the particular crime by the authorising statute, the trend is to not impose a state action requirement in international criminal law and international humanitarian law.

The *Čelebići, Furundžija, Kunarac* and *Kvočka* Judgments have held that when a person is raped with an intent to inflict severe pain or suffering on the victim for a prohibited purpose – such as for punishment, intimidation, coercion, discrimination, humiliation or to secure information – the crime may be prosecuted as torture. The *Akayesu* Judgment also recognised rape as a form of torture.

Other international and regional bodies or commissions, such as the Inter-American Commission on Human Rights, the European Court of Human Rights and the UN Special Rapporteur on Torture have also recognised that rape may constitute torture.[53]

D   Persecution

In addition to the prerequisite elements applicable to establishing that a crime against humanity has been committed, the ICTY *Tadić* Trial Chamber articulated three basic

---

48   *Ibid.*, [139].

49   *Čelebići* Trial Chamber Judgment, above n 2 [470].

50   *Furundžija* Trial Chamber Judgment, above n 2 [162].

51   *Čelebići* Trial Chamber Judgment, above n 2 [470].

52   *Kunarac* Trial Chamber Judgment, above n 2 [816].

53   See for example, *Fernando Mejia Egocheaga and Raquel Martin de Mejia v. Peru*, Case 10.970, Inter-American Commission on Human Rights 157, OEA/Ser. L/V/II.91, doc. 7 rev. (1996); *Aydin v. Turkey*, European Court of Human Rights, 1997-VI Eur. Ct. Human Rights 1866, 25 EHRR 251 (1997); *Report by the Special Rapporteur on Torture*, 44 UN ESCOR, UN Doc E/CN.4/1992/SR.21 (1992) [35].

requirements for the crime of persecution: 1) a discriminatory act or omission; 2) the act or omission founded on the basis of race, religion or politics, as imposed by the ICTY Statute; and 3) the intent to infringe an individual's enjoyment of a basic or fundamental right.[54]

The ICTY *Kupreškić* Trial Chamber defined persecution as 'the gross or blatant denial, on discriminatory grounds, of a fundamental right, laid down in customary or treaty law, reaching the same level of gravity as the other acts prohibited' in the crimes against humanity proscriptions.[55] This definition is consistent with the treatment of crimes against humanity in post-World War II trials. For example, in the *Einsatzgruppen* trial conducted by the Allied victors under the auspices of Control Council Law No. 10, as a supplement the Nuremberg Trial, the judgment stated:

> The Einsatzkommandos committed a crime which, from a moral point of view, was perhaps even worse than their own directly committed murders, that is, their inciting of the population to abuse, maltreat, and slay their fellow citizens. To invade a foreign country, seize innocent inhabitants, and shoot them is a crime.... But to stir up passion, hate, violence, and destruction among the people themselves, aims at breaking the moral backbone, even of those the invader chooses to spare. It sows seeds of crime which the invader intends to bear continuous fruit, even after he is driven out.[56]

Thus, persecution may encompass acts not specifically enumerated within the terms of the Statute, including acts that separately may not even constitute criminal activity. The *Tadić* Trial Chamber made clear that in 'addition to the acts enumerated elsewhere in the Statute, persecution may also encompass other acts if they 'seek to subject individuals or groups of individuals to a kind of life in which enjoyment of some of their basic rights is repeatedly or constantly denied".[57] To reinforce the point that acts do not have to be specifically enumerated, the Trial Chamber gave an example of the severity of acts covered, ranging 'from killing to a limitation on the type of professions open to the targeted group'.[58] The *Tadić* Trial Chamber explained that persecu-

---

54   *Prosecutor v. Tadić* (Judgment), Case No. IT-94-1-T, 7 May 1997 <http://www.un.org/icty/tadic/trialc2/judgement/tad-tsj70507JT2-e.pdf> ('*Tadić* Trial Chamber Judgment') [715]. The *Kupreškić* Trial Chamber enunciated the elements of persecution somewhat differently, although substantively imposing essentially the same requirements, as:
    (a) those elements required for all crimes against humanity under the Statute;
    (b) a gross or blatant denial of a fundamental right reaching the same level of gravity as the other acts prohibited under [the crimes against humanity provision of the Statute];
    (c) discriminatory grounds.
    Prosecutor v. Kupreškić (Judgment), Case No. IT-95-16-T, 14 January 2000 <http://www.un.org/kupreskic/trialc2/judgement/kup-tj000114e.pdf> ('*Kupreškić* Trial Chamber judgment') [627].

55   *Kupreškić* Trial Chamber judgment [621].

56   *US v. Otto Ohlendorf et al., Trials of War Criminals Before the Nuremberg Military Tribunals Under Control Council Law No. 10 – Vol. IV* (1950) 435.

57   *Tadić* Trial Chamber Judgment, above n 54 [703] (quoting ILC 1991 Report [236]).

58   *Ibid.,* [704].

tion 'encompasses a variety of acts, including, *inter alia*, those of a physical, economic or judicial nature, that violate an individual's right to the equal enjoyment of his basic rights'.[59]

In the ICC Statute and UNTAET Regulations, persecution is defined as 'the intentional and severe deprivation of fundamental rights contrary to international law by reason of the identity of the group or collectivity'.[60] These authorities grant jurisdiction for '[p]ersecution against any identifiable group or collectivity on political, racial, national, ethnic, cultural, religious, gender ... or other grounds that are universally recognised as impermissible under international law, in conjunction with any act referred to in this paragraph or any crime within the jurisdiction of the panels'.[61] The term 'gender' is stipulated to 'refer to the two sexes, male and female, within the context of society'.[62] While it is significant that 'gender' is expressly listed as a prosecutable form of persecution, it is unfortunate that persecution must be committed in conjunction with another crime or discriminatory act in order to be justiciable.

The ICTY *Kupreškić* Trial Chamber, in considering the ICC's requirement that persecution be linked to other crimes within the ICC Statute, determined that such a requirement is 'not consonant with customary international law' and explicitly stated that it 'rejects the notion that persecution must be linked to crimes found elsewhere in the [ICTY] Statute'.[63] As a practical matter, persecution tends to be committed through a series of human rights violations or international crimes, including sexual violence and other forms of gender-related persecution.

The ICTY *Krstić* and *Kvočka* Trial Chambers have found that rape and other forms of sexual violence may be committed with persecutorial intent.[64] Indeed, in *Krstić*, even though the rape crimes were not necessarily systematic (as they were found to be incidental to crimes intentionally planned through the joint criminal enterprise), they were still found to be a foreseeable consequence to the persecution committed as part of the criminal enterprise, and thus liability for the rape crimes was

---

59   *Ibid.*, [710].

60   *ICC Statute*, above n 3, Article 7(2)(g); *UNTAET Reg. 2000/15*, above n 5, Section 5.2, crimes against humanity.

61   *ICC Statute*, above n 3, Article 7(1)(h); *UNTAET Reg. 2000/15*, above n 5, Section 5.1(h), crimes against humanity.

62   *UNTAET Reg. 2000/15*, above n 5, Section 5.3.

63   *Kupreškić* Trial Chamber Judgment, above n 54 [580]-[581]. The Tribunal found: '[t]o the extent that it is required that persecution be connected with war crimes or the crime of aggression, this requirement is especially striking in the light of the fact that the ICC Statute reflects customary international law in abolishing the nexus between crimes against humanity and armed conflict. Furthermore this restriction might easily be circumvented by charging persecution in connection with 'other inhumane acts of a similar character intentionally causing great suffering, or serious injury to body or to mental or physical health' under Article 7(1)(k)' [580]. However, it stressed that there must be 'clearly defined limits on the types of acts which qualify as persecution' [618] (emphasis in original deleted.)

64   *Prosecutor v. Radislav Krstić* (Judgment), Case No. IT-98-33-T, 2 August 2001 <http://www.un.org/icty/krstic/trialc1/judgement/krs-tj010802e.pdf> ('*Krstić* Trial Chamber Judgment') [617]-[618], *Kvočka* Trial Chamber Judgment, above n 2 [189]-[190].

attributable to the defendant, General Krstić.[65] Similarly, in *Kvočka*, participants in a joint criminal endeavour were held responsible for all foreseeable consequences of the endeavour, including rape crimes, regardless of whether the participants knew the crimes were being committed.[66]

The *Blaškić* Trial Chamber described the *mens rea* specific to persecution as justiciable in the ICTY:

> The underlying offence of persecution requires the existence of a *mens rea* from which it obtains its specificity. As set down in Article 5 of the Statute, it must be committed for specific reasons whether these be linked to political views, racial background or religious convictions. It is the specific intent to cause injury to a human being because he belongs to a particular community or group, rather than the means employed to achieve it, that bestows on it its individual nature and gravity and which justifies its being able to constitute criminal acts which might appear in themselves not to infringe directly upon the most elementary rights of a human being, for example, attacks on property. In other words, the perpetrator of the acts of persecution does not initially target the individual but rather membership in a specific ... [protected] group.[67]

The ICTY *Kordić* Trial Chamber stated that with the crime of persecution 'a particular intent is required, in addition to the *specific intent* (to commit the act and produce its consequences) and the *general intent* (objective knowledge of the context in which the accused acted). This intent – the discriminatory intent – is what sets the crime of persecution apart' from other crimes against humanity.[68]

The *Tadić* Trial Chamber explained that the discriminatory act could result from positive or negative criteria.[69] A person could be targeted because of their membership in a group or because they do not belong to a particular group. The *Kvočka* Trial Chamber emphasised that inaccurate assumptions about group membership does not preclude persecution: '[P]ersons suspected of being members of these groups are also covered as possible victims of discrimination .... Additionally, if a person was targeted for abuse because she was suspected of belonging to the Muslim group, the discrimination element is met even if the suspicion proves inaccurate.'[70]

In convicting the accused after applying negative criteria, the *Kvočka* Trial Chamber held:

---

65   *Krstić* Trial Chamber Judgment, above n 64 [617].

66   *Kvočka* Trial Chamber Judgment, above n 2 [327].

67   *Prosecutor v. Tihomir Blaškić*, (Judgment) Case No. IT-95-14-T, 3 March 2000 <http://www.un.org/icty/blaskic/trial1/judgement/bla-tj000303e.pdf> ('*Blaskić* Trial Chamber Judgment') [235].

68   *Prosecutor v. Dario Kordić et al*, (Judgment) Case No. IT-94-14/2-T, 26 February 2001 <http://www.un.org/icty/kordic/trial1/judgement/kor-tj010226e.pdf> ('*Kordić* Trial Chamber Judgment') [212] (emphasis in original).

69   *Tadić* Trial Chamber Judgment, above n 54 [652]; *Prosecutor v. Goran Jelisic*, (Judgment) Case No. IT-95-10-T, 14 December 1999 <http://www.un.org/icty/jelisic/trial1/judgement/jel-tj991214e.pdf> ('*Jelisic* Trial Chamber Judgment') [71].

70   *Kvočka* Trial Chamber Judgment, above n 2 [195].

While discriminatory grounds form the requisite criteria, not membership in a particular group, the discriminatory grounds in this case are founded upon exclusion from membership in a group, the Serb group. Based on the totality of the evidence, it is clear that murder, torture, rape, beatings and other forms of physical and mental violence were strategically and systematically committed against non-Serbs in Omarska.[71]

The discriminatory grounds, while not specifically articulated, can be based on gender discrimination. The *Kvočka* Trial Chamber found that 'intentionally directing attacks exclusively against non-Serbs detained in Omarska camp (or their sympathisers), on the basis of their being (or supporting) non-Serbs, constitutes discrimination within the meaning of persecution'.[72] Similarly, sexual attacks directed against persons on the basis of their gender or sex would constitute discriminatory persecution. Prosecuting gender-based persecution explicitly will be possible under the terms of the Sierra Leone Special Court Statute and the UNTAET Regulations, as they enumerate 'gender' as a prohibited form of persecution.

The *Kupreškić* Trial Chamber recognised that 'persecution may take diverse forms, and does not necessarily require a physical element'.[73] Indeed, as an example, the *Kvočka* Trial Chamber stated that '[i]n addition to the harassment, humiliation, and psychological trauma endured by the detainees as part of their daily life in the camp, psychological abuse was also inflicted upon them through having to see and hear torturous interrogations and random brutality perpetrated on fellow inmates', which satisfied the *actus reus* of persecution.[74] *Kupreškić* also concluded that under customary international law, victims can be not only civilians, but also military personnel.[75]

During periods of war, mass violence or oppression, many crimes are committed with a persecutory intent, including gender-based persecution. If women are targeted for sexual abuse on account of their sex or gender (most likely, they will also be targeted for other reasons as well, such as political views, activist proclivities or relationship to a targeted group), the crimes can be prosecuted as persecution on the basis of gender. Gender very often overlaps with ethnicity, religion, race and other factors (such as age, attractiveness, vulnerability and virginity) in causing women and girls to be selected or targeted for sexual violence and each bases for the persecution should be highlighted.

E   Forced Pregnancy

Forced pregnancy has not been explicitly prosecuted as an international crime. Its listing in the ICC Statute as justiciable as a crime against humanity and war crime represents the first time the crime was listed as such in an international instrument. It is also formally listed in the UNTAET Regulations and the Statute of the Special Court for Sierra Leone.

---

71   *Ibid.*, [197].
72   *Ibid.*, [196].
73   *Kupreškić* Trial Chamber Judgment, above n 54 [568].
74   *Kvočka* Trial Chamber Judgment, above n 2 [192].
75   *Kupreškić* Trial Chamber Judgment, above n 54 [568].

The ICC Statute and the UNTAET Regulations define forced pregnancy as 'the unlawful confinement of a woman forcibly made pregnant, with the intent of affecting the ethnic composition of any population or carrying out other grave violations of international law'.[76] The latter alternative of the definition/element – 'or carrying out other grave violations of international law' – will be crucial to the prosecution of forced pregnancy, as it will be relatively rare that a woman is forcibly made pregnant with the intent to affect the ethnic composition of a population. Such an intent would primarily be found in societies where the ethnicity of the father determines the ethnicity of the child. Indeed, in the Yugoslav conflict, there have been reports that some Bosnian Muslim and Bosnian Croat women and girls were systematically raped by Bosnian Serbs with the intent that the victims would become pregnant; they were then detained until past the point of abortion, so that the women would bear the child of the ethnicity of the rapist.[77]

If a woman was raped with the intent to discriminate against her, to persecute her, to torture her or to commit any other grave violation of international law, and she became pregnant as a result of the rape, the pregnancy could probably be prosecuted successfully as forced pregnancy. The victimiser merely needs to intend to engage in the conduct, the sexual activity, not intend the pregnancy. Further, one of the natural and foreseeable consequences of sex is pregnancy. Pregnancy is a clearly foreseeable result of sex and hence rape. This is especially true with the rape of a woman of child-bearing age without the use of a contraceptive. Multiple or gang rapes would multiply the likelihood of pregnancy. There is no requirement that the woman reject the pregnancy (that is, wish to abort the fetus or put the child born of the rape up for adoption). The element is satisfied if rape (or perhaps some medical procedure to impregnate) is intended and pregnancy results. Thus, even if the pregnancy results in abortion, the crime is still committed. Even if the woman bears, keeps and loves the child borne of the rape, she was still the victim of forced pregnancy.

If a perpetrator used contraception, an assertion would likely be made that the perpetrator did not intend the sexual act to result in pregnancy. Nonetheless, if he intends to engage in the conduct of sex – even if he does not intend to cause the pregnancy – if pregnancy can still be considered to be a consequence which 'will occur in the ordinary course of events' (to use the UNTAET *mens rea* requirements), he can still be found guilty.[78]

---

76   *ICC Statute*, above n 3, Article 7(2)(f); UNTAET Regulation 2000/15, above n 5, Section 5.2(e). The provisions also specify that '[t]his definition shall not in any way be interpreted as affecting national laws relating to pregnancy'.

77   See for example, reports of 'genocidal rape' in Bosnia in Catharine MacKinnon, 'Turning Rape into Pornography: Postmodern Genocide, in Alexandra Stiglmayer (ed.) *Mass Rape: The War Against Women in Bosnia-Herzegovina* (1994). See also mention of forced pregnancy in *Prosecutor v. Radovan Karadzic & Ratko Mladic*, (Order) 5 July 1996 <http://www.un.org/icty/karadzic&mladic/trialc/decision-e/60705MS113750.htm> ('*Rule 61 Decision*').

78   *UNTAET Reg. 2000/15*, above n 5, Section 18(b) and (c). Section 18(b) states that the person 'means to cause that consequence *or* is aware that it will occur in the ordinary course of events' (emphasis added).

An expert witness who can testify to the likelihood of pregnancy resulting from whichever contraception was used would be useful to the court. Additionally, particularly in situations where women are injected with some invasive drug and simply informed that it is intended to prevent pregnancy, such statements should not be automatically authoritative or conclusive, especially when reported by a rapist. If a pregnancy results, despite the fact that contraception was purportedly used, that should warrant a charge of forced pregnancy.

F   Enforced Sterilisation

Enforced sterilisation has not been explicitly prosecuted as an independent crime in an international tribunal. The crime was mentioned in the Nuremberg trials, however, and could be considered implicitly prosecuted. Both the Nuremberg Trial of major war criminals and certain subsequent trials conducted in Nuremberg under the auspices of CCL10 referred to the systematic practice of forcibly sterilising certain groups or conducting sterilisation experiments on victims in concentration camps.[79]

The ICC Elements of Crimes give the elements of enforced sterilisation as:

1.   The perpetrator deprived one or more persons of biological reproductive capacity.
2.   The conduct was neither justified by the medical or hospital treatment of the person or persons concerned nor carried out with their genuine consent.[80]

The provisions also clarify that the 'deprivation is not intended to include birth-control measures which have a non-permanent effect in practice'. Thus, only measures intended to be permanent are covered.

Element 2 implies that the sterilisation results from some sort of medical procedure or practice, although a broader interpretation is not precluded. Many women and men were intentionally sterilised as a result of medical Nazi procedures conducted in Europe during the Second World War. In Asia, however, many women and young girls were also rendered sterile as a result of 'treatment' and abuses inflicted on them. Some women lost their reproductive capacity as a result of sexual violence that damaged their reproductive organs or genitalia, some as a result of sexually transmitted diseases incurred as a result of rapes, some as a result of drugs or devises intended to prevent pregnancy and others as a result of forced or botched abortions. It is reasonably foreseeable that each of these acts could result in forcible sterilisation. Indeed, a majority of the former 'comfort women' who were subjected to sexual slavery by the

---

79   See for example especially, *US v. Karl Brandt et al.*, *Trials of War Criminals Before the Nuremberg Military Tribunal Under Control Council Law No. 10 – Vols. 1-2* (the *Medical Case*: includes forced sterilisation and castration). *IMT Documents* – Vol. I <http://www.yale.edu/lawweb/avalon/imt/imt.htm> 45 (sterilisation of women at Auschwitz and at Ravensbruck concentration camps.)

80   *ICC Elements*, above n 14, Article 7(1)(g)-5. A footnote stipulates that 'It is understood that "genuine consent" does not include consent obtained through deception.'

Japanese military lost their reproductive ability as a result of the abuses inflicted upon them.[81]

It might be considered inherently contradictory to assert, on the one hand, that forced pregnancy is a foreseeable consequence of rape, and on the other hand, that enforced sterilisation is also a foreseeable consequence of rape and certain other forms of sexual violence (such as sexual mutilation). The apparent contradiction breaks down, however, when viewed in the context of sexual slavery, gang rape, multiple rapes, rape of virgins or young girls, rape with foreign objects or particularly violent rapes. Both forced pregnancy and enforced sterilisation are recognised as forms of sexual violence in which harmful reproductive consequences can be reasonably anticipated. It is foreseeable that violent sex or sex inflicted by diseased individuals would cause damage to reproductive organs or capacity.

It is also possible that enforced sterilisation could be used to capture crimes such as castration. It could also encompass various other forms of sexual mutilation if the mutilation is committed with the intent to destroy reproductive capacity. It should also be used to cover crimes in which women or men were knowingly, or perhaps negligently, exposed to chemicals or treatment which would render them sterile.

The IMT documents contain evidence of forced sterilisation committed in Nazi concentration camps. For example, one witness testified:

> As to the experiments, I have seen ... the queue of young Jewesses from Salonika who stood waiting in front of the X-ray room for sterilisation. I also know that they performed castration operations in the men's camp.... . They sterilised women either by injections or by operation or with rays. I saw and knew several women who had been sterilised. There was a very high mortality rate among those operated upon.... . They said that they were trying to find the best method for sterilising so as to replace the native population in the occupied countries by Germans after one generation, once they had made use of the inhabitants as slaves.[82]

Enforced sterilisation should be prosecuted if women lost their reproductive capacity as a direct result of acts of violence, illicit exposure to chemicals or drugs that could be expected to impact sterility or unlawful medical procedures or treatments.

G   Sexual Violence

The ICTR Tribunal defined sexual violence as 'any act of a sexual nature which is committed on a person under circumstances which are coercive. Sexual violence is not limited to physical invasion of the human body and may include acts which do not involve penetration or even physical contact'.[83] Thus, sexual violence is broadly defined to capture an array of crimes of a sexual nature that are not otherwise specified in the particular authorising legislation of a court.

---

81   See for example, 'Comfort Women' Judgment, above n 9 [403]-[409].

82   IMT Documents, Vol. VI, transcript 211 <http://www.yale.edu/lawweb/avalon/imt/imt.htm>.

83   *Akayesu* Trial Chamber Judgment, above n 2 [688].

The ICC Elements put forth the following elements for sexual violence:

1. The perpetrator committed an act of a sexual nature against one or more persons or caused such person or persons to engage in an act of a sexual nature by force, or by threat of force or coercion, such as that caused by fear of violence, duress, detention, psychological oppression or abuse of power, against such person or persons or another person, or by taking advantage of a coercive environment or such person's or persons' incapacity to give genuine consent.

2. Such conduct was of a gravity comparable to the other offences in article 7, paragraph 1 (g), of the [ICC] Statute.

3. The perpetrator was aware of the factual circumstances that established the gravity of the conduct.[84]

Unless otherwise specified, other courts are not bound by the ICC's formulation of elements, which were rigorously negotiated by State delegates and intended to serve as guidelines for adjudicating crimes within the jurisdiction of the International Criminal Court.

As pointed out in the *Furundžija* case,

[I]international criminal rules punish not only rape but also any serious sexual assault falling short of actual penetration. It would seem that the prohibition embraces all serious abuses of a sexual nature inflicted upon the physical and moral integrity of a person by means of coercion, threat of force or intimidation in a way that is degrading and humiliating for the victim's dignity. As both these categories of acts are criminalised in international law, the distinction between them is one that is primarily material for the purposes of sentencing.[85]

Other forms of sexual violence that have been named as crimes, but not yet explicitly defined or listed by an authoritative body, are briefly considered below.

1 Forced Nudity

In *Akayesu*, an ICTR Trial Chamber gave forced nudity as an example of sexual violence and found the accused guilty of inhumane acts for sexual violence committed in Taba. Because the term 'sexual violence' is not enumerated as a crime explicitly within the jurisdiction of the ICTR, the accused could not be convicted of sexual violence *per se*.

In the *Akayesu* case, the forced nudity was typically committed as a distinct offence separate from the rape crimes. Women and girls were forced to march or stand nude in public for the entertainment of militia and/or to humiliate them, for example, or a young girl was forced to do gymnastics naked before a crowd of onlookers, sometimes before or after being raped.[86] In *Kunarac*, forced nudity was found to constitute

---

84   *ICC Elements*, above n 14, Article 7(1)(g)-6.

85   *Furundžija* Trial Chamber Judgment, above n 2 [186].

86   *Akayesu* Trial Chamber Judgment, above n 2 [697]. The Tribunal cited separate instances of 'forced undressing', 'the forced undressing and public marching of [the victim] naked' and 'the forcing of the women to perform exercises naked in public'.

an outrage upon personal dignity when young women and girls were forced to dance nude on a table for the entertainment of soldiers/enslavers.

It is unclear if, for example, prior to a rape a woman was forced to take off all her clothes, that it would constitute the crime of forced nudity in addition to the rape crime. In such a context, it is likely that the forced nudity would add to the humiliating or traumatising aspect of the rape, particularly in societies where notions of modesty dictates the preferred behaviour of women. In virtually all societies, nudity, especially forced or coerced nudity, makes people feel inherently more vulnerable and defenceless. They might be less likely to call for help or flee the scene in order to prevent others from seeing their nudity.

The presence of others – not necessarily a large group – beside the perpetrator, whether strangers, family members or militia, would strengthen the potential for a successful claim for forced nudity charged as sexual violence. Prosecuting forced nudity would also have support from the *Furundžija* case, in which the Trial Chamber noted that being nude and sexually assaulted in front of laughing soldiers and a man known by the victim added to her humiliation.

In addition to the above crimes, the *Kvočka* Trial Chamber also cited sexual mutilation, forced marriage and forced abortion as constituting crimes of sexual violence. These crimes will be briefly considered below.

2   Sexual Mutilation

Sexual mutilation could be regarded as mutilation of the sexual organs or a body part considered to be intrinsically sexual, such as breasts.

Documentary evidence from the Nuremberg Trial revealed that women and young girls in detention facilities 'were subjected to particularly outrageous forms of torture. They were raped, their breasts cut off' and had other violence and indignities inflicted upon their bodies.[87]

Arguably, the prosecution of sexual mutilation should focus on acts in which a perpetrator intended to harm a victim for non-cultural reasons and the mutilation was not performed by a person with cultural authority to perform ceremonial practices. For example, if a member of the militia used a knife or machete to slice a woman's breasts or genitalia or to castrate a man in order to harm or intimidate the victim, it should constitute sexual mutilation as a form of sexual violence. If female genital cutting was performed for cultural reasons by a person authorised by the community – particularly female family members – to perform the cutting, however, such traditional acts – despite their condemnation by human rights organisations and UN bodies – are likely not the type of crime intended to come before international tribunals prosecuting international crimes. Nonetheless, an argument can be made that cutting – mutilating – female genitalia for any non-medical reason, including for cultural reasons, constitutes a serious human rights violation rising to the level of an international crime. To be justiciable in the ICC, however, it would need to be com-

---

87   *IMT Documents*, Vol VII, transcript 494. <http://www.yale.edu/lawweb/avalon/imt/imt.htm>. Other examples include: Vol VII, transcript 455 (after they raped a woman, the Germans 'stabbed her through both breasts, and sadistically bored them out').

mitted in conjunction with a war crime, crime against humanity or genocide. The Indictment could charge the crime as a crime against humanity under other forms of sexual violence, namely sexual mutilation.

3 Forced Marriage

Forced marriage could be regarded as a form of sexual slavery that has a more intimate, familial nature. As an example, during the Rwanda genocide, a leading human rights organisation asserted that Tutsi women were forced into marriage to Hutu soldiers – they were 'held in sexual slavery (either collectively or through forced 'marriage')'.[88] Often, the woman's husband or family was killed and she was taken by a soldier for his exclusive use to cook, clean and do household chores for him during the day and to provide sex at night. Although initially forced, in some instances, the woman eventually chose to remain with the soldier, typically because she had nowhere else to go or would be rejected by her family if she attempted to return.[89]

In forced marriage, the woman or girl typically performs services a domestic partner might otherwise perform, physical and sexual. Forced marriage is a form of sexual slavery that tends to take on a more exclusive nature than most sexual slavery practices, such that the woman or girl does not sexually service an array of men in a group facility, but instead would tend to provide sexual (and possibly other) services to one man in relatively familial-type intimate quarters. Sometimes a military person forces a woman into his exclusive sexual servitude, or sometimes the military group or government plays a formal or informal role in marrying, securing or assigning a woman or girl to a member of the armed forces. The servitude may be for a temporary or more permanent period of time.

Forced marriage should be criminal for as long as the 'marriage' remains 'forced'. If at some point the woman becomes genuinely free and able to leave, but chooses to remain in the 'marriage' (often because she has nowhere else to go), it ceases to be the crime of forced marriage. The past conduct, however, remains actionable.

Forced marriage would clearly be encompassed by sexual slavery. Yet forced marriage describes and defines more precisely a more exclusive form of sexual activity. It can be distinguished from the more common form of sexual slavery, when a victim is typically required to provide sexual services to a series of men or a single man who may use, trade, sell or loan her sexual services. While it may be less onerous to prosecute forced marriage simply as 'sexual violence' than as an independent crime, the form the sexual violence takes should be made explicit in the pleadings. There is some hope that forced marriage will be explicitly prosecuted in places where it was common and the authorising legislation permits adjudication of 'other forms of sexual violence'. This includes Sierra Leone and East Timor and perhaps Cambodia. Further, the ICC can prosecute forced marriage as 'other forms of sexual violence' when committed in places such as the Congo and Uganda. The Indictment could charge the crime as a

---

88   Human Rights Watch, *Human Rights Watch World Report 1997* (1998) 343.

89   See an extensive discussion of 'forced marriage' in Human Rights Watch, *Shattered Lives: Sexual Violence During the Rwanda Genocide and its Aftermath* (1996).

crime against humanity under other forms of sexual violence, namely forced marriage.

4   Forced Abortion

Forced abortion could be considered to be treatment, whether medically induced or otherwise, which results in a woman losing her pregnancy against her will and in violation of international norms.

In the Nuremberg Trial, when a pregnant woman was tortured and the abuse resulted in a miscarriage, it was referred to as 'criminal abortion':

> [W]omen were subjected to the same treatment as men. To the physical pain, the sadism of the torturers added the moral anguish, especially mortifying for a woman or young girl, of being stripped nude by her torturers. Pregnancy did not save them from lashes. When brutality brought about a miscarriage, they were left without any care, exposed to all the hazards and complications of these criminal abortions.[90]

Also during the Second World War, transcripts of the Nuremberg, CCL10 and Tokyo trials, contain evidence of atrocities including acts in which a pregnant woman is intentionally subjected to mistreatment until she 'aborts' or miscarries the pregnancy.[91] This may result from a variety of inflictions upon her body, including medical procedures, drugs, chemicals, beating or stomping the stomach area or rape. The *Akayesu* Judgment reported the testimony concerning a rape victim who was several months pregnant and went into premature delivery while being publicly gang raped.[92] While it is not uncommon to receive reports of pregnant women having their wombs sliced open and the foetus removed, murder would be the more appropriate charge because these cases virtually always result in death of both the mother and the unborn child.

According to the IMT transcripts, in the Nazi concentration camps: 'The Jewish women, when they arrived in the first months of pregnancy, were subjected to abortion. When their pregnancy was near the end, after confinement, the babies were drowned in a bucket of water'.[93] The IMT also received evidence that an official announcement was included as part of official Nazi policy that 'every case of pregnancy of non-German women was to be reported, and in all such cases these women were to be obliged to have their child "removed by operation in a hospital"'.[94]

The 'Comfort Women' Tribunal heard considerable evidence of forced abortion/miscarriage, including a particularly egregious example reported by one witness who

---

90   *IMT Documents*, Vol. VI, <http://www.yale.edu/lawweb/avalon/imt/imt.htm> 170.

91   For example, *US v. Oswald Pohl et al.* above n 37, *Trials of War Criminals Before the Nuremberg Military Tribunal Under Control Council Law No. 10* – Vol 5 (1949) (the *Pohl Case*: evidence of forced abortion resulting from mistreatment); *US v. Ulrich Greifelt et al.*, *Trials of War Criminals Before the Nuremberg Military Tribunal Under Control Council Law No. 10* – Vols. *4-5* (1948) (the *RuSHA Case*: evidence of forced abortions).

92   *Akayesu* Trial Chamber Judgment, above n 2 [437].

93   *IMT Documents*, Vol. VI, transcript, 212 <http://www.yale.edu/lawweb/avalon/imt/imt. htm>.

94   *IMT Documents*, Vol. VIII, transcript, 133 <http://www.yale.edu/lawweb/avalon/imt/imt. htm>.

testified that she 'was forced to have an abortion at age 14 by Chikada, the 'comfort station' manager. Because she was already five months pregnant, the 'medicine' used for abortion did not work, and so they pressed on her abdomen till the baby came out'.[95]

If a woman is subjected to violence, including sexual violence, which results in a miscarriage, that act could be prosecuted as forced abortion if the pregnancy was known or obvious and the miscarriage is a foreseeable outcome of the violence. The physical violence would presumably need to be inflicted toward a part of the body, such as the abdomen, that could reasonably result in harm to the foetus. It is more foreseeable that a pregnant woman would miscarry as a result of being beaten in the stomach than from being hit on the head or arm. Nonetheless, there are certain instances in which loss of a pregnancy is a foreseeable consequence of any form of mental, physical or sexual violence or abuse. Being forced to watch the rape of her young daughter or the torture of her husband, for example, could foreseeably cause a pregnant woman such distress that she miscarries. The Indictment could charge the crime as a crime against humanity under other forms of sexual violence, namely forced abortion.

H   Other Crimes: Inhumane Acts, Outrages upon Personal Dignity, Cruel Treatment

As mentioned previously, the crime that more precisely describes, in layperson's terms, the act committed should, as a general rule, be the preferred charge. The other more obscurely named crimes should be reserved to capture crimes that do not fit within other more specifically enumerated crimes. There may be times, however, when due to sensitivities of the survivors or other legitimate reasons, the sexual nature of the crime should not be emphasised. There are several broader crimes which encompass many forms of gender-related offences. They should also be used to capture crimes committed in addition to another crime, such as when grossly offensive conduct is committed as a prelude to or aftermath of a rape. There are numerous offences which are not widely recognised as named crimes and yet constitute conduct clearly prohibited and deserving of punishment. This category of other crimes could cover, for example, instances of sexual humiliation. If a woman is forced into humiliating situations before, during or after a rape, they should be charged in addition to the rape crime. These provisions could also cover pornography if the women were filmed or photographed. The broader, catch-all proscriptions could be used to cover many acts which do not rise to the level of torture but which are designed to cause suffering or humiliation to the victim or a third person. For example, the *Čelebići* Trial Chamber found an accused guilty of cruel treatment when a burning fuse cord was placed around a male detainee's genitals. The *Kunarac* Trial Chamber found an accused guilty of outrages upon personal dignity when he forced girls to dance nude on a table for his entertainment. The *Akayesu* Trial Chamber found the defendant guilty of inhumane acts for instances of forced nudity.

Such provisions could also likely be used to cover some offences, such as 'aborted' rape (which may be different than 'attempted' rape). An example could be in instances where the potential perpetrator had a definite intent to rape, but the woman managed

---

95   'Comfort Women' Judgment, above n 9 [320].

to talk him out of it because she was, for example, menstruating at the time or at least asserted she was. If he did any significant act in furtherance of the rape (which would naturally be inherently threatening, distressing or traumatising), such activity can be prosecuted as an outrage upon personal dignity, particularly if he made a comment such as that he would not have her because she was dirty or disgusting. The main point here is that a person who intended to rape and was only persuaded against the act because of intervening factors should not escape liability if their intent caused serious harm to the victim. As noted above, the *Kvočka* Judgment found that threats to rape cause severe trauma.

If the legislation authorises it, such activity could also be prosecuted as attempted rape. For example, UNTAET Regulations authorise prosecuting:

> attempts to commit ... a crime by taking action that commences its execution by means of a substantial step, but the crime does not occur because of circumstances independent of the person's intentions. However, a person who abandons the effort to commit the crime or otherwise prevents the completion of the crime shall not be liable for punishment under the present regulation for the attempt to commit that crime if that person completely and voluntarily gave up the criminal purpose.[96]

In most instances of abusive treatment, a number of different gender-related crimes will be committed and the broader provisions can be used to capture offences not already covered by other crimes.

III   Conclusion

There is a wealth of jurisprudence available to aid the prosecution of the gender-related crimes. Rape has been prosecuted as genocide, a crime against humanity, a war crime, a form of torture and a means of persecution and enslavement in the Yugoslav and Rwanda Tribunals. Other forms of sexual violence have been explicitly or implicitly prosecuted as well. Nonetheless, numerous sex crimes have been wholly ignored by international criminal justice systems and the number of victims-survivors receiving direct redress is small.

The Tribunals have convicted physical perpetrators of gender crimes; persons who have aided and abetted, ordered, instigated, planned, encouraged or otherwise facilitated the crimes; and superiors who have failed to take adequate steps to prevent, halt or punish sex crimes committed by subordinates. They have also convicted persons of sex crimes who have knowingly participated in joint criminal enterprises when the crimes were known, foreseeable, incidental to or natural consequences of the joint criminal enterprise. Each of these things, and all of these things, can be used in the ICC and hybrid courts to secure redress for gender-related crimes. Because of the centuries of neglect, it is important for justice systems to respond creatively to sex crimes and prosecute the crime actually committed, not some vague or broad crime which implicitly captures the conduct. Sexual violence is now widely recognised as a

---

96   *UNTAET Regulation 2000/15*, above n 5, Section 14(3)(f).

weapon of war and an instrument of terror. Focusing on preventing and punishing such crimes is paramount.

Justice systems have an obligation to ensure that the gender-related crimes are appropriately redressed. Respect for the rule of law requires that the victims of serious crimes, including women, have the crimes committed against them thoroughly investigated, appropriately indicted and rigorously prosecuted. Until justice and accountability are rendered, lasting peace and real progress are unlikely. And until the harmful stereotypes surrounding sex crimes are addressed, women will continue to be wrongfully silenced, shamed and re-victimised by the justice system and by society.

Gender justice has made enormous strides in a relatively short period of time. The presence of women in decision-making positions – and persistent lobbying by women's rights groups – have greatly impacted the prosecution of gender crimes. It is increasingly acknowledged in international criminal court statutes and UN documents that women must be included in positions of power in peace, justice and accountability mechanisms in order to effectuate real change. But major obstacles, including failing to indict or arrest leaders most responsible and failing to take gender crimes seriously, remain.

13

The Other Voices:
Interpreters and Investigators of Sexual Violence in International Criminal Prosecutions

Patricia Viseur-Sellers *

I Introduction

The *ad hoc* Tribunals for the former Yugoslavia[1] and for Rwanda[2] ushered in a period of unprecedented diligence into the investigation, prosecution and adjudication of sexual assaults under humanitarian law and international criminal law. The now familiar litany of cases, such as *Akayesu*,[3] *Kunarac*,[4] *Furundžija*[5] and *Kvočka*[6] testify to a rec-

---

* Patricia Viseur-Sellers is the Legal Advisor for Gender-related Crimes and a Trial Attorney in the Office of the Prosecutor for the ICTY. This article is written in Ms. Sellers' personal capacity. The views expressed herein do not represent the official policies of the Office of the Prosecutor of the International Criminal Tribunal for the former Yugoslavia nor the official policies of the United Nations. The author wishes to thank the contributions of the investigators and interpreters who graciously reflected upon their professional experience. This article is dedicated to those professionals and their colleagues.

1 International Criminal Tribunal for the former Yugoslavia, SC Res 827, 48 UN SCOR (3217th mtg at 29), UN Doc S/827/1993 (1993) (Statute contained in UN Doc. S/25704, Annex (1993), attached to the 'Report on the Secretary-General Pursuant to Paragraph 2 of Security Council Resolution 808'), 32 ILM 1159 (1993) ('Statute of the ICTY').

2 International Criminal Tribunal for Rwanda, SC Res 955, 49 UN SCOR (3453d mtg at 15), UN Doc S/INF/50 Annex (1994), 33 ILM 1598 (1994) – Statute of the International Criminal Tribunal for Rwanda, attached to Prosecution of Persons Responsible for Genocide and Other Serious Violations of International Humanitarian Committed in the Territory of Rwanda and Rwandan citizens responsible for genocide and other such violations committed in the territory of neighbouring States, between 1 January 1994 and 31 December 1994, ('Statute of the ICTR').

3 *Prosecutor v. Jean-Paul Akayesu*, (Judgment), Case No. ICTR-96-4-T, 2 September 1998, <http://www.ictr.org/default.htm> ('*Akayesu* Trial Chamber Judgment')

4 *Prosecutor v. Dragoljub Kunarac et al.* (Judgment), Case No. IT-96-23-T & IT-96-23/1-T, 22 February 2001 <http://www.un.org/icty/kunarac/trialc2/judgement/kun-tj010222e.pdf> ('*Kunarac* Trial Chamber Judgment').

5-6 [See next page.]

Helen Durham and Tracey Gurd (eds.), Listening to the Silences: Women and War, *pp. 155-164.*
© *2005 Koninklijke Brill BV. Printed in The Netherlands.* ISBN 90 04 14365 3.

ognition that sexualised violence, including rapes, torture or sexual enslavement can constitute war crimes,[7] crimes against humanity[8] and acts of genocide.[9] The statutes of the more recently established mixed, national and international courts in Sierra Leone[10] and East Timor,[11] and certainly the International Criminal Court,[12] expand upon the enumeration of sexual assaults crimes and offer the prospect that international community will persist in redressing sex-based crimes and accord a more gendered[13] consciousness to the enforcement of international law.

As the primary source of evidence, Tribunal judgments necessitate the admission and weighing of the voices of sexual assault witnesses which must be assessed in light of other evidence, including plausible defences, in order to determine the guilt or innocence of an accused. Before becoming in-court testimony, a witness' re-counting of a defendant's criminal conduct must pass through a standard process of investigation and interpretation. During the investigation stage the witness is interviewed about alleged sexual violence. The direct words of the witness are first interpreted from their original language into English or French, the official languages of the Tribunals and then are incorporated into official prosecution statements. At trial, the witness verbally responds in direct examination and cross-examination to questions posed by the prosecution and defence lawyers, or to questions from the bench. In the courtroom, the witness' live testimony is again interpreted into English or French. To transform the witness' original words into an official prosecution statement, and then the

---

5   *Prosecutor v. Anto Furundžija* (Judgment), IT-95-17/1-T, 10 December 1998 <http://www. un.org/furundzija/trialc2/judgement/fur-tj981210e.pdf> ('*Furundžija* Trial Chamber Judgment').

6   *Prosecutor v. Miroslav Kvočka et al.* (Judgment), IT-98-30-T, 2 November 2001 <http:// www.un.org/icty/kvocka/trialc/judgement/kvo-tj011002e.pdf> ('*Kvočka* Trial Chamber Judgment').

7   *Prosecutor v. Zejnil Delalić et al.,* (Judgment), Case No. IT-96-21-T, 16 November 1998, <http://www.un.org/icty/celebici/trialc2/judgement/cel-tj981116e.pdf> ('*Čelebići* Trial Chamber Judgment').

8   *Prosecutor v. Radislav Krstić* (Judgment), Case No. IT-98-33-T, 2 August 2001 <http:// www.un.org/icty/krstic/trialc1/judgement/krs-tj010802e.pdf> ('*Krstić* Trial Chamber Judgment').

9   *Akayesu,* above n 3, [731].

10   *Statute of the Special Court for Sierra Leone,* 16 January 2002, established by *Report of the Secretary-General on the Establishment of the Special Court for Sierra Leone* (the Statute is contained in the report's Annex – an *Agreement between the United Nations and the Government of Sierra Leone pursuant to Security Council resolution 1315 (2000)* of 14 August 2000), UN Doc. S/2000/915 (2000), UN website, <http://ods-dds-ny.un.org/doc/UNDOC/GEN/ N00/661/77/PDF/N0066177.pdf?OpenElement>.

11   *Establishment of Panels with Exclusive Jurisdiction Over Serious Criminal Offences (East Timor)* UNTAET/REG/2000/15, 6 June 2000.

12   *Rome Statute of the International Criminal Court,* opened for signature 9 October 1998, UN Doc. A/CONF.183/9 (1998), 37 ILM 999 (1998) (entered into force 1 July 2002) ('*ICC Statute*').

13   The term gendered signals an acute awareness that the sexual autonomy of females and males, of all ages are subject to sexual violations under humanitarian law and international criminal law.

witness' voice into testimony understood by the trier of fact, requires the utilisation of the professional skills of investigators and interpreters.

This chapter attempts to acknowledge the voices of these professionals who skilfully assure a crucial sequence in the enforcement of sexual violence under humanitarian law and international criminal law. Although much has been written, and rightly so, about witnesses, witness rights, witness protection and about the maturing of the sexual assault jurisprudence under international law, little attention has been extended to investigators of sexual assault crimes at the international level or to the official interpreters, who literally construct the access to the witness' evidence. This article commences a humble endeavour to understand the role of investigators and interpreters and to listen to these – the other voices.

In the following two sections, this chapter will outline the work of investigators and interpreters of sexual violence in the Tribunals. The final section will then focus on the individual experiences and thoughts of interpreters and investigators. This last section is the product of interviews conducted by the author with women investigators and interpreters, primarily working at the ICTY, during the first few months of 2004. It is not intended to represent a homogenous or definitive view of the opinions or experiences of professional interpreters or investigators working in this area. Instead, it aims to provide a forum for individual women to express their thoughts and stories accumulated during many years of work at the Tribunals. This is an invaluable addition to the scholarship already available on the issue of sexual violence. It offers a 'behind-the-scene' insight into the work done by the people who have gathered the evidence necessary to ensure that landmark sexual assault cases such as *Akayesu*, *Furundžija*, *Kvočka* and *Kunarac* could exist.

II   Investigators of Sexual Violence

The statute of the Yugoslav Tribunal expressly enumerated a sexual assault crime – rape – only once under the Article 5 crimes against humanity provision. Nevertheless, the Secretary General's Report to the Security Council erased any scepticism that sexual assaults were squarely secured within the Tribunal's mandate.[14] To execute that mandate, the Office of the Prosecutor (OTP) undertook several policy measures such as naming a Legal Advisor for Gender related Crimes to develop a legal framework for the prosecution of sexual assault crimes. The Investigation Unit of the OTP also recruited investigators, endeavouring to hire female and male investigators competent in sexual assault investigations and simultaneously to gender integrate each investigation team. Investigators are organised in teams that are supervised by an investigative team leader. The team leader is responsible to a commander or deputy who reports directly to the Chief of Investigations,[15] who reports to the Prosecutor.

---

14   Richard Goldstone, 'Prosecuting Rape as a War Crime', (2002) 34(3) *Case Western Journal of International Law* 278. See also Patricia Sellers and Kaoru Okuizumi, 'International Prosecution of Sexual Assaults' (1997) 7(1) *Transnational Law and Contemporary Problems* 45.

15   In the structure of the OTP Investigation Unit, two female investigators have held commander posts whereby they supervised the investigations conducted by several investiga-

Several female investigators were hired or 'loaned' by donor governments to 'jump start' the Tribunal's work in its first year of existence. During the past ten years, about thirty female investigators have worked in the Investigation Unit. Each investigator is an experienced law enforcement officer capable of applying investigative expertise to the complex crimes that come under the mandate of the statute. Approximately half of the female investigators who have worked at the Tribunal have spent a considerable amount of their OTP tenure involved with aspects of sexual assault investigations. Some female investigators were principally involved in sexual assault investigations. It is paramount to acknowledge that many male investigators willingly and competently devoted long hours to uncover and investigate sexual assault evidence. Together with their female colleagues, male investigators have provided evidence to substantiate the sexual assault charges in indictments such as the *Češić*,[16] *Kvočka*,[17] *Plavsic*,[18] *Milosevic*[19] and *Stankovic*.[20]

The investigator who is tasked with ensuring that sexual assault evidence can support the charges in an indictment and can withstand scrutiny at trial must develop a professional and credible relationship with the witnesses. First, the investigator must generate a sense of confidence and trust. Second, the investigator must proceed with arrangements to take a formal OTP statement. In most instances, the sexual assault witness – and especially the victim/survivor's statement – is a 'best-evidence' source for the sexual violence and possibly for other potentially pertinent information, such as killings, deportation or detention.

With the establishment of professional trust a witness is encouraged to simply state the truth, as they remember it, about the alleged infliction of sexual violence. An experienced investigator can draw upon an array of techniques to accomplish this mission. When the investigator drops stereotypical notions about 'who' is a victim – including assumptions about age, sex, status, appearance, intelligence, class or ethnicity, the witness' story – no matter how incredulous or simple – can emerge. Likewise, the witness' ability to recount their story depends on the confidence s/he extends to the investigator, 'who' could be a female from South Africa, the Netherlands, Ireland, Nepal or any country other than the former Yugoslavia. If there is no mutual rapport between investigator and the witness, wariness could emerge to the detriment of the evidence collection.

The standard procedure executed to produce OTP witness statements includes creating an appropriate atmosphere at the interview location. The investigator con-

---

tion teams and reported directly to the Chief of Investigations. Two female investigators have also held the post of team leader of an investigation team.

16   *Prosecutor v. Ranko Češić* (Third Amended Indictment) Case No. IT-95-10/1-PT, 26 November 2002 <http://www.un.org/icty/indictment/english/ces-3aio21126e.htm>.

17   *Prosecutor v. Miroslav Kvočka* (Amended Indictment) Case No. IT-98-30/1, 21 August 2000, <http://www.un.org/icty/indictment/english/kvo-aio01026e.htm>.

18   *Prosecutor v. Biljana Plavsic*, (Sentencing Judgement) Case No. IT-00-39&40/1-S, 27 February 2003, <http://www.un.org/icty/plavsic/trialc/judgement/pla-tj030227e.pdf>.

19   *Prosecutor v. Milosevic* et al. (Second Amended Indictment) Case No. IT-99-37-PT, 29 October 2001, <http://www.un.org/icty/indictment/english/mil-2aio11029e.htm>.

20   *Prosecutor v. Radovan Stankovic*, (Third Amended Indictment), Case No. IT-96-23/2, 9 February 2004 (not available on the ICTY website as at July 2004).

ducts interviews with witnesses who usually have been forcibly removed from their pre-war homes. Some witness, therefore, will be lodged in temporary dwellings, overcrowded refugee camps, with relatives or with other who are similarly displaced and distressed. Some potential witnesses may have willingly migrated to foreign countries or been relocated abroad for protection reasons. Investigators may hence attempt to arrange interview locations that offer a sense of privacy and comfort.

Next, investigators must explain to a witness the potential uses of the statement at the Tribunal or more recently, in local war crimes prosecutions. The investigator must then conduct a meticulous interview and draft a witness statement. Drafting a witness statement – in particular statements that involve traumatic sexual assault – can last over a period of one to several days. In certain instances, additional statements might be solicited. For the witness, the statement entails recounting a truth that often traverses delicate and difficult personal territory. It is only because of its characterisation as an international crime that the Tribunal, through the investigator, must present the story to the public. To ensure that the statement could be used at trial and to refresh or further substantiate witness testimony, the investigator must verify the content of the statement in what is commonly called a read-back. Then, if in agreement with its content, the witness signs the statement. Ultimately, the genuine search for solid evidence is what the investigator aims to capture in the witness statement. Finally, the investigator must discuss with the witness the availability of court-ordered protective measures.

After securing a witness statement, investigators periodically contact witnesses to explain case-related developments, such as the arrest of an accused or the approach of a trial date. The investigator ensures that a witness remains willing and able to come to The Hague to testify. During the trial, investigators retain constant and close contact with witnesses, especially during the witnesses' preparation for testimony and after the Trial Chamber releases them from the witness stand. After the witness returns home, especially in the case of protective re-location, the investigator periodically checks on the witness' well-being and updates them on further case developments, such as the issuance of the judgment and the verdict. It is apparent that the interaction between witnesses and investigators can span many years and usually passes through several crucial stages in post-war lives of witnesses.

III   Interpreters of Sexual Violence

Virtually all interaction with victims and witnesses require the professional presence of interpreters. Interpreters whose mother tongue or fluency is in Bosnian-Croat-Serb (BCS) are the linguistic mediators between the victim/witness and the Tribunal investigators, lawyers and judges. The vast majority of BCS interpreters employed by the Registry's Conference and Language Section (CLS) are women who come from, or are descendants of nationals from, the republics of the former Yugoslavia, Croatia, Slovenia, Serbia, Bosnia or more rarely, from Kosovo. Some lived in the former Yugoslavia during the armed conflict and later worked as interpreters for international agencies. Others had left the former Yugoslavia for myriad reasons, such as university studies, prior to the outbreak of war. For the most part, they are women, close in age to many of the female victim/witness of sexual violence.

Interpreters are engaged throughout the investigation phase. Within OTP investigative teams, language assistants provide written translations and interpret routine and emergency telephone conversations between investigators and witnesses. At the OTP offices in Sarajevo, Zagreb, Belgrade or Pristina, free-lance interpreters work with field-based investigators. Other free-lance interpreters join The Hague-based investigators or lawyers who travel on missions to visit witnesses who reside in countries outside the former Yugoslavia.

The interpreter's dominion of the witness' language is crucial to securing the verbal evidence contained in the witness statement. The perceived shared historical background of both interpreter and witness injects another dynamic into the investigation stage. Similar to the trust that must be cultivated between the witness and investigator, who originate from different countries, the interpreter/witness relationship might be complicated by the ethnic-based contentions that fomented the civil war in the former Yugoslavia. The background of the interpreter or the witness could sub-consciously either shred, or facilitate, the narrative. Does the witness question whether the interpreter's accent attests that she is from the 'enemy' side? Is there apprehension about where the interpreter was during the armed conflict? Did the interpreter suffer in war as the witness did, or was she, somehow, safeguarded? Does the interpreter possibly already know something about the witness and thus hinder the witness' sense of security that she is talking anonymously? Is the interpreter a security risk for the witness or her family?

These reservations often arise. The interpreter professionally deals them with in the first stages of their introductory contact. Together, the interpreter and investigator determine how to resolve any misapprehension. Accordingly, pairing an interpreter and witnesses from the same ethnic background, or an interpreter from a perceived neutral background (such as a Serbian interpreter working with a Bosnian Croat witness who suffered crimes committed by Bosnian Muslims) often are the best working combinations. Through this reflective prism, the interpreter assesses and creates the confidence needed to ensure the success of the interview.

The interpreter is fully engaged in developing the sexual assault witness statement as detailed above. It is the interpreter who, through accurate selection of terminology and emotion, is responsible for carefully conveying the investigator's questions and the sexual assault witness' responses. The witness, very possibly, is telling about the rapes for the first time to someone – and that someone is literally the interpreter. The interpreter simultaneously hears the witness' words and receives the emotional impact. The interpreter must accurately relay painful or traumatic experiences into the language of the investigator, while remaining faithful to the witness' version. The interpreter often transmits the witness' meaning that injects another element into the investigator's perception of the crime. Sometimes, this causes the questioning to refocus on previously minimised details, such as a certain peculiarity of the accused or his position in the *de facto* command structure. After the successful read-back or verification of the written statement, the witness must sign the statement while the witness, investigator and interpreter must initial each page of the statement. At the end of each statement, the interpreter must sign and certify that the Tribunal Registry has approved of their ability to interpret BCS into English. The interpreter must also confirm the witness' ability to understand the translation and must attest that the witness statement was acknowledged as true to the best of the witness' recollection. These are serious professional undertakings in the Tribunal's process that become part of the official OTP statement and contribute to the witness' credibility before the judges at trial.

Interpreters also work with the lawyers and investigators when witnesses come to the Tribunal. Trial attorneys conduct proofing sessions to prepare witnesses to testify. At these sessions that can last for several hours or days, interpreters must again establish that operative trust. In those sessions, the lawyers, interpreters and witnesses review the questions that will eventually be asked of the witness in the courtroom by the prosecutors. They also go through potential cross-examination questions which may be used by the defence counsel. Once the witness is called to the stand to give sworn testimony, the conference or booth interpreters utilise their professional skills of simultaneous translation to relay the prosecution and defence questions to the witness, and then the witness' testimony to the judges. In that instant, the interpreter literally becomes the voice of the witness.

IV   Voices of Investigators and Interpreters

What are the real life reactions, comments and emotions that the investigators and the interpreters experience in performing their professional duties *vis a vis* the investigation and interpretation of sexual assault evidence? Below are the voices of six of those women, spoken to individually and chosen because of their long tenure, primarily at the Yugoslav Tribunal, and their work with landmark sexual assault cases. The questions and answers do not represent a scientific survey. Male investigators/interpreters are not included, although this selection does not negate their experience. It only turns the initial attention to their female colleagues. The following personal accounts and experiences of women involved in sexual violence cases demonstrates that these professionals do not speak with a unified voice, but each have highly unique and individual reactions to their daily interaction with tales of horror and depravity. Each voice, however, evidences the strength of character and determination that these behind-the-scenes professionals exhibit on a daily basis.

A   Why Did They Apply Their Skills to Sexual Assault Victims?
Though investigators and interpreters tended to highlight the tough or demanding nature of the job, each seemed to perceive their role as having a greater purpose. One interpreter, for example, told me that her role was 'part of what needed to be done'. She considered her job a 'contribution to the process of justice' and that the process 'made sense' to her. For others, the process of getting past the horrors took more time. An investigator told me that her first year on the job was 'tough'. During that time, she interviewed ten to fifteen sexual assault witnesses and it took a great toll on her. By the second year, however, things improved because she felt as though she could psychologically understand the witnesses better as she interviewed them. For others still, the desire to apply their skills came out of a sense of solidarity with the witnesses them-

selves. One interpreter recalled a complicated sexual assault case, from which other interpreters eventually asked to be transferred because they could no longer bear the stories. This particular interpreter firmly countered, 'If they [the witnesses] could tell their story, I can tell it'. In each case, the decision of the women to apply their skills to this area took an enormous amount of energy and commitment.

B   *What Were the Reations of the Investigators and the Interpreters to the Nature and Impact of the Sexual Assaults on the Witnesses?*

A unifying theme, which emerged throughout the interviews with investigators/ interpreters, appeared to be their recognition of both emotional distress and inner strength that seemed to permeate the demeanour of victims and witnesses of sexual assaults. One interpreter said that the sexual assault witness, compared to other witnesses, tended to be more severely affected by the overall ordeal, placing them into a different category of witness altogether. An investigator, who noted that sexual assaults rendered witnesses 'intensely unhappy', further corroborated this concept. It tended to detrimentally affect the personal relations of the victim/witness for years – especially with men. Yet despite the anguish experienced by many victims and witnesses in conveying their stories, this investigator would still encourage girls and women to testify for their own sake, since they all gained strength from the process. Another interpreter noted that testifying led to closure for witnesses rather than re-traumatisation, especially those who had received therapy. For those who did not have the benefit of therapy, testifying was the beginning – a 'justification to tell it to the old respectable judges'.

C   *What Were the Investigators and Interpreters' Observations of the Sexual Assault Witness as an Individual?*

For some of the women interviewed, the unique experiences of common gender roles impacted on the ways in which they related to, and understood, the victim or witness. One investigator said that after she became a mother, she especially understood how vulnerable some witnesses felt when they were unable to protect their children while living in camps during armed conflict. Another investigator said that she could identify with the women, and particularly Bosnian women, because she came from an Asian country that culturally separated genders. An interpreter who came from the former Yugoslavia found that working with the witnesses allowed her to see that she, too, has been a victim of war. Fortunately, the work permitted her to understand, confront and integrate fragments of her past.

D   *As Professionals, How Did the Sexual Assault Witness Test the Professional Skills of the Investigators and Interpreters?*

The emotionally and physically devastating experiences of sexual assault victims/witnesses seemed to be the issue that tested the professional skills of a number of the investigators/interpreters interviewed. Feeling another's sorrow and pain tended to be a recurring theme in interviewee responses. One interpreter who worked from the language booths in the courtroom, said that during a trial where 17 witnesses told individual sexual assault stories, the difficulty was not interpreting the prosecutor's or judge's question, but waiting for the witness to answer – then, as a professional, to use a strong voice to ask the next question. In one case, she was interpreting the questions for a mother whose eleven-year-old daughter disappeared. She hit the mute button so as not to break down. When a colleague offered to continue for her, she insisted that as a professional she would continue, but noted that this was 'the most difficult thing that I ever did'. One investigator recounted that in dealing with sexual assault witnesses, she changed as a person. She felt she could do anything. 'Insider witnesses or sensitive source witnesses are nothing compared to the sexual assault witness who requires so much investigative skill, each and every time'. The way in which interpreters and investigators have dealt with these issues in the Tribunal has, for some, required focussing on the physical and vocal details of the interaction with the victim/witness in order to enable them to do their job professionally. When taking a statement or participating in proofing a witness, one interpreter purposely creates a physical distance but a professional closeness. She would position herself across the table and not along side of the witness, focussing on the language so that what she interpreted could be said in a very accurate way. When victims or witnesses recounted shocking events, however, the interpreter needed breaks for her mental and emotional well being.

*E   What Are Some of the Poignant Memories that Investigators Received from Sexual
       Assault Witnesses?*
Surprisingly, for many of the interpreters and investigators, the memories that stand out are not necessarily about sexual violence but about other humane aspects of the person. One investigator recounted that one particular witness centred less on her ordeal of tens of rapes and focussed more on the trauma of seeing her father being killed. She wanted to make sure that the international community knew that 'he was the best father in the world'. One investigator cannot remove the memory of a photo of a dead little girl in a blue dress, or a woman who was slaughtered – from a distance, the image of the woman looked like a goat. During a proofing session, that same investigator learned not to underestimate the continued awareness and sharpness of the sexual assault witness. When she asked one witness what kind of skirt she was wearing when raped, the witness looked at her and said, 'It was longer than yours'.

F   What Emotional Toll Has the Work Taken on the Investigators and Interpreters?
One interpreter said that it was hard to leave her work behind at the end of the day. Sometimes at night she has dreamed about the person's hands for whom she was interpreting. Another interpreter found it difficult not to break down when she watched victim/witness' faces as they told their tragic stories of sexual violence. She now prefers to interpret subjects, such as military documents, that are 'mind-breaking but not heartbreaking'.

*G   What Would the Interpreters and Investigators Say to Those Sexual Assault
       Witnesses ho Testified during the Past Ten Years at the Tribunal?*
One investigator wishes the women well in their effort to achieve normalcy as they struggle to survive today. An interpreter said that after working with sexual assault witnesses she admired them for their 'strength and courage' but mostly the 'willing-

ness to go on with their lives'. Another interpreter urged the witnesses to 'go on with your lives because it is important not to give up'. She added that 'it starts as a routine, then you start living again, so keep going, especially the rape victim'.

H   What Would the Interpreters and Investigators Want to Say to Those Perpetrators of Rapes, Forced Nudity, Sexual Threats to Coerce Family Members to Flee and Sexual Mutilations?

Most expressed exasperated horror at the perpetrators' deeds and implored them to think of their own daughters and wives as victims, or to think about the intensity of evil that they unleashed. One investigator wrote the following answer that embodies the disgust directed at the majority of perpetrators who wore military or police uniforms. Please, all perpetrators, hear this lucid, other voice that has humanely served the countless victim/survivor witnesses of your crimes.

> By threatening, humiliating, beating, robbing, assaulting, raping and killing civilians – notably women and children under colour of uniform, you committed a variety of acts of dishonour. Firstly, as a human being acting against a fellow human being. None of the acts ...can be excused by poor upbringing, unfair treatment in the past, personal anger at the current situation or physical need. Secondly, as police officers you have likely sworn to protect the state, however, it is the public you serve and the public you owe. In committing criminal acts under colour of uniform you have brought shame on the service, have violated the public trust and are not worthy of the title police officer as no honourable officer in any country will consider you a colleague. Third, as soldiers you have sworn allegiance to a government and a nation against all foes foreign and domestic, and you have taken up the burden of upholding the conventions relating to the behaviours during the war. There are no conventions or customs allowing for such misconduct. You have broken the honour of the soldier, universally and nationally and joined a cadre of bandits who cannot be trusted and who cannot trust each other.
>
> ...
>
> Your debt is great, to your victims from whom you have taken so much, to your service which you have brought shame and disrepute, to your nation who you promised to serve but betrayed, and to mankind in that you have become the least of us all.'[21]

---

21   The opinions and statements of the interpreters and the investigators derive from their personal views, and do not express the official views of the ICTY, nor the United Nations. On behalf of their colleagues, the victims/survivors and the international community I extend my grateful acknowledgement of their invaluable contribution to international justice.

14

Small Conversations Can Lead to Big Changes

*Georgina McEncroe**

I think I will always remember the night I decided that I had to do something about the treatment of women during armed conflict. It was 1994 and I was listening to the radio to a story about rape camps allegedly operating in former Yugoslavia. I stood in my little kitchen in Melbourne, washing up after dinner, listening stunned and horrified to stories of conquerors raping their female enemies, systematically, as means of further humiliating and eradicating the opposition. The radio commentator was quoting from an American academic who was talking about rape as a tool of ethnic cleansing – genocide.

When the program finished, I sat in my house wondering what I could do to help these women and to stop these atrocities. I was an English teacher with a background in bio-ethics and feminism. I had spent a year teaching in Istanbul with the war going on in the Balkans, just a few hundred kilometres away. Unlike Melbourne, the military presence in Istanbul is huge and my male students were all preparing to enter the military as a part of Turkey's compulsory national service. The war, the soldiers, the guns and the military prisons seemed very real and very close. My students discussed with me the terrible possibility of an Islamic Block of states, unified by their persecution in a world where the most powerful nations were non-Muslim and indifferent to the slaughter of Muslims. I had argued that the world *did* care but sometimes it had been impossible to convince myself, let alone those teenage boys and girls who were hearing about it and worrying about it every day.

Upon returning to Australia that feeling of closeness to the conflict had not evaporated. I felt something had to be done and as unskilled and naïve as I was, I was prepared to at least try to help the situation. I was willing to bake, sew, write letters, organise petitions, raise money, talk on street corners – anything to help the people suffering. I especially wanted to help women because I could, to some degree, imagine

---

* Georgina McEncroe is a writer and teacher who is studying editing and professional writing whilst raising her four children. She writes for Amnesty International Human Rights Defender Magazine, The Age, The Australian, The Big Issue and parenting magazines. She was the welfare coordinator at a secondary school in Melbourne for several years and has worked for many years supporting people with disabilities.

Helen Durham and Tracey Gurd (eds.), Listening to the Silences: Women and War, *pp. 165-169.*
© 2005 *Koninklijke Brill BV. Printed in The Netherlands.* ISBN 90 04 14365 3.

myself, my sisters, my mother, being sexually assaulted. It is a vague muddy fear worn by every woman no matter how rich, educated or powerful she seems. It seemed that the women in armed conflict are so very vulnerable.

I rang some friends. I had to talk about this. I had friends who were academics, feminists, lawyers and aid workers. They too were feeling very anxious and angry. We met for a drink and to talk through the issues. We gathered information and discussed strategies. We read articles by journalists, academics and feminists. We looked up relevant sections of international law and sought advice from experts who were also very concerned about the situation in the Balkans. We also decided to join a group designed specifically to assist women refugees. It was called Women's Interlink and it was an offshoot of a refugee agency in Melbourne called Austcare. That made us feel as though we were doing something practical but it still wasn't enough.

When I joined Women's Interlink, I discovered that Austcare had already organised for a member – a psychologist Jane Gronow – to be sent to a refugee camp in Zagreb to offer counselling. At meetings in a comfortable suburban home, we would read the faxes from Jane and listen as she described her life in Zagreb and the sorts of issues the women there were facing. Women's Interlink had sent luxury care packages to refugees which included things like bras, tampons, sanitary pads, lipsticks and deodorant. These were items which we hoped would make these people feel more human in a place where their humanity had been denied. Jane and the women she was working with were very grateful for these things but they wanted something more, something much harder to supply even with the best intentions in the world. The women Jane was helping wanted justice. They wanted the world to know what had happened to them and their communities and they wanted the perpetrators to be brought before the international community and condemned for their actions. And so the Australian Committee of Investigation Into War Crimes (ACIWC) was born.

ACIWC wanted to join the small but insistent chorus of women from all parts of the world who were claiming that sexual assault is more than a tragic, unavoidable consequence of war. Instead it is a powerful tool, capable of causing pain and fear among the enemy long after the 'peace' agreements have been signed. We discovered through the women in Zagreb that the aim of sexual assault in certain armed conflicts is to assist with genocide.

Our aim was to locate women who had survived sexual assault in the former Yugoslavia, and invite them to make statements that could be submitted to the International Criminal Tribunal for the former Yugoslavia (ICTY). We knew that the Australian Government had allowed some 4,000 refugees from the Balkan region into the country and we assumed that some of these refugees would have stories they would be willing to share. By gathering their stories we hoped that perpetrators of these assaults would be prosecuted and a legal precedent would be established. We did eventually achieve our aims but we found that women willing to speak about the subject of sexual assault were hard to find. Having said that however, some of the evidence ACIWC gathered was used to successfully prosecute perpetrators of sexual violence against women. Our research helped identify witnesses who supported the prosecution of Tadić and others in the Prijedor region, especially those operating in the infamous Omaska Camp.

We know that many women never came forward because rape is such a powerful silencer. Rape is especially powerful in cultures where women are seen as being in some way responsible for the crime and somehow permanently dishonoured by it. For some women to talk about their experiences would have meant risking being ostracised by family and friends. Some women chose not to discuss their experiences because of the shame it can bring to the family and the community and because they believe that going over those memories is too difficult. Many women consider that there is little point in making statements because nothing will change if they do.

ACIWC's screening process was opened up to include men. Witnesses to any war crime were invited to give their statements. ACIWC believed that a peaceful relocation into a new country would best be achieved if wounds could be healed through telling the stories of injustice. All injustice stands in the way of peace.

ACIWC encountered many challenges as we developed. In order to invite survivors to come forward we had to first reach them and gain their trust. We relied heavily upon existing community groups and their leaders to take our message to relevant people and to support the efforts of ICTY. ACIWC soon discovered that many of these communities and their leaders felt victimised by the international community and they wanted ACIWC to see things from a particular cultural point of view. The various ethnic groups were suspicious of our motives and our desire to seek evidence. Once ACIWC established that we were not looking for war criminals and that all people who felt they had suffered a war crime – men, women, Catholic, Muslim or Serbian Orthodox – were invited to speak to us, some of the tension dissipated.

We were, of course, dealing with people who were over-worked, under-resourced and deeply saddened, angry and worried about events taking place in their respective homelands. They felt betrayed or victimised by the world's armed forces and media and had given up hope of justice.

ACIWC also found that some people who claimed to be community leaders did not in fact have the support of the people they claimed to represent. They usually had risen to power by having an excellent command of English. This, combined with the fact that there were often no elections for these unpaid positions, meant that ACIWC sometimes found that it had wasted valuable time and energy on someone who had little influence over his or her community.

We often worked in an atmosphere of real terror. The people we spoke to were still thinking and behaving like people at war. Although they knew in one sense that they were safe, they found it very hard to feel in any way peaceful. We had to have very clear guidelines to ensure that we protected the security of witnesses. ACIWC had excellent advice from a former federal policeman regarding security issues.

In order to gain the trust of the interviewees we had to first become worthy. We interviewed witnesses at a secure neutral location where a security guard was employed. We organised transport for witnesses and paid for their cab fares so they would not have to wait alone for public transport. Most importantly, the statements given never bore the name of the witness. The statement had a random number on the top of the page and the person's name was kept in a separate, secure safety box. The statement itself was kept in a separate place and the two documents were never placed together. We made sure that ACIWC members interviewed in teams so we were never alone with witnesses.

Providing the suitable interpreters was also very difficult at times. It brought home to us the very real fear that the witnesses experienced. ACIWC had an incident at the beginning of an interview one evening when a Bosnian Muslim woman was coming to give her statement. The witness was sitting with her support person and when the translator began to speak our witness got up and left the room. She was very upset and frightened. We later discovered that despite asking for a translator who was Bosnian Muslim, we had been sent a translator who had been raised in Serbia and who apparently had a Serbian accent. We did our best to find women translators for female witnesses and male translators for male witnesses. We tried to always match the culture of the witness with the interpreter. Sometimes, however, it was impossible and it was not always important to the witness.

Many of the people we were dealing with had heard terrible stories and the propaganda on all sides of the conflict was extremely powerful. Refugees in Australia heard of war criminals escaping to Australia using the stolen documents of their murdered victims. Some stories told of victims seeing their torturers in the supermarket. Other refugees told us that they'd heard they shouldn't come forward because the day after someone spoke with ACIWC, his cousin was killed in a camp in Hungary. The level of fear was very high and it affected ACIWC members too, although not nearly to the same degree.

ACIWC recognised that the witnesses giving statements could be suffering from trauma. ACIWC arranged with the Foundation for the Survivors of Torture and Trauma for it to provide free counselling and therapy. Members of ACIWC also experienced some degree of trauma through being involved in this process and immersing ourselves in the pain of these witnesses. Although our screening kit asked limited questions, we could observe and begin to imagine the horror suffered simply by being with a witness. On one occasion a man entered the room to give a statement and I assumed he was about 65 years of age. When he gave his date of birth, I began to shake from head to toe. He was younger than me. I was 26 at the time. He had been held at a notorious camp for several months. He required two walking sticks just to stand up.

Over 15 months ACIWC screened 20 witnesses to assist the ICTY. The Office of the Prosecutor thanked us for our work and Graham Blewitt, Deputy Prosecutor, wrote:

> 'The work of the ACIWC in Australia has lead to the discovery of several important witnesses and ... ACIWC is one of the most professional NGOs that the Tribunal is currently dealing with and I applaud the work that it is doing'.[1]

These days I am a housewife. I have four children. My days consist of shopping, cooking, cleaning, getting little people ready for school, taking them to swimming lessons and growling at them for hurting each other or being impolite to people. But when I

---

1   This was sent to the Chairperson of ACCIWC. A copy of the letter is on file with author.

think about this very humdrum, suburban life I lead and start to feel a bit depressed by the ordinariness of it all, I think about how many people in the world are literally dying for such an ordinary life of kids, family and peaceful normality.

We were amateurs with nothing to guide us but our own sense of duty and obligation. We received no money, no training and no regular guidance and yet we seem to have mirrored, in many respects, the work done by the investigators commissioned by the ICTY. I say that not to boast, but simply to reflect upon the way in which civil society can come up with strategies and systems for dealing with injustices, through conversation and sheer energy. We encountered the same difficulties as those described by Patricia Viseur Sellers in her article about the role of translators and investigators assisting with the Rwanda Trials and former Yugoslavia. I am proud of what we achieved and although much remains to be done to improve the rights of women especially during armed conflict, I have seen with my own eyes how small conversations can lead to very big changes. Outrage alone cannot achieve much, but outrage combined with integrity, intelligence and respect for the rule of law, can do a great deal.

15

Facilitating Women's Voices in Truth Recovery: An Assessment of Women's Participation and the Integration of a Gender Perspective in Truth Commissions

*Hayli Millar**

I Introduction

This chapter provides a critical assessment of the gendered dimensions of truth commissions[1] drawing primarily on the South African Truth and Reconciliation Commission (1995-2002) as an instructive example of women's experiences with one truth commission. Towards the end of the chapter, selective comparisons are made with other truth commissions including the historically prominent Argentinean (1983-1984), Chilean (1990-1991), El Salvadoran (1992-1993), Haitian (1995-1996) and Guatemalan (1997-1999) commissions as well as more recently established entities such as the Sierra Leone Truth and Reconciliation Commission (2002-present) and East Timor Commission for Reception, Truth and Reconciliation (2002-present).

---

* BA, MA (Simon Fraser University). PhD Candidate, Faculty of Law, University of Melbourne; expected submission February 2005. Much of the research for this article was conducted in 2001, with some updating of materials in October through December 2003.

1 See generally Priscilla Hayner, 'Fifteen Truth Commissions – 1974 to 1994: A Comparative Study' (1994) 16 *Human Rights Quarterly* 597, 600-611; Siri Gloppen, *Reconciliation and Democratisation: Outlining the Research Field* (2002) 17-19, fn 27. There is no one accepted definition of a truth commission and varying classification schemes suggest the need for greater conceptual precision to differentiate truth commissions from other forms of inquiry. The present assessment regards a truth commission as an official investigatory body convened by a successor or transitional government or inter-governmental authority to examine a history of serious international humanitarian and human rights law violations. A truth commission may investigate past violations committed solely by or on behalf of a previous regime or in addition to violations committed by opposition groups. The notion that a truth commission is able to investigate a broad historical pattern of repression, including the origins and consequences of past violations, is an integral feature of such bodies. A truth commission generally is adjunct to existing state institutions and transitory, functioning for a fixed period. Usually truth commissions possess both investigatory *and* advisory functions. Truth commissions are characterised as non-judicial or extra-legal bodies in the sense that they typically do not determine individual criminal responsibility and lack prosecutorial powers.

Helen Durham and Tracey Gurd (eds.), Listening to the Silences: Women and War, *pp. 171-222*.
© 2005 *Koninklijke Brill BV. Printed in The Netherlands. ISBN 90 04 14365 3.*

The author explores three basic questions about women and truth commissions. Do women participate in accountability decision-making, especially the policy choice to establish a truth commission and by extention in its legislative or institutional design? Are truth commissions emulating the positive jurisprudential and structural gains for women that have been achieved in 'hard' international criminal law? Do truth commissions address the diversity of women's conflict experiences and the differential effects of armed or political conflict for women?

Propelled by scant attention to the transitional justice needs of women, a partial gender analysis is undertaken focusing exclusively on women.[2] Consistent with other approaches to women and international law, particular emphasis is placed on examining the treatment of sexual and gender-based violence directed against women. The assessment is not exhaustive and should be regarded as a starting point for further discussion and exploration. Its aim is to establish some baseline data about women and truth commissions.

The gendered dimensions of truth commissions are not always obvious from the available public record. At times, it is difficult to ascertain women's participation in truth commissions beyond a somewhat superficial numeric level. As this assessment illustrates, women's presence, whether as signatories to peace agreement provisions establishing truth commissions or as truth commissioners, may increase the likelihood – but does not guarantee – that gender-specific concerns are addressed.

The South African Truth and Reconciliation Commission (TRC) was chosen to exemplify women's experiences because it is considered one of the most widely consultative commissions to date, with substantial contributions from civil society. The South African TRC is internationally renowned and has been the subject of intensive scholarly interest; consequently there is an abundance of published literature to draw on in addition to readily accessible primary data. In spite of a compelling formal gender submission, the South African TRC highlights various challenges associated with facilitating women's participation and integrating a gender perspective – especially when accommodations are 'grafted on' after enabling legislation has been enacted or proceedings have commenced. The failure to integrate gender in its original legislation – and the subsequent modification of its processes to partially address women's concerns – is significant when one contemplates that the South African TRC is promoted as an international model for the formulation of truth commissions in other jurisdictions. Given that the South African TRC can be regarded roughly as a midpoint in the sequential development of truth commissions, it represents an appropriate juncture to reflect on the participation of women and gender integration.[3]

---

2   The term 'women' is used in this chapter to refer to both women and girls.

3   See 'Annex I: List of Truth Commissions Established or Proposed 1982-2003' at the end of this chapter for a chronological listing of the truth commissions surveyed for this assessment.

A   *The Literature on Women and Truth Commissions*

In her recent book, *Unspeakable Truths: Confronting State Terror and Atrocity*, Priscilla Hayner surveys 21 official truth commissions established between 1974 and 1999. She noted at the time that as many as 16 other jurisdictions were contemplating the creation of a truth commission to address their past conflicts.[4] The contemporary importance of truth commissions is underscored by a March 2001 report of the United Nations Secretary General requesting that 'the Security Council consider the establishment of arrangements addressing impunity and, as appropriate, *for truth and reconciliation*, during the crafting of peacekeeping mandates (emphasis added)' especially in situations where violations of international humanitarian and human rights law are widespread and systematic.[5]

While truth commissions clearly have emerged as an accepted alternative – or with increasing frequency as a complementary accountability mechanism to criminal prosecution – there has been limited systematic study of women's experiences with truth commissions. Scholarly interest concerning women and transitional justice has focused predominantly on prosecutorial remedies for serious violations of international humanitarian and human rights law. Comparatively less attention has been devoted to the examination of women and non-prosecutorial remedies, even while recognising that state obligations under international law to confront past violations are much more comprehensive than simply prosecution and punishment[6] and that punitive measures do not fully address the needs of women.

The prominence given to prosecutorial remedies for gender violations of international humanitarian and human rights law is reproduced in the accountability provisions of UN Security Council Resolution 1325 (2000) on Women, Peace and Security. In addition to calling for an amnesty exclusion, these provisions emphasise the responsibility of states to prosecute those responsible 'for genocide, crimes against humanity, and war crimes including those relating to sexual and other violence against women and girls', yet are silent on complementary forms of redress.[7] Correspondingly, the

---

4   See Priscilla Hayner, *Unspeakable Truths: Confronting State Terror and Atrocity* (2001) 14, 23 fn 26, 32-71.

5   *Report of the Secretary-General on the Protection of Civilians in Armed Conflict*, 53 UN SCOR, UN Doc S/2001/331 (2001) [13] Recommendation 2.

6   See especially Paul van Zyl, 'Justice Without Punishment: Guaranteeing Human Rights in Transitional Societies' in Charles Villa-Vicencio and Wilhelm Verwoerd (eds), *Looking Back Reaching Forward: Reflections on the Truth and Reconciliation Commission of South Africa* (2000) 42, 49 who outlines five affirmative state obligations in international law, including the duty to firstly establish the fate of victims and secondly the identity of perpetrators, thirdly to compensate victims, fourthly to take affirmative measures to prevent non-repetition, and fifthly to prosecute and punish those found guilty.

7   *Resolution on Women, Peace and Security*, SC Res 1325, 55 UN SCOR (4213ᵗʰ mtg), UN Doc S/RES/1325 (2000) [11]. This comment is not meant to detract from the momentous progress that the resolution represents as an authoritative declaration against impunity for violations perpetrated against women and girls, but rather to highlight the expectation that redress options for women should be as *comprehensive* as possible.

Secretary-General's 2002 study on Women, Peace and Security[8] and the Independent Experts' Assessment on the Impact of Armed Conflict on Women and Women's Role in Peace Building[9] place greater emphasis on criminal prosecution than truth commissions, reparations or other forms of justice.

Gender perspectives including women's experiences are marginalised in contemporary writings on truth commissions. The scant literature on women and truth commissions nevertheless identifies two specific concerns.[10] The first of these concerns is the underreporting of sexual violence offences, including rape, experienced by women. The second concern encompasses differential patterns of testimony between women and men, whereby women deponents devalue their own victimisation and instead relate the indirect victimisation experiences of their male family members. In comparison, men recount their direct victimisation experiences. It follows that truth commissions may portray the violations experienced by women as a relatively small percentage of the total violations reported to the commission.

At a practical level, the failure of truth commissions to fully integrate women's experiences is troubling because it leads to a distorted historical record of 'truth' and may well restrict women's entitlement to additional forms of legal redress. In South Africa, for instance, entitlement to reparations is limited to those formally declared victims[11] by the TRC. In view of their reluctance to disclose victimisation or speak about direct victimisation, women either will be ineligible or must rely on their secondary status as the 'relatives or dependents' of formally recognised victims to seek reparations. As others have argued more generically in relation to women and conflict transformation,[12] the exclusion of women and non-integration of a gender perspective in truth commission structures and processes is equally troubling because it perpetuates existing power asymmetries between women and men and is less likely to contribute to sustainable peace building.

Taking into account the identified concerns about women and truth commissions, the assessment is framed in terms of three broad questions adapted from the

---

8   See *Women, Peace and Security, Study submitted by the Secretary-General pursuant to Security Council resolution 1325*, (2000), 57 UN SCOR, UN Doc S/2002/1154 (2002) [116]-[161], [343]-[345] (*'UN Study'*).

9   See Elisabeth Rehn and Ellen Johnson Sirleaf, *Women, War and Peace: The Independent Experts' Assessment on the Impact of Armed Conflict on Women and Women's Role in Peacebuilding* (2002), UNIFEM website <http://www.unifem.undp.org/resources/assessment/index.html> 93-101.

10 See especially Hayner, above n 4, 77-79; Donna Pankhurst, *Mainstreaming Gender in Peacebuilding: A Framework for Action* (From the Village Council to the Negotiating Table: The International Campaign to Promote the Role of Women in Peacebuilding, Women Building Peace, 1999) 24. See also Rehn and Sirleaf, above n 9, (2002) 99-100 who essentially restate these concerns.

11 The term victim corresponds with the terminology used by the *Promotion of National Unity and Reconciliation Act 1995* (South Africa) as well as the Truth and Reconciliation Commission. For this assessment, the term 'victim' encompasses victims and survivors.

12 See, for example, Diana Francis, 'Culture, Power Asymmetries and Gender in Conflict Transformation' (Berghof Handbook for Conflict Transformation, Berghof Research Centre for Constructive Conflict Management, 2001) 9.

women and peace building, women and international law and women and armed conflict literature.

1. *Do women participate in accountability decision-making extending to the policy choice to establish a truth commission?* In the women and peace building literature, it is widely observed that women are actively engaged as informal peace activists yet excluded as participants in formal peace negotiation processes.[13] Such exclusion, it is argued, extends to decisions about post-conflict reconstruction, including decisions about accountability arrangements,[14] resulting in the adoption of policies that either completely ignore women's needs or fail to account for the policy's differential effects on women and men.[15] As Elisabeth Rehn and Ellen Johnson Sirleaf maintain, '[rarely] have women been consulted about the form, scope and modalities for seeking accountability'.[16] Amid renewed emphasis on the greater participation of women at all levels of conflict-to-peace decision-making,[17] one of the key issues addressed by the present assessment is whether women participate in *accountability* decision-making extending to the policy choice to establish a truth commission and in the formulation of truth commission legislation or institutional design. If women participate in accountability decision-making, what form does women's participation take and what effect does it have on the integration of a gender perspective? This question is well timed because there are few published accounts systematically deconstructing the role of women as participants in accountability policymaking processes.[18]

2. *Are truth commissions replicating the positive jurisprudential and structural gains that women have achieved in 'hard' international criminal law?* Largely as the result of intensive advocacy efforts by women's organisations, there have been several positive jurisprudential and structural advances for women in 'hard' international criminal law. These advances involve the emergence of more precise legal standards on rape and gender-based violence as elements of war crimes, crimes against humanity, genocide, torture and enslavement[19] as well as the statutory integration

---

13   See for example, Li Fung's chapter 'Engendering the Peace Process: Women's Role in Peace Building and Conflict Resolution' later in this book; cf discussion in Swanee Hunt's chapter 'Moving Beyond Silence: Women Waging Peace' at the end of this collection, and insights contained in Luz Méndez's chapter 'Women's Role in Peacemaking: A Personal Experience' in the first section of this book.

14   Drawing on the description offered by Rehn and Sirleaf, above n 9, 7, accountability is conceived as *answerability to women* who have been violated in the context of past armed or political conflict.

15   See especially Pankhurst, above n 10, 6-7, 23-24.

16   Rehn and Sirleaf, above n 9, 89.

17   See *UN Study*, above n 8, [1]-[2].

18   The comparatively well-documented Women's Caucus for Gender Justice in the ICC concerning the Rome Statute for the International Criminal Court and the NGO Working Group on Women, Peace and Security which lobbied for the accountability provisions contained in UN Security Council Resolution 1325 (2000) may be the exceptions to this.

19   See *Integration of the Human Rights of Women and the Gender Perspective: Violence Against Women, Report of the Special Rapporteur on violence against women, its causes and consequences*, 57 UN ESCOR, UN Doc E/CN.4/2001/73 (2001) [9]-[40] ('*Violence Against Women Report*').

of special measures to encourage the participation and protection of women victims and witnesses in international criminal justice processes.[20] The January 2001 report of the Special Rapporteur on Violence against Women surveying these developments from 1997 to 2000 in relation to statutes and case law for the ad hoc criminal tribunals and the Rome Statute for the International Criminal Court[21] provokes the question of whether similar approaches are being used in 'soft' international criminal law. To what extent are women's concerns integrated in truth commission legislation or institutional design? Are truth commissions expressly mandated, or otherwise willing, to investigate and make findings of sexual and/or gender violence violations concerning genocide, war crimes or crimes against humanity? Do truth commission statutes embody principles of non-discrimination? Do fair gender representation criteria guide the appointment of truth commissioners and truth commission staff? Are gender experts or advisers assigned to truth commissions? Do truth commissions adopt special measures to encourage women's testimony, especially as victims or survivors of sexual violence? Finally, do truth commissions implement special procedures for the enhanced protection or privacy of women who are victims and witnesses, or make available specialised psycho-social support services for women victims and witnesses?

3. *Are truth commissions attentive to the varied and complex roles of women in conflict and the differential effects of armed or political conflict on women?* The observation that conflict affects women in ways that are quantitatively and qualitatively different from men is well documented.[22] Until now, however, there has been limited analysis of the manner in which *accountability* processes acknowledge the varied experiences of women during conflict or the differential consequences of armed or political conflict for women. The present assessment explores whether truth commissions, in their investigative and reporting capacities, embrace the diversity of women's conflict experiences not only as victims/survivors but also as activists, combatants and perpetrators. Additionally it is queried whether truth commissions, in their advisory role, recommend reparative and ameliorative measures that sufficiently address the harmful consequences of armed or political conflict for women.

Each of these areas of inquiry is explored in some detail below with regard to women's experience with the South African TRC, followed by selective comparisons with other historically prominent and more recently established truth commissions.

---

20   See for example, Women's Caucus for Gender Justice, *International Criminal Court Fact Sheet* (undated) Women's International League for Peace and Freedom <http://www.peacewomen.org/un/icj/icc.html> at 4 November 2003.

21   See *Violence Against Women Report*, above n 19, [9]-[40].

22   See for example Charlotte Lindsey, 'Women and War' (2000) 839 *International Review of the Red Cross* 561.

II   Women and the South African Truth and
Reconciliation Commission

The South African TRC was established by the *Promotion of National Unity and Reconciliation Act 1995* (South Africa) which took effect with the appointment of commissioners in December 1995.[23] Originally intended to function for a period not exceeding two years, the Commission was extended in a modified form following the October 1998 publication of its five volume Report to accommodate the finalisation of amnesty hearings. The TRC was formally dissolved on 31 March 2002 after approximately six-and-a-half years of operation. Two codicil volumes of the Report concerning amnesty and victim findings were published in March 2003.[24]

A   *Women and the South African Decision to Establish a Truth Commission*

By most accounts, South African women's organisations mobilised an effective cross-sectoral lobby to ensure that women's concerns were integrated as part of the political transition process (1990-1994) and in the new constitutional arrangements.[25] On the evidence available, the voice of women and women's organisations seems to have been more muted in accountability decision-making extending to the policy choice to establish a TRC and the formulation of draft legislation for the truth commission.

South African accountability policy is encapsulated in the 'National Unity and Reconciliation' postamble of the interim Constitution of 1993.[26] The postamble guarantees that amnesty will be granted for past political acts in order to advance reconciliation and reconstruction. Drafting of the amnesty clause apparently took place outside of established consultative structures in what has been described as a 'closed and secretive' process.[27] Different persons are credited with the actual crafting of the

---

23   See *Truth and Reconciliation Commission of South Africa Report* (1999) vol 1, 53.

24   The five volume *Truth and Reconciliation Commission of South Africa Report* (1999) was widely distributed and the final two volumes, Volumes 6 and 7, published in March 2003, are electronically accessible at <http://www.doj/gov.sa/trc/trc_frameset.htm>. The South African Department of Justice maintains a Truth and Reconciliation Commission (TRC) link <http://www.doj.gov.sa/trc> which hosts original documentation for the Commission including enabling legislation and legislative amendments, amnesty decisions and transcripts, human rights hearing transcripts, various submissions to the Commission and press reports. For discussion of the operations of the commission from October 1998 until March 2002, see especially *Truth and Reconciliation Commission of South Africa Report* (2003) vol 6, 733-734.

25   See generally Catherine Albertyn, 'Women and the Transition to Democracy in South Africa' in Christina Murray (ed), *Gender and the New South African Legal Order* (1994) 39; Brigitte Mabandla, 'Women in South Africa and the Constitution-Making Process' in Julie Peters and Andrea Wolper (eds), *Women's Rights Human Rights: International Feminist Perspectives* (1995) 67, 68-71; Sheila Meintjes, 'The Women's Struggle for Equality During South Africa's Transition to Democracy' (1996) 30 *Transformation* 47.

26   See *Constitution of the Republic of South Africa, Act 200, 1993*. The interim Constitution came into effect on 27 April 1994.

27   See Richard A Wilson, *The Politics of Truth and Reconciliation in South Africa: Legitimising the Post-Apartheid State* (2001) 8 who discusses negotiating irregularities and the absence

postamble and the most likely negotiators of the political amnesty agreement are men.[28] Still it is difficult to be precise about the role of women and women's organisations in relation to the amnesty pact given the irregularity and secrecy of its negotiation. Catherine Albertyn's[29] assessment of women's participation and the advocacy of gender interests in the political negotiations process leading to adoption of the interim Constitution would suggest it is unlikely that women and women's organisations participated in any meaningful way in negotiating the amnesty postamble. Despite the achievement of women's numeric presence at the negotiating table as delegates and advisors, and as members of the technical committees in the Multi-Party Negotiating Process, Albertyn describes the progressive marginalisation of women and gender interests especially from bilateral negotiations in which crucial decisions were made.

There is no explicit reference to a TRC in the interim Constitution. Rather, the National Unity and Reconciliation postamble left Parliament to determine the particular mechanisms 'including tribunals' to confer amnesty. Even so, many South Africans anticipated the establishment of a truth commission and it is plausible that the National Party as 'caretaker' government and the ANC as 'government in waiting' made a gentleman's agreement to grant amnesty in exchange for truth.[30]

While it seems clear that an elite group of men led the truth commission lobby and legislative drafting process,[31] individual women and women's organisations sup-

---

of transparency and open debate on the agreement. See also Lourens du Plessis, 'Legal Analysis' in Alex Boraine, Janet Levy and Ronel Scheffer (eds), *Dealing With the Past: Truth and Reconciliation in South Africa* (1997) 109 for description of negotiation inconsistencies.

28   See for example, Wilson, above n 27, 8. Richard Wilson maintains that technical committee members Mr Fanie van der Merwe (NP) and Mr Mac Maharaj (ANC) were tasked by the National Party and ANC chief negotiators, Mr Roelf Meyer and Mr Cyril Ramaphosa, to draft the postamble amnesty clause. Various persons have claimed authorship of the amnesty clause though it is generally accepted that either or both Kader Asmal and Albie Sachs were involved in writing the agreement.

29   See Albertyn, above n 25, 39, 53-57, 57-60. In fairness, Albertyn concedes that women's demands were not sufficiently prepared ahead of the interim Constitution negotiations. Moreover, as Albertyn highlights, women's advocacy efforts tended to centre on the highly contentious issue of incorporating traditional/customary law provisions in the Constitution.

30   See especially Lynn Berat and Yossi Shain, 'Retribution or Truth-Telling in South Africa? Legacies of the Transitional Phase' (1995) 20 *Law and Social Inquiry* 163, 183. Berat and Shain recount negotiations between the government, security forces and the ANC, arguing that the ANC agreed to a comprehensive, though individualised, amnesty in exchange for a truth commission.

31   See Alex Boraine, *A Country Unmasked. Inside South Africa's Truth and Reconciliation Commission* (2000) 49; Justice in Transition Database (copy on file with author), personal communication with Ms Paddy Clark, Personal Assistant to Dr Alex Boraine (Cape Town, 11 October 2001). The informal drafting committee consisted of Dullah Omar, Medard Rwelamira, Johnny de Lange, Willie Hofmeyr, Enver Daniels, and Alex Boraine. Organisations and individuals that provided advice to the drafting committee and/or commented on the draft bill include: the Black Lawyers Association, Lawyers for Human Rights, the Legal Resources Centre, the National Association of Democratic Lawyers,

ported the idea of a truth commission and made important contributions in the period of debate and amendment leading to the adoption of the *Promotion of National Unity and Reconciliation Act* in 1995. Domestic women's human rights organisations, most noticeably the Black Sash,[32] publicly expressed their support for the concept of an investigatory or truth commission on various occasions between 1992 and 1994. Individual women participated in the 1992 IDASA sponsored study tour to Eastern Europe examining transitional justice options.[33] Several South African women participated in the two main conferences, an IDASA-sponsored international conference in February 1994 and a national conference organised by Justice in Transition in July 1994, that were convened to discuss transitional justice options for South Africa.[34] It can be surmised that women took part individually and collectively in the draft bill public education initiatives organised by Justice in Transition, encompassing country-wide seminars and workshops. The Black Sash was among the organisations that lobbied for specific amendments to the Promotion of National Unity and Reconciliation Bill and made representations to the Portfolio Committee on Justice.[35]

Nevertheless the pattern of women's engagement with the truth commission lobby, like that of civil society organisations more generally, was largely *invitational* and *reactive*. As Hugo van der Merwe, Polly Dewhirst and Brandon Hamber[36] describe more generally in relation to the participation of civil society in the months preceding establishment of the TRC, it was often individuals rather than their organisations who were *invited* to contribute. Moreover, these authors contend, civil society organisations exercised comparatively greater influence lobbying for changes *in response* to the draft bill than in proactively crafting the legislation. The public record reveals also that the participation of women and women's organisations in the legislative negotiations process was more likely to be *indirect* with Justice in Transition functioning as a conduit between civil society and the Minister of Justice. A well-organised and

---

Advocate George Bizos, (Judge) Mohammed Navsa, (Judge) Richard Goldstone, and (Judge) Albie Sachs. External actors who submitted comments on the draft bill include Carl Norgaard, Jose Zalaquet, Robert Howse and Priscilla Hayner. Of the identified individuals, the only woman is Priscilla Hayner.

32   See Black Sash, 'Who We Are', <http://www.blacksash.org.sa/Who.html>. The Black Sash began in 1955 as a women's antiapartheid human rights movement and generally is regarded as South Africa's oldest human rights organisation. The Black Sash was extensively engaged in documenting human rights violations during apartheid.

33   See Boraine, above n 31, 14, fn 11. These women include Elsie Nair, Sarah Pienaar and Charlene Smith.

34   See for example, Boraine, Levy and Scheffer, above n 27, 156-159; Boraine, above n 31, 16-17, 43-44. Justice in Transition is a non-partisan NGO created to facilitate the truth commission legislative drafting and public consultation process.

35   See eg Enrico Kemp, 'Truth (News Feature)' (26 January 1995) African National Congress <http://www.anc.org.sa/newsbrief/1995/news0127> at 4 April 2002; Boraine, above n 31, 51-52.

36   See Hugo van der Merwe, Polly Dewhirst and Brandon Hamber, *Non-governmental Organisations and the Truth and Reconciliation Commission: An Impact Assessment* (1999) [Lobbying in Response to the Draft Legislation] Centre for the Study of Violence and Reconciliation <http://www.wits.ac.sa/csvr/papers/paphvp&b.htm> at 28 March 2001.

unified voice concerning the participation of women and the integration of a gender perspective in truth commission institutional design did not emerge until after the *Promotion of National Unity and Reconciliation Act 1995* was enacted.

1   A Gender Neutral Promotion of National Unity and Reconciliation Act 1995

The *Promotion of National Unity and Reconciliation Act 1995* is essentially gender neutral. The preamble of the Act refers to 'sex' within the context of a 'future founded on the recognition of human rights, democracy and peaceful co-existence for all South Africans irrespective of colour, race, class, belief or sex'. The sole reference to gender is found in the section 11 guiding principles for the treatment of victims, which provides *inter alia* that victims should be treated equally and without discrimination based on several enumerated grounds including gender, sex or sexual orientation. The *Promotion of National Unity and Reconciliation Act 1995* makes no specific reference to women or for that matter to sexual or gender-based violence offences.

Gender concerns were partially addressed following the commencement of Commission proceedings in December 1995. In May 1996, shortly after the first human rights violation hearing had been held, Beth Goldblatt and Sheila Meintjes from the University of Witwatersrand made a formal gender submission to the TRC.[37] The gender submission was based on an earlier March 1996 workshop and augmented by in depth interviews with a number of prominent South African women victims/ survivors. The purpose of the submission was to assist the Commission in thinking about 'how gender forms part of the truth and reconciliation process'. The submission identified 'ways in which the Commission might be missing some of the truth',[38] among other things providing a detailed historical analysis of women's experiences under apartheid and the human rights violations suffered by women within the context of political violence. The submission offered a number of specific proposals for the greater integration of a gender perspective in truth commission processes, in particular stressing the need for adjustments to the definition of gross violations of human rights as well as the amnesty and reparation provisions of the *Promotion of National Unity and Reconciliation Act 1995*.

Commissioners Yasmin Sooka and Glenda Wildschut, both women, were required to advise the TRC on how to respond to the gender submission and two workshops were organised to discuss ways of 'bringing more women into the TRC process'.[39] In August 1996, some eight months after the commencement of TRC operations, the Commission reportedly agreed to several of the gender submission proposals including the need to convene special hearings for women in each of four regions and explore special mechanisms to facilitate women's testimony; provide gender train-

---

37   See Beth Goldblatt and Sheila Meintjes, *Gender and the Truth Commission: A Submission to the Truth and Reconciliation Commission* (1996) [A] and [B] Truth and Reconciliation Commission (South Africa) (hereafter referred to as the 'gender submission') <http:// www.truth.org.sa/submit/gender.htm> at 17 June 2002.

38   *Truth and Reconciliation Commission of South Africa Report* (1999) vol 4, 282.

39   *Ibid.*, 282-283.

ing for commissioners; focus on women accused of being perpetrators, and; develop a gender-attentive reparations policy.[40]

B   *Jurisprudential and Structural Accommodations for South African Women*

1   Gender and Gross Violations of Human Rights

The *Promotion of National Unity and Reconciliation Act 1995* mandated the TRC to investigate gross violations of human rights committed within or outside of South Africa between 1 March 1960 and 5 December 1993, later extended to 10 May 1994. Gross violations of human rights were legislatively defined by section 1 of the *Promotion of National Unity and Reconciliation Act 1995* as the 'killing abduction, torture or severe ill treatment' of any person or the 'attempt, conspiracy, incitement, instigation, command or procurement' to commit such acts. As further provided by section 1, and in addition to the specified geographic and time constraints, the behaviour in question must have originated in the conflicts of the past and been 'advised, planned, directed, commanded or ordered' by a person acting with a political motive. Consequently, to qualify as a gross human rights violation, it was necessary to establish a nexus between the act and its political context and motivation.[41]

The definition of gross violations of human rights proved to be controversial for its limited focus on post-1960 violations and narrow construction of apartheid, encapsulating contraventions of 'bodily integrity rights' rather than the system of apartheid.[42] From a gender perspective,[43] the definition was problematic for its evident neglect of women's gender-specific experiences under apartheid. The need for an expansive interpretation of the definition of gross violations of human rights was central to the gender submission, particularly since entitlement to reparations was contingent on a formal finding of victimisation by the Commission. The gender submission suggested that the concept of 'severe ill treatment' be broadly read to embrace the full range of violations suffered by women such as detention without trial, unjust imprisonment, forced removals, pass arrests, land confiscation, disruptions to family life, and enforced racial education.

In practice, the TRC interpreted torture and severe ill treatment to encompass many though not all of the sexual and gender-based violence dimensions of gross human rights violations identified by the gender submission.[44] As conceded by the

---

40   See *Truth and Reconciliation Commission,* 'South Africa: TRC and Gender' (Press Release, 15 August 1996) [Recommendations] Africa Action <http://www.africaaction.org/docs96/ trc9608.htm> at 25 November 2003.

41   See *Truth and Reconciliation Commission of South Africa Report* (1999) vol 1, 82.

42   See for example, ibid, 29, 64.

43   See Goldblatt and Meintjes, above n 37, [D].

44   See *Truth and Reconciliation Commission of South Africa Report* (1999) vol 1, 78-81; vol 5, 18-22. For example, the operative definitions of torture and severe ill treatment, when taken together, captured 'beating' including assaults of genitals, breasts and pregnant victims; 'deprivation' including the withholding of food and medical care; 'electric shock' including those administered to the genitals or breasts; 'psychological or mental torture' including solitary confinement, degradation, disinformation; 'mutilation' including of the genitals;

TRC, the final definition of gross violations of human rights may not be perceived to have fully addressed gender concerns as the entirety of women's experiences under apartheid, for example with respect to pass control laws, enforced education and land confiscation, were not embraced. In the words of the Commission:

> To integrate gender fully ... would have required the Commission to amend its understanding of its mandate and how it defined gross human rights violations ... The Commission's relative neglect of the effects of the "ordinary" workings of apartheid has a gender bias, as well as a racial one.[45]

The Commission states further that:

> the definition of gross violation of human rights adopted by the Commission resulted in a blindness to the types of abuse predominantly experienced by women. In this respect, the full report of the Commission and the evidence presented to it can be compared to reports on South African poverty, which make it very clear that while women were not the only sufferers, they bear the brunt of the suffering.[46]

These assessments are not inconsequential. In essence, they conclude that the TRC failed to incorporate gender adequately into its operations and its jurisprudential framework so that the extent of women's suffering under apartheid remained unacknowledged and unaddressed. The enormity of these findings become evident when, as will be discussed in more detail below, the TRC is used as a model for more recent truth commission initiatives. The gravity of these issues is further compounded when the TRC's jurisprudential findings are assessed for their gender sensitivity. One of the most crucial areas, in this respect, has been the construction of rape charges and whether rape could be classified as a 'politically motivated' offence.

(a)   The Question of Rape Under the Promotion of National Unity and Reconciliation Act 1995
The construction of particular crimes as 'politically motivated' had important implications for both the alleged perpetrator and the victim/survivor in the TRC. The ascription of 'political motivation' could entitle the perpetrator to apply for amnesty. It could also enable the victim/survivor to place her/his experience within the broader political context of apartheid and, if the TRC found in her/his favour, she/he could be officially categorised as a 'victim' and thus entitled to reparations. Yet some confusion existed as to whether rape was considered a 'politically motivated' offence by the TRC.

---

and 'sexual assault and abuse' including physical assaults on breasts and genitals, rape, forced sexual acts, insertion of foreign objects or substances, use of animals, threats of rape, touching, nakedness, comments or insults, enticement, and deprivation of sanitary facilities. Additionally, the definition of 'severe ill treatment' encompassed 'banning or banishment' and 'detention without charge or trial', with intimidation and harassment categorised as 'associated violations'.

45   *Truth and Reconciliation Commission of South Africa Report* (1999) vol 4, 287-288.
46   *Ibid.*, 316.

Prima facie, the *Promotion of National Unity and Reconciliation Act 1995* does not preclude applications for amnesty where the act, omission or offence was rape or another sexual violence offence. According to section 18(1) of the *Promotion of National Unity and Reconciliation Act 1995* (South Africa) *any person* was eligible to apply for amnesty 'in respect of any act, omission or offence ... associated with a political objective'. Under section 20(3), however, any act that was committed 'for personal gain' or 'out of malice, ill-will or spite' was considered non-political and consequently disqualified for amnesty.

The gender submission identified two principal but competing concerns on the issue of amnesty.[47] On one hand, a decision to grant amnesty for rape would signify tolerance for women's oppression and the permissibility of rape in certain circumstances. On the other hand, in view of women's testimony that described the personal, malice, ill will or spite *and* political motivations of rape, the gender submission surmised that the Amnesty Committee would be unable to conceive of rape as strictly a political act targeting women for political and strategic purposes.

A review of published amnesty decisions reveals that the Amnesty Committee did not grant amnesty for rape.[48] Cursory analysis of the reasons for decision, though, suggests that the Amnesty Committee's refusal to grant amnesty may not be as simple as the outright rejection of rape as a politically motivated offence. In two of the cases, it was the deceased victim rather than the amnesty applicants who allegedly committed rape. In the four other decisions, amnesty was refused, *inter alia*, for the offence of rape. In AC/2000/168, amnesty was refused for failure to make full disclosure. In AC/99/0222 and AC/99/0332 amnesty was refused for failure to make full disclosure *and* because the Amnesty Committee was not satisfied that the rape was committed for a political objective. In the first of these decisions, AC/99/0222, in rejecting the political objective of rape, the Amnesty Committee characterised the offence as being personally motivated stating: 'His silent condonation of the rape as bystander and his failure even to try and reprimand his companion clearly indicated malice and/ or ill will or spite towards the then helpless victim'. In the second of these decisions, AC99/0332, the rape was deemed non-political because the applicant committed the offence before, rather than after, receiving his political orders. Only in AC/2000/155 was amnesty refused *solely* on the basis that the rape did not have a political objective. Regrettably, the Amnesty Committee appears not to have published detailed reasons for this last decision.

Notwithstanding the limited number of amnesty decisions in which rape was considered, six decisions in total, the interpretation of rape as a non-political offence is troublesome. Firstly, it raises questions of internal consistency within the TRC since

---

47   See Goldblatt and Meintjes, above n 37, [E].

48   Published amnesty decisions available at the TRC website <http://www.truth.org.sa> (visited on 8 May 2001) were searched for the terms rape, sexual assault, sexual harassment, sexual abuse, sexual mutilation, sexual violence and/or sexual torture yielding a total of six decisions invoking the words rape or sexual assault (transcripts on file with author). There appears to be nothing in the recently published *Truth and Reconciliation Commission of South Africa Report* (2003) vol 6, 1–91 to contradict these findings.

the Human Rights Violation Committee was willing to consider rape as being politically motivated within the context of finding gross violations of human rights while the Amnesty Committee ostensibly was not. Secondly, such an interpretation may be awkward if truth commissions are rendering decisions at odds with the jurisprudential developments for women in 'hard' international criminal law where the statutes for the international criminal tribunals, subsequent prosecutorial actions and judicial decisions, as well as the *Rome Statute* expressly recognise rape and other gender-based violence offences as war crimes, crimes against humanity, and as elements of genocide, torture and enslavement.[49]

In comparison with truth commissions elsewhere, the South African TRC provides limited jurisprudential analysis of gender and sexual violence to support the particular conclusions that it reached. While acknowledging the conundrum faced by the Amnesty Committee, an interpretation that severs rape from its political motivations in the context of armed or political conflict reifies the public/private divide in international law where violence against women is viewed as a private matter, committed for personal gratification.[50]

This analysis suggests that it would be useful for designers of truth commissions in other countries to ensure that the commissioners receive training in gender awareness – including gender-sensitive developments in international criminal law – to help inform decision-making in the truth commission context.

2   Gender Composition of the Commission

Even though the *Promotion of National Unity and Reconciliation Act 1995* does not explicitly incorporate fair gender representation criteria, it is likely that the actual selection of commissioners was guided by principles of race, gender, political affiliation and geography.[51] Such an interpretation is consistent with other provisions of the Act, specifically sections 13(2), 17(1) and 24(3), requiring the appointment of committee members 'broadly representative' of the South African community.

Seven (41 percent) women and ten (59 percent) men were appointed as Commissioners through a public nominations and screening process. Even though the seventeen appointed commissioners are described as a reasonably representative group, particularly in terms of their political affiliation, Dorothy Shea has observed that the racial and gender composition of the Commission were not 'strictly proportional' to the demographic structure of South Africa.[52] Proportional gender representation would have required that nine (51 percent) of the appointed commissioners be women.

The executive for the TRC, appointed by President Mandela, was composed of two men, Chairperson Archbishop Desmond Tutu and Vice-Chairperson Dr Alex

---

49   See *Violence Against Women Report*, above n 19, [10].

50   See Joan Fitzpatrick, 'The Use of International Human Rights Norms to Combat Violence Against Women' in Rebecca J Cook (ed), *Human Rights of Women: National and International Perspectives* (1994) 532, 544.

51   See for example, Dorothy Shea, *The South African Truth Commission: The Politics of Reconciliation* (2000) 25.

52   *Ibid.*, 25.

Boraine. In fact, men dominated the executive and administrative structure for the Commission. Male Commissioners headed two of three statutory committees.[53] The position of Chief Executive Officer was staffed by a man and, apart from one unit, men headed all units for the Commission extending to the investigative; witness protection; legal services; research; media and communications; finance and support services units. The Commission executive secretary, Paul van Zyl, as well as the executive secretaries for the three statutory committees were men. Women's leadership of the Reparation and Rehabilitation Committee, Vice-chairpersonship of the Human Rights Violation Committee, and management of the Human Resources Unit in addition to two of four regional offices stand out as the main exceptions to the executive dominance of men on the Commission.[54]

The TRC performed its functions through three statutory committees: the Human Rights Violation Committee, the Amnesty Committee, and the Reparation and Rehabilitation Committee. Of the three committees, the Amnesty Committee had the fewest and the Reparation and Rehabilitation Committee the greatest number of women as a proportion of the total configuration of the committee.[55] The disproportionate representation of women on the Reparation and Rehabilitation Committee led one commentator to characterise reparation and reconciliation as 'women's issues'.[56] The gender configuration of the Reparation and Rehabilitation Committee is striking as well since, in comparison with the other two committees and especially the Amnesty Committee, which performed a quasi-judicial function, its powers were essentially advisory.

3   Special Measures for the Protection and Support of South African Women Victims and Witnesses

The *Promotion of National Unity and Reconciliation Act 1995* does not incorporate any gender-specific provisions for the protection and support of women victims and witnesses.[57] Victim testimony was gathered through five types of hearings (many of

---

53   Archbishop Desmond Tutu was Chairperson of the Human Rights Violation Committee, with Mr Wynand Malan serving as one of two Vice-Chairpersons for this committee. Judge Hassen Mall was appointed as the Amnesty Committee Chairperson, with Judge Andrew Wilson serving as Vice-Chairperson.

54   For an overview of the original organisational structure of the Commission, see *Truth and Reconciliation Commission of South Africa Report* (1999) vol 1, 258-259.

55   These comments on gender representation are based on original appointments to statutory committees. It is important to emphasise that the configuration of statutory committees changed substantially during the life of the Commission, especially in relation to the Amnesty Committee, which expanded from an initial five members in 1995 to 11, and then 19 members in 1997.

56   Antjie Krog, *Country of My Skull: Guilt, Sorrow, and the Limits of Forgiveness in the New South Africa* (2000) 311.

57   The exception being the section 11 guiding principles for the treatment of victims, which provide *inter alia* that victims should be treated equally and without discrimination based on gender or sex.

which were open to the public) and a statement taking process.[58] The TRC process in fact was distinguished by its very public nature, including extensive media – television, radio, and newspaper – coverage of its proceedings. Recognising that the public nature of proceedings likely would prevent women from coming forward to speak about their direct victimisation experiences – especially as victims of sexual violence – and underscoring the available statutory provisions for privacy and confidentiality at the disposal of the Commission, the gender submission made specific recommendations regarding gender-sensitive statement taking procedures and the questioning of victims. The submission also proposed a number of special measures to increase women's participation in the truth seeking process, including that the Commission consider utilising women statement takers, closed hearings, single-gender forums, same sex commissioners, third party testimony, group hearings and the provision of psycho-social support services for women deponents. The Commission was also encouraged to work with the media in order to give prominence to gender in the TRC process.[59] In the end, the gender submission achieved two very practical concessions for women victims and witnesses. The first was the addition of special hearings for women. The second was the amendment of the statement taking protocol to alert women to the importance of recounting direct victimisation experiences.

(a) The Addition of Special Hearings for Women
The Human Rights Violation Committee, responsible for investigating human rights violations, held special hearings for women in three of its four regional centres: Cape Town (7 August 1996), Durban (25 October 1996), and Johannesburg (28-29 July 1997). The omission of a women's hearing in the Eastern Cape is conceded by the Commission to be potentially significant since some of the worst custodial violence occurred there.[60] The August 1996 Cape Town hearing consisted of women-only Commissioners. At the Cape Town hearing, women spoke of family members who were killed and their personal experiences being tortured and harassed, including threats of rape, while in detention. Women testified about the long-term effects of trauma and need for psycho-social support and assistance for victims.[61] The October 1996 Durban hear-

---

58   See especially *Truth and Reconciliation Commission of South Africa Report* (1999) vol 1, 54, 135-157; Audrey Chapman and Patrick Ball, 'The Truth of Truth Commissions: Comparative Lessons from Haiti, South Africa, and Guatemala' (2001) 23 *Human Rights Quarterly* 8, 23 for elaboration of the commission's methodology. The five types of hearings included victim hearings, event hearings, special hearings, institutional hearings and political party hearings. A relatively small proportion of victims, approximately 1800 persons, testified in person at the human rights violations hearings.

59   See Goldblatt and Meintjes, above n 37 [G].

60   See *Truth and Reconciliation Commission of South Africa Report* (1999) vol 4, 283.

61   See South African Press Association, 'Women to Testify on Abuse Before TRC', (6 August 1996) Truth and Reconciliation Commission (South Africa) <http://www.truth.org.sa/media/1996/9608/s960806g.htm> at 19 May 2001; South African Press Association, 'TRC Hears of Violations Suffered by Women' (7 August 1996) Truth and Reconciliation Commission (South Africa) <http://www.truth.org.sa/media/1996/9608/s960807k.htm> at 19 May 2001.

ing is described by the press as being held 'in camera'; it was open only to women, with men situated in an adjoining room to hear testimony. Ten women recounted their personal victimisation experiences at the Durban hearing, including rape, gang rape, sexual slavery, harassment by youth gangs, and harassment and humiliation while detained by the state. Three women spoke of their experiences as women activists. A number of the deponents requested counselling services.[62] The July 1997 Johannesburg hearing reveals that three of an approximate 19 deponents were men who spoke of women family members who were killed. The women deponents who testified at the Johannesburg hearing spoke of rape and sexual harassment as well as the difficulties they faced as the family breadwinner when their husbands and sons were killed because of state repression.[63] Although the special hearings for women enabled South African women to give testimony before women commissioners in closed session, it remains questionable whether the hearings improved the protection of privacy for women deponents since the press reported on the Cape Town and Durban hearings and transcripts for the Johannesburg hearing are publicly accessible.[64] Despite these privacy concerns, the fact that these special hearings existed marked an important shift in the gender-consciousness and sensitivity of the Commission. While future commissions will need to work on the details which marred this experience, the inclusion of this type of women-specific hearings should be encouraged and applauded in the planning of future commissions.

(b) Witness Support and Protection

As emphasised by the gender submission, the TRC had a number of statutory provisions for privacy and confidentiality at its disposal that could be used to increase women's participation in truth commission proceedings by affording women victims/survivors, witnesses and amnesty applicants greater protection. This included provision for 'in camera' proceedings. There is no evidence, however, to suggest that in camera hearings were used specifically to facilitate women's testimony.[65]

---

62   See South African Press Association, 'Women Testify In Camera Before Truth Commission' (25 October 1996) Truth and Reconciliation Commission (South Africa) <http://www.truth.org.sa/media/1996/9610/s961025e.htm> at 19 May 2001; South African Press Association, 'First TRC Hearing for Women Recounts 80s Ordeals' (25 October 1996) Truth and Reconciliation Commission (South Africa) <http://www.truth.org. sa/media/1996/9610/s961025h.htm> at 19 May 2001. See also *Truth and Reconciliation Commission of South Africa Report* (1999) vol 1, 419.

63   See *Truth and Reconciliation Commission of South Africa Report* (1999) vol 1, 446.

64   Published women's hearings transcripts are available for the Johannesburg hearings only and can be found at the former Truth and Reconciliation Commission website, now hosted by the Department of Justice <http://www.doj.gov.za/trc/trc_framesct.htm> (originally visited on 5 March 2001) (transcripts on file with author). The Johannesburg transcript identifies deponents by name. The personal identity of seven of nine women deponents is disclosed in the news reports that were reviewed.

65   This conclusion is based on a review of the Truth and Reconciliation Commission report. References to in camera or so-called section 29 hearings are found in *Truth and Reconciliation Commission of South Africa Report* (1999) vol 1, 151; vol 2, 38, 191, 221, 255, 258, 276, 343, 348, 355, 358, 362, 512, 592; vol 3, 182, 193, 194, 196, 200, 207, 209, 230, 303, 627; and vol 5, 262, 265.

Also available were provisions for a limited witness protection program (section 35) and discretionary provisions allowing non-disclosure of witness identity (section 37). Again there is no evidence to suggest these provisions were used for the special benefit of women.[66] In fact, the Commission decided that, 'every person found to have been a victim of a gross violation had the right to have their name and a brief account of the violation in the Report of the Commission'.[67] Victim findings have since been published as volume 7 of the codicil to the Report. The victim findings volume, *inter alia*, documents incidents of rape, sexual abuse, sexual mutilation, sexual assault and sexual torture perpetrated against individually named women and men. This has problematic implications for the protection of witness privacy if in fact individually named deponents did not give their express permission to have their violations made public.

According to Priscilla Hayner, the South African TRC 'went further than any other commission in incorporating psychological support into its operational structures'.[68] Yet a 1998 study, in which women constituted a majority of the participants, assessing survivor perceptions following the conclusion of the Human Rights Violation Committee hearings process reveals ongoing victim/witness concern with personal security, particularly at the local level, as well as the need for long-term counseling and trauma support services.[69] Other witnesses have remarked on the inadequacy of, and need for ongoing support services for women following the women's special hearings.[70] Like the witness protection programme and privacy provisions, the impact of ostensibly gender-neutral psycho-social support services for South African women victims/survivors provided by the South African Truth and Reconciliation merits further assessment.

(c)   The Differential Engagement of South African Women in the Truth Recovery Process
The differential pattern of women's testimony in the Human Rights Violation Committee process was confirmed early in the life of the TRC. As the Commission

---

66   There do not appear to be any assessments that directly address whether the witness protection or non-disclosure provisions of the *Promotion of National Unity and Reconciliation Act 1995* were used specifically to benefit women. The first mention of a South African strategy for the protection of women witnesses appears to be associated with the Department of Justice, Justice Vision 2000.

67   *Truth and Reconciliation Commission of South Africa Report* (1999) vol 5, 14; (2003) vol 7, 2-3. Named victims were identified based on statements to the Human Rights Violation Committee and amnesty applications to the Amnesty Committee. According to the Report, all persons making a statement to the Commission received written acknowledgement of their statement and were notified of the Commission's findings. The Commission informed individuals of the application procedure for reparations if the individual was determined to be a victim of a gross violation of human rights.

68   Hayner, above n 4, 145. See also *Truth and Reconciliation Commission of South Africa Report* (1999) vol 1, 289-291 regarding the provision of generic psycho-social support services.

69   See the Centre for the Study of Violence and Reconciliation and the Khulumani Support Group, *Submission to the Truth and Reconciliation Commission: Survivors' Perceptions of the Truth and Reconciliation Commission and Suggestions for the Final Report* (1998) 1-2, 8, 11-12.

70   See especially the comments of Thenjiwe Mtintso as cited in the *Truth and Reconciliation of South Africa Report* (1999) vol 5, 355.

reflects, 'while the overwhelming majority of women spoke as the relatives and dependents of those (mainly males) who had directly suffered human rights violations, most of the men spoke as direct victims.'[71]

The TRC amended the statement taking protocol in April 1997 to incorporate the following caution:

> IMPORTANT: Some women testify about violations of human rights that happened to family members or friends, but they have also suffered abuses. Don't forget to tell us what happened to you yourself if you were the victim of a gross human rights abuse.[72]

This amendment was significant in its recognition of the way in which many women recount their experiences of conflict. The extent to which this shift in the TRC's gender conciousness affected women's willingness to report their own violations to the Commission remains unclear. Nonetheless, this inclusion does mark an increased awareness within the TRC of the need to open space for previously marginalised voices and experiences of women. This is turn can act as an important lesson in gender awareness in the creation of future truth commissions.

Despite amendments to the protocol regarding the manner in which statements were taken, and the addition of three special hearings for women, the gendered pattern of reporting, with both women and men for the most part recounting the human rights violation experiences of men, continued for the duration of the Human Rights Violation Committee hearings.

Women constituted a majority (11 271 or 52.9 percent) of the 21 297 deponents who gave statements to the Commission.[73] Still, there are obvious differences in the reporting patterns of women and men. In providing statements to the Commission, men overwhelmingly reported about violations to themselves, with only half as many women doing so. The number of women's statements exceeded the number of men's in all instances involving the reporting of violations *experienced by another person*. In terms of women's overall reporting patterns about gross violations of human rights, women were most likely to report killing, followed by severe ill treatment, attempted killing and then torture. When themselves the *direct* victim of a gross violation, women were most likely to report severe ill treatment, then torture and attempted killing.[74]

---

71   *Truth and Reconciliation Commission of South Africa Report* (1999) vol 4, 283. For general discussion of 'women's silences', see also *Truth and Reconciliation Commission of South Africa Report* (1999), vol 4, 293-294; (2003) vol 7, 8-9.

72   *Truth and Reconciliation Commission of South Africa Report* (1999) vol 4, 283.

73   See *Truth and Reconciliation Commission of South Africa Report* (1999) vol 1, 169, 170-171. There are observable racial and geographic differences in South African women's reporting of violations that merit further study.

74   See *Truth and Reconciliation Commission of South Africa Report* (1999) vol 3, 5-6; vol 4, 287. There are clear age differences between the women and men who reported violations, with a much higher proportion of older women deponents giving statements to the Commission as compared with men.

Even though more women than men gave statements to the Commission, the gender profile of human rights *victimisation* portrayed by the Commission is predominantly male. As the Commission observes 'males dominate as the victims of killings, torture, abduction and severe ill treatment'.[75] Based on the statements it received, the Commission documented close to 38,000 gross violations of human rights. A majority (61.1 percent) of the victims of these violations, for both fatal and non-fatal violations, were men. Women were the victims in less than one-quarter (23.7 percent) of these violations. Of these reported violations, men account for 15.9 percent of fatal violations and 45.3 percent of non-fatal violations. In comparison, women account for 2.7 percent of fatal violations and 20.9 percent of non-fatal violations.[76] The victim profile provided by the Commission indicates that most persons killed and tortured were young men aged 13 to 36.[77] Nevertheless, it is clear from the findings presented in the Report that, just as women suffered gross violations of human rights as direct victims to a lesser extent than men did, women experienced the complete array of violations and were victimised by both state and non-state actors.[78]

The silence of South African women concerning their own experience as victims of gross violations of human rights during apartheid extends to the reporting of sexual violence, including rape. As Beth Goldblatt and Sheila Meintjes remark, 'few women gave evidence of sexual violence in the TRC hearings' and 'most women who spoke of sexual violence did so within the context of the special hearings for women'.[79] Of the statements received by the Commission, 446 (2.1 percent) involve sexual abuse of which 158 (less than one percent) concerned women victims. Rape, considered as 'severe ill treatment' by the Commission, was mentioned in 140 cases. Sexual abuse, including rape, against women is thought to have been much more extensive than what was actually reported to the Commission.

In view of the limited number of sexual violence cases that it documented, the TRC's three principal findings on women are somewhat surprising because of the relative prominence given to women's sexual victimisation. The Commission concludes that women were the victims of severe ill treatment, including harassment, committed by the state while in custody. The Commission found that women were the victims of gendered human rights abuses 'specifically exploiting their vulnerabilities as women', such as rape and threat of rape committed by state security forces. Relative to violations committed by the liberation movements, the Commission found that women were subjected to sexual abuse, including rape, and harassment in the camps.[80]

The findings of the TRC on women perpetrators are equally revealing concerning the silence of women. According to the report, only 56 (less than one percent) of the

75   *Truth and Reconciliation Commission of South Africa Report* (2003) vol 7, 7-9.

76   See *Truth and Reconciliation Commission of South Africa Report* (1999) vol 1, 171.

77   See *Truth and Reconciliation Commission of South Africa Report* (1999) vol 3, 5.

78   See *Truth and Reconciliation Commission of South Africa Report* (1999) vol 4, 290.

79   Goldblatt and Meintjes, 'Dealing with the Aftermath – Sexual Violence and the Truth and Reconciliation Commission' (2000) 43 *Agenda* [para Where were the Women?] <http://www.agenda.org.sa/BETH.htm> at 22 August 2001.

80   See Truth and Reconciliation Commission of South Africa Report (1999) vol 5, 256.

recorded 7 128 amnesty applicants are women.[81] This percentage is perhaps less than one might expect given that women constituted approximately 14 percent of the permanent South African Defence Force (SADF) and about 20 percent of Umkhonto weSiswe (MK), the African National Congress' armed wing between 1976 and 1989[82] when some of the worst apartheid violence was perpetrated. Assessment of women's participation as perpetrators of the apartheid violence merits further assessment and investigation.

C   Recognising South African Women's Varied Roles and the Differential Consequences of Conflict for Women

1   Women in the Truth and Reconciliation Commission of South Africa Report

The TRC was asked to prepare a comprehensive final report setting forth its activities, findings and recommendations. The provisions of the *Promotion of National Unity and Reconciliation Act 1995* (South Africa) pertaining to the reporting obligations of the Commission are gender neutral.[83] All the same, the statute places importance on compiling a report providing 'as comprehensive an account as possible of the activities and findings of the Commission'. The preamble and other sections of the guiding statute reflect similar emphasis calling for the establishment of 'as complete a picture as possible of the nature, causes and extent' of gross violations of human rights. Considering these provisions, it is possible to construe the reporting obligations of the Commission in a manner that would embrace a gendered analysis of the past political conflicts. The gender submission in fact anticipated that a final report would benefit from a specific research project examining the role of gender in past abuses.[84] The Commission's Research Department identified research on gender concerns as one of fourteen strategic research themes. Evidently, the Research Department carried out some research in preparation for the special hearing on women as well as on gender differentiation in relation to the consequences of gross violations of human rights, and others credit the Commission with having conducted some gender research.[85]

The five-volume TRC Report, published in October 1998, contains a separate chapter on women focusing on the issues and findings revealed in the three special hearings for women. The Commission was cognisant of the optics of presenting a standalone chapter on women, commenting: 'The inclusion of a separate chapter on gender will be understood by some readers as sidelining, rather than, mainstreaming, the issue. Women will again be seen as having been portrayed as a "special inter-

---

81   The figure of 7 128 is based on data presented in volume four of the Report. Different total figures regarding the number of amnesty applications received by the commission are cited in other volumes of the Report.

82   See Jacklyn Cock, *Women and War in South Africa* (1992) 161.

83   See *Promotion of National Unity and Reconciliation Act 1995* (South Africa) preamble, ss 3(1)(d), 4(e), 14(2), 25(2), 43, 44.

84   See Goldblatt and Meintjes, above n 37 [G].

85   See *Truth and Reconciliation Commission of South Africa Report* (1999) Vol 1, 292, 375-376, 378. See also van der Merwe, Dewhirst and Hamber, above n 36, [NGO Impact on TRC Operations] who assert that one of the positive contributions of the gender submission was that it 'pushed' the TRC to do its own gender research.

est group", rather than as "normal" members of the society'.[86] Although the women's chapter incorporates some mention of women activists and perpetrators, much of the chapter concentrates on women's victimisation experiences. There is insufficient attention given to the role of women as combatants within the armed forces and liberation movements, as activists, or as perpetrators, as well as racial, class and economic differences among women who experienced political violence under apartheid.[87]

Consideration of women is not restricted to the chapter on women, with women's testimony and findings on women scattered throughout other volumes of the Report. Moreover, the Commission's research on the 'consequences of gross violations of human rights' includes examination of gender differentiation and these findings are integrated in the main text of that chapter as well as in the chapter on women.

Excluding the chapter on women, sex disaggregated data are presented for 19 (13 percent) of 147 human rights violations tables.[88] There remains a need for greater sex disaggregation of data across all findings; in particular with respect to the *type* of human rights violations suffered by women, the *distinction between violations perpetrated against women by state security as opposed to liberation forces*, as well as more comprehensive regional data – especially for the Eastern Cape in addition to Natal, KwaZulu and Orange Free State – for human rights violations experienced by women. A major shortcoming of the Report is the presentation of sex-disaggregated statistics as percentages without benefit of corresponding whole numbers.

The final codicil volume of the TRC, though commenting specifically about victim summaries, provides an eloquent précis of the deficiencies of the Report *vis-à-vis* the complexities of women's experiences under apartheid:

> In many ways, women's experiences in the political conflicts of the past are not evident … Males dominate as victims within the narrow mandate of violations examined by the Commission … What is not adequately captured is the story of the thousands of women in South Africa who were left behind to fend for themselves and who experienced the brutality of the apartheid system … Another story that is untold is that of

---

86   *Truth and Reconciliation Commission of South Africa Report* (1999) vol 4, 287.

87   See for example, *Truth and Reconciliation Commission of South Africa Report* (1999) vol 4, 79-86. The chapter on women contains intermittent references to women activists and a small section on women perpetrators, in comparison with its separate sections on sexual abuse, other physical abuse, psychological abuse, and non-prison abuse. The chapter also includes consideration of 'gendered roles and socialisation' but does not really speak to race, class and economic differences in relation to political violence against women, even though this point was emphasised in the gender submission. See also the *Truth and Reconciliation Commission of South Africa Report*, (1999) vol 5, 259-303 chapter on 'Causes, Motives and Perspectives of Perpetrators', which is quite male-centred in its presentation of findings and the conceptual explanations provided. The findings of the Commission's research on gender variation and the 'consequences of gross violations of human rights' are presented in volume 5 of the Report, describing *inter alia* the psychological, physical, family and community effects of such violations on men and women.

88   See *Truth and Reconciliation Commission of South Africa Report* (1999) vol 1, ix-xii, 'List of tables of Human Rights Violations'.

the many women who went into exile to join the liberation movements. We have not been able to do justice to them. This remains unfinished business.[89]

The disturbing silence of women should not be taken lightly. Future truth commissions could greatly benefit from heeding this analysis in the creation of their own institutions to ensure that an historically accurate record is created through listening to the voices and personal stories of individual women.

2 Repairing the Harm to South African Women

As authorised by section 25 of the *Promotion of National Unity and Reconciliation Act 1995* (South Africa), the Reparation and Rehabilitation Committee was empowered to make recommendations to the President for the granting of urgent interim measures and a general policy of reparation to victims. Specifically, the Reparation and Rehabilitation Committee was authorised to recommend the 'policy which should be followed or measures which should be taken with regard to the granting of reparation to victims or the taking of other measures aimed at rehabilitating and restoring the human and civil dignity of victims' as well as measures 'to grant urgent interim reparation to victims'.[90] The *Promotion of National Unity and Reconciliation Act 1995* reparation provisions attracted controversy from the outset because these provisions require persons seeking reparations to make a formal application, with entitlement to reparations based on an official finding of victimisation by the Commission within the narrow definition of gross violations of human rights.[91] In addition, the Reparation and Rehabilitation Committee chose to adopt a finite or 'closed list' policy for the identification of victims. This, in effect, limited payment of reparations to those victims who made statements to the Commission before 15 December 1997.[92] The reparation provisions have remained highly contentious because, as described by the TRC, implementation of non-urgent measures has been 'considerably delayed'.[93] Political commitment to the provision of individual reparation grants has occurred only very recently, and suggests an amount that is substantially less than the grant amount originally proposed by the Commission.[94]

---

89 *Truth and Reconciliation Commission of South Africa Report* (2003) vol 7, 9.

90 *Promotion of National Unity and Reconciliation Act 1995* (South Africa) section 4(f).

91 See especially ibid, sections 26(1), 15(1) and 22.

92 For discussion of the closed list approach, see *Truth and Reconciliation Commission of South Africa Report* (1999) vol 1, 86; (2003) vol 6, 732. The Commission has since acknowledged the limits of the closed list approach requesting that the government review this policy.

93 See especially *Truth and Reconciliation Commission of South Africa Report* (2003) vol 6, 92-164, 99-100. Volume 6 of the Report sets forth considerably strengthened legal and moral arguments for the granting of reparations. According to the Commission, the statutory obligations imposed by section 26 of the *Promotion of National Unity and Reconciliation Act* create a 'legitimate expectation' and give rise to legally enforceable rights for reparations on the part of victims.

94 See *Truth and Reconciliation Commission of South Africa Report* (1999) vol 5, 184-185; Southern Africa Documentation and Cooperation Centre, 'South Africa: Reparation for Apartheid Victims Announced by State President' (16 April 2003) <http://www.sadocc. at/news/2003-116.shtml> at 24 November 2003. The original proposed benchmark amount

The gendered dimensions of each of the three formal requirements for access to reparations – prescribed application procedures, a limited definition of gross violations of human rights, and the closed list policy – were, and have remained, a particular concern for women. The gender submission advanced several cautions in 1996 concerning women and reparations, arguing the need for a gender-sensitive reparation policy. Based on the differential pattern of women's testimony, and in particular the reluctance of women to come forward and speak of their own victimisation, the submission proposed that more flexible measures be adopted to encourage women's access to reparations. In a similar vein, the gender submission expressed concern that the narrow construction of gross violations of human rights would affect women's right to seek reparations given that many violations experienced by women under apartheid fell outside the definition and that a majority of women deponents spoke of indirect rather than direct victimisation. The submission proposed that the 'special needs and interests of women' be integrated in the design of the reparation and rehabilitation policy. In this sense, the reparation policy should take into account the differential effects of past political conflicts for women including women's decreased earning capacity through loss of male wage earners. Moreover, the gender submission highlighted the need for the Reparation and Rehabilitation Committee to carefully avoid gender bias in any policy measure requiring the quantification of a monetary award since women's unpaid labour often is overlooked.[95]

The policy recommendations of the Reparation and Rehabilitation Committee were presented to the President as part of the TRC of South Africa Report in October 1998. The proposed reparation and rehabilitation framework consists of five elements emphasising both individual and collective measures: (1) urgent interim reparation; (2) individual reparation grants; (3) symbolic reparation, including legal and administrative measures; (4) community rehabilitation programmes; and (5) institutional reform. Although the Reparation and Rehabilitation Committee consisted of a majority of women Commissioners, there is no mention of women or gender in the proposed urgent interim reparation or reparation and rehabilitation policy framework.[96] The neglect of gender in these policy proposals is all the more remarkable because the TRC ostensibly committed itself in August 1996 to a reparation policy that would not ignore women's concerns. A number of principles guide the reparation and rehabilitation policy yet gender is not among them. Nor does the proposed reparation framework surmount the formal requirements anticipated to be the greatest obstacle

---

was R 21 700 per victim per annum over six years, for an approximate total grant of R 130 200 per officially recognised victim. In April 2003, four-and-a-half years after the policy was first officially presented, President Mbeki announced that the government will provide a once-off grant of R 30 000 for each officially designated victim.

95   See Goldblatt and Meintjes, above n 37, [F].

96   See Truth and Reconciliation Commission (South Africa), *Policy Framework for Urgent Interim Reparation Measures; A Summary of Reparation and Rehabilitation Policy, Including Proposals to be Considered by the President* <http://www.truth.org.sa/reparations/index. htm> at 7 April 2001. See also *Truth and Reconciliation Commission of South Africa Report* (1999) vol 5, 175-176, 180-181; (2003) vol 6, 94-96.

to women's access to reparations; namely fixed application procedures, a narrow definition of gross human rights violations or the 'closed list' of victims. The Individual Reparation Grant (IRG) scheme remains one of the most divisive aspects of the entire TRC process, largely because it is yet to be implemented.[97] The recommended symbolic reparation and community rehabilitation measures, while relatively comprehensive in scope, similarly lack robust gender-specificity to address the special needs and interests of women, including, for instance, on matters of housing, education and health services.[98]

On the positive side, the definition of 'victim' provided by section 1 of the *Promotion of National Unity and Reconciliation Act 1995* and reinforced by the Reparation and Rehabilitation Committee is comparatively expansive, embracing relatives and dependants. This, in theory, allows women to access reparations whose disclosed victimisation is indirect rather than direct. In addition, the suggested formula for calculating the quantum of individual reparation grants, if adopted by the South African government, takes into account rural access to services, number of dependents and urban costs of living. In these ways, it should not adversely discriminate against rural women or women with large numbers of dependants.[99] By November 2002, the Commission had awarded urgent interim measures in the amount of R50 million to assist close to 17 000 individuals to access services and facilities, even though the precise benefit of urgent interim reparations for women applicants is not documented by the Commission.[100]

3   Preventing the Recurrence of Human Rights Violations against South African Women

The Reparation and Rehabilitation Committee was empowered by section 25 of the *Promotion of National Unity and Reconciliation Act 1995* to make recommendations to the President concerning institutional, administrative and legislative reform measures designed to prevent the recurrence of future human rights violations. As further provided by section 3 of the Act, the Commission was granted broad latitude to make recommendations 'concerning any matter with a view to promoting or achieving national unity and reconciliation.' While the Act did not specifically task the Commission

---

97   See *Truth and Reconciliation Commission of South Africa Report* (2003) vol 6, 159; Case Watch, 'International Law Suit Filed on Behalf of Apartheid Victims, Khulumani et al v. Barclays et al' [1] (Cohen, Milstein, Hausfeld and Toll, PLLC) <http://www.cmht.com/casewatch/cases/cwapartheid1.html> at 24 November 2003. There has been a strong civil society campaign for the implementation of reparations led by the Khulumani Support Group. In November 2002, Khulumani and other civil society groups filed a lawsuit on behalf of apartheid victims in a New York Federal District Court against 22 businesses 'for aiding and abetting the apartheid regime in South Africa in furtherance of the commission of the crimes of apartheid, forced labor, genocide, extrajudicial killing, torture, *sexual assault*, and unlawful detention' (emphasis added).

98   See *Truth and Reconciliation Commission of South Africa Report* (1999) vol 5, 188-193.

99   See ibid, 1/6, 184-185.

100 See *Truth and Reconciliation Commission of South Africa Report* (2003) vol 6, 97, 179-180. A total of 16 855 payments were made but there is no sex disaggregation of these data.

with making gender-specific proposals, an expansive reading of its statutory provisions, specifically section 4 enabling recommendations for the creation of institutions *conducive to a stable and fair society* (emphasis added), conceivably would allow for such recommendations to be made.

The TRC provides numerous recommendations in its final Report for institutional, administrative and legislative reforms, albeit with rather limited attention to gender. Gender is incorporated within recommendations for the promotion of a human rights culture; business sector responsibility for restitution; training for members of the administration of justice; composition of the judiciary; gender balance in the media; and, representivity of statutory health councils. Of note, the Report presents no specific recommendations for women, as were provided for other social and institutional sectors.[101]

The lack of gender-specific recommendations is quite bewildering in view of the Commission's acknowledgement of the differential engagement of women in the truth-seeking process and the silence of women especially concerning personal sexual victimisation experiences. There is no recognition, for instance, of the particular needs of women or victims of sexual violence in witness protection measures proposed by the Commission. The Commission provides no specific policy proposals for the treatment or eradication of violence against women, despite its principal victimisation findings concerning women (including that women were the victims of severe ill treatment and gendered human rights abuses extending to sexual violence and rape). As evidenced by the Commission's statistics, a majority of deponents who came before the Commission to attest to human rights violations were women; many of whom would in the Commission's own words 'bear the brunt of the suffering'. The Commission expressly documents the disparate social and economic effects of past political conflicts for women overtly recognising the difficulties faced by women through the loss of male wage earners, yet offers no reform proposals to ameliorate these negative economic effects other than a gender neutral reparation policy.

A statement in the *reconciliation* chapter of the South African Truth and Reconciliation Report says much about the perceived inadequacy of reform measures proposed by the Commission in meeting the needs of women. Under the topic of 'building a democracy where men and women can be at home', Tthenjiwe Mtintso singles out the compelling need to engage South African society to eradicate epidemic levels of violence against women and children associated with the aftermath of armed conflict.[102] It can only be surmised that the Commission felt there were adequate mechanisms outside of the TRC process, such as the Reconstruction and Development Program, the Commission on Gender Equality, Youth Commission, Human Rights Commission, South African Law Commission, and the Land Claims Courts and Commission to address gender-specific concerns.

---

101   See *Truth and Reconciliation Commission of South Africa Report* (1999) vol 5, 304-349.
102   *Truth and Reconciliation Commission of South Africa Report* (1999) vol 5, 355.

D   Assessing Women's Participation and the Integration of a Gender Perspective in the South African Context

The South African TRC has become a vanguard for emerging truth commissions in other jurisdictions that are seeking to reproduce its comparatively extensive engagement of civil society in legislative design; democratic nomination and selection process for commissioners; public hearings and media coverage; quasi-judicial powers; victim and witness programme; and psychological support structures.[103] Both the Sierra Leone Truth and Reconciliation Commission (2002 to present) and the East Timor Commission for Reception, Truth and Reconciliation (2002 to present) are loosely modelled on the South African TRC. But, is the South African TRC an appropriate *international model* for the participation of women and integration of a gender perspective in truth commission structures and processes? The report card on women's participation and the integration of a gender perspective *vis-à-vis* the South African TRC is somewhat mixed.

At the time it was created, the South African TRC was quite forward thinking and arguably went considerably further than many of the earlier truth commissions in overtly trying to accommodate the participation of women and a gender perspective. Overall, South Africa fares relatively well in relation to the participation of civil society, extending to *individual* women and women's organisations, in truth commission legislative design. In addition, the South African legislative design experience demonstrates the positive contributions of civil society, including women, in shaping the public nominations and selection process for commissioners. South Africa remains one of the most gender balanced truth commissions established to date with seven (41 percent) women commissioners, an achievement which is all the more remarkable in the absence of legislatively stipulated criteria for fair gender representation or gender quotas.

The highly persuasive gender submission is regarded as one of the most successful civil society lobby efforts to influence the operations of the Commission. The gender submission encouraged the Commission to interpret an otherwise neutral mandate to incorporate sexual and gender violence; to amend its statement taking procedures to encourage women's testimony of direct victimisation; to conduct its own gender research; and to mobilise special hearings for women.[104] The TRC of South Africa Report also rates well for its inclusion of a chapter on women, which devotes some attention to the varied roles of women as victims and perpetrators in past political conflicts, as well as its modest sex disaggregation of data.

All the same, the South African experience illustrates the complexity of achieving women's participation in accountability policy-making. The South African decision to

---

103 See Shea, above n 51, 45-68, for assessment of the conceptual (public ownership, mandate, independence, deliverables) and logistical (administration, safeguards) benchmarks set by the South African Truth and Reconciliation Commission. See also Gloppen, above n 1, 22-23 on the topic of the South African Commission as an international model.

104 See especially van der Merwe, Dewhirst and Hamber, above n 36, [NGO Impact on TRC Operations]; *Truth and Reconciliation Commission of South Africa Report* (1999) vol 4, 282-283, 287-288.

establish a truth commission is embedded in two separate yet interconnected political decision-making processes – the peace negotiations process (1990-1994) and the interim government parliamentary process (1994-1997). Catherine Albertyn's observation concerning the exclusion of South African women from bilateral peace negotiations highlights the conundrum that women's participation at the peace table may be a necessary yet insufficient benchmark for women's voices to be heard. In South Africa, crucial accountability policy decisions were made bilaterally outside of established negotiating protocols and in largely non-transparent and non-inclusive ways. Of note, the South African accountability policy choice of amnesty in exchange for truth seems to have been taken largely at the prerogative of men. Members of civil society, including individual women and women's organisations, were *invited* to *react* to already drafted legislation in a policy context offering *indirect* access to political decision-makers. Another valuable lesson of South Africa is that accountability concessions were made relatively *early* in the political transition suggesting that if women wish to *proactively* influence accountability policy decisions they will need to mobilise very early on.

Above all, the South African Truth and Reconciliation experience exemplifies that women's concerns may not be addressed unless integrated in enabling truth commission legislation or terms of reference. Jurisprudentially there is no reason why the legislative mandate for the TRC could not have incorporated some reference to sexual or gender violence offences since the statutes for the International Criminal Tribunal for the former Yugoslavia (1993) and Rwanda (1994) already had begun to establish standards for this. The language of the Promotion of National Unity and Reconciliation Act 1995 reflects political rather than legal considerations.[105] The disparate approach taken by the Amnesty Committee on the question of whether rape is a political offence in the context of armed or political conflict underscores the need for legislative integration in addition to gender training of truth commissioners and/or the appointment of gender experts to advise truth commissions on such matters.

The TRC, in its response to the gender submission, made more commitments to address the special needs and interests of women than it actually was able to uphold. Despite the willingness of the South African TRC to add special mechanisms to encourage women's testimony after proceedings had commenced, the South African victim and perpetrator data demonstrate that much more needs to be done to overcome the differential engagement of women in truth commission processes. Provisions of the statutes for the two ad hoc tribunals and the Rome Statute for the International Criminal Court for the protection and support of women victims and witnesses may offer valuable approaches in this regard, particularly in view of the South Africa TRC's apparent reluctance to use generic statutory powers to afford greater privacy protection to women victims and witnesses. Finally, the South African TRC experience reveals that, unless statutorily directed to do so, it seems unlikely that a truth

---

105 See *Truth and Reconciliation Commission of South Africa Report* (2003) vol 6, 589. According to the Commission, the statutory language used to define gross violations of human rights 'deliberately avoided the use of terms associated with legal definitions of crimes in South African law'.

commission will consider the differential consequences of armed or political conflict for women in the design of reparation policy or institutional reform measures.

III   Selective Comparisons with Other Truth Commissions

Juxtaposed against the three basic areas of inquiry presented at the beginning of the chapter – women's participation in accountability decision-making, replication of positive jurisprudential and structural developments for women, recognition of the differential consequences of armed conflict for women – this section considers women's experience with the South African TRC in selective comparison with other historically prominent truth commissions, such as those in Argentina and Chile, as well as more recently established entities. Even as newly established truth commissions in Sierra Leone, East Timor and Peru represent positive developments for women's participation in accountability decision-making and the integration of a gender perspective in legislative or institutional design, truth commission developments in other jurisdictions suggest the need for much more concerted gender advocacy efforts to ensure that women's concerns and interests are taken into account.

A   Women's Participation in Accountability Decision-Making

A survey of 26 truth commissions established or formally proposed between 1982 and 2003 reveals variation in the official creating authority or institution for truth commissions. Consistent with Priscilla Hayner's observation,[106] most truth commissions are created by executive order and then most often by presidential decree. At least six truth commissions have been created by or are associated with the provisions of a peace agreement. A slightly fewer number of commissions have been created by Parliament, and even fewer still by an inter-governmental body such as the United Nations or the Organisation of African Unity.[107] Relative to women's participation in the decision to establish a truth commission, three women presidents have established truth commissions and women participated as signatories to the truth commission provisions of peace agreements for El Salvador (1991), Guatemala (1994) and Sierra Leone (1999).[108]

---

106 See Hayner, above n 4, 214. See also Gloppen, above n 1, 18.

107 Truth commissions for Bolivia, Argentina, Philippines, Uganda, Nepal, Chile, Chad, Sri Lanka, Haiti, Nigeria, Uruguay, South Korea, Panama, Serbia and Montenegro, and Peru were created by executive order. Truth commissions created by, or associated with peace agreement provisions include: El Salvador, Guatemala, South Africa, Sierra Leone, Burundi and Liberia. At the time of writing, two of these truth commissions – Burundi and Liberia – had not commenced operation. Truth commissions created by Parliament include: Germany, South Africa, South Korea, Sierra Leone and Ghana. The UN Security Council created an International Commission of Inquiry for Burundi in 1995 by means of a resolution. In late 1998, the Organisation of African Unity established an International Panel of Eminent Personalities to Investigate the 1994 Genocide in Rwanda and the Surrounding Events.

108 President Corazon Aquino established the Philippine Presidential Committee on Human Rights in 1986. President Chandrika Bandaranaike Kumaratunga of Sri Lanka established

The role of civil society organisations in lobbying for accountability preferences including truth commissions often is well documented as a matter of public record. As the foregoing analysis of South Africa demonstrates, what frequently is less obvious and more difficult to unravel is the participation of women and women's organisations in accountability decision-making processes. Having said this, on the evidence available it seems clear that women *proactively* and *directly* participated in significant ways in the process of creating the East Timor Commission for Reception, Truth and Reconciliation (2001-present). Consequently, the UNTAET regulation for the CAVR is unrivalled as a model that expressly facilitates women's participation and the integration of a gender perspective.

1   East Timor and the Direct Participation of Women in the Decision to Establish a Truth Commission

Accountability policy direction for East Timor was set by the UN Commission on Human Rights in September 1999 and the UN Security Council in October 1999 in their resolutions calling for the perpetrators of serious violations of international humanitarian law and human rights to be brought to justice. These resolutions additionally recognised and supported East Timorese reconciliation efforts.[109] One might add that the Commission on Human Rights and Security Council resolutions were for the most part negotiated between the United Nations and the Republic of Indonesia to the relative exclusion of the East Timorese. In particular, the Republic of Indonesia ostensibly sought to avoid the establishment of an international criminal tribunal in exchange for bringing those responsible for past violations to justice within its own national justice system. Notably, East Timorese women and women's groups were not *direct* participants in either of these accountability decision-making forums given that East Timor was not an independent or UN member state at the time.

Like South Africa, the most vocal proponents for an East Timorese truth commission were men.[110] East Timorese women's groups, relatively well organised in advance of the 1999 political transition, have had a more visible presence advocating for legal (retributive) justice for past serious violations of international humanitarian and human rights law, in particular calling for the establishment of an international

---

the Commission of Inquiry into Involuntary Removal or Disappearances of Persons in 1994. President Mireya Moscoso established the Panamanian Truth Commission in 2001. Ana Guadalupe Martínez was one of the FMLN signatories to the 1991 El Salvador Mexico Agreement. Luz Mendez Gutierrez was one of the UNRG signatories to the 1994 Oslo Agreement for Guatemala. Adwoa Coleman was the OAU signatory to the 1999 Lomé Accord for Sierra Leone.

109 See *Resolution on the Situation of Human Rights in East Timor*, CHR Res, Fourth Special Session, UN Doc 1999/S-4/1 (1999) [4, 5 and 7]; *Resolution on the Situation in East Timor*, SC Res 1272, 54 UN SCOR (4057th mtg), UN Doc S/RES/1272 (1999) preamble [16].

110 Jose Ramos Horta foreshadowed the possibility of a truth and reconciliation process like that in South Africa in his April 1997 speech to the Commission on Human Rights. Jose Ramos Horta, Xanana Gusmao, and Bishop Belo have been three of the most vocal supporters of an East Timorese truth commission.

criminal tribunal.[111] International women, most notably Mary Robinson, then UN High Commissioner for Human Rights, and women's groups also strongly lobbied for the creation of an international criminal tribunal.[112] This is not to say that women and women's groups opposed the creation of a truth commission for East Timor. On the contrary, East Timorese and international women broadly supported the establishment of a truth commission albeit in combination with, rather than at the expense of formal legal justice.[113] Institutional accountability arrangements for East Timor thus reflect complementary serious crimes prosecution and truth recovery efforts.

Unlike South Africa, East Timorese and international women *directly* engaged at all decision-making stages leading to the legislative creation of the Commission for Reception, Truth and Reconciliation. At the grassroots level, the views of East Timorese women concerning justice and reconciliation for past international humanitarian and human rights law violations were actively sought in the context of UN fact-findings missions between November 1999 and January 2000.[114] Likewise, then UN High Commissioner for Human Rights, Mary Robinson, made a concerted effort to gather the views of women on justice and reconciliation extending to the question of a truth commission.[115] The idea for a truth commission was seriously discussed in political circles as well as at various conferences in East Timor from February 2000 onwards and women and women's organisations actively took part in these discussions.[116] Two East Timorese women's organisations, Fokupers and ETWAVE, participated as members of the Steering Committee that was formed in August 2000 by the UNTAET Human Rights Unit to guide the legislative drafting and public consultation process. International women also participated on the Steering Committee both directly and in an advisory capacity. The Steering Committee undertook a comprehensive community consultation process from September 2000 to February 2001.

---

111 See for example, Rate Laek, 'Widows Group Demands International Tribunal' (24 August 2002), Rede Feto, 'East Timor Women's Network Demands Justice' (25 August 2002) East Timor Action Network <http://etan.org/action/issues/women.htm> at 27 November 2003.

112 See for example, *Report of the UN High Commissioner on the Human Rights Situation in East Timor*, 51 UN ESCOR, UN Doc E/CN.4/S-4/CRP.1 (1999) See also *Note by the UN Secretary General to the General Assembly Regarding the Special Rapporteurs Report on the Situation of Human Rights in East Timor*, UN Doc A/54/660 (1999).

113 See for example, *Report of the UN High Commissioner for Human Rights, Question of the Violation of Human Rights and Fundamental Freedoms in Any Part of the World, Situation of Human Rights in East Timor*, UN Doc E/CN.4/2000/27 (2000).

114 See especially *Note by the UN Secretary General*, above n 112; *Report of the UN Secretary-General to the Security Council and General Assembly Regarding the Findings of the International Inquiry on East Timor*, UN Doc A/54/726 – S/2000/59 (2000).

115 See for example, *Note by the UN Secretary General*, above n 112; *Report of the UN High Commissioner for Human Rights*, above n 113, [31]-[33].

116 See for example, *Human Rights and the Future of East Timor* (Report on Joint UNTAET Human Rights Unit and East Timor Jurists Association Workshop, Dili, 7-8 August 2000) East Timor Action Network <http://etan.org/action/issues/9-00reprt.htm> at 2 June 2001.

Individual women and women's organisations participated in several of the 20 community consultation meetings that were convened in each of the 13 districts.[117]

The UN High Commissioner for Human Rights, Mary Robinson, and her office, together with UNTAET Human Rights Unit staff, including women, assumed a significant role in providing technical assistance during the approximate 18 month legislative drafting and community consultation process, extending from the establishment of a steering committee in August 2000 to an interim truth commission office in August 2001 to organise the public selection process for commissioners who were formally appointed in January 2002. At the political level, East Timorese women participated as members of the CNRT National Congress that unanimously endorsed the proposal to establish a truth commission in August 2000.[118] Two women, one East Timorese and the other a UN international staff member, participated as members of the Transitional Cabinet that agreed in mid-December 2000 to establish a truth commission and which endorsed the draft regulation at the end of February 2001.[119] Thirteen East Timorese women were members of the 36-member National Council of East Timor that unanimously passed the regulation in June 2001.[120]

The UN Transitional Administrator promulgated UNTAET Regulation 2001 on the Establishment of a Commission for Reception, Truth and Reconciliation in July 2001 and the Commission commenced operations with the appointment of Commissioners in January 2002. As discussed below, the CAVR regulation is unprecedented in its integration of a gender perspective.

B   *Jurisprudential and Structural Accommodations for Women*

1   The Integration of a Gender Perspective in Truth Commission Mandates

As was the case with the South African TRC, truth commissions typically have *not* been formally mandated to investigate sexual and gender violence. Some truth commissions have been willing to interpret their mandate to investigate and make findings of sexual and gender-based violations, while others evidently have not. Jurisprudentially there is nothing to prevent the integration of sexual and gender-based violence offences

---

117   See *Consultation Report on the Commission for Reception, Truth and Reconciliation* (unpublished, 2001) (copy on file with author). See also Commission for Reception, Truth and Reconciliation in East Timor 'Background, Chronology' <http://www.easttimor-reconciliation.org/bgd.htm> at 11 December 2003.

118   See eg United Nations Transitional Administration in East Timor, 'UNTAET Recommends Human Rights Principles' (24 August 2000) East Timor Action Network <http://etan.org/et2000c/august/20-26/24unaet.htm> at 2 May 2003.

119   See UN Newservice, 'East Timor Cabinet Agrees to Establish Truth Commission' (13 December 2000) East Timor Action Network <east-timor@igc.apc.org> at 20 December 2000; UNTAET Daily Briefing, 'Cabinet Endorses Truth and Reconciliation Commission' (28 February 2001) East Timor Action Network <east-timor@igc.apc.org> at 18 March 2001.

120   UN News Centre, 'East Timor: National Council Sets Up Truth Commission to Probe Rights' (21 June 2001) Justwatch Listserv <justwatch-l@listserv.acsu.buffalo.edu> at 21 June 2001.

in the statutory mandates or terms of reference for truth commissions. Guiding principles for extra-judicial inquiries prepared by Louis Joinet and published in 1997 specifically recommend that extra-judicial commission of inquiry terms of reference *as a matter of priority* focus on 'violations that constitute serious crimes under international law' and 'pay particular attention to violations of the basic rights of women (emphasis added)'.[121] Additionally, the 1993 and 1994 statutes for the two ad hoc criminal tribunals established benchmarks for the legislative recognition of sexual and gender-based violence, including rape, which presumably could be extended to 'soft' international criminal law. Still as the South African legislative experience demonstrates, and as has been observed by others,[122] truth commission mandates often are shaped by political considerations rather than jurisprudential developments.

Traditionally truth commission mandates have been framed in gender-neutral language using broad investigatory categories like 'forced disappearances', 'serious acts of violence', or 'past human rights violations'. If sub-categories of violations are legislatively stipulated, they often are framed in conventional language relating to, for example, killings, abductions, torture, disappearances or extrajudicial executions, without reference to sexual or gender violence. The legal basis of truth commissions – whether authorised by presidential decree, peace agreement, national legislation or resolution – seems to have no bearing on the gender-neutrality of truth commission mandates. Nor have UN Security Council Resolution 1325 (2000), the Secretary-General's study on Women Peace and Security (2002) or the Independent Experts Assessment on the Impact of Armed Conflict on Women (2002) apparently yet had an effect in the statutory integration of a gender perspective. Of concern, the National Reconciliation Commission Act (Act 611) passed by the Parliament of the Republic of Ghana in early 2002, Article 4, mandates the National Reconciliation Commission to investigate violations and abuses of human rights relating to killings, abductions, disappearances, detentions, torture, ill treatment and seizure of properties but contains no reference to women or gender, or to sexual or gender based violations. Equally disconcerting, Article XIII of the 2003 Comprehensive Peace Agreement for Liberia, providing for the establishment of a Truth and Reconciliation Commission, mandates the commission 'in the spirit of national reconciliation' to 'deal with the root causes of the crises in Liberia, including human rights violations'. Even though widespread rape and sexual violence against women and girls in Liberia are well documented, the Article XIII provision does not explicitly recognise women or gender, sexual or gender violence.

Up to now – few truth commissions have been officially mandated to investigate sexual or gender violence offences. The Haitian National Commission of Truth and Justice (1995-1996) was authorised by Article 3 of its presidential decree to pay detailed

---

121 *The Administration of Justice and the Human Rights of Detainees, Question of the Impunity of Perpetrators of Human Rights Violations (Civil and Political), Revised Final Report prepared by Mr Joinet pursuant to Sub-Commission Decision 1996/119*, 49 UN ESCOR, UN Doc E/CN.4/Sub.2/1997/Rev.1 (1997) [Annex II, Principle 7(e)] (*'The Administration of Justice and the Human Rights of Detainees Report'*).

122 See for example, Patrick Ball and Audrey Chapman, *The Truth of Truth Commissions: Comparative Lessons from Haiti, South Africa, and Guatemala* (2001) 12.

attention to violations of human rights and crimes against humanity committed by individuals or groups of individuals *in particular against women victims of crimes or sexual aggression for political purposes.*[123] The Truth and Reconciliation Commission Act (2000) directs the Sierra Leonean Truth and Reconciliation Commission to give 'special attention to the subject of sexual abuses ... within the armed conflict' in performing its functions.[124] UNTAET Regulation 2001/10 (2001) empowers the East Timor Commission for Reception, Truth and Reconciliation to pay particular attention to sexual offences in performing its truth seeking function.[125]

As prefaced, even if not formally mandated, some truth commissions have been willing to expansively interpret their mandate to investigate sexual and gender-based violations. In addition to South Africa, the Guatemalan Commission for Historical Clarification (1997-1999) and the Peruvian Truth and Reconciliation Commission (2001-2003) overtly interpreted their mandate in this way. On the other hand, some truth commissions have been reluctant to read beyond the 'literal boundaries' of their formal mandate. As a result, these commissions have provided very limited investigation of violence against women. The Chilean National Commission for Truth and Reconciliation (1990-1991) and the Burundi International Commission of Inquiry (1995-1996) for instance, in interpreting their respective mandates, appear not to have deviated from the original wording of their terms of reference. Both reports contain only sporadic references to violence against women, although the Chilean Commission report does mention rape and sexual abuse. Equally troubling, the truth commission interpretation of rape as a non-political offence was not isolated to the South African context. Priscilla Hayner describes the historically prominent UN Commission of the Truth for El Salvador (1992-1993) as having chosen not to report the rape of women in its main report since, in the absence of political orders, rape committed by state armed forces was judged to fall beyond its mandate of 'politically motivated acts'.[126]

The challenge in leaving truth commissions to volitionally interpret gender into their mandate or terms of reference is that truth commissions, as non- or quasi-judicial bodies, are not bound to apply international humanitarian and human rights law in the same way as courts. There is in fact enormous variation in the level of legal analyses that truth commissions perform. Whereas the Haitian and Guatemalan commissions undertook comparatively extensive analyses of international humanitarian and human rights law in defining their mandates and making findings concerning sexual violence against women,[127] the South African Truth and Reconciliation Commission's treat-

---

123   See *Haiti Rapport de la Commission Nationale de Vérité et de Justice* (1996) [Chapitre 5: Présentation Générale des Cas, Les Enquêtes Spéciales, Violence Contra les Femmes] <http://www.Haiti.org/truth/table.htm> at 18 June 2001. Article three of the decree establishing the Commission outlines the 'Duty Applicable to Rape and Sexual Violence Perpetrated against Women'.

124   *The Truth and Reconciliation Commission Act of Sierra Leone 2000* (2000), article 6(2).

125   See *Regulation 2001/10 on the Establishment of a Commission for Reception, Truth and Reconciliation in East Timor*, UNTAET REG/2001/10 2001 Article 13.2.

126   Hayner, above n 4, 79.

127   See *Haiti Rapport de la Commission Nationale de Vérité et de Justice* (1996) [Chapitre 5: Présentation Générale des Cas, Les Enquêtes Spéciales, Violence Contra les Femmes]

ment of violence against women is framed almost completely in non-legal terms.[128] In particular, the absence of accompanying legal analysis for the Amnesty Committee decisions that rape is a non-political crime seems an extraordinary omission in view of the fact that all Commissioners appointed to that committee were legally qualified.

One of the most dramatic jurisprudential changes to emerge following the South African Truth and Reconciliation Commission, which in theory could grant amnesty for sexual and other violence offences against women, is increasingly consistent state practice *excluding amnesty* for genocide, crimes against humanity, and war crimes including those relating to sexual and other gender-based violence against women.

Consistent with the emphasis of UN Security Council Resolution 1325 (2000) stressing the need to prosecute those responsible for genocide, war crimes and crimes against humanity including those relating to sexual and other violence against women and girls and to exclude these crimes from amnesty provisions, both Sierra Leone and East Timor have *complementary* prosecution and truth commission schemes.

The Sierra Leone Truth and Reconciliation Commission is able to *investigate and report on* violations of human rights and international humanitarian law, including sexual abuses. However, the Special Court for Sierra Leone retains competence to *prosecute* within specified parameters serious violations of international humanitarian and Sierra Leonean law extending to 'rape, sexual slavery, enforced prostitution, forced pregnancy and any other form of sexual violence' in addition to 'outrages upon personal dignity, in particular humiliating and degrading treatment, rape, enforced prostitution and any form of indecent assault' as well as the abuse of girls.[129] In a similar fashion, the East Timor Commission for Reception, Truth and Reconciliation may investigate and report on human rights violations including sexual offences within the remit of its truth seeking function. However, serious crimes including rape are excluded from its community reconciliation process and the Commission is expressly prohibited from granting immunity for serious crimes. The East Timor Special Panels

---

<http://www.Haiti.org/truth/table.htm> at 18 June 2001; *Guatemala Memoria del Silencio* (1999) [Tomo III, XIII: Violencia Sexual Contra la Mujer] American Association for the Advancement of Science <http://shr.aaas.org/guatemala/ceh/gmds_pdf/cap2_2.pdf> at 5 September 2001.

128 See especially *Truth and Reconciliation Commission of South Africa Report* (1999) vol 1, 58-85, 94-102; vol 4, 282-316; vol 5, 256; (2003) vol 6, 589-613. In the first five volumes of its report, the South African Truth and Reconciliation Commission used international humanitarian and human rights law in its interpretation of the definition of gross violations of human rights, the right to compensation and its assessment of accountability. Even while presenting separate examination of apartheid as a crime against humanity, the Commission does not provide specific legal analysis of sexual or gender violence offences as crimes against humanity, or as war crimes or genocide. The Truth and Reconciliation Commission has subsequently provided a more detailed legal framework based on international law, and especially international humanitarian law, for its interpretation of gross violations of human rights and assessment of accountability. Unfortunately, the extended legal framework does not add anything in the way of legal analyses of sexual or gender based violence against women.

129 See *the Truth and Reconciliation Commission Act of Sierra Leone 2000* (2000) Article 6(2); *Statute of the Special Court for Sierra Leone* (2002) Articles 2, 3, 4 and 5.

for Serious Crimes have exclusive jurisdiction for the prosecution of serious crimes, which include genocide, war crimes, crimes against humanity, torture, murder and sexual offences. The serious crimes regulation expressly defines genocide, crimes against humanity, grave breaches and war crimes to variously include a wide range of sexual and gender based violence offences including 'imposing measures intended to prevent births within the group', rape, sexual slavery, enforced prostitution, forced pregnancy, enforced sterilization, or any other form of sexual violence of comparable gravity, and 'persecution based on gender'.[130]

The Burundi peace agreement provisions (2002) reflect a similar approach wherein the National Truth and Reconciliation Commission, when established, will have jurisdiction over serious acts of violence other than genocide, crimes against humanity and war crimes. A proposed international judicial commission of inquiry will have jurisdiction over genocide, war crimes and other crimes against humanity with a view to the prosecution of these offences by a proposed UN established international criminal tribunal.[131] These amnesty exclusions have not come about by accident but in large part because of the advocacy efforts of women. For instance, the parallel All Party Burundi Women's Peace Conference submitted recommendations to the negotiating parties, many of which were incorporated in the Arusha Peace Accord, specifically calling for the establishment of legal (retributive) justice mechanisms to address past human rights violations, including rape and sexual violence.[132]

The Comprehensive Peace Agreement for Liberia (2003) seems to be an exception to this emerging trend in state practice. The peace agreement potentially allows the granting of *general amnesty* while providing for the establishment of a truth commission to counter impunity. There is no reference in the agreement to the prosecution of, or an amnesty exclusion for genocide, war crimes and crimes against humanity including those relating to sexual and other violence against women and girls.[133]

2   Structural Accommodations for Women

(a) Gender Composition

Similar to South Africa, even when not statutorily required to do so, most truth commissions have appointed women as commissioners. Nevertheless, women commis-

---

130   *Regulation 2001/10*, above n 125, Sections 13.2, 22.2, 32.1; *Regulation 2000/15 on the Establishment of Panels with Exclusive Jurisdiction Over Serious Crimes*, UNTAET REG/2000/15 (6 June 2000) Sections 1.3, 4, 5, 6 and 9.

131   See *Arusha Peace and Reconciliation Agreement for Burundi* (28 August 2000) [Protocol I, Articles 6 and 8] United States Institute of Peace, Peace Agreements Digital Collection <http://www.usip.org/library/pa/burundi/pa_burundi_08282000_toc.html> at 29 October 2003.

132   See Miriam Zoll, 'Women Join Peace Process in Burundi' <http://www.undp.org/dpa/choices/2000/december/p9.htm> at 17 October 2003.

133   See *Comprehensive Peace Agreement Between the Government of Liberia and the Liberians United for Reconciliation and Democracy and the Movement for Democracy in Liberia and the Political Parties*, Accra, Ghana (18 August 2003) [Articles XIII and XXXIV] United States Institute of Peace, Peace Agreements Digital Collection <http://www.usip.org/library/pa/liberia/liberia_08182003_cpa.html> at 22 October 2003.

sioners recurrently are in the minority. The Sierra Leone Truth and Reconciliation, with three (43 percent) women of seven commissioners, and the South Africa Truth and Reconciliation, with seven (41 percent) women of seventeen commissioners, remain the highest gender parity achieving commissions to date. At least five truth commissions have been exclusively composed of men commissioners, two of which – South Korea and Uruguay – were created in 2000. Françoise Boucard as Chair of the (1995-1996) Haitian National Commission of Truth and Justice (CNJV) and Manouri Kokila Muttetuwegama as Chair of the (1995-1997) Sri Lankan Commission of Inquiry into the Involuntary Removal or Disappearance of Persons, Western and Southern Provinces Commission are notable exceptions to the continuing dominance of men as the chairpersons of truth commissions. Women have served as the chief executive or as co-chief executive officer of truth commissions in Bolivia (1982-1984), Argentina (1983-1984), and El Salvador (1992-1993).

More recently, truth commission statutes for Sierra Leone and East Timor have embodied fair gender representation criteria to guide the appointment of commissioners. The selection coordinator and selection panel for the Sierra Leone Truth and Reconciliation Commission were legislatively required to take *gender representation* into account in making their recommendation of four national commissioners to the President.[134] One of four Sierra Leonean commissioners – Vice-Chair Justice Laura Marcus-Jones – is a woman and two of three international commissioners – Ms Yasmin Sooka (South Africa) and Madam Ajaaratou Santang Jow (The Gambia) – are women. In the case of East Timor, the regulation incorporates a gender parity quota for the commission with the intention that at least 30 percent of the national commissioners be women. The selection panel, statutorily required to have a women's organisation representative, was guided by fair gender representation criteria in making its recommendations to the Transitional Administrator. The gender parity quota extended to the appointment of regional commissioners (30 percent in the aggregate) where the selection panel also was guided by gender representation in making its recommendations to the Transitional Administrator.[135] Two of seven national commissioners and 10 of 29 regional commissioners – all East Timorese citizens – are women. Both Sierra Leone and East Timor engaged in broadly consultative public nominations processes for the selection of national commissioners inviting civil society organisations, including women's organisations, to propose the names of Commissioners.

(b) Provisions for the Protection and Support of Women Victims and Witnesses
Patterns of differential reporting between women and men, including non-disclosure of sexual violence offences, were not unique to the South African Truth and Reconciliation Commission. The Guatemalan Historical Clarification Commission (CEH) acknowledged the tendency for women to speak of their indirect rather than direct victimisation experiences. The Historical Clarification Commission observes: 'Though 48 percent of the testimonies received by the CEH belong to women who were direct victims of the repression, the majority focus their testimonies not as vic-

---

134 See *Truth and Reconciliation Commission Act of Sierra Leone 2000* (2000) sch sub-s 1(a)(v).
135 See *Regulation 2001/10*, above n 125, sections 4.1, 4.3, 11.1, 11.4.

tims of the violation of their rights, but as witnesses of what occurred to others'.[136] The CEH report documents serious underreporting of sexual victimisation by women, with the Commission finding that only 14 percent of the recorded 9 411 women victims were sexually violated.[137] The Haitian National Commission of Truth and Justice documented an even fewer number of rape cases, 83 in total, representing less than one percent of the total number of identified victims.[138]

Two truth commissions in particular reflect a surprisingly low rate of female victimisation. The Chilean National Commission for Truth and Reconciliation (1990-1991) indicates that only 5.5 percent (126) of 2 279 victims identified by the commission are women.[139] The South Korean Presidential Truth Commission on Suspicious Deaths (2001-2003) documents two women among 85 suspicious deaths.[140] Whether these findings are an accurate portrayal of the violations directly experienced by women or are a result of underreporting by women victims is open to question. By way of comparison, and more closely resembling the findings of the South Africa TRC that roughly 24 percent of the total number of violations involved women victims, the Argentine National Commission on the Disappearance of People (1983-1984) determined that women accounted for 30 percent of the disappeared and the Guatemalan Historical Clarification Commission (1997-1999) found that women constituted close to 25 percent (9 411) of the 42 275 identified victims.[141] The small proportion of women victims identified by the Chilean National Commission for Truth and Reconciliation is especially troubling because the list of victims compiled by the Commission was relied on by the Government's subsequent reparation programme.[142]

To what extent then have truth commissions other than the South African TRC sought to increase women's participation through the adoption of special measures for the protection and support of women victims and witnesses? Historically, truth commissions, such as Argentina, Chile, El Salvador and Guatemala, have not adopted special measures for the protection and support of women victims and witnesses. Newly created truth commission statutes represent a perceptible shift from these previous gender-neutral arrangements. Section 7(4) of the Truth and Reconciliation Commission Act of Sierra Leone (2000) specifically directs that the commission 'shall take into account the interests of victims and witnesses when inviting them to give statements,

---

136   *Guatemala Memoria del Silencio* (1999) [Tomo III, XIII: Violencia Sexual Contra la Mujer] American Association for the Advancement of Science <http://shr.aaas.org/guatemala/ceh/gmds_pdf/cap2_2.pdf> at 5 September 2001.

137   *Ibid.*

138   See *Haiti Rapport de la Commission Nationale de Vérité et de Justice* (1996) [Chapitre 5: Présentation Générale des Cas, Les Enquêtes Spéciales, Violence Contra les Femmes] <http://www.Haiti.org/truth/table.htm> at 18 June 2001.

139   See *Chile Report of the National Commission on Truth and Reconciliation* (1993) [Appendix II: Statistics] United States Institute of Peace Truth Commissions Digital Collection <http://www.usip.org/library/tc/doc/reports/chile/chile_1993_appendices.html> at 12 December 2003.

140   See *South Korea Presidential Commission on Suspicious Deaths* (2002) [Case Statistics] Truthfinder <http://www.truthfinder.go.kr/eng/p4.htm> at 21 October 2003.

141   See *Guatemala Memoria del Silencio*, above n 136.

142   See for example, Hayner, above n 4, 172.

including the security and other concerns of those who may not wish to recount their stories in public'. The Commission also may 'implement special procedures to address the needs of such particular victims as children or those who have suffered sexual abuses … (emphasis added).' Because of women's advocacy efforts, the Sierra Leone Truth and Reconciliation Commission has added a witness protection programme to encourage women to disclose sex specific abuse.[143] The East Timor regulation goes much further and empowers the commission to create 'gender aware policies' for the performance of its functions and appoint staff with gender expertise. The oath for commissioners contains a non-discrimination clause, as do the guiding principles for the treatment of persons coming before the commission. Like the South African model, the East Timor Commission for Reception, Truth and Reconciliation holds its hearings in public. However, in addition to generic provisions for in camera proceedings, the commission is empowered to 'take special measures' in hearings involving the testimonies of particular groups of victims, including women, and may allow for victim accompaniment by support workers. Victim and witness protection measures authorise the commission to 'take appropriate measures to protect the safety, physical and psychological well being and privacy of victims and witnesses' taking into consideration factors such as gender, and the type of crime including sexual or gender violence.[144]

Thematic or special hearings for women like those initiated by the South African TRC are becoming more commonplace with at least three truth commissions since South Africa utilising this technique. The Peruvian Commission of the Truth and Reconciliation (2001-2003) organised a Thematic Public Hearing to hear the testimonies of women affected by violence and a Citizen's Dialogue on Political Violence and the Violations of Women's Rights to ensure the visibility of women's human rights violations and generate proposals for reform.[145] The East Timor Commission for Reception, Truth and Reconciliation held a two-day public hearing on women and conflict as part of its broader inquiry into women and conflict. The public hearing was intended to expose the human rights violations experienced by women and facilitate public education about women's human rights. Women and conflict is a main research theme of the truth-seeking division of the East Timor Commission and the results of the broader inquiry together with recommendations are supposed to be included in the final report.[146] The Sierra Leone Truth and Reconciliation Commission convened

143   See UNIFEM, Sierra Leone – Country Page (2003) [What UNIFEM is Doing in Sierra Leone] UNIFEM Portal on Women, Peace and Security <http://www.womenwarpeace.org/sierra_leone/sierra_leone.htm> at 30 November 2003.

144   *Regulation 2001/10*, above n 125, Sections 3.4, 5.1, 11.5, 12.1, 16.1-16.4, 35.1 and 36.1.

145   See Perú Comisíon de la Verdad y Reconciliacíon, 'Commission for Truth to Hear Testimonies of Women Affected by Violence' (Press Release 118, September 2002); Special Hearings End Political Violence and Crimes against Women' (Press Release 126, September 2002) <http://www.cverdad.org.pe/ingles/informacion/nprensa/notas.php> at 21 October 2003.

146   See Commission for Reception, Truth and Reconciliation in East Timor, 'Public Hearing on Women and Conflict in East Timor' (Press Release, 22 April 2003) Women's International League for Peace and Freedom <http://www.peacewomen.org/resources/NGO_reports/postconflict/TimorCAVR.html> at 21 October 2003.

a three day Special Hearing on Sexual Violence focusing on the effects of the war on women and girls. Among other things, the hearing generated specific recommendations concerning customary and common-law reform directed at the eradication of violence against women.[147]

Other interesting innovations to emerge post-South Africa include the creation of a Women's Task Force concerning the Truth and Reconciliation Commission and Special Court for Sierra Leone. The Task Force is composed of domestic and international women's representatives. The purpose of the Task Force is 'to create an enabling environment to encourage the participation of women at all levels' of the Truth and Reconciliation Commission and the Special Court.[148] The Task Force specifically lobbied for gender balance on the commission.[149] In addition, women's organisations in Sierra Leone have started a technical support initiative to provide training to the Truth and Reconciliation Commission on the impact of armed conflict on women and children. This initiative provided its first training workshop on gender based human rights violations for the Sierra Leone TRC in preparation for the commencement of the public hearings phase of the Commission's work.[150]

C   Recognition of Women's Varied Roles and the Differential Consequences of Armed Conflict for Women

The approach of the South African TRC to the separate presentation of women in its report is not unique. A number of other truth commission reports – Argentina (1984), Chad (1992), El Salvador (1993), Haiti (1996), Guatemala (1999), Rwanda (2000), Peru (2003) – have incorporated discussion of women or gender-based violence either as a discrete chapter or as a substantial section of a chapter.[151] There appears to be a strong association between the presentation of an entire special chapter on violence against women and truth commission terms of reference. Those truth commissions that have produced whole chapters on violence against women – South Africa, Haiti,

---

147   See UNIFEM, 'Sierra Leone – Country Page' (2003) [Women's Peace-Building Activities in Sierra Leone] UNIFEM Portal on Women, Peace and Security <http://www.women-warpeace.org/sierra_leone/sierra_leone.htm> at 30 November 2003.

148   See International Human Rights Law Group, 'IHRLG in Sierra Leone: Promoting the Protection of Women's Human Rights' <http://www.hrlawgroup.org/country_programs/sierra_leone/womens_rights.asp> at 25 November 2003.

149   See Richard Bennett, 'The Evolution of the Sierra Leone Truth and Reconciliation Commission' in *Truth and Reconciliation in Sierra Leone: A Booklet on the Truth and Reconciliation Commission* (2001) Truth and Reconciliation Commission (Sierra Leone) <http://www.sierra-leone.org/trc-documents.html> at 8 October 2003.

150   See UNIFEM, 'UNIFEM and Urgent Action Fund Support Peace-Building Process in Sierra Leone, New Initiative Launched to Strengthen Capacity of Sierra Leone's Truth and Reconciliation Commission' (Press Release, 17 April 2003) <http://www.unifem.undp.org/newsroom/press/pr_030417_sierra_leone.html> at 26 November 2003.

151   The 1984 report of the Argentinean National Commission on Disappeared Persons, for instance, provides separate discussion of 'children and pregnant women who disappeared' in its chapter on victims. The 1992 report of the Chad Commission of Inquiry Commission of Inquiry into Crimes and Misappropriations Committed by Ex-President Habré, His

Guatemala and Peru – are the same truth commissions that were specifically mandated or willing to interpret their mandate to investigate violence against women. It is anticipated that Sierra Leone and East Timor will produce chapters on violence against women in their reports since these commissions were explicitly mandated to seek the truth about past sexual abuse and organised thematic hearings on violence against women.

Though some truth commissions perfunctorily acknowledge the positive role of women in opposing repression or the negative consequences of armed conflict for women, common to many truth commission reports is a visible emphasis on women as victims, and in particular as victims of sexual violence. In view of the well recognised role of women as combatants in Sierra Leone and Liberia, as well as women's contribution to the resistance in East Timor, it will be intriguing to see if these truth commission reports when produced are better able to represent the diversity of women's experience in armed or political conflict.

Several truth commission reports, among them Argentina (1984), Chile (1991), Guatemala (1999) and Peru (2003), have incorporated some sex-disaggregated statistics. The presentation of sex-disaggregated statistics by truth commissions highlights the need for further investigation of gender variation in the human rights violation experiences of women and men. As UNIFEM observes in relation to Guatemala:

> Men experienced four times as much arbitrary executions, torture, forced disappearance, detention. The same number of women and men died due to forced displacement. Women, however, were subjected to 99 percent of the sexual violations. The age of females who have experienced violations of all types is known in only 51 percent of cases. Of these cases, 35 percent are girls under the age of 18, 62 percent are women between the ages of 18 and 59, and 3 percent were identified as women 60 and over. Because sexual violations are usually targeted at women and girls, it is crucial that this be investigated further to understand who the women were (and are) and who experienced these violations.[152]

Concerning recommendations, the Guatemalan Historical Clarification Commission adopted a somewhat unusual approach by consulting civil society in the preparation

---

Accomplices and-or Accessories includes a section on 'widows' within its chapter on the social consequences of repression. The 1993 report of the Commission on Truth for El Salvador provides a separate section on 'The American Churchwomen (1980)' within its chapter on 'Extrajudicial Executions'. The 1996 report of the Haitian National Commission for Truth and Justice presents a separate section on violence against women as part of its special investigations chapter. The 1999 Guatemalan Historical Clarification Commission report includes a separate chapter on sexual violence against women. The 2000 report of the Rwandan International Panel of Eminent Personalities to investigate the 1994 Genocide in Rwanda and the Surrounding Events Report includes a chapter on 'The Plight of Women and Children'. The 2003 report of the Peruvian Truth and Reconciliation Commission includes a standalone chapter on sexual violence against women.

152   UNIFEM, 'Guatemala – Country Page' (2003) [para Political and Security Impact] UNIFEM Portal on Women, Peace and Security <http://www.womenwarpeace.org/guatemala/guatemala.htm> at 30 November 2003.

of its recommendations and convening a National Forum on Recommendations for civil society organisations to reflect on the proposals made. The Guatemalan reparation proposals stand out as a possible template for future truth commissions because the beneficiary provisions of the proposed National Reparation Programme expressly recognise the economic and social severity of human rights violations, instructing that particular attention be given to 'the elderly, widows, minors or those who are found to be disadvantaged in any other way'. The proposed measures also call for a women's organisation representative to sit on the Board of Directors for the National Reparation Programme.[153] Yet, as Costa Rican lawyer Alda Facio cautions on Guatemala, none of the Historical Clarification Commission recommendations deals with rape 'even though many thousands of women are thought to have been the victims of multiple rapes during the armed conflict and hundreds of women came forward to give testimony to the CEH'.[154]

The Haitian National Commission of Truth and Justice is one of the few truth commissions to present separate recommendations on rape and sexual violence against women. The reform measures proposed by the Haitian Commission are relatively comprehensive and include modification of the penal code classification of rape; improvements to protective and rehabilitative services for sexual violence victims; education and training courses for administration of justice personnel; public education to increase awareness of sexual violence against women; ratification of human rights instruments relating to the elimination of violence against women; the prosecution and punishment of perpetrators of sexual violence; and, compensation for the victims of sexual violence.[155] The Peruvian Commission of Truth and Reconciliation (CVR) also proposes both institutional reform and reparative measures to benefit women and sexual violence victims. Among a variety of measures, the CVR calls for the comprehensive reparations programme to give preferential treatment to 'the widows' and 'women victims of sexual violence' in addition to proposing monetary grants for victims of sexual violence, whether women or men or children.[156]

The East Timor Commission for Reception, Truth and Reconciliation represents a departure from the previous practice of state-sponsored reparations. In compliance with a community reconciliation process, individual perpetrators alleged to have committed less serious crimes are required to engage in an act of reconciliation which

153 *See Guatemala: Memory of Silence: Report of the Commission for Historical Clarification, Conclusions and Recommendations (English Summary)* (1999) [Recommendations, III: Reparatory Measures paras 14, 16] American Association for the Advancement of Science <http://hrdata.aaas.org/ceh/report/english/> at 15 December 2003.

154 Jessika Rang Schmidt, 'The Gender Dimension of the Rome Statute and the ICC, a Talk with Alda Facio, Costa Rica' (Swedish NGO for Human Rights, 10 February 2003) <http://wwwqweb.kvinnoforum.se/misc/seminar/AldaFacio.pdf> at 28 November 2003.

155 See *Haiti Rapport de la Commission Nationale de Vérité et de Justice* (1996) [Chapitre 8: Des Recommandations, Viols et Violences Sexuelles Contre Les Femmes] <http://www.Haiti.org/truth/table.htm> at 28 November 2003.

156 *Peru Comisión de la Verdad y Reconciliación Informe Final* (2003) [Tomo IX, Capitulo 2, Recomendaciones] <http://www.cverdad.org.pe/ifinal/pdf/PORTADA.pdf> at 21 October 2003.

may consist of community service, *reparation*, public apology or another act of contrition.[157] The East Timorese community reconciliation process would seem to satisfy some of the principal concerns expressed by South African victims/survivors on the subject of reconciliation, wherein victims/survivors felt strongly that perpetrators 'must be made to contribute materially and financially toward the reparation and rehabilitation of victims.' While endorsing state compensation for access to psychological and medical services, South African victims/survivors proposed that a reparations fund be established so that beneficiaries and especially perpetrators could *directly* contribute.[158] The CAVR regulation stipulates 'appropriate gender representation' on community reconciliation panels that are convened to hear cases.[159] It remains to be assessed how well the more community-based East Timorese reconciliation process benefits women victims.

For the most part, truth commission recommendation and reparation provisions have not been especially attentive to the special needs and interests of women. Of note, truth commission statutes evidently have not integrated gender within reporting and recommendation requirements. This statutory omission is puzzling when viewed against the Joinet principles for extra-judicial inquiries that specifically endorse gender-specific reparative and preventive measures for women.[160] There remains a critical need to ensure that the findings of truth commissions on violence against women are appropriately complemented by gender-specific recommendations for reparative and ameliorative action.

D   Assessing Women's Participation and the Integration of a Gender Perspective in Comparative Context

A selective comparison of truth commissions established or proposed between 1982 and 2003 suggests some quite positive developments for the participation of women and integration of a gender perspective in truth commission structures and processes.

Women are participating in the decision to establish truth commissions and in legislative or institutional design, for example as members of working groups convened to draft enabling legislation or as members of executive and legislative bodies that debate and approve truth commission legislation. Some truth commissions are being legislatively mandated to investigate sexual violence offences committed in the context of past armed or political conflict. Up to now, the mainstreaming of a gender perspective in the regulation for the establishment of an East Timorese Commission

---

157   See *Regulation 2001/10*, above n 125, section 27.7.

158   The Centre for the Study of Violence and Reconciliation and the Khulumani Support Group, *Submission to the Truth and Reconciliation Commission: Survivors' Perceptions of the Truth and Reconciliation Commission and Suggestions for the Final Report* (1998) 11-13.

159   See *Regulation 2001/10*, above n 125, section 26.1.

160   See *The Administration of Justice and the Human Rights of Detainees Report*, above n 121, [Annex II, Principle 11]. Principle 11 on the advisory functions of commissions encourages 'setting out legislative or other measures … where applicable, reparation for violations of the fundamental rights of women and prevention of their recurrence'.

for Reception, Truth and Reconciliation is unparalleled. The regulation embodies principles for non-discrimination; expressly mandates the commission to pay particular attention to sexual offences in performing its truth seeking function; includes fair gender representation criteria for the appointment of commissioners and community reconciliation panels; calls for the appointment of staff with gender expertise and enables the commission to make gender-aware policies; and allows the Commission to take special measures to protect and support women victims and witnesses especially in relation to sexual or gender violence. Congruent with the emphasis of UN Security Council Resolution 1325, there is increasingly consistent state practice *excluding amnesty* for genocide, crimes against humanity and war crimes including those relating to sexual and other violence against women. At least three jurisdictions – Sierra Leone, East Timor and Burundi – have implemented or formally proposed *complementary* truth commission and prosecution schemes.

The utilisation of thematic or special hearings for women represents another interesting trend. Thematic hearings in Peru, East Timor and Sierra Leone illustrate that this procedure is being used not just to encourage women to come forward and testify about their own victimisation experiences but also to generate gender-specific proposals for reform. It is anticipated that this type of hearing increasingly will address the full range of women's experiences during conflict, not only as victims but also as activists, combatants and perpetrators, in addition to the negative social and economic consequences of armed or political conflict for women. The addition of a witness protection programme to encourage women to disclose sex specific abuse, the creation of a Women's Task Force to promote women's participation at all levels of the Truth and Reconciliation Commission process, and the provision of gender violence training for truth commissioners in Sierra Leone also represent positive advances.

In terms of ameliorative and reparative measures, the Guatemalan, Haitian and Peruvian experiences demonstrate that it is possible for truth commissions to propose comprehensive institutional reforms aimed at the eradication of violence against women and to stipulate criteria for the preferential treatment of particular groups, including widows and victims of sexual violence, in the awarding of monetary compensation.

Despite these positive developments, we have yet to achieve the *comprehensive* participation of women and integration of a gender perspective in truth commission structures and processes. Generally, women's participation in *accountability* decision-making remains largely at the technical rather than the political negotiations level. In this sense, women are more likely to participate in legislative or institutional design negotiations than in the political forums that make accountability policy decisions. Consistent with resolution 1325 (2000), increasing women's representation at all levels of conflict-to-peace decision-making in national, regional and international institutions is vital since accountability policy may be determined by the parties to a peace agreement but equally by the executive or legislative branches of government or by an inter-governmental body. Other options to promote the inclusion of women's concerns and interests in accountability decisions include the development of gender-specific proposals through parallel forums as was done in the Burundi peace negotiations.

As the lesson of South Africa suggests, increasing women's participation at the peace table is a necessary yet *insufficient* condition for the inclusion of women's concerns and interests in accountability decision-making. Accountability decisions may be negotiated outside of established procedures and in ways that are largely non-transparent and exclusionary. Women will need to lobby for greater openness and inclusivity in accountability decision-making, or alternatively seek access to the processes or persons who make these decisions. We also need to be *extremely cautious* about thinking of truth commissions and other accountability mechanisms as 'post conflict' reconstruction issues.[161] As the experiences of South Africa, Sierra Leone, East Timor and Burundi demonstrate, accountability policy decisions including the decision to establish a truth commission may be negotiated near the beginning of a political transition and perhaps well in advance of a formal peace settlement. Women will need to mobilise early if they wish to ensure that their demands are on the table when accountability decisions are made.

Comprehensive integration of gender equity provisions in enabling truth commission legislation is the exception rather than the rule. Other than East Timor and to a much lesser extent Sierra Leone, a gender perspective has not been mainstreamed in truth commission legislation or institutional design. Only rarely have truth commissions been explicitly mandated to investigate sexual and gender-based violence. The UN Secretary-General's study on women, peace and security (2002) goes part way in suggesting change to the jurisprudential practices of truth commissions, proposing that judicial and *quasi-judicial* mechanisms *established by the Security Council* interpret and apply the international legal framework relating to armed conflict in a consistent and gender sensitive manner.[162] Certainly, the experiences of South Africa and Sierra Leone demonstrate that it is possible to achieve concessions to accommodate women's concerns and interests after truth commission legislation has been enacted or proceedings have commenced. Yet, these concessions have been relatively modest and not nearly as extensive as the accommodations thought necessary to adequately address women's concerns and interests.

The legislative integration of special measures for the protection and support of women victims and witnesses has been particularly limited. Consequently, women have had to lobby for the addition of special measures like witness protection programmes as an afterthought rather than as an integral design feature of truth commissions. Here, we need to draw on the lessons of 'hard' international criminal law where women have purposefully campaigned for the legislative integration of gender attentive witness protection provisions in the Rome Statute of the International Criminal Court and hybrid tribunals such as those for Sierra Leone and East Timor. The UN Secretary-General's study on women, peace and security (2002) proposes exactly this type of action to the Security Council:

> Ensure ... that the mandates of domestic mechanisms of redress, such as truth and reconciliation commissions .... clearly reflect gender perspectives, respond to the

---

161 See *UN Study*, above n 8, 39, 50, 113, which appears to make this conceptual distinction.
162 See *ibid.*, 50 [Action 9].

needs, concerns and experiences of women and girl victims of armed conflict, and include special measures for victim and witness protection, especially of sexual crimes and violence; and ensure during all stages of ... other redress procedures, measures to protect their safety, physical and psychological well-being, dignity and privacy, and gender-sensitive care and protection ....[163]

One of the most disappointing features of truth commissions to date is the non-achievement of proportionate representation of women as truth commissioners, or within truth commission executive and management structures. Public nominations and selection processes, as were undertaken in South Africa, Sierra Leone and East Timor, enabling women and women's organisations to submit the names of commissioners and participate as members of selection panels in the recommendation of commissioners, seem to have a positive influence on the gender composition of truth commissions. While it is possible to legislatively stipulate fair gender representation, as was done for Sierra Leone and East Timor, this criterion is often counterbalanced against other factors such as regional representation. Another alternative is to set legislative quotas or targets for gender representation. The UNTAET regulation for East Timor does this with the result that the gender representation quotas – women to constitute 30 percent of national and regional commissioners – were met. The UN Secretary-General's study on women, peace and security (2002) supports such an approach proposing that targets be set for 'gender balance in the composition of truth and reconciliation commissions'.[164] The question is whether those involved in future legislative or institutional design processes for truth commissions will be willing to set targets that are proportional to the gender composition of their society. It also remains to be seen whether the pattern of political appointments will change so that an equal number of women are appointed as truth commission chairpersons and to executive and management positions.

The other singularly disappointing feature of truth commission practice has been the apparent reluctance of most truth commissions to confront violence against women when proposing reparative or preventive remedies. In comparison with other forms of redress, the probity of a truth commission lies not only in its ability to officially acknowledge a pattern of past international humanitarian and human rights law violations, including the origins and consequences of such violations, but to propose institutional reforms to prevent non-repetition and in some instances recommend or provide reparative measures. In view of the often epidemic levels of violence against women both during *and* after armed or political conflict, it seems clear that the elimination of violence against women should be a central tenet of the *remedial* function of truth commissions.

In this assessment, three basic questions about women and truth commissions were explored primarily in relation to the South African TRC as well as in selective com-

IV   Facilitating Women's Voices in Truth Recovery

In this assessment, three basic questions about women and truth commissions were explored primarily in relation to the South African TRC as well as in selective com-

163   See *ibid.*, 50 [Action 6].
164   See *ibid.*, 49 [Action 5].

parison with other historically prominent and some recently established truth commissions. The three questions were: (1) Do women participate in accountability decision-making, including the choice to establish a truth commission and by extension in its legislative or institutional design? (2) Are truth commissions emulating the positive jurisprudential and structural advances that women have achieved in 'hard' international criminal law? (3) Do truth commissions address the diversity of women's conflict experiences and the consequences of armed or political conflict for women?

The South African TRC experience exemplifies that women and women's organizations played a somewhat peripheral role in the decision to establish a truth commission and in its legislative design. In response to an essentially gender-neutral truth commission statute, women successfully campaigned to have gender-specific procedures attached to already set processes. Even with the addition of special procedures to draw more women in, the South African TRC was not able to overcome the differential engagement of women in its structures and processes. Ultimately a majority of South African truth commissioners and the truth commission executive were men; a majority of the Human Rights Violation Committee and Amnesty Committee members were men; women's testimony centred on indirect rather than direct victimisation; few women spoke about their sexual victimisation experiences; few women activists testified before the commission; and few women disclosed their role as perpetrators of gross human rights violations. Sally Baden, Shireen Hasim and Sheila Meintjes evaluate the gender outcome of the South African TRC process in the following way:

> The outcome of the TRC process has been to create awareness of the terrible atrocities of the past and, at least in the public mind, to assert the need for a new human rights culture. The connection between women's rights and human rights has not been fully absorbed into the emerging democratic thinking in South Africa. However, the gender advocacy lobby did receive considerable media attention and were persistent in their efforts to ensure that the TRC kept 'gender questions' to the fore. Nevertheless, gender issues were often ... an 'add-on' factor rather than integrated into the thinking of the TRC.[165]

Recently created truth commissions in Peru, Sierra Leone and East Timor symbolise positive gender developments, with much more overt women's participation in the deliberations concerning the establishment of these truth commissions and in the crafting of truth commission legislation. The Sierra Leone and East Timor truth commission statutes, in particular, reflect enhanced gender awareness and expanded prospects for the protection and support of women victims and witnesses, especially victims of sexual violence. But just as these truth commissions represent advancements for women, some post-2000 truth commission developments give pause for concern. The appointment of exclusively male truth commissioners and negotiation of gender neutral peace agreement provisions for truth commissions underscore the need

---

165 Sally Baden, Shireen Hasim and Sheila Meintjes, *Country Gender Profile: South Africa* (Report No 45, BRIDGE Development-Gender, 1998, revised) 37.

for much more concerted gender advocacy efforts to ensure women's participation and the integration of a gender perspective.

This assessment is conceived as a starting point for further discussion and exploration; its aim was to establish some baseline data about women and truth commissions. The assessment reveals a number of critical areas that require further investigation. At a general level, there is a need for more research on women and transitional justice and especially non-judicial remedies, including but not limited to truth commissions. At a more specific level, there has been limited published research deconstructing the role of women in accountability decision-making. For instance, do women support truth commissions as having virtue in their own right or simply as a counter impunity measure? Is there gender variation in accountability preferences; do women favour legal (retributive) justice while men support more politically expedient measures like truth commissions and amnesty? As identified by the assessment, a number of specific facets about women and truth commissions merit further examination. How do the media portray women *vis-à-vis* truth commissions? Do generic support and protective services benefit women? What are the implications of gender variation in the victimisation experiences of women and men?

It is clear that women's inclusion in decisions about accountability and the jurisprudential and structural gains accomplished for women in 'soft' and 'hard' international criminal law have not been automatic but have come about as the result of intensive and unified gender advocacy efforts. The Women's Caucus for Gender Justice in the International Criminal Court and the Women Building Peace Campaign to Promote the Role of Women in Peacebuilding exemplify just how effective women's advocacy efforts can be, given the success of these campaigns in ensuring the integration of women's concerns and a gender perspective in the Rome Statute for the International Criminal Court and, among other things, counter impunity measures in UN Security Council Resolution 1325 on Women, Peace and Security. It is likely, at least in the immediate future, that the gender advocacy lobby will need to continue its vigilance to ensure that women affected by conflict and serious violations of humanitarian and human rights law are afforded the opportunity to voice their needs and participate in the accountability decisions that affect them. Now, it is imperative that gender advocacy groups consciously extend their advocacy interventions beyond predominantly prosecutorial remedies to ensure that women's participation and a gender perspective are integrated in the full range of judicial *and non-judicial* remedies for serious violations of international humanitarian and human rights law.

The assessment of women's experiences with truth commissions to date highlights at least three essential areas for gender advocacy. Firstly, there is a need to ensure that women *directly* and *indirectly* participate in accountability decision-making *for all forms of redress*. At the same time, there is a critical need to increase awareness of women's concerns and a gender perspective among policy makers whether peace negotiators, the executive, legislators, or members of inter-governmental institutions. Secondly, much more needs to be done to ensure women's participation and the integration of a gender perspective in truth commission legislative or institutional design extending but not limited to the incorporation of sexual and gender based violence in truth commission terms of reference, fair gender representation criteria and gender targets for truth commissioners and staff, and special measures for the protection and support of women victims and witnesses. Thirdly, truth commissions need to be unambiguously authorised to *comprehensively report* on the varied experiences of women in armed or political conflict and to remedy, through recommended reparative and other institutional reform or policy measures, the consequences of armed and political violence for women.

Relative to the differential engagement of women in truth commission processes, numerous techniques have been suggested to encourage women's testimony as the victims of gender and sexual violence in the aftermath of armed or political conflict ranging from better assurances of confidentiality to more extreme long-term protective measures such as resettlement or asylum.[166] There is a need to assess whether recent innovations including the use of thematic hearings for women by truth commissions have any marked effect in encouraging women to come forward and testify and in generating gender-specific recommendations for reparation and reform. Additional suggestions to advance gender inclusion within truth commission structures and processes might comprise increased cross-fertilisation of gender expertise between truth commissions and prosecutorial/judicial bodies.

The large-scale impact assessments on women and armed conflict that were authorised by the International Committee for the Red Cross[167] and the United Nations Security Council[168] present additional recommendations to improve women's access to justice and reconciliation for past serious violations of international humanitarian and human rights law. The Independent Experts on Women and Peacebuilding, Elisabeth Rehn and Ellen Johnson Sirleaf, provide one of the more intriguing recommendations, proposing the creation of an international Truth and Reconciliation Commission on violence against women in armed conflict. The commission would be convened by civil society, with international support, 'to fill the historical gap that is left when crimes against women in armed conflict are unrecorded and unaddressed'.[169] Before creating such an institution, exactly how it will contribute to sustainable peace-building and meet the needs of women must be carefully considered.

One option that has not been seriously explored is the development of gender guidelines for the creation and operation of truth commissions. At various times, guidelines articulating minimal requirements for truth commissions have been produced although few of these guidelines have directly addressed the participation of women or the integration of a gender perspective.[170] The Joinet principles for extra-judicial commissions of inquiry, published in 1997, are an exception because they

---

166　See for example, Rehn and Sirleaf, above n 9, 100; *Violence Against Women Report*, above n 19, [42].

167　See Lindsey, above n 22.

168　See SC Res 1325, above n 7; *UN Study*, above n 8; Rehn and Sirleaf, above n 9.

169　See Rehn and Sirleaf, above n 9, X, 10, 30.

170　See especially Priscilla Hayner, 'International Guidelines for the Creation and Operation of Truth Commissions: A Preliminary Proposal' (1996) 59 *Law and Contemporary Problems* 173, 178-180; John Dugard, 'Reconciliation and Justice: The South African Experience' (1998) 8 *Transnational Law and Contemporary Problems* 277, 289.

embody some gender-inclusive measures concerning commission terms of reference, protection and support of sexual abuse victims, and the advisory functions of commissions.[171] On the other hand the recently revised Basic Principles and Guidelines on the Right to a Remedy and Reparation for Victims of Violations of International Human Rights and Humanitarian Law (Rev. 15 August 2003) are somewhat disappointing, containing a singular reference to 'gender' in the 'non-discrimination among victims' provision.[172] As a first step, existing international guidelines pertaining to redress for violations of international humanitarian and human rights law need to be systematically reviewed from a gender perspective to determine whether separate gender guidelines for truth commissions would be beneficial.

In thinking about the future of accountability or answerability to women for past violations, in a way that will promote sustainable peace, it is imperative that we think longitudinally, comprehensively, creatively and contextually.[173] As South Africa so eloquently demonstrates, redressing past violations of international humanitarian and human rights law is a long-term process and victim/survivor demands for accountability do not diminish with time. Knowing that singular remedies, whether prosecution or truth, do not fully address the needs of women, we need to think more holistically about accountability. State obligations under international law are much broader than simply prosecution and punishment, encompassing as well the duty to investigate the fate of victims and identify perpetrators, provide reparation or compensation to victims, and take measures to prevent non-repetition. In responding to the complex needs of women victims/survivors of past political violence, we need to think in terms of the full range of judicial and non-judicial remedies,[174] keeping in mind that women victim/survivor needs are not uniform and likely will change over time. Rama Mani's conceptualisation of three distinct yet overlapping dimensions of justice – legal, rectificatory *and distributive* – is particularly insightful in this regard.[175] Truth commission *models* should be regarded with some caution. In particular, we need to be more attuned to how well any one model addresses women's concerns and

---

171   See *The Administration of Justice and the Human Rights of Detainees Report*, above n 121 [Annex II: Principles 7(e), 9, 11].

172   See also *The Right to Restitution, Compensation and Rehabilitation for Victims of Gross Violations of Human Rights and Fundamental Freedoms, Final Report of the Special Rapporteur, Mr M Cherif Bassiouni, submitted in accordance with Commission resolution 1999/33*, 52 UN ESCOR, UN Doc E/CN.4/2000/62 (2000) [Annex]; M Cherif Bassiouni, 'Proposed Guiding Principles for Combating Impunity for International Crimes' in M Cherif Bassiouni (ed), *Post Conflict Justice* (2002) 255, 268-272.

173   See generally John Paul Lederach, *Building Peace: Sustainable Reconciliation in Divided Societies* (1997); John G Cockell, 'Conceptualising Peacebuilding: Human Security and Sustainable Peace' in Michael Pugh (ed), *Regeneration of War-Torn Societies* (2000) 15.

174   See especially Gloppen, above n 1, for discussion of this point. Gloppen's main research findings on accountability suggest that: (1) 'there is no superior strategy or institutional model'; (2) timing is critical; (3) 'local ownership and legitimacy are crucial'; and (4) a singular strategy is likely to be insufficient.

175   See Rama Mani, 'The Rule of Law or the Rule of Might? Restoring Legal Justice in the Aftermath of Conflict' in Michael Pugh (ed), *Regeneration of War-Torn Societies* (2000) 90; Rama Mani, *Beyond Retribution. Seeking Justice in the Shadows of War* (2002).

the integration of a gender perspective before transplanting it from one jurisdiction to the next. Accountability mechanisms, whether truth commissions or some other institutional strategy, must be *contextually responsive* and meet the needs of the women directly affected by past political violence. Above all, women affected by past armed or political conflict must have a voice in accountability policymaking and a role in designing, implementing and monitoring accountability mechanisms such as truth commissions.[176]

Annex I   List of Truth Commissions Established or Formally Proposed (1982-2003)[177]

1. BOLIVIA: National Commission of Inquiry into Disappearances (1982-1984)
2. ARGENTINA: National Commission on the Disappearance of People (1983-1984)
3. PHILIPPINES: Presidential Committee on Human Rights (1986-1987)
4. UGANDA: Commission of Inquiry into Violations of Human Rights (1986-1995)
5. NEPAL: Commission of Inquiry to Find the Disappeared Persons (1990-1991)
6. CHILE: National Commission for Truth and Reconciliation (1990-1991)
7. CHAD: Commission of Inquiry into Crimes and Misappropriations Committed by Ex-President Habré, His Accomplices and-or Accessories (1991-1992)
8. EL SALVADOR: (UN) Commission on the Truth for El Salvador (1992-1993)
9. GERMANY: Study Commission for the Assessment of History and Consequences of SED Dictatorship in Germany (1992 1994)
10. HAITI: National Commission of Truth and Justice (CNJV) (1995-1996)
11. SRI LANKA: Commissions of Inquiry into the Involuntary Removal or Disappearance of Persons (1995-1997)
12. GUATEMALA: Commission to Clarify Past Human Rights Violations and Acts of Violence that Have Caused the Guatemalan People to Suffer (1997-1999)
13. BURUNDI: International Commission of Inquiry (1995-1996)
14. SOUTH AFRICA: Truth and Reconciliation Commission (1995-2002)

---

176 See eg Naomi Roht-Arriaza, 'Civil Society Processes in Accountability' in M Cherif Bassiouni, above n 172, 97.

177 For simplicity, truth commissions are referred to by the English translation of their original title. Truth commissions are listed in roughly chronological order with the specified years reflecting the period in which the commission was *operational*. In most instances, the truth commission was officially endorsed in advance of its commencement of operations.

15. RWANDA: International Panel of Eminent Personalities to Investigate the 1994 Genocide in Rwanda and the Surrounding Events (1999-2000)
16. NIGERIA: Commission of Inquiry for the Investigation of Human Rights Violations (1999-?)
17. URUGUAY: National Peace Commission (2000-2002)
18. PANAMÁ: Truth Commission (2001-2002)
19. SOUTH KOREA: Presidential Truth Commission on Suspicious Deaths (2001-2002)
20. PERU: Truth and Reconciliation Commission (CVR) (2001-2003)
21. SERBIA AND MONTENEGRO: Truth and Reconciliation Commission (2001-?)
22. SIERRA LEONE: Truth and Reconciliation Commission (2002-present)
23. EAST TIMOR: Commission for Reception, Truth and Reconciliation (2002-present)
24. GHANA: National Reconciliation Commission (2002-present)
25. BURUNDI: National Truth and Reconciliation Commission (not yet operational at the time of writing)
26. LIBERIA: Truth and Reconciliation Commission (not yet operational at the time of writing)

Part III

How Can We Use Women's Voices to Create and Perpetuate Peace and Security?

The final section of the book explores the lessons learned from a number of the pieces in the book and reviews how these voices can be used in the construction of peace and security. Obviously the impact of armed conflict is not eradicated when the fighting stops. For many, women in particular, the hard work begins when the phase of reconstruction and re-building commences. What is being done to include women in the range of political, social and economic developments post-conflict? How does the local context and culture impact upon this process? What international instruments have been created to assist, and how practical are they? These are some of the themes explored in Section III.

Li Fung, Pacific Program Officer at Oxfam Community Aid Abroad, introduces the section with an in-depth examination of the significant Security Council Resolution 1325 that deals with 'Women, Peace and Security'. Li looks at the aims and substance of this resolution as well as the practical work done on this subject matter in the Pacific. Next Rina Amiri, Political Affairs Officer at the United Nations Assistance Mission to Afghanistan, writes about the role of women in peace-building and reconstruction in Afghanistan after years of armed conflict. Noting the need for a pragmatic approach, Rina highlights the important role played by religious interpretation and the requirement of men's support if the there is to be a change in the position of women in Afghani society.

In conclusion, Ambassador Swanee Hunt, Director of the Women and Public Policy Program at Harvard, highlights the advantages – and challenges – of developing a new model of 'inclusive security' that is built firmly on women's active participation in peace-building at grassroots and policy levels.

16

Engendering the Peace Process: Women's Role in Peace-building and Conflict Resolution

*Li Fung**

I Introduction

In recent years, the international community has increasingly recognised the differential impact of armed conflict on women, and women's experiences of conflict.[1] Much of this attention has focused on the negative effects of conflict on women and the need for special protection and assistance.[2] Around the globe, women are subjected to unacceptable violence and human rights violations during the course of armed conflict and suffer long after the cessation of hostilities. Armed conflict has a devastating and continued impact upon women, but it is wrong to perceive women solely as passive victims of conflict. They are agents of change and play an important role in forging and maintaining national and international peace and security.

In the international arena, the long silence surrounding women's role in the peace process has been broken through key documents such as Security Council Resolution 1325 (2000).[3] Women's contributions to peace, however, continue to be marginalised. Despite international recognition of the importance of increasing the participation

---

*   BA(Hons) LLB (Adel) LLM (Melb). Li Fung is Pacific Program Officer at Oxfam Community Aid Abroad, and has previously worked in Australia and Vanuatu as a judge's associate, commercial lawyer and government legal adviser. The views expressed in this chapter are her own, and do not necessarily reflect those of Oxfam Community Aid Abroad.
1   See, for example, International Committee of the Red Cross, *Women Facing War* (2001); *Women, Peace, and Security: Study Submitted by the Secretary-General Pursuant to Security Council Resolution 1325*, 57 UN SCOR, UN Doc S/2002/1154 (2002) (*'UN Study'*); and Elisabeth Rehn and Ellen Johnson Sirleaf, *Women, War and Peace: The Independent Experts' Assessment on the Impact of Armed Conflict on Women and Women's Role in Peace-building* (2002).
2   Judith Gardam and Hilary Charlesworth note that the focus on violence – particularly sexual violence – has tended to obscure other aspects of women's experiences of armed conflict: see Judith Gardam and Hilary Charlesworth, 'Protection of Women in Armed Conflict' (2000) 22(1) *Human Rights Quarterly* 148, 148.
3   SC Res 1325, UN SCOR (4213th mtg), UN Doc S/RES/1325 (2000).

Helen Durham and Tracey Gurd (eds.), Listening to the Silences: Women and War, *pp. 225-241.*
© 2005 *Koninklijke Brill BV. Printed in The Netherlands.* ISBN 90 04 14365 3.

of women in decision-making roles and integrating a gender perspective in the peace process,[4] women are still largely excluded from decision-making in matters relating to peace and security.[5] Women's marginalisation is reinforced by structural inequalities that support gender-based discrimination[6] and also by a dichotomy between 'public' and 'private' spheres of the peace process that restricts women's access to the realms of national and international politics.[7] This chapter will suggest that it is in the interests of the international community to avail itself of the skills of women peace-builders and peace-makers.

Conflict exacerbates existing inequalities within societies and, as a result, has a disproportionate impact on the least powerful and most vulnerable members of society.[8] To build sustainable and inclusive peace, the peace process should aim to empower those who are most adversely impacted by conflict, breaking down discriminatory barriers based on unequal power relations. As illustrated in the chapters of Luz Méndez and Swanee Hunt,[9] the participation of women in the peace process empowers women, enabling them to counter the destructive impacts of armed conflict and contribute to decision-making regarding long-term peace and security in their own communities and in the international community.

For sustainable peace and security to take root, we must integrate a gender perspective in the peace process, addressing the inequities of gender-blind decision-making and making room for women's full and effective participation in all aspects of political, social, economic and cultural life. Making visible women's experiences with conflict, particularly their contributions to peace and security, is the first step towards engendering the peace process and creating a space for women's participation.

II   Redefining Peace and Security

Gendered concepts of peace and security have contributed to women's marginalisation from the peace table. If peace and security are the ultimate goals of the peace process, it is necessary to redefine these terms in order to examine how women and men can contribute to their achievement.

---

4   See SC Res 1325, above n 3 and *UN Study*, above n 1, Actions 7-9.

5   See *Report of the Secretary-General on Women's Equal Participation in Conflict Prevention, Management and Conflict Resolution and in Post-Conflict Peace-Building*, 55 UN ESCOR, UN Doc. E/CN.6/2004/10 (2003) [11]-[14].

6   See Judith Gardam and Michelle Jarvis, *Women, Armed Conflict and International Law* (2001) 7-9, 251.

7   See Regina Graycar and Jenny Morgan, *Hidden Gender of Law* (2nd ed, 2002); Hilary Charlesworth, 'Worlds Apart: Public/Private Distinctions in International Law' in Margaret Thornton (ed) *Public and Private: Feminist Legal Debates* (1995) 243; and Christine Chinkin, 'A Critique of the Public/Private Dimension' (1999) 10(2) *European Journal of International Law* 387.

8   Gardam and Charlesworth, above n 2, 150.

9   Luz Méndez, 'Women's Role In Peacemaking: A Personal Experience' earlier in this collection and Swanee Hunt, 'Moving Beyond Silence: Women Waging Peace' later in this section.

'Peace' is traditionally characterised as the absence of war or armed conflict.[10] Likewise, 'security' is typically defined by reference to territorial integrity and defence from armed attack.[11] Being heavily centred on military interests, traditional definitions of peace and security are gender-blind, and fail to acknowledge women's aspirations for peace. Further, by asserting that peace and security are military matters, these definitions reinforce existing inequalities and balances of decision-making power within societies, and have operated to exclude women from formal peace processes on the basis that peace talks are concerned with the end of hostilities and women have no experience in military matters.

It is now widely recognised that peace is not only the absence of armed conflict, but a more holistic concept linked to the enjoyment of human rights and elimination of all forms of violence. The *Nairobi Forward-Looking Strategies for the Advancement of Women*, adopted at the Third World Conference on Women, defines peace to include 'not only the absence of war, violence and hostilities at the national and international levels, but also the enjoyment of economic and social justice, equality and the entire range of human rights and fundamental freedoms within society'.[12] This definition of peace is inextricably linked with gender equality and women's equal participation in political, economic and social life, particularly in decision-making processes.[13]

Similarly, security has been recast in terms of human security, reflecting a people-centred approach which relates to the needs and aspirations of individuals and communities. The Secretary-General of the United Nations, Kofi Annan, has described human security as encompassing economic development, social justice, environmental protection, democratisation, disarmament and respect for human rights and the rule of law.[14]

Fundamental to this human-centred redefinition of peace and security are the principles of human rights, gender equality and women's empowerment. The close relationship between peace, human rights and gender equality has long been recognised by women peace activists. In 1915, at the first International Congress of Women at The Hague, 1,000 women from 12 countries emphasised that permanent peace

---

10   Johan Galtung defines peace as the 'absence of violence', and distinguishes between 'negative peace', meaning the absence of personal or direct violence (including war), and 'positive peace', meaning the absence of structural violence. see Johan Galtung, 'Violence, Peace, and Peace Research' [1969] *Journal of Peace Research* 167, 167, 183.

11   See, for example, Jeffrey Elliot and Robert Reginald, *The Arms Control, Disarmament and Military Security Dictionary* (1989), 71, 106, who define 'national security' as freedom from armed attack or political or economic sabotage, and 'collective security' as a system by which states renounce the use of force and agree to take common (deterrence and military) action against states that breach the peace.

12   The *Nairobi Forward-looking Strategies for the Advancement of Women*, adopted by the World Conference to Review and Appraise the Achievements of the United Nations Decade for Women: Equality, Development and Peace, Nairobi, 15-16 July 1985, UN Doc DPI/926-41761 (1993) 8.

13   See also the *Beijing Platform for Action*, adopted at the Fourth World Conference on Women, Beijing, 4-15 September 1995, UN Doc DPI/1766/Wom (1995), [131].

14   Kofi Annan, 'Towards a culture of peace', UNESCO website, <http://www.unesco.org/opi2/lettres/TextAnglais/AnnanE.html>.

could only be built on the basis of equal rights – including equal rights between men and women – and justice within and between nations.[15]

If peace and security are redefined by reference to the enjoyment of human rights and achievement of equality and justice, then the whole of society has a role to play in building and maintaining peace and security, not only combatants and political players. Further, if gender equality, peace and security are intrinsically linked, women must be key actors in the peace process. Swanee Hunt and Cristina Posa have argued that just as warfare has become inclusive, impacting on civilians and combatants, so too must our approach to peace and conflict resolution; and all of society – particularly women – must be involved in forging 'inclusive security'.[16]

III   Women, Peace and Security

Women's experiences with conflict, peace and security are multi-faceted. Women suffer disproportionately in times of conflict, but they are also instrumental in sowing the seeds of peace within their communities, advocating for justice and an end to violence, and building peaceful, just and equitable societies. The landmark Security Council Resolution 1325 has played a critical role in making visible the multitude of women's perspectives on war and peace.

On 31 October 2000, following an Open Debate on Women, Peace and Security, the United Nations Security Council unanimously passed Resolution 1325,[17] recognising women's varied experiences in armed conflict and promoting their role in building and maintaining peace and security. This was the first time in history that the Security Council – the body with primary responsibility for the maintenance of international peace and security – had dedicated an entire session to a discussion of women's experiences in conflict and post-conflict situations as well as their contributions to peace. It was a turning point in viewing peace and security through a gender lens and promoting women's agency.

Resolution 1325 recognises the disproportionate impact of armed conflict on women and girls and the need to ensure the implementation of international humanitarian and human rights law protecting their rights. The emphasis of the resolution, however, is on the role of women in preventing conflict, promoting peace and assisting in post-conflict reconstruction, and the importance of women's equal participation and full involvement in all aspects of the peace process. By recognising the vital role women play in building, restoring and maintaining peace, Resolution 1325 marks a shift away from the historical perception of women as 'needing protection'[18] to the realisation of their potential as key actors in all matters relating to peace and security.

---

15   Marilee Karl, *Women and Empowerment: Participation and Decision Making* (1995) 26.
16   Swanee Hunt and Cristina Posa, 'Women Waging Peace' (2001) *Foreign Policy* 38 available at <http://www.foreignpolicy.com/issue_mayjune_2001/Hunt.html>.
17   SC Res 1325, above n 3.
18   Gardam and Charlesworth argue that the rules of international humanitarian law dealing specifically with women are couched in terms of protection rather than prohibition: above n 2, 159. According to Gardam and Jarvis, the special protection afforded to women is

Resolution 1325 provides a broad framework for women's engagement in peace and security, emphasising the need for the increased representation of women in decision-making, integration of a gender perspective in the peace process and the promotion of gender equality.

A   Increased Participation in Decision-making Relating to Peace and Security

The full and effective participation of women in decision-making processes is central to Resolution 1325. Reaffirming the vital role played by women in the maintenance and promotion of peace and security, the resolution stresses the importance of their equal participation in the peace process and the need to increase their role in decision-making with regard to conflict prevention and resolution.

Resolution 1325 calls upon member states to ensure the increased representation of women at all levels of decision-making relating to the prevention, management and resolution of conflict. It urges the Secretary-General to increase the participation of women at decision-making levels in conflict resolution and peace processes and appoint more women as special representatives and envoys. These calls for women's increased representation and participation in peace processes echo the Beijing Platform for Action, which sets a strategic objective of increasing the participation of women in conflict resolution at decision-making levels.[19]

By increasing the representation of women throughout peace processes, Resolution 1325 is striving to achieve greater gender balance and a critical mass of women in decision-making relating to peace and security. The rationale is two-fold: first, there is a need to engender the peace process and make it representative of women's concerns and priorities, and second, by doing so, the peace process benefits from women's perspectives and contributions.

Unless women are adequately represented throughout the peace process, their aspirations and priorities for peace will continue to be masked by the power struggles of (male) politicians and combatants. Women's perspectives on peace-building and conflict resolution are influenced by their experiences in times of conflict. Given the stark realities faced by many women in armed conflict, women are more likely to express their aspirations for peace in terms of meeting basic human security needs and building a sustainable future for their communities.[20] Therefore, women have the potential to revitalise and refocus the peace process by bringing fresh perspectives and priorities to the peace table and grounding negotiations in an understanding of the day-to-day realities of the civilian population. This can advance the prospects for sustainable peace by ensuring that peace agreements respond to the needs and priorities

---

based on assumed 'feminine' characteristics such as chastity, modesty, frailty and dependence: above n 6, 11, 62-68.

19   *Beijing Platform for Action*, above n 13, Strategic Objective E.1.

20   United Nations Development Fund for Women (UNIFEM), Portal on Women, Peace and Security <http://www.womenwarpeace.org/issues/peace_process.htm>. See also Hunt, above n 9, 235 and Rehn and Johnson Sirleaf, above n 1, 2, 4.

of society as a whole and that the peace negotiated is 'owned' by those who have to make it a reality in their lives.[21]

While women have different perspectives on and aspirations for the peace process, it is problematic to assert that women are inherently peaceful by nature. It is important to avoid essentialism and recognise the many facets to women's experiences and involvement in peace and security.[22] Inger Skjelsbæk has suggested it is more accurate to say that women are potential bearers of peaceful thinking, and while women are not inherently more 'peaceful' than men, the increased participation of women in decision-making may increase the likelihood of changing the value system which justifies war.[23]

B   Integrating a Gender Perspective in the Peace Process

Although the increased participation of women in the peace process encourages the inclusion of a gender perspective, greater numbers of women at the peace table do not guarantee that the peace process will be more equitable or that it will result in a more sustainable peace. It does not suffice to simply 'add women and stir': merely increasing the number of women in political processes will not bring about qualitative change in policy and decision-making. As the Secretary-General noted in his report on Women, Peace and Security, submitted to the Security Council in accordance with Resolution 1325, the presence of women at peace negotiations does not ensure attention to gender issues.[24]

As it cannot be assumed that all women involved in political processes will give priority to gender issues, achieving gender balance cannot be a goal in and of itself. Drude Dahlerup has suggested that rather than focusing purely on critical mass, it would be better to concentrate on 'critical acts' which change the position of women considerably and lead to further changes in policy.[25] 'Critical acts' which promote gender equity and positive outcomes for women may be initiated by both women and men – this shift in perception acknowledges that men, as well as women, may be actors in initiatives to advance the position of women.

Recognising this fact, Resolution 1325 calls upon all actors in the peace process to adopt a gender perspective in the negotiation and implementation of peace agreements. Measures which further a gender perspective in the peace process include support for local women's peace initiatives and the involvement of women in all aspects of the imple-

---

21   Sanam Naraghi Anderlini, *Women at the Peace Table: Making a Difference* (2000) 7, 55. Méndez notes that women bring different themes to the negotiating table and their participation in peace negotiations is essential to ensure women's concerns, needs and demands are included in peace agreements: above n 9, 47.

22   See Gardam and Charlesworth, above n 2, 165.

23   Inger Skjelsbæk, 'Is Feminism Inherently Peaceful? The Construction of Femininity in War' in Inger Skjelsbæk and Dan Smith (eds) *Gender, Peace and Conflict* (2001) 65.

24   *UN Study*, above n 1, [29].

25   Drude Dahlerup, 'Women in Political Decisionmaking: From Critical Mass to Critical Acts in Scandinavia' in Skjelsbæk and Smith (eds), above n 23, 115.

mentation of peace agreements. Promoting women's contributions to peace and security is an important aspect of gender mainstreaming and advancing gender equality.[26]

C   *Promoting Gender Equality and Women's Empowerment*

Women's participation in the peace process is critical to ensure that the negotiated political, economic, social and security structures facilitate the achievement of greater gender equality.[27] Throughout Resolution 1325, there is an emphasis on gender equality and empowering women. The resolution makes the quest for gender equality relevant to each and every stage of the peace process, recognising that gender equality and women's empowerment are vital steps on the road to peace. As noted in the Beijing Platform for Action, the equal access and full participation of women in power structures and their full involvement in all efforts for the prevention and resolution of conflicts is essential for the maintenance and promotion of peace and security.[28]

Capacity-building is an essential aspect of empowerment, as women require training, skills and opportunities to break through the barriers of gender discrimination and participate effectively in the peace process. The Secretary-General's report on Women, Peace and Security emphasises the need to enhance women's capacities as participants and leaders in peace negotiations through measures such as the provision of training on formal peace processes.[29] It is also important to foster an enabling environment for women's participation: women require safety, resources, political space and access to decision-makers in order to participate effectively in peace processes.[30]

Resolution 1325 is an important tool for promoting women's full and active participation in the peace process. It has played a vital function in making visible the scope and nature of women's role in peace-building and conflict resolution. Two years following its adoption, the Independent Experts' Assessment commissioned by UNIFEM found that the resolution has given political legitimacy to a long history of women's peace activity and has been seized with vigour by women around the globe to assist in their pursuit of gender equality in peace and security.[31]

IV   Public/Private Distinctions in the Peace Process

In the context of conflict resolution and the maintenance of peace and security, a distinction is often drawn between community peace-building initiatives and formal peace negotiations.[32] This distinction is similar to the dichotomy which, some femi-

---

26   See *Report of the Secretary-General on Women's Equal Participation in Conflict Prevention, Management and Conflict Resolution and in Post-Conflict Peace-Building*, above n 5, 3.

27   *UN Study*, above n 1, [4], [26].

28   *Beijing Platform for Action*, above n 13, Strategic Objectives E.1 and E.4 [134].

29   *UN Study*, above n 1, Action 9.

30   Rehn and Johnson Sirleaf, above n 1, 79, 85.

31   *Ibid.*, 3.

32   The *Report of the Secretary-General on Women's Equal Participation in Conflict Prevention, Management and Conflict Resolution and in Post-Conflict Peace-Building* notes that while

nists have argued, divides the 'public' sphere of politics, government and the state, and the 'private' sphere of the home and family.[33]

As peace and security have traditionally been defined in military-focused and gender-blind terms, the maintenance of national and international peace and security is often perceived to fall within the public sphere of political and military decision-making. Thus peace negotiations have typically brought together predominantly male combatants and political players, excluding women and civil society organisations. Conversely, grassroots organising is seen as an extension of women's 'traditional' role in the community and responsibility for the health and well-being of their families.[34] Thus women's participation in the peace process has largely been confined to the private sphere of community-based peace initiatives.

Due to this artificial distinction, women experience difficulties gaining access to decision-making processes and are often marginalised from formal peace negotiations and political structures.[35] In periods of conflict, the prevailing culture of militarism can reinforce gender-based discrimination,[36] making it even more difficult for women to access and participate in political decision-making.[37]

Distinguishing between conflict resolution initiatives undertaken at a community level and those undertaken at a national or international level creates a hierarchy of people's contribution to peace.[38] As a result, community peace-building work is often undervalued and perceived as secondary or peripheral to formal peace negotiations. This disregards the value and impact of community peace-building and reconciliation and ignores that a peaceful society must be built from the ground up, addressing the causes of conflict and laying the foundations for lasting peace.

This dichotomy is based upon an assumption that a strict divide can be drawn between community peace-building and formal peace negotiations, presuming that actions taken on a community level have no impact on the national level and vice

---

women are active in 'informal peace initiatives', they are largely absent from 'formal processes': above n 5, 6.

33   See generally Graycar and Morgan, above n 7.

34   Karl, above n 15, 19.

35   The *Report of the Secretary-General on Women's Equal Participation in Conflict Prevention, Management and Conflict Resolution and in Post-Conflict Peace-Building* notes that the prevailing focus on formal peace processes is a challenge to the promotion of gender equality and women's participation in peace processes: above n 5, 5-6.

36   Anderlini, above n 21, 11.

37   Several authors have noted that armed conflict can be a time of empowerment for some women, creating opportunities to move out of the private into the public sphere, and take on roles traditionally performed by men. However, these gains are usually lost upon the cessation of hostilities. See Gardam and Charlesworth, above n 2, 152, Gardam and Jarvis, above n 6, 51 and Hunt, above n 9, 238.

38   See Christine Chinkin, *Peace Agreements as a Means for Promoting Gender Equality and Ensuring Participation of Women*, background paper to the United Nations Division for the Advancement of Women Expert Group Meeting on 'Peace Agreements as a Means for Promoting Gender Equality and Ensuring Participation of Women – A Framework of Model Provisions', Ottawa, 10-13 November 2003, UN Doc EGM/PEACE/2003/BP.1 (2003) 4.

versa. In reality, there is no clear-cut distinction between informal and formal peace processes – each influences and impacts upon the other. In particular, as illustrated by Méndez, community-based activism and peace-building initiatives play a critical role in building momentum for broader change and building lasting peace.[39]

The dichotomy between public and private aspects of the peace process supports existing structural inequalities and power imbalances within societies, maintaining segregated gender roles.[40] In doing so, it arbitrarily restricts women's access to decision-making spheres, denying them the opportunity to be heard in formal decision-making processes that affect their lives. To maintain such a distinction reinforces the erroneous image of women as victims, passively affected by armed conflict. It fails to recognise women as powerful agents of change, capable of transforming society at the 'macro' national and international levels as well as at the 'micro' community level.

V   Analysis of Women's Engagement across the Peace Process

Owing to their limited access to traditional avenues to power such as political processes, women have used alternative structures such as civil society organisations to influence the peace process. Through the formation of organisations and networks at local, national, regional and international levels, women have played a major role in de-escalating conflict and mitigating its impacts. This role is illustrated in Méndez's account of the Guatemalan peace process[41] and in the case studies in Part VI of this chapter.

At a community level, women have been instrumental in rebuilding relationships, bridging the gap between different ethnic, religious and political groups, and sowing the seeds of peace and reconciliation. Through community peace-building, women can begin to play an active role in determining how conflict affects their lives, and how it can be resolved. As one commentator has noted, processes that may lead towards conflict resolution should begin at the local level, involving those hardest hit by conflict – the civilian populations living in conflict zones, in particular, women.[42]

While women play a crucial part in fostering reconciliation at a local level, women's participation should not be limited to this role. Rebuilding relationships and confidence within communities is the basis for sustainable peace, but women must also be involved in formal negotiations and decision-making, guiding the direction of the peace process in order for 'peace' to be successfully implemented at the local level.

The peace process does not come to an end upon the cessation of hostilities and conclusion of a peace agreement. Post-conflict reconstruction is a critical stage in

---

39   Méndez, above n 9.

40   Women are often excluded from formal peace negotiations because they are not combatants, military leaders or political decision-makers, they are assumed to lack the expertise to negotiate, or because of discrimination and stereotypical thinking: see *UN Study*, above n 1, [28].

41   Méndez, above n 9.

42   Kumudini Samuel, 'Gender Difference in Conflict Resolution: The Case of Sri Lanka' in Skjelsbæk and Smith (eds), above n 23, 200.

building sustainable peace and human security. Méndez emphasises the importance of women's continued involvement in the post-conflict stage and the need for measures to address structural and institutional obstacles to women's participation in the political sphere.[43] The transition from conflict to peace offers a unique window of opportunity to install a gender-responsive framework for the reconstruction of society, addressing structural inequalities that discriminate against women and promoting gender equality.

Women often encounter difficulties making the transition from community peace-building to peace negotiations, post-conflict reconstruction and political decision-making. This is due in part to the lack of training and support, but also to the fact that the prevailing political and social environment often reflects gender inequalities and is not conducive to women's equal participation in political structures.[44] To create an enabling environment for women's participation across the spectrum of the peace process, it is necessary to invest in women and promote their leadership.[45] The existence of a strong civil society and women's movement plays an important role in this regard, cultivating skills and broadening opportunities for women to gain entry to the peace process.[46] However, it is also essential to instil gender awareness within political structures, to ensure that women participate effectively in political processes and are not just token inclusions.[47]

The equal participation of women in peace-building, conflict resolution and post-conflict reconstruction is critical to the maintenance of national and international peace and security.[48] In order to effect a qualitative change on the peace process, it is necessary to promote women's effective participation throughout the spectrum of the peace process, and to recognise and validate how they have contributed to the restoration and maintenance of peace and security within their communities and countries. The stories of women from around the globe demonstrate the vital role of women in building and maintaining peace and security, and the following case studies illustrate the contributions of women to fostering peace in the Pacific.

VI   Building Peace in the Pacific

In recent years, civil unrest and conflict have plagued Melanesia,[49] particularly Bougainville in Papua New Guinea, and the Solomon Islands. Women and wom-

---

43   Méndez, above n 9, 45, 47.

44   See *UN Study*, above n 1 [28].

45   See *Ibid.,* [32] and Action 9.

46   See Rehn and Johnson Sirleaf, above n 1, 79 and Méndez, above n 9, 43.

47   See Rehn and Johnson Sirleaf, above n 1, 82-84.

48   The *Report of the Secretary-General on Women's Equal Participation in Conflict Prevention, Management and Conflict Resolution and in Post-Conflict Peace-Building* notes that gender equality is crucial to achieving sustainable peace: above n 5, 7. See also Hunt, above n 9, 230.

49   Melanesia is one of three sub-regions within the Pacific region, and comprises Papua New Guinea, Solomon Islands, Vanuatu, Kanaky (New Caledonia) and Fiji.

en's organisations have been instrumental in promoting reconciliation and building a momentum for peace, paving the way for the conclusion of formal peace agreements. Despite the vital contribution of women, the following case studies from Bougainville and the Solomon Islands demonstrate that there is yet a significant distance to be travelled before women are fully integrated into the peace process, particularly at the peace table and in post-conflict reconstruction.

A   Bougainville

From 1989 to 1998, Bougainville[50] was gripped by a protracted armed conflict between the separatist Bougainville Revolutionary Army (BRA) and the Papua New Guinean Defence Force, after disputes over the control of land and mineral resources escalated into a broader conflict about the political status of Bougainville. The conflict divided the province into BRA and government controlled areas, and the Papua New Guinean Defence Force effected a total air, sea and land blockade cutting off medical and other essential supplies to BRA-controlled areas. During the nine-year conflict, up to 20,000 people died, including thousands of civilians as a result of the blockade, and tens of thousands were displaced.

Throughout the period of conflict, Bougainvillean women and women's organisations worked tirelessly to build a culture of peace in the war-torn province, rejecting the prevailing culture of violence. Working within communities, they tried to build an understanding that no matter which side of the conflict they found themselves on, they were all people of Bougainville, and reconciliation was needed to achieve genuine peace.

Leitana Nehan Women's Development Agency (Leitana Nehan) is one of the organisations that played an instrumental role in restoring peace to Bougainville. In 1992, a group of Bougainvillean women formed Leitana Nehan in response to the armed conflict that was destroying their communities. Using the motto 'Women Weaving Bougainville Together', they began rebuilding trust and relationships within and between communities, and reaching out to 'their men' to demonstrate that violence was not the only option, and peace was attainable. Leitana Nehan's strategy was to actively pursue sons, husbands and brothers, calling them to come back to their communities, sit down and think about non-violent ways of negotiating with the government.[51] By demonstrating to those bearing arms that violence was not the only method for achieving their goals, Leitana Nehan and other Bougainvillean women's organisations built a momentum for peace within the province, and laid the groundwork for the formal peace negotiations that followed.[52]

---

50   The name 'Bougainville' is commonly used to refer to Bougainville, Buka and other islands which make up the North Solomons province of Papua New Guinea. Geographically and culturally, Bougainville is closer to the Solomon Islands than to Papua New Guinea.

51   fem'Linkpacific, interview with Agnes Titus, co-founder of Leitana Nehan Women's Development Agency (Suva, Fiji, 12 March 2001), <http://lyris.spc.int/read/messages ?id=8335#8335>.

52   Bougainville Inter-Church Women's Forum (BICWF) and Bougainville Women for Peace and Freedom (BWPF) were also active in building peace among Bougainvilleans.

Nine years of conflict have had wide-ranging impacts on the population of Bougainville, and even though the conflict has ended, much work remains to be done in order to build sustainable peace in Bougainville. The absence of war does not mean the end of violence, and as Helen Hakena of Leitana Nehan notes, 'Even when the guns are silent there is still war in communities'.[53] A culture of violence, exacerbated by the abuse of homebrew liquor, continues to jeopardise peace at a community level, with women bearing the brunt of much of the violence.[54] In order to foster a culture of peace, Leitana Nehan is continuing to work within communities to break down community-level violence and heal the deep rifts caused by the war, laying the foundation for more peaceful communities in post-conflict Bougainville.

On 8 March 2001, International Women's Day, the inaugural Millennium Peace Prize for Women was presented to Leitana Nehan, honouring its cross-community work for peace during and after the nine year conflict in Bougainville.[55] The prize was the first of its kind to specifically recognise the impact of women's contributions to resolving and preventing conflicts, and maintaining peace and security. Helen Hakena accepted the prize on behalf of all Bougainvillean women who worked for peace, acknowledging that it was through all of their efforts that the conflict was ended.

Women's peace-building initiatives encouraged the development of a momentum for peace within Bougainville, and played an important role bringing the plight of the province to the attention of the international community. This illustrates the wider impact of community peace-building, and demonstrates how 'informal' and 'formal' peace processes are intrinsically interwoven and inseparable. The recognition of women's community peace-building work empowered them to voice their experiences and views in formal fora, and participate in official peace negotiations. In 1997, a delegation of women leaders attended the Burnham peace talks, and a year later, fifty women attended the Lincoln peace negotiations, issuing a joint statement on peace which called for greater inclusion in the peace process. Their statement declared, 'We, the women, hold custodial rights of our land by clan inheritance. We insist that women leaders must be party to all stages of the political process in determining the future of Bougainville'.[56]

In 1996, BICWF organised a Women's Peace Forum which brought together 700 women from across Bougainville to find lasting solutions to the crisis. BWPF ran human rights training workshops in blockaded areas of Bougainville, and provided support for women to undergo diplomacy training.

53   Shoba Rao, 'Women weaving Bougainville together' (2001) Australian Centre for Independent Journalism, University of Technology, Sydney, website, <http://www.report-age.uts.edu.au/stories/2001/may01/07bougainville.html>.

54   In a speech given on International Women's Day 2003, Helen Hakena noted that the abuse of homebrew alcohol has led to increased violence within communities, in particular gender violence – see <http://www.peacewomen.org/resources/Bougainville/HakenaIWD2003.html>.

55   Jointly sponsored by UNIFEM and International Alert, the Millenium Peace Prize for Women also honoured Flora Brovina of Kosovo, Veneranda Nzambazamariya of Rwanda (post-humous), Asma Jahangir and Hina Jilani of Pakistan, Ruta Pacifica de las Mujeres of Colombia, and Women in Black.

56   Sister Lorraine Garasu, 'The role of women in promoting peace and reconciliation' (2002) 12 *Accord* <http://www.c-r.org/accord/boug/accord12/women.shtml>.

Since the conclusion of the formal agreements that ended the nine-year conflict, women have continued to advocate for their equal participation in the reconstruction of Bougainvillean society and the movement towards autonomy from Papua New Guinea. However, despite women's achievements in community peace-building and their engagement in peace negotiations, Bougainvillean women continue to be marginalised from formal political processes and post-conflict reconstruction. Helen Hakena says that while women's role in peace-building and conflict resolution was recognised during the period of conflict, women are now being sidelined from political processes.[57] Women were under-represented in the post-peace agreement political structures, such as the Bougainville People's Congress and Bougainville Interim Provincial Government, and in official talks on autonomy, referendum and weapons disposal. The excuse given was that the time was 'not yet right' for greater female representation.[58] Despite women demonstrating that they are willing and able to play an equal role in the reconstruction of Bougainville, this trend has continued.

In May 2003, 165 women attended a meeting of women leaders, expressing concern regarding their exclusion from peace and constitutional reform processes. The women issued a series of recommendations, including calls for women's involvement in weapons disposal talks, the integration of a gender perspective in the new constitution, and a quota of seats for women in the new autonomous government. However, to date these demands remain unmet. Only three women are represented on the Bougainville Constitutional Commission that is drafting the new constitution, and Helen Hakena says they are not able to play an effective role, as they are not included in meetings. Further, no women were included in the final stage of the weapons disposal which took place in late November 2003. When Leitana Nehan put forward the names of ten female participants, ex-combatants said the talks did not concern women, as they did not own guns. However, the women said they were victimised by those guns, and had the right to be there.[59]

Women's peace-building efforts in Bougainville demonstrate how community engagement can build momentum for peace and empower women to participate in formal peace processes. However, political players must recognise that peace is not a process which ends upon the conclusion of a formal peace agreement, but rather an ongoing goal towards which societies strive, and which includes a place for women at all stages. This is the challenge now facing Bougainville. In order to build sustainable peace and inclusive security in Bougainville, it is necessary to make room for the effective participation of women in political decision-making and post-conflict reconstruction. As Helen Hakena says, 'We can softly and silently break the cycle of violence by putting women in positions of power'.[60]

---

57   Telephone communication with Helen Hakena, co-founder of Leitana Nehan Women's Development Agency (25 November 2003) (transcript of conversation on file with author).

58   Garasu, above n 56.

59   Hakena, above n 57.

60   Chris Richards, 'Making Waves: Interview with Helen Hakena' (2002) 350 *New Internationalist*, available at <http://www.peacewomen.org/resources/Bougainville/MakingWavesHakena.html>.

B   Solomon Islands

Bougainville's neighbour, the Solomon Islands, is also emerging from a bitter conflict that has brought the effective functioning of the country to a standstill over the last five years. During what is termed 'the tension' by Solomon Islanders, rival militant groups – Isatabu Freedom Movement (IFM) from Guadalcanal island and Malaita Eagle Force (MEF) from Malaita island – waged a conflict that crippled the country's government and resulted in over 200 deaths and 30,000 internally displaced persons. The tension culminated in an attempted coup on 5 June 2000, during which MEF militants raided police armouries and forced Prime Minister Bart Ulufa'alu to resign. Whilst commonly referred to or dismissed as an ethnic dispute, the tension had its roots in inequalities in the distribution of land and economic opportunities around the nation's capital, Honiara, on Guadalcanal island.

Women have played an active and important role in defusing the tension and promoting conflict resolution in the Solomon Islands. They mobilised for peace, bringing together people from different ethnic communities, and risking their lives to go to militants' camps to persuade combatants to lay down their weapons. At a time when formal peace talks were far from the horizon, the government was paralysed, and militants on each side were refusing to budge, women took it upon themselves to promote peace within communities, heal the rifts caused by the conflict, and reach out to those affected by the tension, such as internally displaced persons.

At the height of the tension, in May 2000, women held a roundtable discussion in Honiara to discuss how, together, they could work more effectively towards peace in the Solomon Islands. The result of this meeting was the Women's Communiqué on Peace, a document setting out activities women would undertake to contribute in a meaningful way to the peace process. Soon afterwards, the Women for Peace group was formed, uniting women from all walks of life to actively and effectively support and encourage women's initiatives in search of a peaceful solution to the crisis gripping the Solomon Islands.[61] Women for Peace members sought out both IFM and MEF militants to encourage them to forgo violence, and undertook visits to families displaced by the tension. This provided an outlet for women affected by the conflict to work towards peace and the end of hostilities. For example, after losing two sons during the tension – one at the hands of IFM militants, and the other at the hands of MEF militants – Bethery Kiepo joined Women for Peace and visited camps, talking to militants and working to end the culture of violence that was tearing communities apart.[62] In many different ways, women helped to restore peace and promote recon-

---

61   For further information on Women for Peace and its activities, see Alice A Pollard, 'Resolving Conflict in Solomon Islands: The Women for Peace Approach' (2000) *Development Bulletin* 53, and Ruth Liloqula and Alice Aruhe'eta Pollard, 'Understanding conflict in Solomon Islands: a practical means to peacemaking' (State, Society and Governance in Melanesia Discussion Paper 00/7, Research School of Pacific and Asian Studies, Australian National University, 2000).

62   See Oxfam Community Aid Abroad, 'The Solomon Islands – Healing the Wounds', *Oxfam Horizons*, December 2001 (Copy on file with author).

ciliation in the Solomon Islands, defusing the tension and building momentum for peace within communities.[63]

Despite the recognition of women's efforts in building peace and promoting reconciliation in the Solomon Islands, women have been marginalised from formal peace processes. In August 2000, women's groups participated in a National Peace Conference which brought together 150 Solomon Islands civil society representatives on board the New Zealand navy frigate HMNZS Te Kaha. However, women and civil society organisations were excluded from the Townsville Peace Conference in October 2000, at which the formal peace agreement was brokered. Focusing on the surrender of weapons and competing demands of militants and the government, the negotiations failed to adopt an inclusive approach, and addressed neither the priorities of those working towards peace nor the needs of those affected by the conflict.

Despite the conclusion of the Townsville Peace Agreement and return of some weapons, peace did not return to the Solomon Islands. Kidnappings, killings and persecution continued on both sides, and in this atmosphere of fear and lawlessness, thousands of internally displaced persons continued to flood into Honiara from the Weather Coast of Guadalcanal, or to flee Honiara for other islands. The failure of the Townsville Peace Agreement demonstrates that without wide consultation or real commitment, the mere conclusion of a formal peace agreement will not guarantee the return of peace to a country.

In July 2003, another critical episode in the life of the peace process began when the Regional Assistance Mission to the Solomon Islands (RAMSI) was deployed in response to a request by Prime Minister Allan Kemakeza for assistance to restore peace to the troubled nation. A regional peace-keeping force comprising military and police personnel from Australia, New Zealand, Papua New Guinea, Fiji, Samoa and Tonga conducted a mission to collect and dispose of weapons, and restore law and order to Honiara and the islands. Four to five months later, the military component of RAMSI started to withdraw, having collected thousands of weapons and made hundreds of arrests, including the heads of the IFM and MEF, Harold Keke and Jimmy Rasta. While RAMSI is widely credited with having restored law and order to the streets of Honiara, or at least the appearance of such, the real work to build lasting peace in the Solomon Islands is just beginning. Peace will not come unless the root causes of the conflict are addressed and human security is achieved.

A key window of opportunity has now been opened to address the mistakes of the past and create a space for women's active participation in post-conflict reconstruction. This is a unique chance to integrate a gender perspective into the reconstruction of the Solomon Islands, rebuilding the nation on the basis of human rights, gender equality and the equal participation of women. However, to date, RAMSI has

---

63 The National Council of Women appealed to militants for peace and organised exchanges of food and essential supplies between women of different ethnic groups. Since the conclusion of the Townsville Peace Agreement, the National Council of Women has run restorative justice training programmes, building communities' capacity for conflict resolution. Vois Blong Mere Solomon ('Voice of Solomon Women', formerly known as the Solomon Islands Women's Information Network) has used radio as a medium for promoting awareness of human rights, gender issues and peace.

not engaged in specific consultations with women, although a group of prominent women has met with representatives of the regional assistance mission.[64] To achieve true peace, it is important to call upon women's experience and skills in conflict resolution and reconciliation, and ensure that they participate in steering the Solomon Islands towards lasting peace and security.

C   Promoting Women's Role in Peace and Security

As part of its global Peace and Security Programme,[65] UNIFEM is implementing the 'Women, Peace and Security in Melanesia' project, aiming to increase, strengthen and support women's work in conflict prevention, conflict resolution and peace-building. This six-year project makes visible women's efforts in building and sustaining peace in Papua New Guinea, Solomon Islands, Fiji and Vanuatu, and focuses on capacity-building to support women's political participation and contribution to conflict resolution.

The project will provide valuable support to Bougainvillean and Solomon Islander women, equipping them with the training and resources to participate more fully in post-conflict reconstruction and engender political structures. Hopefully, it will also serve as a catalyst for the increased participation of women in political processes throughout the Pacific region, and spur on governments and other stakeholders to promote and encourage women's political involvement.

VII   Conclusion

Peace and human security are concepts that address the needs and aspirations of society as a whole. The objective of the peace process is not solely the cessation of hostilities, but also the construction of a more just society where all members can enjoy their basic human rights. Therefore, to achieve sustainable peace and security, women and all of civil society must guide the peace process, not only the parties to armed conflicts.

While there has been increasing recognition of women's role in peace and security in international fora and policy documents, progress remains slow on the ground. Women continue to encounter barriers to their equal participation in political aspects of the peace process, particularly in post-conflict reconstruction. To mask or marginalise the voices of women in this way suppresses a powerful force for peace and compromises the goals of human security. Therefore, to address the invisibility of women at the peace table, it is imperative to break down gendered notions of what is public and private, masculine and feminine, and all other barriers to women's participation in the

---

64   Email communication with Ruth Liloqula, Under-Secretary for the Solomon Islands Ministry of Justice and co-founder of Women for Peace (19 November 2003).

65   The Peace and Security Programme specifically addresses Security Council Resolution 1325, and promotes early warning and prevention, protection and assistance during conflict, women's participation in the peace process, and gender justice in post-conflict reconstruction.

peace process. By moving away from dichotomous thinking, energies can be focused on devising strategies that will empower women and correct their perceived status as passive victims of armed conflict.

To engender the peace process, a necessary step is to expose women's invisibility in the promotion of peace and security. However, to truly mainstream gender in peace and security, it is essential to empower women in all stages of the peace process, and create an enabling environment to support women's full and effective participation in political decision-making. Promoting women's agency and leadership is critical to achieving gender equality, and a fundamental step in the process of building inclusive peace and security based on the equal enjoyment of human rights. While women need access to the peace table in order to advance the goal of gender equality, the peace process also requires women's participation to lay the foundations for sustainable peace and security.

17

Fine Lines of Transformation:
Afghan Women Working for Peace

*Rina Amiri**

I   Introduction

In the last decade, the hapless image of Afghan women shrouded in burkas has often been used to signify the tragic situation of Afghanistan. The defeat of the Taliban and the establishment of the Interim Administration during the Bonn Agreement[1] in December 2001 were heralded as an opportunity for the country to make its way forward on the long road back to peace and stability. The international community centred on the re-institution of women's rights and their participation in public life as a key indicator of the country's move toward democratic change. In the last two years, the media has continued to focus upon the situation of women in gauging the pace of progress in the Afghan peace process. This chapter begins with this premise, reflecting on the status of Afghan women and considering the extent to which the advancement of women's rights has broader implications for Afghanistan's road to peace.

II   The Status of Afghan Women

Nancy Dupree, a leading Afghan expert, describes the situation of Afghan women as follows:

> It is useful perhaps to view the totality of Afghan women as a pyramid. The sound base is broad and consists of a majority who live in rural areas cherishing aspirations that are almost exclusively oriented towards children and family. Their needs lie in all aspects of basic and non-formal education, in health and in skills training for better

---

*   Rina Amiri is the Political Affairs Officer at the United Nations Assistance Mission in Afghanistan.

1   In late 2001, after the Taliban was ousted from power in Afghanistan, representatives of various Afghan factions met in Bonn, Germany. Under the auspices of the Special Representative of the Secretary-General for Afghanistan, these delegates attempted to map out Afghanistan's future. The negotiations resulted in the *Bonn Agreement*, which was signed on 5 December 2001.

Helen Durham and Tracey Gurd (eds.), Listening to the Silences: Women and War, *pp. 243-250.*
© *2005 Koninklijke Brill BV. Printed in The Netherlands.* ISBN *90 04 14365 3.*

family welfare. Here some progress, albeit slow, is taking place in a non-confrontational manner. At the tip are the small number of Western-oriented, assertive working women who have taken a leading part in the emancipation process begun in 1959. They have become accustomed to formal employment in mixed environments, often in association with foreigners who are now joined in battle on their behalf. These women call for the right to participate fully at all levels of decision-making. They bear the full brunt of Taliban ire. In the centre is the solid core of professional teachers, medical practitioners, engineers, judges, administrators, businesswomen, social workers and civil servants of every sort which has grown in magnitude and strength since the beginning of the century.[2]

This description of women's status and roles in society continues to accurately depict the situation of Afghan women in society. Women from throughout Afghanistan face similar restrictions and difficulties. They have borne the brunt of the 23 years of war and conflict, suffering from extreme devastation, displacement, violence and the physical and material destruction of their family lives. But there are key differences in how their social patterns were impacted by the years of instability and conflict.

The lives of rural women, who make up 85 percent of the total female population, are limited to the confines of the extended family compound. Women in such communities are largely illiterate and have been excluded from opportunities for formal employment and education. Their way of life remained largely unchanged during the decades of war because they had been left out of discussions and debates centering on women's rights and opportunities. In contrast, urban women – who would be seen as the tip and middle of the pyramid analogy that Nancy Dupree applies – enjoyed education, employment and decision-making opportunities during the period of the monarchy and the Soviet Invasion. They were drastically affected by the increasingly conservative policies imposed by the Mujahideen (freedom fighters) and were the targets of the Taliban's repressive social policies. Women belonging to families which had the resources and means, became part of the millions of refugees in Iran, Pakistan and the West. Over the years of displacement, they benefited from training, educational and vocation programs offered in the refugee camps. The crowded conditions in the camps also allowed women from different ethnic groups and regions to mix and share common experiences. They learned the fine balancing act of functioning in the public sphere while reassuring their community that they adhered to Islamic and Afghan traditional values. In the last two years, many have returned with their families and resettled largely in the urban centers of Afghanistan, particularly in Kabul. These are the majority of women who have emerged as political leaders, activists, human rights workers and NGO organisers in the new social and political landscape of Afghan society.

This cadre of women's leadership recognises that the donor and international community has opened a small window of opportunity for Afghan women. After the systematic exclusion of women from all aspects of public life, the international community weighed in and ensured that the Bonn Agreement included specific provisions

---

2   Nancy Dupree, 'Afghanistan Under the Taliban' in William Maley (ed) *Fundamentalism Reborn: Afghanistan and the Taliban* (1998) 165-166.

to ensure that Afghan women would benefit from the country's peace and reconstruction activities. A Ministry of Women's Affairs was created for the first time in Afghan history and women were ensured representation in the Interim Government and the Emergency Loya Jirga.[3] Heralded as key steps in securing women's claims to a place in public life and participation in the peace process in Afghanistan have been a) the return of women to government offices, universities, schools; b) new work and training opportunities targeting women and c) the commitment of the donor community.

While these measures served as a promising beginning, women have faced an uphill battle in taking advantage of the new rights and opportunities accorded to them. Insecurity is rife in many parts of the country and it remains the prime reason why women are hesitant to partake in the new possibilities offered to them. In some areas, women and girls are prevented from attending school for fear of violence and rape. Women's schools have been the target of arson attacks in several areas around the country. There has also been a radicalisation of Afghan culture in the decades of political upheaval and war. The Taliban may be gone, but its repressive policies have left its mark on society.

Women leaders and outspoken activists face harassment and intimidation in many parts of the country. There have been several instances in which politically active women have been threatened for their roles. Perhaps the most notorious example is the case of Dr. Seema Samar, former Minister of Women's Affairs. During the Emergency Loya Jirga Assembly, copies of a letter accusing Dr. Samar of blasphemy were circulated among the delegates. Soon after, Dr. Samar received death threats. On the evening of the closing of the Loya Jirga elections, she was forced to leave her home and seek refuge to escape a death threat. On 22 June 2002, Dr. Samar was summoned to appear in a Kabul court to face a blasphemy charge. Although the charges were dropped, Dr. Samar continued to face threats and intimidation. She eventually stepped down as the Minister of Women's Affairs and assumed the position of Chair of the newly formed Independent Afghan Human Rights Commission.

The international community, which has actively supported aid projects targeting women, approaches women's issues with some level of trepidation. They are keenly aware that the issue of women's honour has been used as a rallying point repeatedly throughout history to mobilise public sentiment against foreign presence in the country. It was one of the key issues used to whip up public support in the war against the Soviet Union. In the last two years, radical elements have once again attempted to use this issue to incite violence and insurrections against the international community. Pamphlets have been distributed in eastern Afghanistan and outlaying areas around Kabul encouraging a holy war against internationals to protect the honour of Afghan women.

Women are also wary about solely relying on the government to support their rights. They bear in mind short-lived periods when women were briefly emancipated by elite leaders, only to have subsequent conservative governments reverse such policies. This saga has repeatedly played out in Afghan history, beginning in the 1920s

---

3   The National Assembly to elect the next government.

with the progressive King Amanullah Khan and continuing with the current Karzai regime. The consequence of these battles have been oscillations in the roles of women from modernist-led periods where women have represented more than 60 percent of the educated and professional population to traditionalist-based rule in which women have been rendered powerless and invisible.

Afghan women ruefully acknowledge that with all the donor dollars and political pressure from the international community, women's rights will not be advanced without the leadership of women themselves. To succeed, the pyramid model must be turned on its head. Women leaders must find a way to reach beyond Kabul and close the chasm between rural and urban women, the educated and uneducated and across the ethnic divide. In short, they must mobilise a grassroots movement for change in order to transform the rigidity and radicalism that has been used to imprison women.

The Minister of Women's Affairs, the State Minister of Women's Affairs and the NGO community have taken a number of steps to transform this aspiration into a reality. Women from the provinces are being invited to Kabul for seminars and conferences and those from Kabul are travelling to the provinces. To further institutionalise this exchange, NGOs are opening up centres in areas throughout Afghanistan. The Ministry of Women's Affairs has opened up satellite offices throughout the country. The Independent Human Rights Commission is now established in eight regional centres and in the main urban centres in Afghanistan. Organisations like Afghan Women's Network and Afghan Women Judges Association regularly hold training programs and seminars in various provinces. These initiatives are helping to overcome stereotypes and prejudices. Rural women are gradually recognising that urban women hold similar values and that they can play a key role in advocating on their behalf. Urban women are slowly learning to discard age-old prejudices about the backwardness of rural women. Women are not immune to the factionalisation and ethnic divisions that have that have taken root in the decades of war, but they have learned to set aside some of these differences to advance women's rights. Even as they fall into opposing camps on issues related to party politics, ethnic issues and matters of national debate, women usually fall into line in supporting women's rights on a number of fronts, including access to education, health care, employment opportunities and access to political space.

They have also learned to be strategic and have identified how women from different sectors can coordinate to advance their rights. Women's NGOs working across multiple sectors are working together to capitalise on what each brings to the table. Afghan Women's Network, Afghan Women Judges Association, Voices of Afghan Women and Afghan Women in Global Media are some of the key women's networks that serve as umbrella organisations, bringing women professionals from key sectors together to increase awareness of women's rights. Women in government and NGOs are turning to women journalists like Jamilla Mujahid – editor of the women's magazine *Malalai* and the director of a women's radio station – to carry their voice and message. The Ministry of Women's Affairs is using women's NGOs to undertake training and public awareness efforts in support of women.

Women also learned the advantages of unity and coalition-building during the Constitutional Loya Jirga,[4] where they comprised more than 20 percent of the delegates. In the days prior to convening the assembly, they organised a number of meetings, gathering women delegates to identify who, among them, would be most effective in running for leadership positions in the Constitutional Loya Jirga Secretariat Bureau (the body that would play a leadership role in all aspects of managing the three week long event). They identified the key leaders among them and agreed to vote as a block in support of the woman who had the largest constituency among men. Despite a number of discussions, women leaders could not agree among themselves on one candidate. The female delegate from the eastern region insisted that she was supported by the largest constituency, particularly among tribal elders. One of the Hazara women leaders held that she could gather a large number of votes from minorities. The female delegate from Kabul argued as vehemently that she could mobilise a large number of urban votes. In the end, several women submitted their candidacy and predictably, the female vote was divided and male candidates received the highest number of votes for all the Bureau positions. Even as they understood that the results were due to their own failure as a group, women delegates decided that they would not accept an all male Bureau and raised their voices, lobbying the entire assembly to include women. The Chair of the assembly relented and the three women with the highest number of votes were accepted as part of the Bureau as a deputy chair and rapporteurs.

The delegates also succeeded in making a number of key amendments in the constitution. They succeeded in arguing for gender specific provisions in the constitution. The new constitution affords that all 'citizens of Afghanistan – men and women – have equal rights and duties before the law'.[5] Perhaps their greatest moment was when they succeeded in increasing the representation of women in the National Assembly by 50 percent. At a critical time when the delegates were bitterly divided along regional and ethnic lines, the women delegates succeeded in begrudgingly setting aside their differences on other constitutional issues and organising themselves to demand greater representation for women in the future national assembly. They submitted a petition and heavily lobbied the government, other delegates, the United Nations and donors to support their position. In the end, the new constitution was amended to increase the number of seats allotted to women in the national assembly from one to two per province, resulting in women securing 25 percent of the total National Assembly seats.

III   What Is Their Impact on Society?

The various strands of women's leadership are gradually consolidating into a women's consciousness and increasing women's profile. The inclusion of women's voices is reverberating beyond gender interests and having, albeit incremental, an ultimately transformative impact on society. At the very least, the reintegration of women into public space is making a dent towards 'normalising' society. In the decades of war,

---

4   The National Assembly which was elected to ratify the new constitution.

5   The original draft read that 'citizens of Afghanistan have equal rights before the law'.

women were markedly absent from the public arena. During the period of the civil war, citing fears of violence and rape, the Mujahideen restricted women's activities and their participation in the public arena. When the Taliban took hold of the country, they made the removal of women from all public spaces a national policy, provoking an international outcry and gaining notoriety as the most gender repressive regime in the world. Women's re-entry in public space is often invoked by politicians and the international media as a marker of stability and normalcy in the country.

The role of women has been helpful in fueling national debate among government officials as well as between the government and civil society. In the bazaars and in mosques, on the airwaves and in the centres of government, moderates and religious elements are engaged in an intense debate over what kind of country Afghanistan should become, the face of Islam that reflect Afghanistan's values and the role that religion should have in it. The rights of women often serve as a centerpiece in these exchanges. The government of President Hamid Karzai has been active in this debate. In the last two years, a series of public battles have taken place over women's issues between moderate elements of President Karzai's government and conservative religious fundamentalists. The government has engaged in a series of tussles with the conservative-led Supreme Court on issues such as the broadcasting of women's voices on radio and television. While such debates have centred on women's participation in society, they have extended to a larger discussion about the rights of the media and press, the role of the government in civil society and broader concerns about human rights.

Women are playing more than a symbolic role. Many are using the narrow space that has been allotted to them to broaden the space of public debate and to challenge the status quo. The culture of war that gripped Afghan society for decades has resulted in a society that eulogises the conservative Mujahideen – sometimes at the expense of truth or justice. While some consider these figures holy warriors for defeating the Soviet Union in the 1980s, others consider them warlords for fermenting civil war in the 1990s. Many Afghans privately note that the warlords and militia, who wrap themselves in the sanctity of serving as freedom fighters, are the same figures who were responsible for human rights atrocities such as raping, pillaging and the victimisation of innocent civilians. A curtain of silence hangs over these injustices. Those who speak about the travesties committed in the name of 'jihad'[6] do so bitterly under their breath. The few exceptions to this complicity of silence are women.

In the Emergency Loya Jirga, it was a handful of women who stood up and railed against the warlords for destroying the country, pillaging the country's natural gems, its museums and its resources to line their pockets. In the Constitutional Loya Jirga, one young woman, Malalai Joya stood and spoke the minds of many Afghans when she challenged the Chair of the event, criticising him for allowing warlords who had destroyed the country to take part in the Loya Jirga. 'These people should be standing before an International Tribunal,' her voice rang out. Malalai Joya received death threats

---

6   The term refers to the concept of 'holy war' used by the Mujahideen during the decades of war. In Islam, Jihad also refers to the struggle against one's own evil and unrighteous inclinations.

and was nearly thrown out of the National Assembly. The rest of the country celebrated her courage and she became the centre of a nationwide debate. Students in the provinces of Farah, Mazar, Herat and Kabul demonstrated in support of her and the radio airwaves throughout the country repeatedly carried her voice and openly discussed what had been a taboo subject for the last two years – the role of the 'jihadis' in society. As a key official said, 'Malalai was accepted and heard because some people felt that she stated the truth'.[7] For a few days, Malalai managed to wedge open a small space for the public to openly discuss and debate the consequences of the decades of war.

While these acts of heroism are celebrated, most Afghan women take a more cautious and moderate approach, recognising that loosening the grip of radical elements will be a slow and difficult struggle. To avoid a backlash from conservative elements, women leaders reach out to men – particularly from conservative and religious elements – and go to lengths to demonstrate that even as they advocate for change, they adhere to Islamic and Afghan values. This is reflected in almost any activity women undertake. With their hair neatly drawn under scarves, women punctuate their speeches with references to Islam and pay homage to Afghan culture and values. The patronage of men and the clergy is patiently sought. At women's gatherings, male leaders are often invited as key speakers and they are the first to address the gatherings. Minister of Women's Affairs, Habiba Sarabi, reasons: 'We try to work with the religious community, to draw attention to women's rights. We can never work for women's rights alone. We require men's support. We shouldn't just work with elites and intellectuals. First we need to educate men about women's rights in Islam, particularly the conservative elements in society.'[8] Women are keenly aware that the power of religious interpretation is key to countering the radicalised and repressive cultural norms and traditions that continue to dominate Afghan society today.

In a society of deeply religious people, with close to 80 percent illiteracy, the power of the clergy is formidable. An uneducated population simply has to accept what is said to them by their religious leaders. Even among the educated and literate Afghans, the vast majority do not understand Arabic, the language in which the Quran is written. The fact that the Quran is written in a highly stylised form of Arabic makes the verses even more inaccessible to many Muslims. Moreover, Islamic law is further complicated by the fact that it is based on a vast number of hadiths (the sayings or actions of the holy prophet Muhammed), which are sometimes contradictory. There is a great deal of room for interpretation. Unsurprisingly, conservatives often use interpretations and hadiths that support restrictive social mores and curtail women's rights and other social freedoms.

Throughout Afghan history, the monarchy and the elite leadership have tried to counter the power of religious conservatives. The monarchy and elite turn to Islamic experts in order to argue on the basis of the original precepts of Islam. Afghanistan's comparatively moderate interpretation of Islam allowed for the adoption of a consti-

---

7   Interview, Kabul, 23 December 2003 (Due to privacy concerns, this individual could not be named. A copy of the transcript on file with the author).

8   Interview with Minister Habiba Sarabi, Kabul, 26 December 2003 (copy of transcript on file with author).

tution that guaranteed the basic rights of women in 1964. In the 1970s, prior to the Soviet Invasion and the subsequent emergence of the Mujahideen resistance, women in urban areas – particularly Kabul – comprised more than 40 percent of the doctors and teachers.

The ten years of war transformed the moderate form of Islam practiced in Afghanistan to an ideological movement monopolised by political leaders. In the resistance movement against the Soviets, the Mujahideen used Islam as a rallying point to mobilise Afghan men and women throughout the country and Muslims throughout the world. Years before the emergence of the Taliban, the Mujahideen leaders suspended the constitution and imposed conservative measures and religious decrees limiting social freedom, particularly with respect to the rights of women. The Taliban built upon on this foundation of extremism and introduced such repressive and extreme measures that Islamic governments throughout the world, including Iran, rejected much of the views espoused by the Taliban as 'un-Islamic'.

Women leaders like State Minister of Women's Affairs, Mahbooba Hoqooqmal, bear in mind the Afghanistan of the past and see the current situation as a reaction-ary response to decades of instability. She and other women realise that to lift the veil of oppression, borne in the guise of Islam, the monopoly of interpretation must be cast off. Minister Hooqoqmal uses her role as a leader and academic to teach young Afghan women and men Afghan history and the rights accorded to men and women in Islam. Her organisations – Afghan Women's Lawyers Association alongside a number of other women's organisations – trained over a hundred women activists and sent them to the provinces to teach women and men about Islam and constitu-tional rights. Invoking the verses of the Quran, they defend rights on a wide variety of fronts, from preventing forced and under-age marriages to lobbying for more posi-tions for women in the government.

These efforts serve as a quiet but discernable challenge to the monopoly of power that religious and conservative elements wield in society. Educated Afghan women at Kabul University are enrolling in law programs that include the study of Arabic and law. The Independent Human Rights Commission and the International Human Rights Law Group, among a number of NGOs, are holding discussion groups and seminars on Islam. Young Afghan men and women are advocating for the publica-tion of the Quran and other religious documents in Farsi and Pashto (the main offi-cial languages in the country). They realise that to dismantle repressive traditions and sacrosanct policies, they must equip themselves with the tools and values that were distorted to construct the repression in the first place.

The legacy of 23 years of war in Afghanistan has resulted in a shattered society. Amidst the devastation, women are discovering the cracks and crevices and using these small openings to broaden the space for national dialogue and change. The proc-ess of retracing the steps back towards peace and normalcy is bound to be difficult and complicated. But the fine lines of change are forming and a pattern is becom-ing discernable. Women's collective strength is taking shape, slowly solidifying and the extension of their activities is creating a ripple effect, gradually transforming the isolated voices of a few into a discourse for moderation and the stabilisation of a war-torn society.

18

Moving beyond Silence: Women Waging Peace

*Swanee Hunt**

I Introduction

Around the globe, women play a vital but often unrecognised role in averting violence and resolving conflict. With expertise in grassroots activism, political leadership, investigative journalism, human rights law, military reform, formal and information negotiations, transitional justice and post-conflict reconstruction, these women bring new approaches to the security sphere process. Sustainable peace, and therefore international security, depends on such innovations. But scholarship regarding the work of women peace builders is scarce and women's work in the field of security is largely unrecognised at the institutional and public policy levels.

'Women Waging Peace' was developed to bridge this gap. Launched in 1999 to connect women in conflict areas to one another and to policy shapers, 'Waging' advocates worldwide for the full participation of women in formal and informal peace processes. Connecting women peacemakers and policy shapers is the core of Waging's work. First Lady Hillary Clinton hosted the original roll-out of the initiative at the White House. Since then, through conferences and briefings, Waging has brokered relationships among an extensive network of over 200 women peace builders and 2,000 policy shapers, resulting in new solutions to long-standing conflicts at local, regional and international levels. Government officials, NGO leaders, media professionals and academics are collaborating with Waging network members to explore options for building sustainable peace.

This chapter lays out the case for women's inclusion in peace building, examples of women's peace efforts around the world, as well as our challenges and successes in connecting such women to policymakers to create a new model of 'inclusive security'.

*   Former US Ambassador to Austria (1993-1997), Swanee Hunt directs the Women and Public Policy Program at Harvard University's John F. Kennedy School of Government. Ambassador Hunt is founder of Women Waging Peace and President of Hunt Alternatives Fund. Ambassador Hunt remains grateful for the editorial assistance of Annemarie Brennan while writing this chapter.

Helen Durham and Tracey Gurd (eds.), Listening to the Silences: Women and War, *pp. 251-271.*
© *2005 Koninklijke Brill BV. Printed in The Netherlands.* ISBN 90 04 14365 3.

II   Why Women?

The justification for women's inclusion can be built on several platforms. *Fairness* is the most obvious: women account for half of the population and therefore it's only just that they comprise half the decision makers. Or *compensation*: given how greatly women have been victimised, they deserve to be heard. Or *representation*: leaving women out of the peacemaking process means their concerns are likely to be ignored or bargained away in the negotiation process.

But there's an *efficiency* argument as well. For lasting stability, we need peace promoters, not just warriors, at the table. More often than not, those peace promoters are women. Certainly, heroic and visionary men have changed the course of history with their peacemaking; likewise, belligerent women have made it to the top of the political ladder or, at the grassroots level, have joined the ranks of terrorists. But social science research has demonstrated that women tend to be more cooperative and less aggressive in their styles; and in conflict situations around the world, leaders of UN and other international peace missions have reported to me their frustration at not having access to women in the society, whom they perceived to be the steadiest voices of moderation.

A negotiated settlement must have the buy-in of the masses before it is truly sustainable, and thus stakeholders from throughout the society must be involved in the informal and formal peace process. In domestic policy-making, the mayor of an American city wanting to address race relations would pull together not only minority leaders, but also representatives from the business, religious, education, social welfare, labour and political circles. But foreign policymakers aren't subject to the same electoral pressure to build their work on a broad base. International negotiators have not learned to include individuals from multiple spheres who understand the dynamics of the community in which the agreement must be lived.

Women's perspectives in formal and informal peace processes are often different from men's in at least four key ways:

A   *Women are Adept at Bridging Ethnic, Political and Cultural Divides*

In his address to the 24 October 2000 Open Session of the UN Security Council on Women, Peace and Security, UN Secretary-General Kofi Annan stated that: 'For generations, women have served as peace educators, both in their families and in their societies. They have proved instrumental in building bridges rather than walls.'[1] Former President of the Irish Republic, Mary Robinson, agrees that women are 'instinctively ... less hierarchical'[2] and harness in a cooperative way the energies of those who are like-minded. Scores of women have told me they consider themselves generally more collaborative than men and thus more inclined toward consensus and

---

1   See United Nations, 'Secretary-General Calls for Council Action to Ensure Women are Involved in Peace and Security Decisions', M2 PRESSWIRE, 25 October 2000.

2   *Voices of Women Leaders*, SLANT, New York, (Spring 1997) at <http://www.columbia.edu/cu/sipa/PUBS/SLANT/SPRING97/quotes.html>.

compromise. In fact, when I asked a UN official why there were no women in several African peace talks, he said warlords refused to have women because they were concerned that the women would compromise.

Challengers note that female leaders such as Britain's Margaret Thatcher and Israel's Golda Meier have a leadership style quite similar to men: hierarchical and power-centred. The issue may be one of critical mass. Former European Commissioner Anita Gradin notes that in her Swedish homeland, when women made up 15 percent of the parliament, they behaved more like the men. As their numbers increased to 45 percent, the norm changed. They advocated for more changes important to Swedish women and insisted that a woman be appointed defence minister and men be given responsibilities such as social welfare.[3]

In 1976, women organisers in Northern Ireland won the Nobel Peace Prize for their non-sectarian public demonstrations. Almost two decades later, Monica McWilliams (formerly a member of the Northern Ireland Assembly) and May Blood (now a member of the House of Lords) were told that only leaders of the top ten political parties – all men – would be included in the peace talks. Over the next six weeks, McWilliams and Blood mobilised over 200 women's organisations to create a new party: the Northern Ireland Women's Coalition. They received 10,000 votes in the local elections, winning a place at the peace table.[4]

The Coalition is a non-sectarian, broad-based group of women of all political hues and religious traditions, with an agenda of reconciliation through dialogue and inclusion. Based on prior work with families affected by 'The Troubles,'[5] they drafted key clauses of the Good Friday Agreement to include integrated housing and the needs of young people. They lobbied for the early release and reintegration of political prisoners and pushed for a comprehensive review of the police service. In the subsequent public referendum on the Good Friday Agreement, Mo Mowlam, then British Secretary of State for Northern Ireland, attributed the overwhelming success of the YES Campaign to the canvassing of the Northern Ireland Women's Coalition.

Composed of women on different sides of the conflict, the Coalition has had the cross community credibility to work across lines. Members have helped calm the often deadly 'marching season' by facilitating mediation between Protestant unionists and Catholic nationalists. They have brought together key players from each community, including released prisoners, to work on issues of safety and security, maintaining 24 hour contact across the peacelines. Coalition members are not only idealistic but practical. When the women entered the Forum set up as part of the peace negotiations,

---

3   Personal communication with Anita Gradin, former European Commissioner, March 2003 (copy held on file with author).

4   Sanam Naraghi Anderlini, *Women at the Peace Table: Making a Difference*, (UN Development Fund for Women 2000) 16–17, available at <http://www.unifem.undp. org/resources/ peacebk.pdf>.

5   'The Troubles refers to the period of violent conflict in Northern Ireland beginning with the Civil Rights marches in the late 1960s to the political resolution enshrined in the 1998 Good Friday Agreement. During that time more than 3000 people were killed, most of them civilians.' British Broadcasting Corporation, 'War and Conflict: The Troubles' at the BBC website <www.bbc.co.uk/history/war /troubles>.

some men started moo-ing as if they were cows. The women responded by setting up a blackboard outside their office doors. It was called the 'name 'em and shame 'em' board. Every day, insults hurled at the women were listed for all to see – with attribution. The public insults soon stopped.

Women's progress does not move in a straight line. In November 2003, the Coalition, along with other moderates, lost their Parliamentary seats. They held a retreat within a few days and emerged resolved to stay the course, organising for the continued implementation of the peace process and to get more women elected again.

B   *Women Have Their Fingers on the Pulse of the Community*

Living and working close to the roots of conflict, women are well positioned to provide essential information about activities leading up to violence as well as to gather wartime evidence. Grounded in practicalities of everyday life, they also play a critical role in mobilising their communities to begin post-conflict of reconciliation and rebuilding.

In Kosovo, after paediatric neurologist Vjosa Dobruna was locked out of her hospital office during Milosevic's imposed apartheid, she helped create 'Fe-mail', an email warning and emergency aid system. Having collected evidence from victims at massacre sites, she was targeted for murder or capture by Serb special police. She escaped by jumping out of a second floor window into her garden. Caught up in the flood of refugees in the exodus to Macedonia, Dr. Dobruna administered trauma relief. Subsequently, she was appointed to the UN's Joint Interim Administrative Structure of Kosovo, with responsibility for democracy building and civil society. Her portfolio included establishment of new protocols for free elections and a system of independent news reporting to replace the mendacious media machine that contributed to the destruction of her community. She says having only her car and cell phone as an office for the first six months of her job wasn't a handicap because she held meetings in cafes and homes, where she stayed in close touch with Kosovars' concerns.

Dobruna has won the confidence of Serb and ethnic Albanian Kosovars and has led efforts to create a women's caucus in the new assembly, the only political structure crossing party lines. In July 2002 Hashim Thaci, president of the assembly, said of her work: 'This women's caucus is the only effort to bring together people from all sides. It will be a model, giving us hope that we can live together.'

C   *Women are Innovative Community Leaders With or Without Formal Authority*

Around the world, women are disproportionately represented in grassroots organising, even though (or because?) their work is generally under-funded and overlooked. The good news is that grassroots leaders may set their own agenda outside the close scrutiny of political parties or official establishments.

In stark demographics, women frequently outnumber men in post-conflict populations. They often drive on-the-ground implementation of peace agreements, using techniques such as popular protests, electoral referenda and other citizen-empowering movements whose influence has grown with the spread of democracy. Precisely because they haven't been allowed full participation within power structures, women have learned to work 'outside the box'. Africa offers many examples. With no resources available to them, Sudanese women marched though town naked to protest the abduction of their children as child soldiers. Their songs were played on radio and became popular throughout the region. Going further, during the November 2000 Burundi peace talks, Nelson Mandela encouraged women to withhold 'conjugal rights' ('such as cooking' he quipped) if their rebel husbands picked up arms again.[6] *Lysistrata* revisited.

In Rwanda, 'after the genocide, women rolled up their sleeves and began making society work again,' says President Paul Kagame.[7] A leader among those women is Aloisea Inyumba, Governor of Kigali-Ngali Province and former head of the Commission for Unity and Reconciliation. Born and raised in a refugee camp in neighbouring Uganda, she confronted a society in crisis when she entered her parents' homeland with the Rwandan Patriotic Front in the early 1990s. Inyumba witnessed the genocide of 1994 and at age 26 was made Minister for Families and Gender. She and her co-workers faced the immediate challenge of figuring out how to bury some 800,000 bodies from the massacres that wiped out ten percent of the population in 100 days. As well, she devised a system to care for hundreds of thousands of orphans. 'Each One Take One' was her motto as she urged every mother to add at least one more child to her family. Hutu women adopted Tutsi children and Tutsi women took home Hutus. Inyumba also prepared Rwandan communities for the release of about 100,000 genocidaires from prison. One by one, she visited villages to ready them for the release of prisoners – mostly men – who have been in jail for years without trial because the court system was completely overwhelmed by the catastrophic killing spree.

D   *Women are Highly Invested in Preventing and Stopping Conflict*

The first comment usually offered by casual observers as to why women promote peace is that women are so inclined because of their social and biological roles as nurturers. While most men come to the negotiating table directly from the war room and battlefield, women's experiences usually come from care-giving professions and family care. This notion that women's contributions are linked to being mothers (or being scripted to have been mothers) has been challenged by those who see a line between biology and destiny as confining, dangerous and wrong-headed. But we don't need to argue 'nature or nurture' to make the case that women are motivated by mothering as agents for peace. Women I've interviewed in conflict areas all over the world repeatedly state that they feel driven by the need to ensure security for their families. They describe themselves as different from men with phrases such as 'after all, we bring life into the world so we don't want to see it destroyed'. That theme is picked up by many men, like

---

6   Swanee Hunt and Cristina Posa, 'Women Waging Peace' (2001) *Foreign Policy* 38, 42.

7   Personal communication with Paul Kagame, President of Rwanda, May 2001 (copy held on file with author).

Haris Silajdzic, post-war Prime Minister of Bosnia, who told me in 1996: 'If we'd had women around the table, there would have been no war; women think long and hard before they send their children out to kill other people's children'.

The energy of mothers determined to protect their children inspires Ida Kuklina, who works with over 200 chapters of soldiers' mothers, demanding Russian military reform. Her powerful NGO defends the human rights of servicemen. She and her members confront judges, generals and presidents with the deaths of 3,000–5,000 soldiers who perish each year, not because of war, but because of abuse by their own commanders and peers. In addition, Ida and her colleagues were so vocal criticising the war in Chechnya that the American Ambassador to Russia credited them with Yeltsin's ending of the first Chechen war.

III   Evidence of Efficacy

Policymakers sometimes ask for 'proof' of whether and how women make a difference in peace building. Advocates note that the mayor in the earlier example, putting together a race relations campaign, would not ask for proof that he should include blacks in the initiative planning and implementation. Still, research is turning up a range of new examples of women's effectiveness in dealing with conflict.

A journalist and scholar with the South Asia Forum for Human Rights in Kathmandu, Nepal, Rita Manchanda explores the context in which strong women peace builders emerge, the forces that seek to prevent their leadership in this field and the progress made by women peace builders:

> Traditionally, women have formed the humanitarian front of the war story …. But beyond the passivity and powerlessness of victimhood, conflict has seen South Asian women come out and mobilise resistance, confront the security forces, the administration and the courts. Women have formed Mothers Fronts and coalitions for peace, women have become guerrillas and soldiers and women have emerged as agents of social transformation and conflict resolution.[8]

Adding to the work of Manchada and others, in 2002 Women Waging Peace established a Policy Commision to link gender research and theories of conflict prevention and resolution. The process has included scholars, practitioners, policymakers, grassroots organisers and students analysing topics such as how women use their traditional identities to mobilise peace; the role of women as community builders during warfare; how women adapt indigenous cultural practices to contain violence; and the crucial role of women in healing and reconciliation.

The Policy Commission's analytical body of research strengthens the effectiveness of advocacy work. Case studies address three overarching questions:

---

8   Rita Manchanda, 'Where Are the Women in South Asian Conflicts?' in Rita Manchanda (ed) *Women, War, and Peace in South Asia: Beyond Victimhood to Agency* (2001) 15.

1. How do women contribute to peace processes?
2. How and why is the consideration of gender issues essential to the successful implementation of peace processes?
3. What are the most effective models and examples of the inclusion of women and gender issues in peace processes? What guidelines and recommendations can be provided to policymakers for the design and implementation of international assistance programs?

The research methodology was developed after a scholars meeting and consultations with more than 60 representatives of government institutions, international organisations, leading non-governmental organisations and think tanks. Based on these consultations, the Commission identified as themes:
a) conflict prevention and non-violent transformation;
b) pre-negotiation and negotiation processes; and
c) post-conflict reconstruction, including disarmament, demobilisation and reintegration (DDR); governance and political participation; and transitional justice and reconciliation.

The initial case studies reveal fascinating, untold stories:

1   Strengthening Governance: The Role of Women in Rwanda's Transition[9] examines women's contributions to post-conflict governance. In September 2003, Rwanda held its first multi-party parliamentary elections since the 1994 genocide. Women won 49 percent of the seats and are playing a significant role in politics and governance in the country. The Rwandan government developed innovative mechanisms to increase women's participation in governance and leadership structures at all levels. At national and grassroots levels, Rwandan women have made significant contributions to post-genocide recovery and reconciliation and women in governance have developed models for working across party and ethnic lines, strengthening partnerships with civil society.

2   Adding Value: Women's Contributions to Reintegration and Reconstruction in El Salvador[10] revisits the role of women in the Salvadoran DDR process and subsequent reconstruction efforts. Women's participation in negotiations had a significant impact on the inclusion of women and non-combatants in reintegration benefits programs. Women played an important stabilising role in the early phases of reintegration and are leaders in reconstruction and development despite social and economic constraints.

3   From Combat to Community: Women and Girls of Sierra Leone[11] examines the participation of women and girls in formal and informal processes of DDR. Women

---

9   Elizabeth Powley, *Strengthening Governance: The Role of Women in Rwanda's Transition* (2003) available at the Women Waging Peace website <http://www.womenwagingpeace. net/content/articles/RwandaFullCaseStudy.pdf>.

10 Camille Pampell Conaway and Salomé Martínez, with contributions by Sarah Gammage and Eugenia Piza-Lopez, *Adding Value: Women's Contributions to Reintegration and Reconstruction in El Salvador* (2004) available at Women Waging Peace website <http:// www.womenwagingpeace.net/content/articles/ElSalvadorFullCaseStudy.pdf>.

11 Dyan Mazurana and Khristopher Carlson, with contributions by Sanam Naraghi Anderlini, *From Combat to Community: Women and Girls of Sierra Leone* (2004) available

mobilised public support for peace. They were active militarily in the conflict – particularly within the pro-government Civil Defence Forces – and they have provided a significant, but previously unacknowledged, number of services in the reintegration of ex-fighters, filling many gaps in official programs.

4   Good Governance from the Ground Up: Women's Roles in Post-Conflict Cambodia [12] traces women's contributions to governance and peace through local and national politics as well as civil society. Politics in Cambodia have been characterised by mistrust and a culture of violence persists. But there is growing public support for women's increased political participation since they are perceived to be more trustworthy and competent than men. Women in Cambodia have lobbied for the inclusion of human rights in the constitution, campaigned for peaceful elections, urged accountability in government structures and the establishment of government-civil society partnerships and developed mechanisms to advance their own political participation. Women are breaking new ground by appealing for fresh models of cross-party cooperation and establishing new patterns of public consultation.

5   In the Midst of War: Women's Contributions to Peace in Colombia [13] documents the critical work of women at local, regional, and national levels to mitigate the effects of continued violence on their communities, mobilise for renewed dialogues and prepare for the next cycle of peace. Despite widespread disillusionment in the peace movement, women's groups have developed a process to build consensus and create an agenda addressing the root causes of conflict such as political, social, and economic exclusion. Locally, despite being targeted through violence and repression, women are leading resistance efforts, establishing informal agreements with armed actors and forming 'peace zones' to protect their communities.

Earlier in this book, Li Fung noted the 'dichotomy between 'public' and 'private' spheres, which restricts women's access to the realms of national and international politics'. [14] Women associated with grassroots organising and civil society efforts are often absent or under-represented in official positions – particularly when it comes to peace negotiations. Fung goes on to say when this gender-based discrimination is reinforced during times of conflict, it is more difficult for women to become involved in political processes. [15]

Manchanda takes a different slant:

---

at Women Waging Peace website <http://www.womenwagingpeace.net/content/articles/SierraLeoneFullCaseStudy.pdf>.

12   Sambath Chan, Kate Frieson and Laura McGrew, *Good Governance from the Ground Up: Women's Roles in Post-Conflict Cambodia* (2004). At the time of writing, the study's executive summary is available at the Women Waging Peace website <http://www.womenwagingpeace.net/content/articles/CambodiaExecSummary.pdf>.

13   Catalina Rojas, *In the Midst of War: Women's Contributions to Peace in Colombia* (2004). At time of publication, the study's executive summary is available on the Women Waging Peace website <http://www.womenwagingpeace.net/content/articles/ColombiaExecSummary.pdf>.

14   See Li Fung, 'Engendering the Peace Process: Women's Role in Peace Building and Conflict Resolution' earlier in this collection at 213-215.

15   Ibid.

Violent conflict opens up for women the public sphere predominantly controlled by men ... As we see in the lived narratives of women in the Kashmir conflict or in the Chittagong Hill Tracts of Bangladesh, protracted curfews and high risk security regimes obliged women to innovate survival strategies for the family and community. It was the mothers, wives and sisters who made the rounds of detention centres and torture cells looking for the disappeared and entered into negotiations of power with the institutional power structures, the army, administration and the courts. Women used their traditional invisibility in the public sphere to create space for their activism. As they are seen as less threatening, they are less watched. Violent conflict blurs the divide between the private sphere of the family and the public sphere or men and politics and in so doing calls into question the validity of the divide.[16]

Even when a conflict creates more opportunities than barriers for women, those gains are rarely lasting. When the men return home, women lose their non-traditional jobs and they must often deal with a soaring rate of domestic violence from their soldier husbands.

IV   What Women Peace Builders Need

Given their positions in communities and investment in a peaceful society, women can be amazingly resourceful and creative in designing their work. They still greatly benefit, however, from additional training as well as opportunities to share techniques and make connections.

A   Messaging and Strategic Planning

Often coming from civil society or other fields, women need additional training in negotiation techniques. Such training, as well as other capacity-building programs, not only strengthens women's voices but also equips them to work within the traditionally male policy community.

The war in the Democratic Republic of the Congo has destabilised much of the surrounding region. As a result, conflict resolution experts from across the continent are lending their assistance. Kemi Ogunsanya, originally from Nigeria, is a senior conflict resolution training officer with the African Centre for the Constructive Resolution of Disputes (ACCORD), a conflict management NGO. Originally created to address challenges in South Africa's difficult transition from apartheid to democracy, ACCORD's focus has broadened to include all of Africa, offering innovative and effective solutions to regional challenges.

In 2002, the Congolese Women's Caucus successfully pushed for the inclusion of women in the Inter-Congolese Dialogues. Kemi provided conflict resolution and negotiation training to women participating in the Sun City peace talks, which brought together Congolese representatives from the government, political parties, rebel groups, and civil society. Kemi and other women from conflicts around the world say they are able to apply material from Waging conferences to their own situations,

---

16   Manchanda, above n 8, 15-16.

training local women to hone their messages, using traditional security language in their meetings with policy makers, and applying consistent pressure until they have a voice in the peace process.

B   *Exposure to Fresh Ideas*

A flow of new ideas is key to the solution of long-standing conflicts. Even brilliant and committed activists need the stimulation of hearing the accounts of others.

A civil war, detailed earlier by Neela Marikkar, has gripped Sri Lanka for 20 years. Following the disappearance of one of her sons, a soldier in the Sri Lankan army, Visaka Dharmadasa founded Parents of Servicemen Missing in Action, launching a campaign to require the Sri Lankan army to issue identification tags for soldiers. At a Waging meeting, Dharmadasa met Ida Kuklina, Secretary of the Union of the Committees of the Soldiers' Mothers of Russia. Kuklina inspired Dharmadasa to reach out to mothers on the other side of the conflict line. This outreach to the Tamil Tigers community led Dharmadasa to start peace-building dialogues between members of the two communities. Now one of the few people trusted by officials on both sides of the conflict, she is leading Track Two dialogue processes between the two groups. As she moves in and out of rebel territory in her work, Dharmadasa credits Kuklina with the broadening of the scope of her empathy from other soldiers' families to her entire country,

C   *Coalitions for Strength*

Women benefit from coalitions in which they not only share and develop new ideas but also encourage and support each other. Whether providing practical guidance or inspiration, these coalitions offer women peace builders new perspectives on their own work and cement help from others, often leading to dramatic changes.

Peace agreements signed in 1996 form the base of a comprehensive platform for socio-economic development and democratisation in Guatemala. They also include major shifts toward gender equality. That unusual inclusion is in large part due to the voice of Luz Méndez, author of an earlier chapter in this book. Between 1991 and 1996, Méndez participated in the peace negotiations as part of the delegation of the Guatemalan National Revolutionary Unity; she was the only woman negotiator for the first few years of the talks. Over the course of the negotiations, she began to work closely with representatives of civil society organisations, which had observer status at the talks. When women's groups made proposals about women's rights in the new Guatemala, Méndez backed them, despite the opposition she received from other negotiators. In 1995, she attended the Beijing UN Fourth World Conference on Women. That experience solidified her belief that women's rights are human rights. Later, as General Coordinator of the National Union of Guatemalan Women, Méndez worked for implementation of the peace accords, particularly the gender equality provisions. In 2000, she was a member of UNIFEM's gender experts team at the Burundi peace talks. She insists that in each of these situations, she was emboldened by the presence of other women, who fed her ideas and courage.

D   *Access to Policymakers*

The most important tool for women peace builders is access to the policymakers they are hoping to influence. Training and skills building, crafting new ideas and working within wide coalitions are all useful means of drawing the attention of officials who control budgets and agendas.

It is important to have buy-in from people within the power structure – formal or informal. In the case of women's inclusion, this often means collaborating with men. Li Fung and Rina Amiri note that in Bougainville, the Solomon Islands and Afghanistan, including men in women's efforts to transform the peace-building process was essential. Fung describes how the Women's Development Agency, which played an integral role in ending the conflict in Bougainville, had a strategy to 'actively pursue sons, husbands and brothers, calling them to come back to their communities, sit down and think about non-violent ways of negotiating with the government'.[17] Similarly, Amiri explains the importance of Afghan clergy in furthering her cause. With close to 80 percent of the population illiterate, those who interpret the religious law of the Qu'ran wield a great deal of power. Conservative clerics often favour interpretations that uphold more restrictive customs, limiting the rights or women, among others.[18] Building the right coalition for change is key to success in forcing change.

V   Getting the Words Right

Recent policy statements from the UN Security Council, the Organisation for Security and Cooperation in Europe (OSCE), the Group of Eight Leading Industrialised Nations (G8), the European Union (EU), and the Organisation of American States (OAS) call for the inclusion of women at every stage of local and international efforts to prevent, manage and resolve conflict.

A   *UN Security Council Resolution 1325*

In October 2000, the UN Security Council unanimously passed Resolution 1325 on women, peace and security, urging its member states to ensure the full inclusion of women in all aspects of international peace and security processes. Resolution 1325 recognises that those most negatively affected by war and conflict are civilians – particularly women and children. It also acknowledges, however, the critical role women can play in preventing and resolving conflicts and in building peace. Consequently, the Security Council urges member states to include more women at all levels of decision making and field operations. It asks the Secretary-General and member states to include a gender perspective in peacekeeping operations – both on and off the ground – and to provide training on the protection, rights and needs of women in post-conflict reconstruction. The resolution also urges all parties involved in conflict

---

17   Fung, above n 15, 217.
18   Rina Amiri, 'Fine Lines of Transformation: Afghan Women Working for Peace', the previous chapter in this collection, at 228-229.

resolution to adopt a gender-conscious approach during disarmament, demobilisation and reintegration. The policy statement stresses the responsibility of all actors to protect women from gender-based violence – especially rape – and to prosecute those guilty of perpetrating such crimes. It also calls for the support of women-led peace initiatives and indigenous approaches to conflict resolution. The Secretary-General is responsible for implementation with the mandate to investigate and communicate to all members the impact of armed conflict on women and girls and the overall gender implications of conflict resolution.

B   European Parliament Resolution on Participation of Women in Peaceful Conflict Resolution

In November 2000, the European Parliament passed a resolution calling on member states to guarantee the equal participation of women in conflict resolution at all levels, recruiting and training them for diplomatic positions and requiring negotiation teams to regularly consult women's community-based organisations. Because the reconciliation process presents an opportunity to address deeply rooted conflicts, the resolution promotes constitutional protection of women's equality in peace accords and grassroots encouragement of warring factions to include women and civil society representatives in their negotiation teams, as well as fostering public awareness in conflict zones regarding systematic gender abuse. The goal is to ensure that peace is deeply rooted and that citizens, especially women, are not victimised or marginalised during demobilisation.

To this end, all member states should emphasise the importance of gender sensitivity and awareness in peace and security missions. Women are generally excluded from peace negotiations, although they are the majority of refugees and war victims. They are often targets of sexual violence as a weapon of war and suffer stigmatisation, sexual slavery, child prostitution, trafficking and sexually transmitted diseases. Member states must protect war-affected populations and facilitate international efforts in conflict prevention and resolution. Only with women's participation will negotiations take into account the rights and interests of women and girls and achieve the legitimacy needed for sustainable peace. The resolution also encourages the use of non-military strategies in peacekeeping operations that protect female participants by international human rights standards rather than cultural norms. Member states should classify sexual violence as a grave breach of the *Geneva Conventions* and support the appointment of a UN Special Rapporteur on Women in Armed Conflict Situations.

C   OSCE Action Plan for Gender Issues

In 2000, the OSCE approved a detailed Action Plan for Gender Issues, acknowledging the critical role women play in ensuring security while calling for greater gender equity within its institutions. A central part of the plan is the inclusion of women at all levels of the OSCE. Regular reports, intended to monitor the plan's implementation throughout the organisation, include gender-specific statistics and data on the percentage of women in leadership roles.¹⁹ Training on human rights, gender sensitivity and non-discrimination is a prominent objective of the action plan, involving mission staff, senior staff, human rights workers, police monitors and officers. The action plan also urges all 55 OSCE member states to take similar measures for achieving greater gender equality, and pledges that the OSCE will monitor member states' compliance and encourage cooperation with other organisations to share information and best practices. Finally, the plan mandates that the Office for Democratic Institutions and Human Rights take into account a gender perspective in all of its work. Specific action areas include increasing women's access to public and political life, enabling active participation of women in conflict resolution and management and preventing gender-related violence.

D   *The G8 Statement on Strengthening the Role of Women in Conflict Prevention*

In early 2000, I met with President Clinton to urge him to include on the US agenda the issues of women's role in peace building. Although he enthusiastically agreed and the State Department followed suit, the process was slowed down during the preparatory process and the issue received only passing mention at the meeting in Japan. Although the US Administration changed hands, the State Department under George W. Bush kept up the pressure. At their July 2001 meeting in Rome, the G8 Foreign Ministers agreed on the urgency of the systematic involvement of women in all stages of conflict prevention and resolution. The G8 Foreign Ministers' Official Statement describes the value of women as prime negotiators, peacemakers and advisers who can add creative, alternative approaches to mitigating conflict and sustaining peace. It encourages the appointment of women to national and international operational positions. The G8 foreign ministers call for special attention to the needs of female ex-combatants and urge gender sensitivity in training materials for peacekeeping operations, including military, civilian police and humanitarian personnel. They view women's involvement in bilateral and multilateral aid efforts as contributing to the larger goal of strengthening the role of women in building a peaceful and just society. The statement also highlights the positive role the private sector can play in conflict prevention and peace building. Calling for corporate social responsibility and endorsing collaboration among government, business and civil society, the G8 ministers support the notion of public-private partnerships in response to high-risk conflict situations.

E   *Organisation of American States*

Success breeds success. In a 2003 Declaration on Security in the Americas, the OAS acknowledged the importance of strengthening the participation of women in efforts to promote peace and security; the need to increase women's decision-making role at all levels in relation to conflict prevention, management and resolution; and the neces-

---

19   The first *Report on the Implementation of the Action Plan for Gender Issues* was distributed by the Secretary-General in May 2003.

sity of integrating a gender perspective in every policy, program and activity of inter-American organs, agencies, entities, conferences and processes that deal with matters of hemispheric security.

VI   Walking the Talk

Despite ample policy resolutions, comprehensive analysis to prove the efficacy of women's involvement and important connections made between women peace builders and policy shapers, the full inclusion of women in peace processes remains elusive. As Fung notes in her earlier chapter, women's marginalisation is reinforced by structural inequalities that support gender-based discrimination.[20] The United Nations, for example, is beleaguered by male dominance among permanent representatives and upper level administration; and so, examining UN Resolution 1325, we see interest and intention, but little implementation.

Following the passage of the resolution in 2000, the Inter-Agency Network on Women and Gender Equality established the Inter-Agency Taskforce on Women, Peace and Security, headed by the Special Adviser on Gender Issues, to ensure coordination of implementation throughout the UN system. The Taskforce, which developed an Action Plan for Resolution 1325's implementation, includes representatives from nearly 20 organisations – among them the Department of Disarmament Affairs, Department of Political Affairs, Department of Peacekeeping Operations, Office of the High Commissioner for Human Rights, Office of the Special Adviser for Gender Issues, Office of the Special Representative of the Secretary-General for Children in Armed Conflict, United Nations Development Programme, United Nations High Commissioner for Refugees, United Nations Development Fund for Women. It also includes among its official observers the International Organisation for Migration and the NGO Working Group for Women, Peace and Security.[21]

The Inter-Agency Task Force contributed to the preparation of the Secretary-General's study 'Women, Peace and Security'.[22] Mandated by Resolution 1325, an October 2002 report on this study examines the effect of armed conflict on women and girls; outlines the relevant international legal framework and assesses its implementation; and reviews the gender perspectives in peace processes and missions, humanitarian operations and reconstruction and rehabilitation, including DDR (disarmament, demobilisation and reintegration). With an eye toward further implemen-

---

20   Fung, above n 15, 208.

21   Inter-Agency Network on Women and Gender Equality, *Task Force on Women, Peace, and Security*, Website of the Inter-Agency Network on Women and Gender Equality, United Nations, <http://www.un.org/womenwatch/ianwge/activities/tfwpsecurity.htm>. See also the Office of the Special Adviser on Gender Issues and the Advancement of Women, *Implementation of the Security Council resolution (1325) on Women, Peace and Security*, website of the Office of the Special Adviser on Gender Issues and the Advancement of Women, United Nations, <http://www.un.org/womenwatch/osagi/gmtoolsscnoteres.htm>.

22   *Women, Peace, and Security: Study Submitted by the Secretary-General Pursuant to Security Council Resolution 1325*, 57 UN SCOR, UN Doc S/2002/1154 (16 October 2002).

tation of Resolution 1325, the study includes recommendations for concrete action to ensure greater attention to gender perspectives in each of these areas.[23]

Following the presentation of this report and subsequent debate, the President of the Security Council issued a statement on the Council's behalf that strongly encouraged member states to continue and to increase their efforts at gender mainstreaming, particularly within peacekeeping and reconstruction efforts. The statement urged the Secretary-General to appoint more women to special representative, envoy and gender adviser positions and requested member states to contribute to a database of women candidates for such positions. Noting the important contributions of women in peace building, the statement requested the integration of gender perspectives into all reports presented to the Security Council and into all manuals and training materials for peacekeeping organisations. In an apparent effort to bridge the public-private dichotomy which Fung cites, the President's statement asserts:

> The Security Council recognises the vital role of women in promoting peace, particularly in preserving social order and educating for peace. The Council encourages its Member States and the Secretary-General to establish regular contacts with local women's group and networks in order to utilise their knowledge of both the impact of armed conflict on women and girls, including as victims and ex-combatants, and of peacekeeping operations, to ensure that those groups are actively involved in reconstruction processes, particularly at decision-making levels.[24]

The Security Council's statement also encourages UN member states, civil society organisations and other actors to create clear and detailed strategies and action plans for gender mainstreaming and the integration of gender perspectives into humanitarian, peacekeeping and reconstruction missions, as well as mechanisms that monitor such missions. It also requests that the Secretary-General present a follow-up report in October 2004.[25]

One year after that statement was released, in October 2003, the UN Security Council held an open debate on women, peace and security. Speakers indicated that barriers to implementation had not yet been overcome. Bulgarian Ambassador Tafrov levelled this critique: 'The resolution provides a very important legal framework for action by the Council, but we should not stop there. It must be said that the results of its implementation are meagre indeed.' Ambassador Hannesson of Iceland agreed, saying: 'The Security Council should put the same effort into ensuring the implemen-

---

23   *Ibid.*, 11. See also the Office of the Special Adviser on Gender Issues and the Advancement of Women, *Implementation of the Security Council resolution (1325) on Women, Peace and Security*, website of the Office of the Special Adviser on Gender Issues and the Advancement of Women, United Nations, <http://www.un.org/womenwatch/osagi/gmtoolsscnoteres.htm>.

24   *Statement by the President of the UN Security Council*, UN Doc. S/PRST/2002/32 (2002).

25   *Ibid.*, final paragraph. See also the Office of the Special Adviser on Gender Issues and the Advancement of Women, Implementation of the Security Council resolution (1325) on Women, Peace and Security, website of the Office of the Special Adviser on Gender Issues and the Advancement of Women, United Nations, <http://www.un.org/womenwatch/osagi/gmtoolsscnoteres.htm>. Also see Report of the Secretary General 'Women and Peace and Security', UN Doc. S/2004/814 (2004).

tation of Resolution 1325 (2000) as it puts into all its other resolutions. The effectiveness of the United Nations and its international authority ultimately rest on the extent to which it is seen to implement its own decisions'.[26]

As an innovative way to bring attention to this problem, the United Kingdom Women's National Commission sponsored a Moot Court regarding the implementation of UN Security Council Resolution 1325 on Women, Peace and Security at the Commission on the Status of Women meeting in March 2004. Structured as a tribunal, '1325 on Trial' allowed witnesses and prosecutors to highlight the action – or inaction – of governments and UN entities that have primary responsibility for applying the resolution in war affected countries. The evidence presented made clear that while ad-hoc and one-off efforts have been made by officials, the NGO community has been the greatest force and supporter of Resolution 1325. A packed auditorium of some 200 people voted almost unanimously against the defence. The judge's sentence provided a number of specific recommendations on awareness-raising and implementation, including resources channelled to NGOs, extensive training around Resolution 1325 for government, UN and NGO personnel, and including men and boys in outreach efforts. Other recommendations were to strengthen institutional collaboration and support mechanisms within the UN and among UN member states, civil society organisations and other interested parties. The recommendations also called for gender perspectives and experts at all stages and for explicit references to gender concerns and, when possible, gender units and advisers in peace operation mandates and operations.

VII   Acting As If

While Resolution 1325 remains unimplemented, even without adequate support situations women are playing important roles in stabilising the most recent conflict areas.

A   *East Timor*

In 2002, the UN established a support mission in East Timor. A Special Representative to the Secretary-General headed the mission, which would initially comprise 1,250 civilian police and a military troop strength of 5,000, including 120 military observers. In addition to a focal point for HIV/AIDS, a Civilian Support Group of up to 100 personnel to fill core functions, a Serious Crimes Unit and a Human Rights Unit, it was determined that the civilian component would include a focal point for gender. In

---

26   Felicity Hill, 'Summary of Statements, Actions, Commitments and Recommendations, Security Council Open Debate on Women, Peace, and Security', 29 October 2003 (2003) Portal on Women, Peace, and Security, United Nations Development Fund for Women, <http://www.womenwarpeace.org/summary2003.doc>. For the full text of all statements delivered at the debate, as well as press releases and other collateral materials, see Women's International League for Peace and Freedom, United Nations Security Council Open Debate on Women, Peace, and Security, (2003) website of Women's International League for Peace and Freedom, <http://www.peacewomen.org/un/SCOpenDebate2003/OpenDebate2003index.html>.

addition, the UN High Commission on Refugees sponsored an East Timor Women's Initiative to raise women's profile in post-conflict reconstruction.

B   Afghanistan

The world knows the plight of Afghan women under the Taliban. With international support, great advances have been made since the fall of the regime: more that 20 percent of the delegates to the December 2003 Constitutional Loya Jirga were women. When the female vote split, preventing any women from being elected to the Constitutional Loya Jirga secretariat bureau, individual women successfully lobbied to be included; one was named a deputy chair and two were made rapporteurs. The constitution finalised at the Loya Jirga enshrined the rights of women: 'citizens of Afghanistan – men and women – have equal rights and duties before the law'. Additionally, 25 percent of national assembly seats were set aside for women.

Improvement has been made at the local level as well. Rina Amiri's chapter discusses how networks of women from across the country have begun to work together for the advancement of women's rights. As the Ministry of Women's Affairs and NGOs open offices throughout the country, training sessions and seminars are held in Kabul and throughout the provinces, providing rural and urban women opportunities to meet. Amiri notes that such initiatives are helping different populations in Afghanistan overcome misconceptions and stereotypes about one another. 'Rural women are gradually recognising that urban women hold similar values and that they can play a key role in advocating on their behalf. Urban women are slowly learning to discard age-old prejudices about the backwardness of rural women.'

C   Liberia

In 1994, Mary Brownell, a former elementary teacher, ran a radio advertisement calling all women to attend a meeting at Monrovia City Hall. The resulting Liberian Women's Initiative was pivotal in monitoring the words and actions of warlords. Using their community status as mothers and elderly women, they reprimanded and cajoled fighters into laying down their weapons. When the election of Charles Taylor in 1997, instead of peace, brought international condemnation, Liberian women joined with their counterparts in Sierra Leone and Guinea to form the Mano River Union Peace Network. They organised a major advocacy campaign, targeting the leaders of their three nations, as well as the international community. The group focused on disarming child soldiers, stemming small arms trafficking and addressing inflammatory political issues. Throughout 2002 and 2003, they were key mediators between the various fighting forces, 18 political parties and the government. In recognition of their role, in August 2003 the Network was an official witness and signatory to the peace agreement. The women have continued to work with the UN on disarmament and demobilisation efforts.

D *Iraq*

Women in Iraq, once among the most liberated in the Arab world, faced the erosion of their rights under the regime of Saddam Hussein. The US-led Coalition Provisional Authority made several serious missteps in its earliest days, appointing only a minimal number of women in decision-making positions. As the Iraqi Governing Council began to formulate policy, it looked as though that negative trend would continue. On 29 December 2003, the Governing Council passed Resolution 137 to cancel the Iraqi family law in place since 1959, replacing it with much more restrictive *Shariah* (Islamic) law.

Energised by internal leadership and supported by several outside groups such as UNIFEM, the World Bank, Women for Women and Women Waging Peace, women's groups in Iraq and around the world organised protests, leading to the revocation of Resolution 137. The interim constitution signed on 8 March 2004 states that: 'All Iraqis are equal in their rights without regard to gender, sect, opinion, belief, nationality, religion, or origin and they are equal before the law. Discrimination against an Iraqi citizen on the basis of gender, nationality, religion, or origin is prohibited'.[27]

The interim constitution also set a goal for the new parliament to be 25 percent women but does not guarantee that 25 percent of the seats in parliament will be filled by women. Bush Administration officials, for domestic reasons allergic to the notion of 'affirmative action' protections for minorities, quickly pointed out that target did not create a quota. Still, addressing this critical moment in her nation's history, Iraqi Minister of Municipalities and Public Works Nesreen Berwari noted:

Resolution 137, if signed into law by the CPA Administrator, would have severely diminished the status and benefits Iraqi women enjoy to date. But this resolution was a blessing in disguise. Its passage motivated Iraqi women to organise and demonstrate and successfully represent themselves. The [Governing Council] was moved to retract the resolution, the first and only resolution to be retracted…. The retraction of Resolution 137 and the 25 percent target are achievements in themselves. But more importantly, the process by which they occurred is also an achievement. It's about democracy being public, open, transparent and accountable. The retraction and the target brought Iraqi women together for a common cause. Cooperation and organisation crossed religious and ethnic lines – Shia, Sunni, Christian, Arab, Kurd, Assyrian, Turcomen.[28]

---

27   Iraqi Governing Council, *Law of Administration for the State of Iraq for the Transitional Period*, (2004) Website of the Coalition Provisional Authority, <http://www.cpa-iraq.org/government/TAL.html> Chapter 2, Article 12.

28   Excerpt from remarks of H.E. Nesreen Berwari, Iraqi Minister of Municipalities and Public Works, on International Women's Day, The White House Treaty Room (Washington DC, 8 March 2004) see US Department of State Office of International Women's Issues, *Iraqi Minister's Remarks on International Women's Day* (2004) website of the US Department of State, <http://www.state.gov/g/wi/30247.htm>.

E The Americas

In early 2003, the then US Secretary of State Colin Powell expressed his commitment to women's inclusion, from prevention to negotiations to post-conflict reconstruction. Recognising that women are often marginalised in the aftermath of conflict despite having played leadership roles during war, the then Secretary of State encouraged ambassadors worldwide by highlighting concrete examples of how US agencies have brought women into varying stages of peace-building processes:

- The US Embassy in Côte d'Ivoire supported a two-day seminar on women's decision making in the political arena.
- The US Consulate in Istanbul co-hosted a conference entitled 'A Global Forum for Women' with a panel on women, peace and conflict and helped train women involved in conflict.
- Women attorneys in Nigeria were trained in ways to manage conflict between oil industry interests and local communities.
- Afghan women politicians, human rights advocates and lawyers received training and many of them participated in the first Loya Jirga.
- In Sierra Leone, USAID has helped prepare community leaders to rebuild civil society and government institutions.
- Programs in Serbia-Montenegro have led to increased participation by women and minorities in community development activities and increased inter-ethnic cooperation.
- Vocational training for ex-combatants in Guatemala, including women, was made possible by USAID's demobilisation program.

In addition to these and other US-led actions, in early 2004 the Organisation of American States began initial discussions on implementing various programs to advance women's contributions to peace and security issues in the western hemisphere. A number of individual missions and agencies of the Secretariat, including the Unit for the Promotion of Democracy and the Inter-American Commission for Women, are exploring how programming within the areas of conflict prevention, resolution and post-conflict reconstruction can address women's participation. In preliminary conversations, participants are considering a gender-mapping program to create a portal of all women's organisations working on conflict in the hemisphere, with the eventual outcome of providing more resources for training and capacity for women peace builders.

VIII Conclusion

For all our talk about policy, peace is not only political – it's also personal. Pumla Gobodo-Madikizela is Senior Consultant for Reconciliation at South Africa's Institute for Justice and Reconciliation. In 1996, she joined the Human Rights Violations Committee of the Truth and Reconciliation Commission (TRC), designed to help South Africa overcome its history of apartheid which was marked by violence on the part of both the State and the liberation movement. She not only facilitated public hearings in the Western Cape province, but also developed the TRC's first outreach program, giving victims a chance to speak publicly about their abuse. The large majority of witnesses were women who were determined to foster healing at both individual and community levels.

The most profound experience of Gobodo-Madikizela's time with the TRC was witnessing the forgiveness between victims and perpetrators. The desire of victims to meet their perpetrators was something she had not imagined. Witnessing victims reaching out with forgiveness to perpetrators who had shattered their worlds filled her with hope. Clearly the TRC process had far-reaching consequences, not only for individual victims and perpetrators encountering each other – often for the first time – but also as a model for uniting groups with a history of conflict.

Dr. Gobodo-Madikizela herself is an example of a woman who has reached across conflict lines. She reflects on a series of prison interviews with Eugene de Kock, the commanding officer of apartheid death squads:

> What enables some victims to forgive heinous crimes? What distinguishes them from those who feel unable to do so? In addition to an external context that makes reconciliation normative through the language of restoration – a truth commission, for example, or a counselling agency that focuses on victim-offender encounters, or a national dialogue that begins to put in place the symbols and vocabulary of forgiveness and compromise – there are internal psychological dynamics that impel most of us toward forming an empathic connection with another person in pain, that draw us into his pain, regardless of who that someone is. The possibility of making an empathic connection with someone who has victimised us, as a response to the pain of his remorse, stems significantly from this underlying dynamic. The power of human connectedness, of identification with the other as 'bone of my bone': through the sheer fact of his being human, draws us to 'rescue' others in pain, almost as if this were a learned response embedded deep in our genetic and evolutionary past. We cannot help it.[29]

In a decade of working in conflicts all over the world, I have witnessed such acts of forgiveness among women who say, simply, 'All mothers cry the same tears' as they band together across conflict lines to search for their missing sons and husbands. As Gobodo-Madikizela and other authors and activists in this book can attest, that empathy has a transformative potential, not only for women individually, but for the world. Officials concerned with security would do well to listen and, in turn, transform our foreign policy.

Moving from individual forgiveness to collaborative community work to the policy arena is a giant leap. But in recent years, the construction of a bridge across that gap has begun to be created. The design of the bridge is based on two fundamental principles: that it's smart to try new approaches to long-standing problems; and it makes practical sense to draw on 100 percent of the population when looking for solutions.

---

29   Pumla Gobodo-Madikizela, *A Human Being Died that Night: A South African Story of Forgiveness* (2003) 127.

We can be heartened by resolutions of the Security Council and other international bodies calling for the inclusion of women throughout the peace process. But those same groups are almost exclusively male and they've done stunningly little to walk their talk. So we've still a long row to hoe.

And along the way, as we gradually shift our foreign policy paradigm to include women in peace processes, the lives of those women will change. Their stock will be higher back home when they return from a working session in Washington. Their names will appear on invitation guest lists of other embassies and on the 'too well-known to touch' list in repressive regimes. With those developments, their voices will become stronger and their actions bolder. That is the promise of this incipient social movement stirring within the sphere of foreign policy – the promise of inclusive security. Over the decades, it will be fascinating to watch it grow.

Index

International Humanitarian Law Series

1   Michael J. Kelly, *Restoring and Maintaining Order in Complex Peace Operations: The Search for a Legal Framework*, 1999   ISBN 90 411 1179 4

2   Helen Durham and Timothy L.H. McCormack (eds.), *The Changing Face of Conflict and the Efficacy of International Humanitarian Law*, 1999
                                                                        ISBN 90 411 1180 8

3   Richard May, David Tolbert, John Hocking, Ken Roberts, Bing Bing Jia, Daryl Mundis and Gabriël Oosthuizen (eds.), *Essays on ICTY Procedure and Evidence in Honour of Gabrielle Kirk McDonald*, 2001
                                                                        ISBN 90 411 1482 3

4   Elizabeth Chadwick, *Traditional Neutrality Revisited:Law, Theory and Case Studies*, 2002   ISBN 90 411 1787 3

5   Lal Chand Vohrah, Fausto Pocar, Yvonne Featherstone, Olivier Fourmy, Christine Graham, John Hocking and Nicholas Robson (eds.), *Man's Inhumanity to Man: Essays on International Law in Honour of Antonio Cassese*, 2003
                                                                        ISBN 90 411 1986 8

6   Gideon Boas and William A. Schabas (eds.), *International Criminal Law Developments in the Case Law of the ICTY*, 2003   ISBN 90 411 1987 6

7   Karen Hulme, *War Torn Environment: Interpreting the Legal Threshold*, 2004
                                                                        ISBN 90 04 13848 X

8   Helen Durham and Tracey Gurd (eds.), *Listening to the Silences: Women and War*, 2005   ISBN 90 04 14365 3

9   Marten Zwanenburg, *Accountability of Peace Support Operations*, 2005
                                                                        ISBN 90 04 14350 5

10   Gideon Boas and Hirad Abtahi (eds.), *The Dynamics of International Criminal Justice: Essays in Honour of Sir Richard May, First Presiding Judge of the Milošević Trial*, 2005   ISBN 90 04 14587 7

11   Frits Kalshoven, *Belligerent Reprisals*, 2005   ISBN 90 04 14386 6